Communicating Today
The Essentials

Raymond Zeuschner

California Polytechnic State University
San Luis Obispo

Boston   New York   San Francisco
Mexico City   Montreal   Toronto   London   Madrid   Munich   Paris
Hong Kong   Singapore   Tokyo   Cape Town   Sydney

Executive Editor: *Karon Bowers*
Editorial Assistant: *Jennifer Trebby*
Marketing Manager: *Mandee Eckersley*
Cover Administrator: *Linda Knowles*
Composition Buyer: *Linda Cox*
Manufacturing Buyer: *JoAnne Sweeney*
Production Editor: *Christine Tridente*
Editorial-Production Service: *DMC & Company*
Text Design: *Donna Merrell Chernin*

For related titles and support materials, visit
our online catalog at www.ablongman.com

Library of Congress Cataloging-in-Publication Data
Zeuschner, Raymond F.
  Communicating today : the essentials / Raymond Zeuschner.
      p. cm.
  Includes bibliographical references and index.
  ISBN 0-205-33241-2 (alk. paper)
  1. Communication I. Title.

  P90 .Z47 2003
  302.2--dc21

                                            2002071147

Photo Credits
p. 7: Jose Galvez/PhotoEdit; p. 10: North Wind Picture Archives; p. 48: Paul Conklin/PhotoEdit; p. 71: Y. Karsh/Woodfin Camp & Associates; p. 79: Laimute E Druskis/Pearson Education/PH College; p. 86: Robert Azzi/Woodfin Camp & Associates; p. 105: Dan Budnik/Woodfin Camp & Associates; p. 158: Robert Pham/Pearson Education/PH College; p. 242: Laimute E. Druskis/Pearson Education/PH College; p. 276: Bettmann/CORBIS; p. 301: Laima Druskis/Pearson Education/PH College

Printed in the United States of America

10 11 12 13 14 15 16 17 18 19 20 V036 16 15 14

CONTENTS

Preface   xv

CHAPTER 1: How We Got Here:
          Communication Study in the Past   **1**

Early Education   **2**
    Western Approaches   2
    Non-Western Approaches   6

Communication in the Middle Ages and Renaissance Europe   **8**
    Preservation of Knowledge   8
    The Beginnings of Mass Communication   8

Thinking, Speaking, and Learning   **9**
    Early Renaissance Schools   9
    The Impact of Printing   10

Communication and Political Changes   **11**
    The Birth of Parliament   11
    The Parliamentary Tradition   11
    Government of the People   11

The Revolutionary Tradition   **12**
    Power in Words   13
    Peace or Violence   13

Communication in U.S. Life   **13**
    Free Speech, Free People   14
    The Power of Speech, the Progress of People   14
    Free Expression   14
    Our Voices   15

The Field of Speech Communication   **15**
    Traditions in American Life   16
    The Elocutionists   16
    Academic Discipline   16
    The Modern Emergence of the Discipline   17
    Current and Future Trends in Communication Studies   17

Summary   **18**
Key Terms   **19**
Exercises   **19**
References   **20**

CHAPTER 2: What We Have Learned: Communication Principles 21

A Formal Definition   22

Principles   22
Communication Is a Whole Process   22
Communication Is Inevitable and Irreversible   22
Communication Involves Content and Relationship   23
Communication Happens in a Context   23
Communication Takes Place in a Variety of Settings   24
A Communication Model   26

Communication Apprehension   28
Sources of Anxiety   28
Anxiety Reactions   28
Responses to Anxiety   29
Coping Strategies   30
Research About Communication Apprehension   31

Communication Competence Reviewed   31
Repertoire, Selection, Implementation, Evaluation   31
Knowledge, Feelings, and Skills   32

Summary   33
Key Terms   33
Exercises   34
References   34

CHAPTER 3: What We Know About Listening 35

Listening: The First Communication Event   36
Listening Contexts   36
Effective Listening   37
Active Listening   38
Listening Skills in Context   42

Improving Listening Competency   45
Eliminate the Barriers   45
Responsible Listening   48

Listening Beyond the Classroom   50
Summary   51
Key Terms   51
Exercises   52
References   52

CHAPTER 4: Critical Thinking and Communication   53

Critical Thinking Defined   54

Approaches to Reasoning   56
Deduction   56
Induction   62
The Toulmin Model   65

Informed Decision-Making   68
Evaluating Information   68
Evaluating Sources   70
Evaluating Supporting Materials   70
Critical and Creative Thinking   71
Critical Thinking Competency and Communication   72

Summary   72
Key Terms   73
Exercises   73
References   74

CHAPTER 5: What We Know About Nonverbal Communication   75

A Definition of Nonverbal Communication   76
The Impact of Nonverbal Communication   77
Nonverbal Communication Contexts and Rules   77
Functions   77
Rules   80

Types of Nonverbal Communication   82
Paralanguage   82
Posture   83
Movement   83
Objects   84
Space and Time   85
The Senses   87

Improving Nonverbal Communication Competency   87

Summary   88
Key Terms   88
Exercises   89
References   89

CHAPTER 6: What We Know About Verbal Communication   91

Symbols, Utterances, and Meanings   92
Language as Symbol   92
Semiotics   94

Acquiring Language Skills   96

Speaking and Writing   99

Use and Misuse of Language   99
Mainstream American English   99
Variety in American English   100
Professional, Personal, and Popular Codes   101
Linguistic Oppression   102
Magic, Taboo, and Ritual   104

Improving Linguistic Competency   106

Summary   107

Key Terms   107

Exercises   108

References   108

CHAPTER 7: Intrapersonal Communication   109

A Definition   110

Development of Intrapersonal Communication   111
Experiences   111
Self-Concept   111
Body Image   112
Personal Attributes   112
Social Roles   113
Values, Attitudes, and Beliefs   114
Perception and Self-Concept   116
Expectations   116
Self-Fulfilling Prophecies   117

Thoughts, Feelings, and Dreams   118
Thinking Styles   118
Physical Limitations   119

Functional and Dysfunctional Communication Systems   121
Communication and Mental Health   121
Communication and Achievement   122

Improving Self-Communication Competency   123

Summary   123

Key Terms   123

Exercises   124

References   124

CHAPTER 8: Interpersonal Communication   125

Definition of Interpersonal Communication   126
The Johari Window   127
Inclusion, Affection, and Control Needs   129
Communication and Relationship Development   130
Coming Together   130
Coming Apart   133
Everyday Interpersonal Interactions   135
Communication Climate and Conflict   136
Supportiveness   137
Defensiveness   139
Conflict Management   141
Conflict Is Inevitable   142
Conflict Can Be Constructive   142
Process of Conflict Management   143
Improving Interpersonal Skills   146
Be Assertive   146
Be Considerate   146
Listen   146
Develop Language Skills   146
Be Supportive   147
Summary   147
Key Terms   148
Exercises   148
References   149

CHAPTER 9: Interviewing   151

Defining the Interview   152
Types of Interviews   153
Information Interviews   153
Selection Interviews   153
Appraisal Interviews   154
Problem Solving and Counseling   154
Sales and Persuasion Interviews   155
Interviewing Another Person   156
Structure and Sequence   157
Being Interviewed   159
Preparation for the Interview   159
Responses During the Interview   161
After the Interview   164
Interview Formats   166

Improving Interview Competency   166
Summary   168
Key Terms   169
Exercises   169
References   170

CHAPTER 10: Small-Group Communication   171

Small-Group Communication   172
Size   172
Interaction   174
A Common Purpose   174
Organization   174

Types of Small Groups   175
Social Groups   175
Work Groups   178
Decision-Making Groups   180

Communication Patterns in Groups   183

Environments   185

Phases of Group Development   186
Orientation   186
Conflict   186
Consensus   187
Closure   188

Personal Influences   189
Group-Related Influences   189
Independent Influences   189

Leadership Influences   190

Outcomes and Measurement   191

Organizations: Groups Working Together   192

Improving Small-Group Communication Competency   194

Summary   196
Key Terms   196
Exercises   197
References   197

CHAPTER 11: Preparing Speeches   199

Outlining Principles   200
General Outlines   200
Subordination and Grouping   203
Symbols   206
Efficiency of Expression   207

Organizational Patterns   208
   Sequential Patterns   208
   Topical Patterns   209
   Motivational Patterns   210

Analyzing Your Listeners   212
   Analyzing the Occasion   213
   Analyzing the Environment   214

Using Supporting Materials   214
   Verbal Supporting Materials   215
   Numerical Supporting Materials   217
   Visual Supporting Materials   217

Researching Your Ideas   221
   Finding and Recording Information   222
   Using Personal Resources   222
   Using Library Resources   222
   Using Internet Resources   224
   Broadcast Media Resources   224
   Synthesizing Your Material   224

Summary   225
Key Terms   225
Exercises   225
References   226

CHAPTER 12: Presenting Speeches   227

Types of Presentations   228
   Memorized   228
   Manuscript   229
   Extemporaneous   229
   Impromptu   230

Dealing with Apprehension   231
   Physiological Preparation   232
   Psychological Preparation   234

Effective Public Speaking Skills   236
   Verbal Skills   236
   Nonverbal Skills   239

Evaluating Public Speeches   242
   Standards of Presentation   243
   Adaptation to the Audience   244
   Standards of Ethics   244

Improving Public Communication Competency   245
Summary   247
Key Terms   247
Exercises   248
References   248

CHAPTER 13: Informing Others   249

Types and Purposes of Informative Speaking   251
  Speeches of Definition   251
  Speeches of Demonstration   253
  Speeches of Exposition   255
Patterns of Informative Speaking   256
Evaluating Informative Speeches   259
  Goals as a Listener   259
  Goals as a Critic   259
  Goals as a Consumer of Information   261
Improving Informative Speaking Competency   263
Summary   265
Key Terms   265
Exercises   265
References   266

CHAPTER 14: Persuading Others   267

A Definition of Persuasion   268
Facts, Values, and Policies   268
Attitude Change Theory   270
  Early Approaches   271
  Credibility   271
  Fear Appeals   273
Types of Persuasive Speeches   274
  Speeches to Convince   274
  Speeches to Actuate   275
  Speeches to Reinforce or Inspire   275
  Debates and Public Argumentation   276
  Developing Motivating Supporting Materials   277
  Ethos   277
  Pathos   279
  Logos   279
  Informal Reasoning   280
Developing Persuasive Organization   282
  Logical Patterns   282
  Motivated Sequence   283
Developing Persuasive Language   284
  Imagery   284
  Impact   285

Developing Persuasive Presentation   286

Adapting Persuasive Speeches to Your Audience   287

Evaluating Persuasive Speeches
Listening Goals   288
Critical Goals   289
Consumer Goals   290

Improving Persuasive Communication Competency   290

Summary   291

Key Terms   292

Exercises   292

References   293

CHAPTER 15: Speaking on Special Occasions   295

Speaking to Introduce Another Person   296
Goals of the Introduction Speech   296
Methods of Organization and Presentation   296

Speaking to Commemorate a Person or Event   298
Goals of a Commemorative Speech   298
Methods of Organization and Presentation   298

Speaking to Accept or Thank   301
Goals of the Acceptance Speech   301

Speaking on Short Notice: Impromptu Speeches   302
Goals of Impromptu Speaking   302
Methods of Organization and Presentation   303

Reading Literature Aloud   307
Goals of Performing Literature   307
Methods of Presentation   308
Presentation Methods   309
Evaluation of Performances   310
Readers' Theatre   310
Evaluation of Group Performances   311
Finding Materials to Read   311
Preparing Materials for Reading   313
Cutting and Excerpting Materials for Reading   314

Summary   315

Key Terms   315

Exercises   315

References   316

INDEX   **317**

Optional CD-ROM Chapters

CHAPTER 16: Communicating in Careers   16-1

A Definition of Organizational Communication   16-2
Organizational Behavior   16-2
  Classical   16-2
  Human Relations   16-3
  Social Systems   16-4
  Organizational Cultures   16-6
Organizational Behavior, Norms, and Rules   16-8
Upward and Downward Message Distortions   16-9
Gatekeepers and Facilitators   16-10
  Improving Organizational Rumor Control   16-11
Personal, Small-Group, and Public Careers   16-12
Applying Interviewing Skills   16-12
Improving Career Communication Skills   16-12
Summary   16-14
Exercises   16-14
Key Terms   16-14
References   16-15

CHAPTER 17: Family, Community, and Classroom Communication   17-1

Communicating in the Family   17-2
Parents and Children   17-3
  How Children Acquire Language   17-4
  How Children Acquire Meaning   17-4
Classroom Communication   17-6
Communicating in the Community   17-10
  Participation Means Communication   17-10
Democracy Communicates   17-12
  Citizen Preparation   17-12
  Citizen Participation   17-12
  Improving Community Communication   17-13
Summary   17-13
Exercises   17-14
References   17-14
Key Terms   17-14

CHAPTER 18: Mass Communication and Society   18-1

Mass Communication Defined   18-2

How Mass Communication Works   18-3
One-, Two-, and Three-Step Approaches   18-3
Diffusion, Uses, Gratification   18-3
Gatekeepers, Facilitators, and Opinion Leaders   18-5
The HUB Model   18-5

The Impact of Mass Media on Our Lives   18-7
Entertainment   18-7
Knowledge   18-8
Opinions and Impressions   18-9
Propaganda and Diversion   18-10

Public Relations   18-12
Public Relations Defined   18-12
Types and Functions of Public Relations   18-13
Careers and Consumption   18-14

Improving Mass Communication Competency   18-14

Summary   18-15

Exercises   18-16

Key Terms   18-16

References   18-17

CHAPTER 19: Diversity in Communication   19-1

Intercultural Communication   19-2
Importance of Communicating Across Cultures   19-3
Global Village   19-4
Global Economy   19-5

Learning About Other Cultures   19-6
Filters and Screens   19-6
Cross-Cultural Communication Competency   19-10

Communication and Gender   19-12
Males, Females, and Communication   19-12
Importance of Gender   19-13
Aspects of Gender   19-13
Gender and Communication Competency   19-15

Communication, Age, and Health   19-16
Health and Communication   19-17
Benefits from Improved Health Communication Competency   19-18
Overcoming Communication Barriers Related to
  Age and Health   19-19

Summary   **19-19**
Exercises   **19-20**
Key Terms   **19-20**
References   **19-21**

CHAPTER 20: Communication and Technology   20-1

Communication Technology Defined   20-2

Communication Technology and Civilization   20-2
Access to Communication Technology   20-4
Ethics and Communication Technology   20-5

Personal Communication and Technology   20-8
Intrapersonal Communication   20-8
Interpersonal Communication and Technology   20-8
Interviewing and Technology   20-9
Small-Group Communication and Technology   20-10

Public Communication and Technology   20-11
Public Speaking and Technology   20-11
Career Settings and Communication Technology   20-13

Social Communication and Technology   20-13
Family, School, and Community Settings   20-14
Mass Media and Communication Technology   20-16
Intercultural, Gender, Health, and Age
   Communications and Technology   20-17

Communication Competencies and Technology   20-20
A Final Word   20-20

Summary   **20-21**
Exercises   **20-22**
References   **20-22**
Key Terms   **20-22**

PREFACE

Welcome to *Communicating Today: The Essentials*. This book is the result of focused revising and updating of *Communicating Today*. It is designed to meet the needs and interests of those who want to apply the essential elements of contemporary communication to their everyday lives. It seeks to develop competency, inform about process, explain and apply theory, and provide clear and practical communication skills for the readers.

Features

The main features that distinguish this new book from its predecessors are a shorter length (15 chapters instead of 20), dozens of new references to contemporary scholarship, a compact design with attention to the essential content, and editing for precision.

It has unique insights in the areas of critical thinking, listening, intrapersonal communication, and interviewing, and there is even an introduction to the performance of literature.

Best of all, a new component has been added which makes Chapters 16 through 20 available electronically. These CD-ROM–based chapters deliver the book's message to users through the expanding technology of electronic communication.

Themes

Five themes are woven throughout every chapter through set-off boxes. First, the *Story of Communication* is told by examples and anecdotes from historical and current events. Readers will appreciate the two-thousand-year history of the study of communication through these brief glances into this tradition. Sometimes humorous, sometimes somber, these stories remind us of where we came from and of those who used communication to shape our world.

Second, the *Critical Thinking in Communication* feature found in every chapter challenge readers to apply analysis, logic, and reason to common communication situations. Told with interest and variety, these short vignettes are designed to arouse interest, curiosity, and insight into the role that our critical thinking competencies play in making our communication choices.

The third theme is *Diversity in Communication*, where the rich contributions of individuals and cultures to our communication history and development are presented. A variety of ethnic groups are featured so that all readers can appreciate the contributions made by a wide range of people and cultures to our understanding of the elements of communication.

Technology in Communication spotlights the emerging role of technology in communication development. These pieces touch upon everything from the invention of papyrus for writing to the microchip for information processing. Frequently referring to mass media concepts, this feature has wide appeal to contemporary readers who are increasingly connected to electronic communication outlets.

The final feature in every chapter is *Communication Competency.* The theme of increasing skills and abilities is ever-present throughout the book.

In addition to the chapter content, these five themes appear in each chapter to provide a unifying element, add interest, and provoke thought.

Pedagogy

Every chapter has enhancing communication competency as a goal. In order to reach that goal, you will find a variety of organizational elements.

Chapter Objectives   Each chapter begins with a statement of objectives organized around the Bloom taxonomy of educational goals. There are knowledge-based goals, skill development goals, and affective goals to help the readers develop greater communication competency in the forms of knowledge, actions, and appreciation.

Chapter Summaries   These end-of-chapter recapitulations are designed to link the chapter content back to the goals listed at the opening of each chapter. The communication competency elements of *repertoire, selection, implementation,* and *evaluation* are repeated in each chapter to reinforce student learning and success.

Exercises   Exercises are included at the end of each chapter, many of which have been tested for several years now in a variety of classrooms. They can be used for class assignments, personal development, or simply to initiate thought or discussion.

Plan of the Book

Communicating Today: The Essentials is one of the only books in this area to ground the study of communication in its historical context. Chapter 1 traces two thousand years of communication commentary and education. Starting with our African heritage, the chapter moves to discuss the contribution and effects of Greece and Rome on today's understanding of communication. In addition, Asian, Native American, and other traditions are brought into the narrative.

Chapter 2 summarizes major principles of communication derived from theory building in the discipline. Chapters 3–6 take major areas of communication—listening, critical thinking, nonverbal communication, and verbal communication—and explore their theoretical bases as well as the practical applications that will help readers become competent communicators. Chapters 7–10 move to the major contexts of communication—intrapersonal communication, interpersonal communication, interviewing, and small group communication. Again, the major theoretical underpinnings that inform our knowledge and approaches to these areas are combined with practical applications and emphasis on enhancing communication competencies in each major context. The last five chapters take traditional approaches to public speaking. Preparation and presentation are each given a chapter so students can develop their rhetorical skills. Then applications are made to informative and persuasive speaking. A final chapter looks at speaking on special occasions, such as ceremonies, the granting of awards, and oral readings of literature. This may be the only textbook in this area of study that introduces the fundamentals of performance of literature to basic course students.

Optional CD-ROM Chapters

While fifteen printed chapters constitute the core of communication competency, there are additional materials available on CD-ROM with the purchase of a new textbook (if requested by the instructor; contact your local Allyn & Bacon representative for details). Chapters 16 through 20 round out the study of communication for those who have the time and interest to use them. The chapters are:

- Chapter 16: *Communicating in Careers*
- Chapter 17: *Family, Community, and Classroom Communication*
- Chapter 18: *Mass Communication and Society*
- Chapter 19: *Diversity in Communication*
- Chapter 20: *Communication and Technology*

These chapters provide a route for readers to explore cutting edge topics in an electronic form. They may be used for classroom development, supplemental reading, or personal interest.

Acknowledgments

In preparing this book, I am indebted to all those reviewers and contributors of the first two editions of *Communicating Today*, whose suggestions and insights helped to shape this project as well. I also want to add to that list the many recent reviewers of earlier versions of this manuscript. Specifically, I would like to thank Virginia Chapman, Anderson University; Kelby K. Halone, University of Tennessee; Anna Kaplan, Five Towns College; Steven Todd Mortenson, Georgia Southern University; and Anne Pym, California State University, Hayward. The time, patience, and encouragement of the great Allyn & Bacon staff, especially Karon Bowers and Jennifer Trebby, made this book possible. Finally, I would like to give a big thank-you to all the members of my family for their love and support, especially during the mad moments of final preparation. Thanks for everything, Linda, Jim, Lisa, Ken, and Clara!

Raymond Zeuschner

CHAPTER 1

How We Got Here: Communication Study in the Past

After reading this chapter, you should be able to:

- Describe the historical development of communication study in human societies

- Understand the relationship between communication systems and political systems

- Explain how communication influenced the early development of our country and its traditions and institutions

- Feel connected to a five-thousand-year tradition of studying and applying communication principles and skills

- Realize that the modern field of Speech Communication evolved as our knowledge grew, and continues to expand its methods and concerns

Anthropologists are fairly certain that as ancient peoples of the north-central part of eastern Africa began to gather in groups, they used patterns of verbal and nonverbal signs to communicate. As these groups began to remain in stable clusters, these signs also stabilized and were taught to children by the group and then sometimes shared with others living near. Some signs probably imitated the sounds of nature or were gestures that mimicked more complete actions that they represented; thus a vocabulary developed for each group. The story of the Tower of Babel is probably a good analogy for early language. As the groups interacted, languages were developed. When groups in an area interacted and combined, their languages also merged. While we cannot pinpoint the exact location of the emergence of languages as we know them today, scholars generally agree that a somewhat common language emerged in the Mesopotamia area centered on the modern nations of Iran and Iraq. They call this language **Indo-European**, but it was probably not a real language spoken consistently by any single group. It does, however, permit us to see a link between many modern Western languages, and often the same word in English has a common root with a similar word in Farsi or Greek or Norwegian or Coptic.

As people developed civilizations, they also created ways to record spoken sounds. Writing followed speech as a way to remember, transmit, and express spoken ideas. Both the early forms of cuneiform (which eventually grew into our modern systems of lettering) and hieroglyphics (a picture/letter system) were found in the ancient Middle East. In Asia, the Chinese were developing a pictographic writing system that survives today in modern China, Korea, and Japan.

One trend in these developments is clear. When people began to write and record ideas that were meaningful to them, some of their earliest writings were about the importance of communication education.

EARLY EDUCATION

As civilization advanced, the training of young people to continue the ways of their cultures began to take on regular, if informal, patterns. Children were usually taught at home and in community interactions through events such as meetings, meals, rituals, festivities, and religious exercises. All of these activities served to educate upcoming generations about the group and all depended on oral language. Often the most important person in the group was the one who presided over these events and communicated to the whole group. In other words, the best public speaker was an important person, then as now.

Western Approaches

When we turn to more formal training in this chapter, we look back especially to our roots in Western Civilization and find the teaching of communication skills to be an important event in early Egypt, Greece, and Rome.

Egypt   The earliest fragments of writing we have come from Egypt. Unfortunately, the hieroglyphic inscriptions remained indecipherable for nearly 2000 years, until 1799 when the **Rosetta Stone** was discovered in Egypt. This stone, which is on view today in the British Museum, carried an identical message inscribed in three languages—including Greek and hieroglyphics. Thus, in the 1800s, scholars in Europe were able to translate the writings of these ancient Africans. Among those writings was a part of a lesson from the Egyptian Ptah-Hotep who advised speakers to be clear, talk to the concerns of the listeners, and be careful to have good delivery—that was clear and loud. His advice, although over 3000 years old, still applies to speakers of today. Priests and pharaohs, who depended upon religious authority and a divinely based dictatorial style of government, however, ruled Egypt. Other than for ceremonies, they had little need for effective public speaking to the masses. Although they certainly had discussions and paid attention to nonverbal elements, they did not indicate that these communication areas were formally studied. When the roots of Western Civilization grew out of Africa and reached Greece, especially in the period of 500–300 B.C., public speaking began moving to a prominent position in education.

Greece   About 2600 years ago, the Greeks developed a city-state form of government in which citizens (generally, male property owners) gathered in public meetings to debate and decide matters of policy and to elect leaders. Although this system was a good beginning to democracy (a word based on the Greek terms meaning "people" and "rule"), these meetings usually involved only a small fraction of the population. In Athens, for example, around the time of Socrates, there were only about 12,000 "citizens" in a population of about 120,000.

Because these meetings were both legislative and judicial, a citizen had to be able to speak well. We know of the first public speaking textbook, *Techne*, written about 465 B.C. by Corax, a Greek teacher from Sicily, which was concerned with teaching the art of public speaking—especially persuasion (Ryan, 1992). Small group discussion was certainly a part of daily life in Greece, and the **Socratic Method** of teaching by question and answer dialogue was certainly done best in small groups. However, the Greeks made major decisions in public meetings, and thus focused their communication training on that setting. This focus guided communication education in the West until modern times, and has only recently been challenged by emerging lines of scholarship.

The ancient Greeks engaged in some practices of what we would now call "mass communication" in the form of declarations and announcements, but there was no press. Often, a courier would run with a written message from one place to another, and stories are told that if the news he brought was bad, the receivers would kill the messenger. These first attempts to be critics of mass communication were certainly hard on the couriers. Today, we still see people reacting in the same way when they say, "Hey, don't blame me, I'm just relaying the message!"

Many early Greek scholars devoted their teaching and writing to the study of communication, especially public speaking. While the first Greek academies usually taught four general subjects (rhetoric, mathematics, music, and gymnastics),

TECHNOLOGY AND COMMUNICATION
From Papyrus to Microchips

The development of papyrus and vellum to replace clay tablets as writing surfaces profoundly affected communication development. Easier to store and easier to transport, sheepskin and especially paper made it possible to send letters over great distances and store large volumes of writing in small spaces. Early couriers paved the way for modern postal systems, and you can still visit the library at Ephesus, where St. Paul stopped on his famous journey to Asia Minor. These technologies required that the receiver be able to read and understand the sender's writing, and thus helped to foster standardized forms of language—grammars and vocabularies. These, in turn, promoted commerce, culture, and trade. The same two features—speed and the ability to store more information—motivated the invention of paper along the Nile Valley and the microchip in Silicon Valley.

it was the study of the first, rhetoric, that included much of what we study today. To learn rhetoric, one also needed to be familiar with history, philosophy, grammar, and human nature. This sounds a lot like modern college requirements in general education! One Greek teacher, Isocrates, wrote about the place of good public speaking in society; his words are as true today as they were then:

> Because there has been implanted in us the power to persuade each other and to make clear to each other whatever we desire, not only have we escaped the life of wild beasts, but we have come together and founded cities and made laws and invented arts; and generally speaking, there is no institution devised by man which the power of speech has not helped to establish. (Isocrates, 1929)

Probably the most influential book ever written about speech communication is the *Rhetoric* by **Aristotle**. Building upon ideas from Socrates and Plato, Aristotle added his own keen observation and insight into the topics of finding a subject and supporting materials, organizing them, using an appropriate level in the style of expression, delivering the speech so it has clarity and impact, and using the speaker's and listener's memory of events to make the speech appealing. Because he covered his material soundly and carefully, Aristotle is read widely today in translation, and sometimes in the original. The *Rhetoric* continues to teach new generations of students into the twenty-first century because of the care and depth of its explanation and applications (Cooper, 1932, Solmsen, 1954).

Although ancient Greece had many colorful, dramatic speakers, there was not complete freedom of speech, even for the privileged citizens. Socrates was fond of asking questions, and instilled the same habit in others. Sometimes the questions turned toward existing morals and values as well as the way those in power were behaving. Eventually, Socrates was convicted of corrupting the youth of Athens, and sentenced to death. His thoughts and teachings survive through the writings of his star pupil—Plato.

Teachers of public speaking found a wide and ready market for their classes, and were termed **sophists**, which originally meant simply "wise men" or "teachers." As time went on, and the opportunity for profit in this profession became evident, other teachers also set up shop teaching clever or tricky ways to persuade, and the term sophist took on a negative connotation. Much the same fate has happened to the subject they taught—**rhetoric**. Originally, educated people knew rhetoric to be the study of creating, organizing, supporting, and presenting messages. It applied to written and spoken forms and was at the heart of curriculum then as it is today. Your instructors in Speech, Communication, and English Departments still use the term in its traditional denotation. However, the popular use of the term has come to mean an empty display of superficial, emotional, or exaggerated words. Aristotle (like the teachers of rhetorical principles today) took great care to instill in students the importance of substance, ethics, support, and honesty to communication. So the term "rhetoric" has had a complete reversal in connotation. Even after Rome conquered Greece and made it a part of that empire, the influence of the Greek rhetoricians continued to be felt.

Rome   The Roman armies did more than just conquer territory. They were good at exporting treasures from their new domains back to Rome. When they added Greece to their empire, they added the products of advanced culture and civilization. In early Rome, as in all of the Western World to modern times, knowing how to read, write, and speak Greek was the mark of an intelligent and well-educated person. The Roman armies sent back to Rome hundreds of Greek slaves, many of whom were well educated and were used as tutors in the most prominent families. It was a status symbol to have a Greek tutor in one's home. In Latin, these teachers were known by the term *rhetor*. These tutors taught what they knew best, and that included the rhetorical principles of the sophists.

The Roman *forum*, or marketplace, gives its name to our current practice of exchanging and debating important issues in public. Over time, Roman writers created their own systems for teaching communication skills. Especially notable in this regard were Cicero and Quintillian. The Romans were excellent at organizing and systematizing everything they did, from road building and tax collection, to commerce, trade, and rhetoric. The rhetorical system they established is still used today. It divides the study and practice of rhetoric into five major headings, which the Romans termed **canons** (meaning "laws").

Today, the first of these, **invention**, concerns the discovery of ideas and materials for a speech. When you brainstorm for topics, when you do research, when you try to think up good explanations, you are practicing invention. You need to consider your opinions, your audience, your analysis of the topic, and the ideas and opinions of your potential listeners. You must also consider your strengths and weaknesses. How might they affect the willingness of others to believe what you say?

The second major canon, **organization**, is based on the Latin term *disposition*. This canon is easiest to see in speech and English outlines. A variety of organizational formats is available to put ideas and information into a sensible pattern that you can go through and your audience can follow. Any decisions you make about arranging materials in a speech or an essay involve principles of organization.

Style, the third canon, refers to your use of language. Are your sentences simple or complex or a variety? Graceful or clumsy? Do you use simple vocabulary or challenging terms or do you lose your listeners by using too much jargon? You need to consider yourself, your subject, and your audience when making decisions about style. The Romans referred to this as *elocution*.

The fourth, **memory**, refers to a speaker's ability to read and remember enormous amounts of material. In Greece and Rome, people who depended on their memory to bring up facts, stories, previous cases, and other references delivered most major speeches from memory. With the advent of libraries, manuscripts, notes, overhead projectors, laptops, flipcharts, data banks, and recordings, memory no longer serves the same purpose. However, when you are asked to respond in class to a instructor's question, to explain a complex idea spontaneously, or to write a clear and compelling essay test, you are working in the domain of memory. You may someday have the opportunity to give impromptu speeches, and memory is all you will have.

The last Roman canon was **delivery** and concerned the same elements then as now—voice, articulation, volume, nonverbal cues, and gestures—all which help the listeners understand and appreciate the intellectual and emotional content of your message. The choices you make regarding use of notes, your speaking volume, use of microphone, where you look, and so on, are all based on your sense of delivery.

The Romans' contributions were dominant in over a thousand years of academic study in Western Europe, and because our educational and cultural traditions are so strongly tied to that heritage, they continue to be the perspective of this and other texts in the field. The continued use of these traditions has been called a **Eurocentric perspective**—meaning that we have depended primarily on this Western heritage in our education and research and largely underused ideas and concepts from outside this Greco-Roman-European point of view. Some chapters of this book are direct descendants of the Greek and Roman systems, and cover the five canons outlined above. There were, however, other communication traditions in non-western civilizations. Recently, more and more of these traditions are being studied, appreciated, and incorporated into modern communication study.

Non-Western Approaches

Writings from Asian cultures indicate that some training in public speaking and in communication skills in general were also historically important in those cultures. With the invention of paper in China around A.D. 105, writing on paper replaced writing on silk and bamboo, both of which were less satisfactory due to their expense or weight. Block printing emerged in China in the T'ang Dynasty period (618–906) and, when combined with paper, gave rise to an increased output of recorded information from that time (Carter, 1995). We have fairly extensive written records from Chinese and Japanese civilizations that include advice from Lao-Tsu in China, and from Shotetsu Mongatari in Japan whose book *Zoku Gunsho Ruiju* gave instruction on how to create beautiful and effective communication (deBarry, 1958, 1960). Writing around the year 1405, the Japanese critic Seami tells his readers about the important goal of speaking in public, "the *yugen* (ultimate goal) of discourse lies in a grace of language and complete mastery of the speech of the nobility and gentry, so that even the most casual utterance will be graceful" (deBarry, 1958:280).

Other than the Egyptian and Ethiopian, most early African, Pacific Island, and Native American societies did not leave written records of their ancient history. The Incas developed a recording system of knotted string collections (*quipu*) which registered events and accounting data for goods, production, and census information (Ascher and Ascher, 1981), and thereby created an alternative to writing. The strong oral traditions of these cultures point out the prominent place of the **storyteller** who acted as a sort of living history book. Through the use of memory and delivery, these key members of societies created the very fabric of culture. The most important member of a group was often neither the warrior nor the healer, but the storyteller. In these cultures, people spent much of their time in family or tribal clusters, and instead of libraries as we think of them today, they turned to a revered elder to relate the history and traditions of that group. In his important work, *The Power of Myth*, Joseph Campbell tells us how cultures have developed in every part of the world largely through the myths they developed through their storytelling experiences (Campbell, 1988). In these cultures, many legends, songs,

The storyteller is a living library.

and chants developed into living libraries of information which members of the group passed on to successive generations. In modern times, storytelling still has an active role. Many colleges offer courses in storytelling. Each year, numerous storytelling festivals are held in the United States. The most prominent are those in the Southern Mountain region, where the tradition of storytelling, especially among traditional African American families, remains strong. Some say that the powerful speaking style of leaders such as Martin Luther King, Jr. was founded in the strong oral traditions of the Black community.

Showing those of us with Eurocentric traditions how important the story-telling skill is, Ray Bradbury in his novel *Fahrenheit 451* describes a world where all the books have been burned by the government. A small band of rebels gathers and each one "becomes" a book from the culture, learning it word for word, and reciting it to keep it alive. The storytelling tradition of the past is used here as the vehicle to save literature for future generations in much the same way as traditional cultures passed on their past. Even today, strong social events center around Native American gatherings where storytellers continue the tradition and, in African American communities, you will still find some of the best of modern storytellers (Sawyer, 1962).

COMMUNICATION IN THE MIDDLE AGES AND RENAISSANCE EUROPE

The time between A.D. 500 and 1300 was often a chaotic and troubled time for Europe. Many small nations grew and fell around prominent leaders, and some of these groups spent their energies criss-crossing Europe as bands of destructive armies.

Preservation of Knowledge

Education, culture, literature, and history were kept mostly by the early Christian Church in European monasteries, by the great libraries and universities of the Arab world in North Africa and Spain, and by hundreds of Jewish settlements spread widely from the Mediterranean throughout northern and eastern Europe, and possibly India and China. Each of these groups made important contributions to preserving the study of communication. For example, the early Christian Church, with its Roman/Latin base, preserved and expanded upon the writings of Cicero and Quintillian.

The Beginnings of Mass Communication

Saint Augustine reminded his church that teaching the masses was part of its mission, and that could be done best by effective preaching—public speaking. Literacy was limited, and the only way most of the population would get access to the Bible was through someone else reading it aloud. Saint Isidore of Seville lived in Spain in the early 600s and wrote about many topics, including the importance of language and speech (Brehart, 1912). In the Arab world of this period, great libraries were kept in North Africa and Spain and included many of the early Greek and Latin writings such as Aristotle's *Rhetoric* and Cicero's *De Oratore*. Jewish civilization was intermixed throughout this area, and Jewish teachers (rabbis) were thought to have preserved and passed on principles of clear organization and effective style. History tells us that the beginnings of mass communication were evident in these times, and other communication modes such as nonverbal communication, small group discussion, and interpersonal communication must have been evident. For example, the town crier was a person who presented announcements and read important information, or related current events as a sort of radio broadcaster without the radio. Many councils must have used small group communication, and interpersonal influence certainly affected everyday communication. However, because the formal emphasis was still on one expert or authoritative person speaking to and teaching others, the skills of public speaking for a privileged and elite few continued to occupy the study of communication.

THINKING, SPEAKING, AND LEARNING

With the resurgence of culture and education, beginning in the early 1300s in Italy, the study of communication skills returned to the public arena from its sheltered existence in the church, library, or rabbinical school.

Early Renaissance Schools

Early Italian schools followed much the same model as the first Greek Academies. They were places for the male children of the wealthy to learn important skills and improve their thinking. Business and trade areas were discussed, especially since the great seaport cities of Italy were opening up trade routes to the Middle East and Asia. Literacy expanded with trade and commerce, and more and more of the general population learned about communication in the forms of thinking, speaking, and writing. Universities taught their subjects through a method called *disputations*, which were public debates assigned by the professor. These debates called

CRITICAL THINKING IN COMMUNICATION

The Debate Method

The debate method of teaching thinking and speaking was a strong form. The famous question, "How many angels can dance on the head of a pin?" might have been the topic for two students to dispute. The process of defining the arguments and then making them plausible rested to a large extent on skills of logic. Aristotle used the *syllogism*, especially the shortened form called an *enthymeme* to teach reasoning skills. Medieval debaters followed this tradition by training themselves in clear, critical, logical thinking.

for students who were skilled in thinking and researching as well as in giving clear and compelling presentations. As the Renaissance moved northward, interest and training in communication skills moved with it.

The Impact of Printing

When printing began in Europe around 1450, books became available to many people for the first time in human history. With books and debating skills available to them, people began to ask many new questions—about life, business, government, and religion. While there have been freethinking people throughout history, their numbers increased and they communicated with each other and with the public through printed words that had not been available previously. Other people, who could now read and write, could also check the ideas and opinions against other written works, and debate and discuss their value and impact. Scholarship still remained largely within the church, but was expanded and made it possible for the writings and philosophies of people like Martin Luther to be widely read, discussed, and debated.

All of these factors increased communication. Trade with many different cultures; education of a variety of populations; discussions, arguments, and debates; and interaction across cultures and national borders all helped shape the Protestant Reformation and changed the way the Christian religion was practiced. The development of book printing was so influential to the development of civilization that *Time* magazine's poll in 1999 determined that Johannes Gutenberg was the most important person of the previous millennium.

Gutenberg's press helped to spread literacy.

COMMUNICATION AND POLITICAL CHANGES

For many subsequent political leaders, such as Henry VIII who ruled England from 1509–1547, the changes in religion were potentially dangerous for their survival. After all, most rulers used religion to justify their powers and positions; questions and debates about religion lead to similar examinations about the monarchy. Henry, a first modern monarch in the sense of his education and insight, joined the questioning of the established religion, broke with the existing church, and actually gained power with the momentum of the Protestant reformation.

The Birth of Parliament

The English tradition of a monarch sharing some power with a limited group was already well established by Henry VIII's reign. One of his ancestors, King John (the same one from the tales of *Robin Hood*) was forced by a group of nobles to sign the **Magna Carta** in 1215. This document was the basis for setting up a consultative form of government in England. That form of government then developed into England's **Parliament**, a term derived from the French word *parler*, meaning to speak. Speaking is exactly what government representatives do in Parliament.

The Parliamentary Tradition

Much like their Greek and Roman forebears, members of Parliament debated at great length about the policies of their government. Especially in the British government, upon which we model ours, speaking out freely developed into a protected and expected behavior over several hundred years. For the most part, however, those who became members of Parliament were the kind of people who always spoke in governmental affairs—wealthy, male property owners. They spoke to each other out of a common experience and educational background and out of concern for the protection of the privileged. In 1275, Edward I began the practice of inviting representatives of the merchant class and the town's middle class to sit with Parliament. In turn, Parliament began the custom of voting the king some regular revenues from the trade and export business to run the government. Eventually, two "houses" or sections of Parliament grew out of this practice; they are still known as the House of Commons and the House of Lords. This bicameral system is a forerunner of the U.S. Senate and House of Representatives.

Because it held the power of the purse, Parliament became the center of governmental authority. Although its power rose and fell over the next four hundred years, it always grew stronger in the long run.

Government of the People

It took the English revolution of 1645–60 to give people other than the nobility a substantial role in government. As common people were elected and as its influence

The Story of Communication
British Debate

THERE ARE DOZENS of famous speakers from the British Parliament, where wit, humor, and even clever insults were developed into a fine art. In recent times, Winston Churchill stands out. One of his most antagonistic opponents was Lady Astor, and their exchanges have grown to legendary proportions. One time, the story goes, when Churchill had a little too much to drink, he encountered Lady Astor and remarked, "Madam, you are exceedingly ugly." She responded, "And you, sir, are exceedingly drunk!" Churchill took a deep breath and replied, "That may be true, madam, but in the morning, *I* shall be sober." Infuriated, Lady Astor exclaimed, "Sir, if you were my husband, I would give you poison!" Churchill looked right at her and said, "Madam, if I were your husband, I would *take* poison!"

grew over the centuries, Parliament replaced the monarchy as the locus of power (Smith, 1957). To this day, the Prime Minister of England must be a Member of Parliament. The Prime Minister usually has to climb the seniority ranks before becoming a party leader, and then becomes Prime Minister when that party is elected to a majority.

Free, robust, and eloquent speech became identified with the best of these leaders. A Member of Parliament could be cross-examined by the opposition for hours and was expected to have ready and witty answers. If you have C-SPAN available, you can watch "Question Time" directly from London and experience the parliamentary speaking tradition at its source. It is not surprising that the study of public speaking includes many outstanding orators who spoke in the British Parliament over the past 400 years.

As Britain spread its influence around the world in the period from 1600 to 1900, it also spread its parliamentary model of government. After the loss of the American Colonies between 1776 and 1782, the British began to institute local parliaments in their other colonies. From India to Canada, and from Australia to the Bahamas, much of the world is now governed on this model. In addition, many modern nations have adopted similar systems, some only after long periods of autocratic rule and discord. As history shows, protracted authoritarian governments usually end in revolution. The dramatic changes in Eastern Europe and the former Soviet Union are a continuing step in this long march of people who have wished to speak freely in order to govern themselves.

THE REVOLUTIONARY TRADITION

In addition to the use of public speaking in a formal meeting such as parliament, speakers could also use their abilities to address large groups of listeners and advocate the overthrow of some established group—religious or governmental.

Power in Words

Stories of attempts at revolution in several countries generally focus on one or two prominent speakers who stood in front of crowds and urged them to action. The celebrated oratory of Patrick Henry, or that of the impassioned Vladimir Lenin brings to mind the revolutionary image instantly.

Because literacy was still not widespread in the eighteenth century, the tradition of the effective speaker continued to be an important means of transmitting information. Speaking to the masses has always served the cause of those who want to overthrow the established order. Whole volumes have been written about the Irish speakers who urged rebellion against England for centuries. Latin American history is filled with examples of people, from Juarez in Mexico in the 1800s, to Castro in Cuba in the 1900s, who were able to rally the population to revolt against a powerful ruling group.

Peace or Violence

The ability of a powerful speaker, be it Napoleon in 1800 or Hitler in 1932, to cause ordinary citizens to rise up against the existing government is amply demonstrated across time, country, and culture. This revolutionary tradition is an alternative to the parliamentary tradition. One says that the power of speech must be used to incite the violent overthrow of the system; the other says that the power of speech must be used within the system to bring about change through rational, persuasive discourse.

The United States has some of each heritage—methods of debate from the British Parliament and methods of revolution that established our own forum for change. Most of the revolutionaries of 1776 would have stopped their rebellious activities if the English Parliament had given meaningful representation to the colonies in the government decision-making process. In other words, when the governmental structure does not allow free speech, and government becomes too strong and oppressive, then the revolutionary use of speech will come forth. The stronger the government tries to be, the more likely it will inspire revolution. If, on the other hand, a governmental structure includes a method for free speech to influence decisions and create change, then the parliamentary tradition is likely to emerge. However, even with setbacks, the eventual emergence of free expression seems to be inevitable. The dramatic events of the late 1980s and early 1990s in Eastern Europe and the former Soviet Union are built upon the premise of free expression of ideas. Former rubber stamp parliaments in those countries changed from quiet, docile followers, to arenas of robust comment and dissent.

COMMUNICATION IN U.S. LIFE

It is not surprising, given our heritage and the care and vision of our founders, that one of the first important steps of our new country was to guarantee the freedom of expression. At first, this meant that the reasoned discourse of the educated lawmaker was protected. Anti-government, inflammatory, or personal attack was still frowned upon and not permitted.

Free Speech, Free People

U.S. history has seen a steady expansion of the right to free expression, but it has not been a smooth one. Originally, the free speech clause of the First Amendment applied primarily to spoken words, and somewhat less to printed words; it was still subject to much regulation. The expression of unpopular ideas had to be permitted—that much was recognized.

In the early days, freedom of expression was protected as long as it stayed within bounds of prevailing taste and moral codes. During periods of great national stress—the Civil War for example—the mood in the country and the courts tightened up on these limits. In times of ease and prosperity, the boundaries of free expression seem to expand.

A look at strong, authoritarian governments reveals one element in common among them: They attempt to restrict and control the expression of ideas. Authoritarian governments run the media, whether newspapers or radio or television. For that reason, one of the first activities of a revolution is to take over the media outlets. Totalitarian governments forbid free flow of information and spend enormous resources searching luggage for forbidden books or newspapers, and jamming radio and television signals that are not under their control.

The Power of Speech, the Progress of People

In many ways, U.S. history can be seen as a continuous journey, from early times to the present, of increasing tolerance for the free expression of ideas, no matter how distasteful, idiotic, bizarre, or offensive some may be. Every year, numerous court cases test the limits of free expression and the ability of government to regulate that expression.

Free Expression

One after another, challenges to these restrictions have been upheld by the courts, and the protection of "speech" now includes almost all forms of verbal and nonverbal expression—from the traditional oration and newspaper editorial, to art, film, and even flag-burning and topless dancing. Many people feel that it is precisely because of our tolerance for a range of ideas, opinions, and expressions, that we have usually avoided the violence of the revolutionary tradition (Arnett, 1990). As scholars put it in *Speech Communication in Society*:

> The success of a democratic system depends upon an open and continuing dialogue between the citizenry.... You as an individual not only have the constitutional right to speak freely and to assemble peaceably, but it is often your social responsibility. (Gruner, et al, 1972)

Our Voices

Speakers of every sort have used their public speaking to create and further a cause or campaign. These speakers included the well-known early leaders of Congress as well as seekers and holders of the Presidency, such as Webster, Clay, Calhoun, Randolph, Douglas, and Lincoln. Others, such as Lucy Stone, Susan B. Anthony, Sojourner Truth, and John Brown, created or supported social reform outside of government.. The reform speakers from the late 1800s and through the past century helped to improve social conditions, sparked the labor movement, established political parties, and created the civil rights movement (Duffy and Ryan, 1987a).

Speakers such as Eugene Debs, Emma Goldman, William Jennings Bryan, Frederick Douglass, Margaret Sanger, Clarence Darrow, the Roosevelts—Teddy, Franklin, and Eleanor—Marcus Garvey, and Martin Luther King, Jr. are all remembered for the power of their spoken words. The field of Speech Communication has always been concerned with this power, which has played a continuous role in U.S. life (Duffy and Ryan, 1987b).

THE FIELD OF SPEECH COMMUNICATION

When early settlers from England arrived with their British traditions, they found that Native Americans also included public speaking in their culture. The Iroquois and Algonquin nations had thriving systems of self-government that depended on skill in public speaking. Speakers often addressed a community council, and were expected to follow a standard outline. One famous speaker, known to us today as Red Jacket, is still studied in speech classes as an example

DIVERSITY IN COMMUNICATION
Sojourner Truth

One of the most interesting speakers to arise out of the early 1800s was a woman who named herself Sojourner Truth. As a slave, she knew firsthand the oppression of that system. She had intelligence and ambition, and she escaped. Abolitionists helped her to gain wide audiences for her anti-slavery appeals. A large, imposing woman, she used biblical references, common sense, and powerful personal stories to win over large audiences. She faced double barriers to speaking in public—being a woman and being Black. Neither group was permitted to speak in public in many places, even in the North. She was so powerful, with a deep, resounding voice, that some accused her of being a man dressing as a woman. One story tells us that, upon being shouted down as an impostor at a meeting, she threw open her blouse, exposing her breasts, and then told of how children she had nursed had been taken from her and sold away.

of an orator from this tradition. However, the English brought their own traditions and set up their own schools. When John Harvard endowed a college in Cambridge, Massachusetts in 1636, one of the principal subjects in the curriculum was rhetoric and an important professorship was created especially for a brilliant scholar to teach that subject.

Traditions in American Life

As the number of colleges and universities grew in the following years, speech continued to be a central subject. The link between good oral expression and good written expression was maintained by instructors who taught both subjects, emphasizing the standard Roman canons that had been passed along through the centuries. Free speech and public debate guaranteed that aspiring leaders of political, social, and legal enterprises needed rhetorical training, insights and skills of good research, good organization, and polished presentation. The writing of Thomas Jefferson is a good example of these elements; students study the Declaration of Independence not just for its political ideas, but also for the grace and eloquence of its expression.

The Elocutionists

A revived interest in Classical Greece began to compete for attention with the Roman tradition in the late 1700s and early 1800s. This Greek revival affected art, literature, architecture, and even public speaking. The shift of attention to the Greeks involved special interest in their ideas about beauty. Keats's "Ode to a Grecian Urn" is but one example that proclaimed the idea that "Truth Is Beauty."

Unfortunately, this single-minded attention to beauty meant that in public speaking that grand gesture, elegant vocabulary, and flowing vocal tones received so much attention that matters of substance, thought, research, and precision were nearly forgotten in many schools. The teachers of this florid style were called **elocutionists,** and their schools dominated speech education for most of the 1800s. Movies set in this period often feature a stereotyped politician or preacher who becomes puffed up with grand oratory.

Traveling groups of performers criss-crossed the country during this period, performing *chautauqua* programs, named after a series of summer seminars started in the town of Chautauqua, New York at an Episcopal summer camp in 1874. These performances often included music, dramatic presentations, poetry recitations, and re-creations of famous speeches from historical figures.

Academic Discipline

It was during this time that U.S. higher education began to take the shape that it has today. As knowledge expanded, academic departments began to form around History, Philosophy, and the Sciences. Eventually English split from departments of Rhetoric to study primarily literature and, to a lesser extent, grammar. These new English departments left behind the often silly extravagances of the Elocutionists thereby aiding the decline of rhetoric's reputation.

Many scholars also were occupied with the emerging disciplines of Psychology and Sociology. These scholars were doing important research around the turn of the twentieth century, and carried with them vivid memories of elocution training that they associated with the study of rhetoric. Since the emerging disciplines were also concerned with an academic approach to communication, they ventured their own research and publications about how people interact with each other.

At the same time, the excesses and shallowness of the elocution movement in public speaking began to be even more apparent, and a new association formed in 1915 for the "Academic Teachers of Public Speaking." This association has grown and changed names several time to become the current National Communication Association. Unfortunately, despite the internal changes in the field, many people still associate speech communication with the old superficial style of presentation without substance.

The Modern Emergence of the Discipline

With the explosion of knowledge in recent history, speech communication has taken on an enormous burden. Studying human communication in all its richness is a difficult and broadly focused task. Since communication impinges upon almost everything we do, and weaves through every part of life, communication scholars must look everywhere to learn about its processes and effects. A definition of the field formulated by the Association for Communication Administrators (1981) gives you a feeling for this area:

> *Speech Communication* is a humanistic and scientific field of study, research, and application. Its focus is upon how, why, and with what effects people communicate through spoken language and associated nonverbal messages. Just as political scientists are concerned with political behavior, and economists with economic behavior, the study of speech communication is concerned with communicative behavior. (p.1)

As we move into the twenty-first century, we find departments of Speech Communication with a variety of names and concerns. Some departments, such as at the University of California, Berkeley, emphasize the classical study of rhetoric and still call themselves by that name. Others, such as the Annenberg Schools of Communication at Pennsylvania and Southern California, are heavily involved in mass media concerns and public policy. Some still have a relationship with Theatre, while others are connected with Journalism or Speech Therapy and Audiology. These departments hold in common an intense interest in humans communicating with each other. Various areas in the field of Speech Communication are defined in the next chapter, along with a model that describes the communication process.

Current and Future Trends in Communication Studies

Although it is difficult to predict the future, the interests of present investigators in the field can provide some clues as to where our study of communication behavior is going.

► **IMPROVING COMPETENCY**

Communication and Careers

Understanding the role of communication in everyday life is a valuable competency. Conduct an informal survey of four or five people—perhaps parents or friends or workers you meet during one day. Ask them to describe briefly the role of communication in their careers. What would happen if they were unable to communicate well? Would they feel a need or a benefit from improving their communication skills? National surveys confirm that communication skills are of primary importance in virtually every career (*Pathways*, 1995).

Currently, in addition to the established areas of rhetoric, public address, performance of literature, speech correction/audiology, linguistics, interpersonal communication, group communication, mass media, nonverbal communication, and organizational communication, many speech communication people are working with communication and gender, multicultural communication, health communication and communication and aging. New perspectives enrich our Eurocentric tradition. Afrocentric and feminist research paradigms in communication are now the focus of many researchers (Asante, 1987). These investigators use a variety of methods to help them study, including historical research; descriptive approaches; critical analysis; empirical observation and fieldwork; and experimental and statistical data gathering and analysis. The impact of technology on our communication behavior and the use of technological tools to study communication are both changing our knowledge of this ancient subject (Wood and Gregg, 1995). It is as complex a field as it is a subject. If you have the time and interest, your school probably offers many opportunities to study in a variety of these areas and approaches.

SUMMARY

From the beginnings of human history to the latest in electronic message processing, speech communication has been at the center of interaction. In a few pages, you have seen some 50,000 years of communication activity bring us to where we are today. How did we get here? Through our ability to communicate. Sometimes our messages were helpful, passing on important knowledge regarding our environment and ourselves. Sometimes they were hurtful, inciting one group to hate or fear or destroy another. Often they were hopeful, inspiring us with a vision for future well being and extending the human spirit.

As Aristotle pointed out, the tools of communication are indifferent to the uses we make of them. Just as a fine new hammer can build a shelter, so can it crush a skull. The hammer does not care—it is amoral; only the user determines its purpose. So it is with the tools of communication—the way you apply your skill and knowledge will determine the outcome of your communication behavior.

Key Terms

Indo-European, **2**
Rosetta Stone, **3**
Socratic Method, **3**
Aristotle, **4**
sophists, **5**
rhetoric, **5**
canons, **5**
invention, **5**
organization, **5**

style, **6**
memory, **6**
delivery, **6**
Eurocentric perspective, **6**
storyteller, **7**
Magna Carta, **11**
Parliament, **11**
elocutionists, **16**

► EXERCISES

1. Go to a large, comprehensive dictionary and find five different words with five different root languages. Most of the words you find will list a Greek or Latin origin, but see if you can find some with Sanskrit, Indo-European, Japanese, Celtic, or African roots. Share your findings in class and see how many different root languages you and your classmates can find which have contributed to the development of modern English.

2. Which is more valuable to civilization—written or spoken communication? Write a two-page essay defending your choice, and then be prepared to read your essay and defend your position to your class.

3. Conduct an interview of ten people from ten different occupations—such as student, professor, librarian, bank teller, service station attendant and ask each one to define "rhetoric." How many included the classical origin of developing, supporting, and expressing messages? How many only talked about the modern media usage? Compare the definitions you gathered with those of a classmate and see if you can pick out the common themes.

4. If you were going to make a career of studying communication, what area would you like to work in—business, health, politics? What particular skills do you think would be important for your "chosen" career? Why?

References

Arnett, Robert. "The Practical Philosophy of Communication Ethics and Free Speech as the Foundation for Speech Communication." *Communication Quarterly* 38, Summer 1990.

Asante, Molefi K. *The Afrocentric Idea*. Philadelphia: Temple University Press, 1987.

Ascher, M. and R. Ascher. *The Code of the Quipu*. Ann Arbor: The University of Michigan Press, 1981.

Beasley, Vanessa B. "The Rhetoric of Ideological Consensus in the United States: American Principles and American Prose in Presidential Inaugurals." *Communication Monographs* 68, 2, June 2001.

Brehart, Ernest. *An Encyclopedist of the Dark Ages— Isidore of Seville*. New York: Burt Franklin, 1912.

Campbell, Joseph (with Bill Moyers). *The Power of Myth*. New York: Doubleday, 1988.

Carter, T. F. "Paper and Block Printing—From China to Europe," *The Invention of Printing in China and Its Spread Westward*. Reprinted in David Crowley and Paul Heyer, *Communication in History— Technology, Culture, Society*. White Plains, NY: Longman, 1995.

Clark, Ruth Anne and David Jones. "A Comparison of Traditional and Online Formats in a Public Speaking Course." *Communication Education* 50, 2, April 2001.

"Communication Careers." Annandale, VA: Association for Communication Administration, 1995.

Cooper, Lane, Translator. *The Rhetoric of Aristotle*. New York: Appleton-Century-Crofts, 1932.

de Barry, William T. *Sources of Japanese Tradition*. New York: Columbia University Press, 1958.

———. *Sources of Chinese Tradition*. New York: Columbia University Press, 1960.

Duffy, Bernard K. and Halford Ryan, Eds. *American Orators Before 1900 and American Orators of the Twentieth Century*. New York: Greenwood Press, 1987.

Gruner, C., C. M. Logue, D.L. Freshley and R. C. Huseman. *Speech Communication in Society*. Boston: Allyn and Bacon, 1972.

Hallstein, D. and Lynn O'Brien. "A Postmodern Caring: Feminist Standpoint Theories, Revisioned Caring, and Communication Ethics." *Western Journal of Communication* 63, 1, Winter 1999.

Isocrates. *Antidosis*. Translated by George Norlin. Cambridge, MA: Harvard University Press, 1929, 2.

Pathways to Careers in Communication. Annandale: Speech Communication Association, 1995.

Ryan, Halford. *Classical Communication for the Contemporary Communicator*. Mountain View, CA: Mayfield, 1992.

Sawyer, Ruth. *The Way of the Storyteller*. New York: Viking, 1962.

Smith, Goldwin. *A History of England*. New York: Charles Scribner's Sons, 1957.

Solmsen, Fredrich, Ed. *The Rhetoric and Poetics of Aristotle*. Translated by W. Rhys Roberts and Ingram Bywater. New York: Random House/Modern Library, 1954.

Wahl-Johnson, Kain. "Letters to the Editor as a Forum for Public Deliberation: Modes of Publicity and Democratic Debate." *Critical Studies in Media Communication* 18, 3, September 2001.

Wood, Julia T. and Richard B. Gregg. *Toward the Twenty-First Century: The Future of Speech Communication*. Creskill: Hampton Press, 1995.

CHAPTER 2

What We Have Learned: Communication Principles

After reading this chapter, you should be able to:

- Provide a formal definition of communication
- Describe three major principles of communication
- Discuss communication competency and the communication model
- Understand sources of, and responses to, communication anxiety
- Apply the formal study of communication to your daily life

From the brief review of the history of communication in Chapter 1, it is evident that communication study has come a long way, and that many great minds have contributed to its development. Because human communication is such a broad field, with application to so many disciplines, a simple definition is difficult to formulate. Therefore, a few approaches may help clarify what is meant by communication not only in this book, but also in most formal works dealing with communication and people. We will begin with a definition of communication in general, follow with an examination of the areas of study, and then look at each part of the communication process.

A FORMAL DEFINITION

Because this book focuses on human communication, other popular uses of the term **communication** will not be considered here (for example, communication between animals and computer interfacing). The definition used in this text emphasizes "the process of people interacting through the use of messages" (Zeuschner, 1994). This interaction takes place in each of the intrapersonal, interpersonal, small group, public, mass communication, organizational communication, and intercultural communications settings described in this chapter.

PRINCIPLES

A formal definition of communication is based on certain principles of communication.

Communication Is a Whole Process

Two contemporary writers about Speech Communication, Malcolm Sillars and Charles Mudd, suggest that communication is a human activity—it is interpersonal; it is purposive; and it is a process (Mudd and Sillars, 1991). The communication process is dynamic, continuous, irreversible, and contextual (Berlo, 1971). It is not possible to participate in any part of the process without implying the existence and functioning of the others.

Communication Is Inevitable and Irreversible

The desire and capacity for communication is inherent in us. People are equipped with both the brain functions and the physical attributes that make communication possible. Even people without the ability to use their voices or their hearing have both the capacity and ability to communicate. Helen Keller, who was both blind and deaf, set a dramatic example, proving that the communication impulse is strong.

DIVERSITY IN COMMUNICATION
The Miracle Worker

Helen Keller is known here and in other countries as the blind and deaf girl in the famous book, *Miracle Worker*. The "worker" was Helen's teacher, Anne Sullivan Macy, herself nearly blind. Sullivan taught Helen the means to *communicate*—and that was the miracle. She opened Helen to the world through the communication link of finger spelling. Helen went on to become a voracious communicator, reading, writing, and graduating from Radcliffe in 1904. For all her impairments, she viewed the ability to communicate as the most wonderful way to participate in the life of the world. She believed that, "Life is either a daring adventure or nothing."

Communication is *inevitable*. It is also *irreversible* which means that once the message goes out, it cannot be called back. Yes, you can try to modify, rescind, neglect, distort, amplify, or apologize for a message, but you cannot delete it. A Greek sage once said that you cannot step into the same stream twice because you are not the same from one moment to the next, and the stream changes as well. So it is with communication: It takes place in a constantly moving stream of time, and time is not reversible.

Communication Involves Content and Relationship

Each message in the communication process tells us about the twin elements of content and relationship. The first, content, is the substance of the message—the meanings and definitions of message parts. The second, relationship, tells us about the sender and the receiver and how they perceive their interaction. For example, consider the difference between the following sentences:

"Excuse me, but I was hoping that the materials belonging to you in this room could be put away, if it wouldn't be too much trouble?"

"Clean up your room!"

The contents of the statements are similar, but the relationship in each one is clearly different. The fact that a person communicates at all indicates some perception of relationship. In an elevator in a large city, you are unlikely to start a conversation with the strangers around you. However, in the university library elevator, you may feel less inhibited about making small talk or a casual remark because you already feel a relationship in general with your fellow students. A *relationship potential* is the possible basis for a connection you sense in a specific context (Caputo, et al., 1994).

Communication Happens in a Context

Communication cannot happen in a vacuum; there is always a setting or *context* in which the communication takes place and derives much of its meaning. The context may be a culture, a location, or a relationship. Waving at someone in

Japan may be a way to call him or her back to you. Waving at someone driving toward an accident may be a way to warn him or her to slow down. Waving to your best friend across a crowded classroom before an examination may be a way of saying, "Good luck!"

The universal principles of communication are constant, and they work in a process that can be delineated for the purpose of definition and study. Note, however, that these parts are not distinct and easily seen in isolation. They are always interacting with each other.

Communication Takes Place in a Variety of Settings

People who study communication usually focus on one of seven major settings: intrapersonal, interpersonal, small group, public communication, organizational communication, mass communication, intercultural communication, and organizational communication. While there may be some overlapping of areas, each can be easily defined.

Intrapersonal Communication   You can probably guess that this term means communicating within yourself. When you think, daydream, solve problems, and imagine, you are in the realm of **intrapersonal communication.** Some investigators also include in this area all physical feedback mechanisms, such as the sensations of hunger, pain, and pleasure.

Interpersonal Communication   This form of communication describes the interactions of two or more people. The most significant setting for **interpersonal communication** is the one-on-one, or dyad. An interview, a conversation, and intimate communications come under this heading. In the broadest sense, all communication involving other people and oneself is interpersonal but it is usually associated with oneself in direct contact with one other person or a few other people. A different set of communication dynamics comes into play when three or more people get together in a discussion, and that is the area of small group communication.

Small-Group Communication   **Small-group communication** requires the following conditions: leadership, somewhat equal sharing of ideas, peer pressures, roles and norms, and focus on a common goal, usually in face-to-face interaction. Although the number of members of a small group is not absolute, most studies show that four to six people maximize small-group potential. Fewer reduce the opportunity to express a broad range of ideas. A group of more than seven members begins to "crowd" the channels of communication, so people get left out of the discussion and may form subgroups or pairs. The small group is one of the most important communication settings. It exists everywhere from the family to interview teams, roommates, workgroups, legislative subcommittees, and military and business groups.

Public Communication   When one person talks to several others, and is the dominant focus of the communication, the communication is in the public setting.

A good example is a speaker and audience. Again, numbers are not that important. A single person could be talking to three or four others, or to 3000 or 4000 others. The defining characteristics of **public communication** are that one person is identified as the primary sender of messages, while others function primarily as receivers of those messages.

Mass Communication   When a message needs "help" to get from its source to its destination, **mass communication** occurs. Usually, some form of medium— one meaning of which is "between"—is needed to connect the sender to the receivers. These media may be print (newspapers or magazines), electrical (radio, television, or video), or even electronic (computer modems). The common characteristics of mass communication are that something comes between the direct communication of the sender and the receivers; there is usually some delay in sending and receiving; and there is often considerable delay in the feedback, if any, that the sender gets from the receivers.

Organizational Communication   This specialized area focuses on interpersonal, small group, public, and mass communication as they interact in a complex, multigroup setting. Especially important to business, government, and educational institutions, **organizational communication** analyzes what happens to messages as they travel up and down and around a large collection of individuals and groups bound together in some formal way.

Intercultural Communication   Sometimes called "cross-cultural" communication, this setting describes what happens when the sender of a message is from a different cultural background than the intended receiver. In reality, **intercultural communication** can be present in any of the previously described settings. Rarely does one "culture" communicate with another "culture." Rather, one person communicates with other people who do not share the same culture. Nevertheless, it is an area of much interest, importance, and study. It is easy to think of the primary settings in which one national or ethnic group meets another. Some intercultural communication studies are also investigating between-gender communication and the more subtle interactions involving various regional and even occupational differences.

Each of these settings is the subject of its own chapter later in this book, but right now you should be aware of how complex and enormous the study of communication can be. Even though they seem to differ greatly in size and attributes, these settings are all subject to the universal principles outlined above, and they all involve very similar qualities.

▶ **IMPROVING COMPETENCY**

Review Your Communication

Keep track of the various communication settings you are in today. Which small groups are you active in? How many people from different cultures do you interact with? Are you part of an organization? The basis for building communication competency is knowledge, so study the definitions from this chapter to see how many apply to your everyday life.

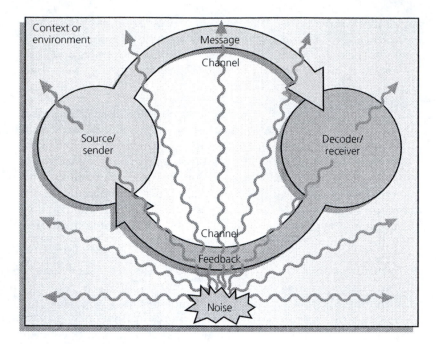

A model of
communication.

A Communication Model

There are seven primary elements in this **communication model**. They include:
contexts, senders/sources, messages, channels, receivers/decoders, interaction,
and feedback/interference/noise. Each of these elements is explained to clarify
the definition of communication.

Context indicates that communication takes place in a setting, sometimes called
an *environment*. That means that there is no communication in a void; the place,
time, surrounding events, physical and psychological climate, what has come
before and what is likely to follow—all of these factors are included in context.

People are an obvious element of communication, given the reference to
senders/sources, but in a technological society the word "communication" is often
used to describe computer interfacing, or machine transmissions to other
machines. For the purposes of this book, electronic messages are not, strictly
speaking, part of the human communication process—a human is always the
originator and the ultimate destination of any message. In other words, people
use machines to help in the transmission of their messages, but, as yet, the
machines do not originate the messages, nor do they define the purpose of the
messages they carry.

Messages are the content of the communication process. They may be verbal
(written or spoken) or nonverbal (everything else from gestures and movements
to smells and objects). Messages can be transmitted through the use of *channels*
such as sound waves, light waves or other sense-stimulating means.

Receivers and decoders are also part of the people orientation in that they are the ultimate goal of any message, and they are needed to translate the message finally into a form that people can comprehend. This link between senders and receivers is where communication interaction happens.

Interaction should call your attention to the "back and forth" nature of communication, sometimes called a "transaction." Even within yourself, you consider and weigh alternatives, so a response is built in. That response may not always be the one you intended, but it is a necessary part of the process. The term *transaction* calls attention to the fact that all parties in the communication event influence and are influenced by the event.

In formal terms, responses, interruptions or blockages to that interaction come under the heading of *feedback/interference* or *noise*. These terms are just what you imagine them to be—the response you have to the message, or the factors that inhibit a clear response. For example, you may give an answer when questioned, you may just think about it, or you may try to respond even though you didn't fully hear or understand the question. The interference or noise can be external or internal. You may have tried to hear a message, but a lawnmower going by the window got in the way. Or you may have been trying to read an article, but someone spilled coffee on the page. Both machine and beverage in these cases constitute a form of external noise. On the other hand, you may be able to see and hear just fine, but you get to daydreaming about a vacation last summer, or worrying about tonight's dinner. Both of these disruptions are internal noise. The next chapter directly addresses the problem of how to handle noise and improve listening skills. Part of the communication model includes the internal noise you generate when you are anxious about communicating. Because the internal anxiety associated with many types of communication can be an important factor in everyone's communication, the next section introduces this topic. More information and methods to respond effectively to this anxiety come in subsequent chapters.

You can see that this simple model of communication has a variety of components, and these components interact with each other. As a convenient way to study the process, we can break it down into sections, and attempt to isolate each section as we define and describe it. But just as a molecule's parts make sense only as they interact, so does the communication model make sense as a whole—not as pieces. The model is a useful guide to help you think about the different aspects of communication, but keep in mind that each aspect implies the existence of the others, and depends on those others for its full meaning. Because noise can be found in any part of the model, it is important to take a moment now and begin our examination of this important idea.

One of the most difficult times to listen effectively is right before you are called on to present your message. Especially if you are just about to give a speech, the internal factors of worry may be so great that your physical and psychological focus is going out of control. The anxiety associated with public communication is well known to everyone who has ever given a speech in public, and was well known to the ancient Greeks as well. We have stories of the great orator, Demosthenes, who worked painfully hard to overcome his inhibitions and perceived limitations as a speaker, shouting out his speeches to the ocean waves, putting pebbles in his mouth to speak more clearly, and continually practicing so that he could finally summon the courage to address the Athenian crowd. Some 2500 years after his death, his speeches are still reprinted and studied as models of excellent oratory. Communication apprehension seems to be a core part of communication, cutting across contexts, situations, cultures, languages, and individuals. It can be seen as a fundamental factor in the study of communication. So, let's take a first look at this problem—speech anxiety—and see what it is and what can be done about it.

COMMUNICATION APPREHENSION

What is commonly called nervousness, stage fright, or even shyness is called **communication apprehension** (CA) by people studying this reaction. Some link it to a broader concept, "performance anxiety," to cover the following situations: athletic performances, music recitals, stage productions, business deadlines, test taking, and even interpersonal situations, such as asking someone for a date.

Sources of Anxiety

The one thing that all these events have in common is that by taking part in them a person's actions will be judged or evaluated. Researchers have demonstrated that a person is likely to suffer an attack of this anxiety in any number of different situations (Richmond and McCroskey, 1995). The more the person cares about the outcome, the greater the anxiety (McCroskey, 1977). Whenever a person begins to dread the possible failure of his or her actions, the anxiety begins to take hold. It is a universal reaction, and its immediate effects are predictable.

Anxiety Reactions

The human body is well equipped to deal with fear. People are genetically programmed to shift into a heightened state when they are, or believe they are, confronted with a threat.

The fear can be of mountain lions or of making a mistake. This reaction is often called the "flight/fight" response, and begins with a message from the brain's danger perception center to the adrenal glands telling them to "start pumping." Adrenaline flows almost instantly into the person's system, making the person ready to run or to fight. Unfortunately, the brain's danger center does not differentiate between reactions appropriate to facing an angry lion and those appropriate to giving a speech; it prepares us the same way for both. Breathing becomes tense and shallow; hands and feet get cold and sweaty; heart rate increases; stomach and digestive system go into spasms; large muscles become tense and may twitch with all the energy flowing into them; the voice tightens; and the mind seems to evaporate.

Each of these reactions may have roots in a survival mechanism needed in a more primitive time. For example, hands and feet get cold because the blood leaves the surface capillaries and flows to the large muscles, allowing for more energy to be available to the arms and legs to do battle or run away. Moreover, with less blood near the surface of the skin, an injured person is less likely to bleed—great protection from the lions, but hardly useful for a business presentation!

Sweaty hands and feet can also help when facing an angry lion because a small amount of moisture increases traction. When turning a page in a book or newspaper what do some people do automatically? Lick their finger. In the past, better traction helped people hold on to a weapon, grab a vine and swing, or scale a tree or a cliff, but traction does not get someone a date for Saturday or a better grade on a class speech.

Blood also leaves the viscera and travels to the large muscles. Tension in the mid-section and shallow breathing also give a person more strength. Think of karate demonstrations. Just before an expert smashes a brick apart, she shouts "HA!" Why? Is she trying to *scare* the brick into breaking? No, she is tightening up her midsection to focus her energy. During a speech, a person's body automatically tries to do the same thing. Tension in the muscles affect the throat; extra energy is bottled up in the large muscles; and some blood flows from the frontal cortex, where the mind operates, and goes to the medulla to help coordinate the right and left sides of the brain. The net result is a person who feels out of control. What can be done?

Responses to Anxiety

After the body has reacted, it is time for the person as a whole to respond. There is no way to prevent communication anxiety, so the best response is to prepare for it. Many students set an unrealistic goal of getting rid of their physical reactions, or conquering them somehow. A better goal is to respond so that you direct the anxiety reaction and eliminate the effects that detract from your performance. Then you can use the rest of the energy to make your communication more interesting, dynamic, and appealing to your listener.

Unfortunately, many people block their own success by falling into traps of "irrational thinking" (Adler and Rodman, 1994; Ellis, 1977). For people in communication situations, these "traps" can be classified as fallacies.

The Fallacy of Catastrophic Failure   Sometimes people focus on the disaster they imagine will happen, often making it happen by their own certainty. They imagine forgetting everything. They think their messages will be rejected so totally that it isn't even worth trying. Yet, in reality, most listeners are sympathetic to a speaker. They want to hear, they try to understand, and they overlook the minor errors almost everyone makes in any message presentation.

The Fallacy of Perfection   This problem is the counterpart and often companion to the first. People who believe this fallacy tell themselves they should be perfect. Not a single "um" is allowed in their presentation. Every word must be precisely

The Story of Communication
Performance Anxiety

UNIVERSALLY RECOGNIZED PERFORMERS are not immune to attacks of anxiety. One of the finest actors of our age, Sir Laurence Olivier, used to tell of being so frightened right before he went on stage that he would run to the bathroom and vomit before every performance. The great opera tenor, Enrico Caruso, spoke of how he would pace nervously in the stage wings waiting for his entrance. A young tenor came up to him and asked, "Why are *you* nervous? You're the great Caruso!"

Caruso replied, "Young man, you can just go out there and sing and all will be fine. But night after night, *I* have to go out there and sound like 'Caruso'!"

in the proper place, given at the best tone and at the best rate; only a perfect score on an exam will do; and all experiments must be flawless. Yet successful communicators are rarely even close to such a level of perfection. Often these people focus on presentation details to a point at which they forget that listeners are interested in *content*. Listeners want to know the value of the message and are only superficially concerned with extraneous slips. Perfection is an unrealistic goal in virtually every human activity, and communication is one of the least perfect of our undertakings. Setting perfection as a goal can become a psychological compulsion that then actually inhibits our ability to do an excellent job.

The Fallacy of Approval   A person who thinks he or she must have 100% agreement or support from everyone is a victim of the fallacy of approval. Everyone needs approval (Schutz, 1958) and seeking it helps people integrate into society. However, it is unrealistic to think that it is possible to please everyone. People who are always trying too hard to be friendly actually drive people away. These people create the opposite effect from the one they seek because they are trapped into thinking that they must always please everyone, which is yet another irrational goal.

The Fallacy of Overgeneralization   In this circumstance, a person holds on to a previous experience or exaggerates it until he or she thinks it is the norm for behavior. Because a previous situation was not as successful as the person had wanted it to be, it is easy to believe that future situations will be just as unpleasant. To counteract this fallacy it helps to recognize that each of us is always changing and growing in experience and ability. No one steps into the same river twice; you are not the same and the river moves on. Moreover, it's possible to take several positive, proactive steps to counter the undesirable effects of communication apprehension.

Coping Strategies

There are ways to counteract these fallacies by focusing on reality, your own potential, and the actual situation. These fallacies can be avoided by taking a rational approach, and thereby become less bothered by the physiological reactions to the stress. This approach includes both physical preparation and psychological preparation (Zeuschner, 1994).

Physical preparation includes deep, relaxing breathing; selective tensing and relaxing of muscles; and movement to burn off excess energy. Psychological preparation involves developing a positive self-image; becoming aware of and mastering the areas of communication competence covered in the next section; and creating confidence through thorough preparation and practice (McCroskey and Richmond, 1982).

Research About Communication Apprehension

After years of studying people who experience communication apprehension, researchers have come to several conclusions about its nature and how to lessen its effects. Communication apprehension is tied closely to self-concept, and for that reason the subject is discussed again in later chapters. For now, you should realize that communication apprehension is widely felt, although most people can and do carry on their communications in spite of it. A critical evaluation of what is probable, likely, and logical can be a way to counteract unproductive anxiety.

Four levels of communication apprehension (CA) are identified in the extensive research done by McCroskey and Richmond. They found that some persons have CA as a general trait. That is, they experience high levels of anxiety in all communication situations. Their condition is extremely limiting, for they may be unable to talk on the telephone, answer a question in class, or even make a request of a store clerk. A second group experiences extensive apprehension in situations requiring some sort of solo presentation or participation in a group discussion, presentation, or speech. Their level of anxiety may change from one situation to another, but it is usually present. The third type of person experiences apprehension in the presence of a given individual or group. For example, a certain instructor, but not instructors in general, will always cause that person anxiety. Along the same lines, a special or significant person—parent, police officer, boss—will always get some people's adrenaline flowing no matter what the circumstances. Some say that falling in love produces a similar reaction. Finally, most people experience CA in a particular situation—for example, when the instructor calls a student in for a conference, when the boss demands an unexpected meeting, or when a person is put on the spot for whatever reason (McCroskey and Richmond, 1998). In all these situations, CA is evident but it is possible to respond to it in a way that limits its negative effects on the ability to send and receive messages.

COMMUNICATION COMPETENCE REVIEWED

Repertoire, Selection, Implementation, Evaluation

The four elements required to be a competent communicator are developing a broad range or *repertoire* of skills and perspectives; learning how to *select* from that background, using appropriate criteria; putting into practice or *implementing* certain skills in the presentation and delivery of the message; and finally, learning *to evaluate* the communication so that you can adjust your future efforts based on an analysis of your past efforts. In an important way, this entire text is aimed at helping you to develop one or more of these competencies. They are somewhat general at this point; so let us consider what experts in the field of Speech Communication have defined as **communication competencies**.

Knowledge, Feelings, and Skills

A widely read educator, Benjamin Bloom, created a system to organize educational goals and outcomes that he called "cognitive, affective and psycho-motor" dimensions of education (Bloom, 1956). Another way to label these ideas is to call them *knowledge, feelings,* and *skills*. These words describe many of the communication abilities covered in this text.

Knowledge as a competency in the field of Speech Communication means gaining information about the subject. It refers to the history of the field, its concern with ethics, its universal principles and applications, and its place in the development of culture, especially Western Civilization. It includes knowledge about the contexts of Speech Communication, from intrapersonal to intercultural, and about the elements of the communication process.

In terms of *feelings*, the field offers an opportunity to experience a growing level of ability and the associated sense of pride that comes from working competently. You should feel both responsible for your messages and for being an effective receiver of other people's messages. You should feel that you play a valuable part in society by being a responsible communicator, and you should be convinced of your own self-worth, the worth of others, and the value of ideas, even if they are different from your own (McBath, 1975).

Skills are the obvious focus of several aspects of this text, and often the reason why schools offer or require courses in communication. "What can I *do* with this class?" is a frequent question from students, their parents, and others in the academic community. Although skills are certainly the most easily measured and observed of these three competencies, they are best used in conjunction with the other two. Someone who is skilled in organizing and presenting messages has surely gained something important; but without a clear understanding of background and principles, coupled with a sense of responsibility and value, these skills are somewhat superficial.

At the end of each of the following chapters, a reference is made to how that chapter contributes to your knowledge, your feelings, and your skills. From those areas, you build your communication competence. Your expanding knowledge and skills increased the choices you have available—your *repertoire*. Some of the chapters discuss different circumstances and applications that are appropriate, helping you to learn about making choices. That communicators are concerned with appropriate choices indicates that they are following the accepted behavior for relationships and contexts (Spitzberg and Cupach 1984).

Other chapters are aimed at building skills—your *implementation*. Finally, *evaluation* is present in the various exercises at the end of the chapters as well as in the various assignments you will complete for the class and the daily interactions you have that involve communication.

SUMMARY

This course is a beginning, designed to launch you in the study of a rich discipline. It is a discipline abundant in history, revealing about ourselves, and useful in every aspect of successful living. The effects of good communication are far-reaching. You have seen how the principles of communication work in a variety of settings. Communication is a whole process, inevitable and irreversible, that involves both content and relationships. The principles of communication operate within everyone; when a person talks to another person; when a person participates in small groups, in meetings, in careers; and when a person is involved with the mass media and people of different cultures. Each message takes place in a context, has a source and destination, travels over a channel, and is subject to internal and external interferences. Feedback is the single most important element in making messages accurate. Communication anxiety is a normal part of the communication process and extreme anxiety can be dealt with so that communication flows more smoothly. Finally, being a competent communicator involves enlarging your pool of resources, selecting carefully from that pool, putting choices into practice, and evaluating performances. By enlarging your repertoire, you will gain knowledge about communication and your feelings of self-worth, and you will enhance your skills. Becoming a competent communicator probably does not happen at any particular point in time, but can be a life-long endeavor. Specific goals, however, are discernible and achievable, even in a single course of study. This book is an effort to lead you farther along the path of your own development.

Key Terms

communication, **22**
intrapersonal communication, **24**
interpersonal communication, **24**
small-group communication, **24**
public communication, **25**
mass communication, **25**

organizational communication, **25**
intercultural communication, **25**
communication model, **26**
communication apprehension (CA), **28**
communication competencies, **32**

EXERCISES

1. Communication is studied in many different disciplines, and each one defines *communication* differently. Find five different dictionaries (e.g., law dictionary, medical dictionary, dictionary of psychological terms, business dictionary, general use dictionary) and record the various definitions you find. Bring them to class for a discussion of the meaning of the term *communication*.

2. Describe how the elements of the communication model work in at least three different communication contexts. In your descriptions, identify each element and indicate how it relates to the other elements in each of the three contexts.

3. What was your most recent experience with communication anxiety? Answering a question in class? Giving a report for an organization you belong to? Asking someone for a date? Being interviewed for a job? What was your reaction to the anxiety? What did you do about it?

4. Make a list of three or four activities in which you think improved communication skills would be most beneficial to you. Keep the list in the back of your notebook for later use.

References

Adler, Ronald and George Rodman. *Understanding Human Communication.* New York: Harcourt Brace, 1994.

Berlo, David K. *The Process of Communication.* New York: Holt, Rinehart and Winston, 1960.

Bloom, B. S. *Taxonomy of Educational Objectives.* New York: McKay, 1956.

Caputo, J. S., H. C. Hazel, and C. McMahon. *Interpersonal Communication.* Boston: Allyn and Bacon, 1994.

Craig, Richard. "Expectations and Elections: How Television Defines Campaign News." *Critical Studies in Media Communication* 17, 1 (March 2000).

Ellis, Albert. *A New Guide to Rational Living.* North Hollywood, CA: Wilshire Books, 1977.

Kelly, Lynne, Robert Duran, and J. Jerome Zolten. "The Effect of Reticence on College Students' Use of Electronic Mail to Communicate with Faculty." *Communication Education 50,* 2 (April 2001).

McBath, James H. *Forensics as Communication.* Skokie: National Textbook Co., 1975: 14.

McCroskey, James. "Oral Communication Apprehension: A Summary of Recent Theory and Research," *Human Communication Research* 4, 1977.

McCroskey, J. C. and V. P. Richmond. *The Quiet Ones: Communication Apprehension and Shyness.* Scottsdale, AZ: Gorsuch Scarisbrick, 1982.

McCroskey, James C. and Virginia P. Richmond. "Communication Apprehension and Small Group Communication" in Robert Cathcart and Larry A. Samovar, *Small Group Communication,* 5th ed., Dubuque: Wm. C. Brown, 1988.

Messman, Susan J. and Jennifer Jones-Corley. "Effects of Communication Environment, Immediacy, and Communication Apprehension on Cognitive and Affective Learning." *Communication Monographs 68,* 2, June 2001.

Mudd, Charles S. and Malcolm O. Sillars. *Speech: Content and Communication,* 5th ed. New York: Crowell and Co., 1991.

Richmond, V. and J. McCroskey. *Communication: Apprehension, Avoidance and Effectiveness,* 4th ed. Scottsdale, AZ: Gorsuch Scarisbrick, 1995.

Schutz, William, *FIRO: A Three Dimensional Theory of Interpersonal Behavior.* New York: Rinehart, 1958.

Spitzberg, B. and W. Cupach, *Interpersonal Communication Competence.* Beverly Hills: Sage, 1984.

Zeuschner, Raymond B. *Building Clear Communication.* Glenview, IL: Scott, Foresman and Co., 1985.

———. *Effective Public Speaking.* Dubuque, IA: Kendall-Hunt, 1994.

CHAPTER 3

What We Know About Listening

After reading this chapter, you should be able to:

- Identify the differences between hearing and listening
- Describe the four steps of active listening
- Understand the similarities in and differences between listening critically, listening for appreciation, and listening to emphasize
- Apply the steps of active listening to your own behavior

Listening is a communication skill that is one of the primary communication interactions. It is vital to the transmission and reception of oral communication. In order to provide feedback, you need to *listen* to the messages. There are at least two ways to listen—passively and actively. There are a variety of reasons for listening: to make sense of potentially important information, for entertainment, to learn in class, and to understand the messages of people who want you to act in a variety of ways. Each of these elements of listening will be discussed as a primary tool of communication (Wolvin and Wolvin, 1991).

LISTENING: THE FIRST COMMUNICATION EVENT

Listening is a "first" in several respects. It is the communication interaction we encounter first. Some research indicates that fetuses react to sounds that reach them in the womb. They can begin to recognize voices and react to them. After birth, listening was the primary means by which we learned to speak. We heard a sound, we paid attention to it, we remembered and recognized it, and finally we tried to imitate it.

But listening is also the "first" communication event in another sense—it occupies more of our time than any other type of communicating. In fact, listening takes up more of our day than *all* other kinds of communication combined (Pauk, 1989), ranging from 60 percent of college students' time as reported in one study, to 53 percent as reported in another (Barker, et al., 1981).

The time you spend listening represents a significant portion of your life. Yet, as with speaking, all of us do it but few of us do it well. A distinction can be made between *adequate* listening, and *effective* listening. You may listen adequately enough to get through the day—following directions fairly well, taking sufficient notes in class to perform decently on tests, and getting along with your associates—but still you could improve in nearly every area. That is your goal—improving your listening so that you use your time and energy effectively. Let's take a deeper look at listening, your first communication skill.

Listening Contexts

There are at least four different reasons we listen: appreciation, empathy, comprehension, and criticism. Each of these contexts applies to activities we do every day (Wolvin & Coakley, 1992). For example, listening for **appreciation** means that enjoyment of the event is your primary purpose. As you listen for recreation to music, you are engaging in appreciative listening. **Empathic listening** is involved when friends share their troubles with you and you respond by giving them your time and attention. You demonstrate care and concern by listening; you communicate empathy. Classroom listening is a clear example of listening for **comprehension**. You take notes and pay attention to the lecture, film, or discussion in an effort to understand the material. Finally, you engage in *critical* listening when you gather information about a new car you might purchase, or when two candidates for office debate in an attempt to win your vote. You apply the principles of critical thinking as you listen to help you make effective decisions. Each type of listening will be discussed further in the sections about improving your listening competency.

Effective Listening

Listening is often not studied simply because it seems so obvious. Unlike trigonometry, which everybody knows that you cannot just "do," but need to learn, effective listening is taken for granted. Even with daily reminders of how wrong that assumption is, we still neglect to train ourselves for the single activity we spend most of our time doing (Sypher et al., 1989). There are several reasons we gloss over the importance of listening. Most of these have to do with several misconceptions about the activity.

First Misconception   Most people assume that listening is the same as **hearing.** Actually, hearing involves only the physical reception of the sound waves by your auditory mechanisms. You are quite capable of receiving many sounds that you do not listen to at all. For example, as you are reading this paragraph there are many sounds around you that your hearing mechanism is picking up, but you are not paying attention to them. These may include cars driving by, people talking at a distance, or a television or radio in another room; even the fluorescent light makes a sound. Sometimes, people hear sounds, and *appear* to be listening, but they may be attending to internal dialogue or noise. This activity is called *pseudo-listening* (Caputo, Hazel, McMahon, 1994).

Of course, the first step in listening *is* hearing—the reception of sound waves by the hearing mechanism in the ear. The next step is paying attention to those sounds and organizing them into a meaningful pattern that begins the process of understanding.

We do not always understand the sounds to which we pay attention. For example, the sounds of an unfamiliar language are sounds we hear but we are simply unable to organize them into meaning. Birdcalls may mean something to the bird, but we probably do not translate them. However, we

> ▶ **IMPROVING COMPETENCY**
> ## Your Listening Profile
>
> Do you think the estimates about your communication time are accurate? Try to review the way you spent today. First, block out time segments on a piece of paper from when you awoke to when you retire. Now estimate whether you were listening, speaking, writing, or reading. TV time, music time, and conversation time all count as listening. Since these averages are gathered from many college students, yours may be slightly different, just as mine are different when I spend an intense day writing. Nevertheless, over the course of several typical days, the same pattern emerges—listening takes up more than half our communication time.

often think that because we *heard* a sound, we understood it. That idea is our second misconception.

Second Misconception   Some people think that understanding comes automatically from paying attention. However, think about listening very hard to movie dialogue in another language. You can concentrate very carefully on every sound, and still not understand much. Comprehension means organizing sounds into meaningful patterns and associations. Unfortunately, we all may speak a language that is "foreign" at one time or another—even to our friends and family. One study of listening comprehension concluded that people grasp only about 50% of what they hear (Steil et al., 1983). As you will explore more thoroughly in a later chapter, we all have different vocabularies and associations with common words. As a result, our everyday interactions are filled with errors in understanding—from slight and unimportant, to large and consequential.

There are ways to counteract these misconceptions and thus increase your ability to understand the sounds you receive. Such systems are often called **active listening**.

Active Listening

By following the four major steps of active listening you can dramatically increase your understanding and retention of the information you hear. This process is: (1) Getting prepared to listen, (2) Staying involved with the communication, (3) Keeping an open mind while listening, and (4) Reviewing and evaluating after the event.

These steps can be applied to each of the four types of listening contexts. Before applying them to everyday types of listening behaviors, let's take a brief look at the steps of active listening.

Getting Prepared   To be fully prepared to listen, get ready both physically and mentally. In terms of physical preparation, you need to be able to *hear* the sounds.

TECHNOLOGY AND COMMUNICATION
Edison's Deafness Gave Us Sound

Hearing sounds is a first step in listening, and those with limited hearing ability have many systems available to increase their reception of sound. Most of these systems owe their existence to America's great inventor, Thomas Edison. Edison was deaf for most of his later life, and the invention of the phonograph came as a result of his efforts to produce a hearing aid. In fact, the horns you see on old Edison phonographs are taken from the "ear trumpets" deaf people used to amplify sound in those days. Edison's expert technological skills and creative insight brought about improvement in the way we understand hearing as well as the development of one the world's greatest tools for entertainment and education—recorded sound.

You might need to move closer to the source, eliminate interfering noises, such as radio or television sounds, or adjust your seat so that you can see better. If you want to remember specific ideas or materials for later use—such as on a test—then bring notepaper, pens, pencils, and sit in a place where you can write. If you don't see well at distances, sit near the front. If you can't hear well, move closer. If you are easily distracted, don't sit next to the open door or near a window. Give yourself as many advantages as possible in your physical placement so that you get the most out of the listening experience.

Mental preparation includes reading about the topic *ahead* of the event if you need some background information, or clearing your thoughts of extraneous ideas. Suppose you are going to listen to a world-famous expert on the Galapagos Islands. You would strengthen your listening ability by first investigating some material about the islands. Even a few minutes of reading in a general encyclopedia would help create a context for the event and vastly increase both the amount of material you can comprehend, and the speed at which you can take it in. In a classroom situation, reading the assigned material before class will make any lecture or discussion much more meaningful. Some students read entire texts for their classes before the term even begins. At a minimum, you can make a commitment to active listening by preparing mentally.

Staying Involved   The next step in active listening is to stay involved. Keeping your attention focused on the speaker may be one of the most difficult parts of the listening process because distractions are everywhere—inside your head and outside. Staying involved requires both physical and mental actions.

Physically, you should keep eye contact with the speaker, watching for important nonverbal cues including facial expressions and gestures. Some speakers make use of visual aids, such as charts or objects or slide projections, that require your attention. Keeping your eyes on the event is an important job because there may be distractions all around, from someone walking by the door to an attractive person three rows over that you'd like to get to know better, or an event happening outside the window. Despite these distractions, you must stay focused on the speaker. You also need to keep yourself alert by assuming good posture. If you get too comfortable, you may drift off. Shift around in your seat to keep from getting settled in any one position. Keep jotting down ideas with your pencil and make certain that you remain where you can hear and see easily. Get up and move if necessary.

Mentally, concentration is your best ally in staying involved. Summarize mentally as the speaker moves from one idea to another. Memory devices can help you associate an idea you are hearing for the first time with something familiar. For example, if the speaker is discussing "dressage," you might associate the "dress" part of the term with "dressy clothes" and remember that *dressage* is a very formal type of competitive horseback riding. Make up any associations that work for you as ways to stay mentally involved, especially when the subject matter is not familiar. If there will be a question time following a presentation, make notes about questions you might like to have answered. It is important to concentrate on the speaker, however, so don't get distracted by making up complex associations or questions. If you do, you may come back to the speaker after several minutes and be lost because there has been a change in the direction of the presentation.

Keeping an Open Mind   One of the major **barriers** to staying involved with a speaker is the tendency to react to something that is said and begin to dwell on it to the extent that the speaker leaves us behind. This reaction, called *quick judgment*, is most likely to occur when the speaker touches on a subject about which we feel strongly. Our minds jump to judgment, and we stop listening. For example, if the speaker uses a term you find offensive, you may pay so much attention to the use of the term that you miss the fact that the speaker also finds the term offensive. Or, you may find that a speaker shares a favorite interest of yours. The speaker makes a comparison to your favorite baseball team, and you react by thinking how wonderful the speaker is to admire the same team you do—but you may not notice that the comparison is faulty and irrelevant.

This third step of active listening—keeping an open mind—is truly a difficult part of good listening, and it must be conscientiously exercised to be effective. Otherwise, you may simply stop listening when the speaker uses terms or references or analogies to which you have very strong reactions. Keep listening for the idea, and then wait to make your judgment.

Keeping an open mind does not mean accepting as true everything you hear. It does mean that you listen as completely and as carefully as you can, but not uncritically. An open mind allows you to take in the complete message before passing judgment. Judgment, however, is an important part of the active listening process. It is *quick* judgment that is the problem, not the evaluation itself.

DIVERSITY IN COMMUNICATION
Are You Invisible?

What are your "button" words? What words make you angry or hurt your feelings? Do you find pejorative references to ethnic groups distracting? Or just when they are about *your* ethnic group? How about favorite sports teams? If you listen to a speaker who is wearing a jersey of the rival team of your favorite, do you find it difficult to listen with an open mind? References to singers, politicians, sports figures, and religious authorities can all have a highly positive effect for the source—the *halo* effect. However, those same references can turn off other listeners and cause them to become resentful. Ralph Ellison, in his book *The Invisible Man*, talked about the frustration he felt when people treated him almost as if he did not exist.

Some speakers feel the same way when they sense that their intended listeners are not paying attention to them. A frequent research finding in studies of gender and communication shows that both male and female instructors respond to boys' answers in class more often than girls' answers (Rowe, 1986). How would (or how does) this experience affect you? Would it (or does it) make you feel invisible?

Reviewing and Evaluating
After an event is over, it is time to review and highlight the main ideas and themes. You may wish to look over your notes and fill in any sketchy areas. It is a good idea to try to remember immediately any of the supporting materials the speaker used. What were the statistics? Stories? Quotations? Examples?

Some students do this type of reviewing daily. When they have a break between classes or when they arrive home for the day, *before* they take off for other

CRITICAL THINKING IN COMMUNICATION
Reacting or Thinking?

You can probably recall the effect of a powerful speaker on your emotions and feelings. Often political speakers will tell an especially moving story, one that gets you angry or sympathetic. While these stories are useful for getting attention, they should enhance, not substitute for content. A critical listener will *think* about the ideas as well as experience the feelings. In a persuasive situation, you should apply your thinking skills, knowing that some-times emotional responses may replace careful evaluation. Pausing, questioning, and testing ideas can all help you to engage your critical thinking skills while you listen.

activities, they quickly go through their class notes for that day and fill in any incomplete phrases, or partial notes they took. In twenty or thirty minutes, they can clean up their class notes. They do not try to study at this point; they just review to eliminate blanks they left as they were listening. Then, when it *is* time to study, they have complete notes from the day.

Others may neglect to review immediately and wait days, or possibly weeks, before trying to recall what was clear once, but now is lost. You probably have a piece of paper next to your telephone right now with a telephone number on it in *your* handwriting. But you forgot to write down the name next to it. Now the number has become a mystery, even though it was perfectly clear at the time you wrote it. Reviewing notes immediately just to fill in content is one of the most powerful study aids for people trying to stay on, or get on, the Dean's List.

Once you have the information clearly and completely in hand, then it is time to evaluate it. There are many ways to evaluate information. You can look at its form, delivery, subject, presentation, use of supporting materials, and fairness or relevance. You can evaluate whether the presenter adapted to the relevant needs and concerns of the listeners. You can look at the recentness of the evidence; determine if there was evidence at all; and note which, if any, experts were cited.

While presentation and delivery skills are often the most immediate items to be evaluated, a careful evaluation does not begin and end with the presentation skills of voice, eye contact, and movement or gesture. Some critics think they have done a good job if they count the "ums" and "uhs" in a speech. To have done that, and missed the content and substance, is a waste of listening time.

It is probably true that great speakers avoid verbal dysfluencies ("ums" and "uhs"), but there is much more to a worthwhile message than a smooth presen-tation. Some very smooth presenters in history have carried the most profoundly evil messages. Adolf Hitler is a case in point. On the other hand, some profound ideas were presented in plain, flat style, as is evident in the newspaper accounts of Lincoln's speech at Gettysburg.

The Story of Communication
The Gettysburg Address

NOVEMBER 19, 1863: "Fourscore and seven years ago our fathers brought forth on this continent a new nation, conceived in liberty and dedicated to the proposition that all men are created equal. Now we are engaged in a great civil war, testing whether that nation or any nation so conceived and so dedicated can long endure. We are met on a great battlefield of that war. We have come to dedicate a portion of that field as a final resting place for those who here gave their lives that that nation might live. It is altogether fitting and proper that we should do this.

But, in a larger sense, we cannot dedicate—we cannot consecrate—we cannot hallow—this ground. The brave men, living and dead, who struggled here, have consecrated it, far above our poor power to add or detract. The world will little note, nor long remember what we say here, but it can never forget what they did here. If is for us the living, rather, to be dedicated here to the unfinished work which they who fought here have thus far so nobly advanced. It is rather for us to be here dedicated to the great task remaining before us—that from these honored dead we take increased devotion to that cause for which they gave the last full measure of devotion—that we here highly resolve that these dead shall not have died in vain—that this nation, under God, shall have a new birth of freedom—and that government of the people, by the people, for the people, shall not perish from the earth."

To summarize, evaluation should help you obtain a complete picture of the message, including both its content and its delivery. Some of the most memorable speakers of all time were able to do justice to both.

It is important to apply the steps of active listening—getting prepared, staying involved, keeping an open mind, and reviewing and evaluating—as much as you can. These steps are ready for you to start using now! Using them is your first communication assignment, an activity you can begin immediately. You will have at least 40 to 60 percent of your day, every day, to try to put principles into practice. To get you started, let's look at the reasons and the places to work on your listening skills.

Listening Skills in Context

The four contexts for listening—appreciative, empathic, comprehensive, and critical—were identified at the beginning of this chapter. Let's examine how the techniques of active listening can be applied in each area.

Listening for Appreciation   Probably the listening event easiest to look forward to is listening for recreation. Your favorite radio station, CD player, or live concerts are quick examples. In the listening for recreation category, you can still apply the principles of active listening. Get yourself ready to relax. You might increase your enjoyment if you know a little about the music or the artist. In fact, many newspaper and magazine articles about recording artists help to fulfill this part of listening preparation. Reviews of concerts or new releases also provide background information that may help you prepare for better recreational listening. Just using headphones or volume controls, or closing your eyes and shutting out distractions help you get involved and stay involved. You may also increase your enjoyment by listening to new or unfamiliar material with an open mind. It might take several attempts before you appreciate a new approach, sound, artist, or style. Finally, you can review the material and decide if you want to hear more, or move on to another listening experience. There are people who constantly flip through radio stations until they finally hear a familiar, favorite song. They give no time to a station unless they recognize the material immediately. A good recreational listener will be more tolerant and withhold quick evaluation in favor of thoughtful review and judgment.

Listening For Empathy   Being part of any social interactions requires that you function as a sender *and* a receiver of information. Remember that communication is a transaction in which meanings and understanding result from the interaction of the communicators. When your primary role in an interaction is to support your relationship with another person, you are probably engaged in **empathic listening**. Empathy means to "feel within" someone else's emotional state. Empathic listening means trying to both understand the content of the message and relate to the feelings behind that message. You might be discussing with a friend or close co-worker some problem or situation in which feelings are important. Suppose your roommate has just received a low grade on an assignment and tells you about it. You could say, "Hey, no big deal, you'll do better next time." Although you might be trying to help, you have not engaged in empathic listening. Instead, if you say, "Sounds like a real let-down," you are letting your friend know that you understand about both the low grade and how your friend feels about the situation. Much counseling—both professional and informal—involves providing empathic listening. When you really like a friend, often it is because that person listens, *really listens,* to you and provides feedback indicating that he or she identifies, understands, and supports your feelings.

Using active listening in an empathic setting may mean putting your communication agenda aside for the moment and getting ready to listen to your partner's message. By being nonjudgmental in this situation, you help your partner to avoid feeling defensive and may invite your partner to explore further his or her ideas and reactions. Keep involved by providing appropriate feedback, making brief references to similar situations or feelings you have experienced, and yet restraining your own talking so that your partner can fully express him or herself. An important part of empathic listening may be to help your partner by providing a summary of what he or she has told you. This feedback may help your partner to clarify and even reevaluate the situation. You can also make your own personal evaluation by considering how your partner's experience applies to your own situation.

Listening for Comprehension   As a student, you spend a major portion of your time in activities that require listening for comprehension. Research indicates that effective listening correlates directly with academic success. Students who tested best on listening skills also had the highest grades (Coakley and Wolvin, 1991). In the classroom, you focus primarily on remembering ideas and content presented by your instructors and others. In a learning environment much of your comprehension depends upon your ability to recall major ideas and their supporting details. You may have to learn complex mathematics; engineering formulae; or historical dates, names, and locations. You may be asked to both remember and criticize. You could be asked not just *when* the French Revolution started, but *why*, and what *you think* might have been done differently. In communication classes, you may be asked to be a critic of other students' speeches or presentations, and your instructors will be seeking both summary *and* evaluation from you.

Classroom listening is difficult because of the many barriers that are potentially at work, interfering with your ability to listen effectively. For example, most classrooms are not furnished with comfortable chairs; the lighting may be poor, or the temperature uncomfortable. Other barriers to good listening may come from your instructors, most of whom have not taken courses in how to lecture effectively. Your mathematics professor may have no idea of how to organize a lecture, how to do effective previews and transitions, or how to enhance content with clear visual aids. Your chemistry instructor may be so involved in working out a formula construction problem that he or she makes no effort to tie fast-appearing work on the board to your note-taking speed. Finally, *you* may provide barriers by having a poor attitude if the class is required for general education and not in your major area of interest. Or you might be preoccupied by an exam coming up next hour in another class. You might be distracted by home or personal concerns that pull your attention away from the subject at hand. Each of these problems is a form of *noise* which we discussed in Chapter Two as part of the communication model. Good listening in the classroom is a challenge, and you will need all the skills of active listening to help you meet that challenge.

Increased attention to comprehensive listening can improve your classroom experience. *Get prepared* by reading the assigned material, having pencil and paper handy for notes, sitting where you can see and hear, and avoiding hunger and fatigue. *Stay involved* by taking notes, rephrasing the ideas, connecting material to other things you know, asking questions, and paying attention to other classroom comments. *Withhold quick evaluation*, as it becomes internal noise to distract you. Avoid mental distractions such as wishing you did not have to take this class or critiquing the appearance or presentation of the instructor. Finally, the best students always *review* shortly after class to refine and complete their notes, connect up ideas to the reading materials, and prepare questions for the next session to clarify ideas they still find unclear or incomplete.

Listening Critically   A major purpose of training in listening is to enable you to become a wise consumer of the information that flows at you daily. If you watch twenty hours of television weekly—a fairly low average for people in the sixteen- to twenty-five-year-old age range—you will be exposed to about 280 commercial messages a week urging you to buy various products or services. Some estimates of commercials viewed go as high as a million commercials by the time you are twenty (Postman, 1981). By the early 1970s, it was estimated that the average college freshman had been exposed to 22,000 hours of television programming (Burmeister, 1974). Most likely, the number has increased since that study. Add hours of radio listening to that number and you have a sizable number of messages designed by professionals trained in persuading you to act in a manner of their design. Not all of these actions are for your benefit; in fact they are likely for the benefit of the advertiser's sales figures. **Critical listening** means taking information and looking at it carefully. It means being able to analyze the content and form of the message so that you make informed decisions. As you follow the steps for active listening, add these items to your mental checklist:

- What was the quality of supporting material?
- How adequate were the reasons expressed?
- Were there reasons that were *not* expressed? Why?
- Were the appeals logical, emotional, or personal?
- What will I gain from the proposed action?
- What will the presenter gain from my action?

Consider these questions while you are involved in listening and at the end of the event, let them form a major part of your evaluation. Does the speaker want you to act immediately, before you have a chance to evaluate the message? What does that say about the speaker's purposes?

Listening happens in almost every waking moment of our lives. It is an event that has great importance for us every day, yet one that is little studied and seldom taught. In this short introduction to listening, you saw how the four steps of active listening can help you to improve your listening abilities. This improvement can lead you to become a better critic of the persuasive messages from advertisers, a more informed classroom receiver of ideas, an enhanced recreational listener, and an empathic friend.

IMPROVING LISTENING COMPETENCY

Let us take a brief look at each part of the communication model to see how barriers are formed and how they can be overcome.

Eliminate the Barriers

The first step in improving listening competency is to remove the **barriers** that prevent active listening. These barriers can be found in any part of the communication transaction as described earlier by the Communication Model.

Contexts   The first part of the model, contexts, can help or hinder your listening ability. When you are in a classroom listening to a lecture, a certain context has been set. You know something about the subject matter and may be familiar with the person speaking and the content of the message. On the other hand, being in church and listening to a sermon probably does not call for notepad and pencil, nor does sitting in a friend's apartment.

Your expectations can set your frame of mind so that you are ready for certain kinds of information, and certain kinds of listening behavior. Feedback in the form of questions may be appropriate, but it is controlled by the requirement of raising your hand in the classroom. However, raising your hand in church is probably not appropriate while, in your friend's room, feedback is spontaneous rather than regulated.

Context then helps to determine how you prepare and how you behave. Barriers to good listening arise when the context is unclear or counter to normal expectations. Award shows on television have run into the problem of an award-winner taking the opportunity to lecture the audience about a favorite cause or issue. The context would normally call for a simple statement of thanks and appreciation, so those who violate the expectations of the audience often find their message received with hostility. In another setting and time, the same message might be well received and perhaps even supported. Paying attention to the context can help increase listening potential and power.

Source   The next part of the Communication Model is the *source/sender*—where the message originates. Usually, the source is another person who creates, or encodes, a message. Because we all have different associations and vocabularies, a problem can arise at this point. If the sender of the message uses a term or sentence construction that is unusual or simply unknown to the listeners, a barrier is created. The source needs to pay attention to the message and the target audience so that clarity is achieved. Being organized; following a clear pattern of development; using transitions and internal summaries; and restating main ideas are ways the source can help improve listening and remove, or at least lower, the barriers to good reception. One of the best ways to help a source respond to your needs as a listener is to provide feedback. You can nod in agreement if you understand, or perhaps ask the sender to stop and rephrase or repeat an idea if you don't understand.

Message   Because the message is an output, or product, of the source, any barriers that are in the message probably stem from the source. The best way to keep the message clear is for the source to check it as part of self-monitoring.

This self-checking occurs when you have a clear message in mind, but when you express it, it just "doesn't come out right." You say something like, "That didn't sound right, let me try it again." Then you rephrase the message. You may rearrange the word order, or substitute one unclear term for a different term you hope better conveys your idea. This process is a form of editing, similar to editing a written paper. In other words, problems that occur in messages are usually just extensions of barriers that originate in the sender.

Channels   One common place for barriers to arise is in the various channels that carry communication. For example, if you cannot see a speaker, you are unable to pay attention to the nonverbal aspects of the message carried on the visual channel. If you cannot hear the message adequately, a problem with the audio channel prevents you from listening effectively.

Often, you can make simple changes to help eliminate these barriers. You can move to a place where you can see better, or turn up the volume on the radio or television. In an audience, you can ask the speaker to be "louder, please!" A good speaker depends on this immediate feedback in order to enhance the presentation. You can also move your chair, turn down the sound of competing or interfering sources, ask others to be quiet or louder, or make any other quick physical changes to clear the main channel of interfering noise.

Receivers/Decoders   The destination of a message is usually another person or group of people who are the focus of your communication. Within each person are potential barriers to good reception of the message. As a receiver, you may not be adequately or properly prepared for the message, or you can let internal thoughts, such as premature evaluation of the message, distract you, or you may give your attention to ideas other than the one being presented at the moment.

When you function in the receiver role, the steps of the active listening process will help you to remove or reduce the barriers of effective listening, and in this sense, you have a great deal of control over this part of the process. It is one of the more difficult areas to control completely, as our minds are constantly active, often moving to areas unrelated to the event at hand.

Feedback/Interference/Noise   Good listening depends upon good **feedback,** both internal and external. Internally, you use feedback when you summarize or link ideas from the source to those that are important or relevant to you. Externally, you provide important feedback through your nonverbal responses to a speaker or your verbal reactions when you make comments or ask questions.

Interference in the feedback process becomes a barrier to good listening when you cannot see the source, or the source cannot react to you. Noise is any disruption that occurs at any place along the process. Noise may be an internal distraction experienced by the sender; it may be a clattering fan in the room or a lawnmower going by outside. It may be a faulty picture tube on a television monitor, or the listener's stray thoughts when his or her attention wanders from the source to personal concerns.

Removing these barriers depends on where they are and your ability to react. You probably cannot change the schedule of the person mowing the lawn, but you can get up and close the window.

Of all the ways to improve listening, *providing feedback* is perhaps the most useful. In each of the barrier situations,

▶ IMPROVING COMPETENCY
Barriers to Listening

As you pay attention to your listening today, try to take one active step to help eliminate a barrier. Get up and close a window deliberately, and think, "I have just helped to eliminate a listening barrier." Or consciously move closer to a speaker if you are having difficulty hearing, and tell yourself what a good job you've done improving your listening. Being aware that you can actively control the listening situation, especially its barriers, will increase your sensitivity to the listening experience and your competence as an effective listener.

Feedback and response complete the communi-cation cycle.

direct feedback, if possible, is an immediate way to lessen the barrier and promote clarity and understanding. By recognizing that barriers arise in many places, you have already taken an important first step toward eliminating them. The princi-ples of active listening, combined with your knowledge about the communication process, can help you to becoming a more effective listener.

Responsible Listening

The improvements you can make in your listening skills are related to both your responsibilities as a listener and your responsibilities as a sender.

Listener Responsibilities   Try viewing your efforts at listening as focusing on the information, focusing on learning, and focusing on wise consumer attitudes.

The focus on information means that you pay attention to the key ideas, and ignore distractions or irrelevancies. You practice active listening to connect ideas in a message, even if the speaker does not. You try to apply ideas to your own experiences and needs. At the end of a lecture, you should be able to review main ideas and a few of the subpoints and supporting information such as examples, personal experiences, stories, or statistics. As a responsible listener, you should try to review at the end of each listening event. You will increase the amount of information at your disposal, and not waste time or energy on the speaker's haircut or clothing choice. Focus on the information. Take the job of listening seriously.

Next, try to keep learning about communication as a goal, even though the message may be about something else. For example, if the speaker is talking about physics and uses an exceptionally clear diagram, make a quick mental note about the qualities of the diagram so that you can emulate them in your next visual aid. You are surrounded by good and not-so-good examples of communication; if you can make use of the situation to help you discover what works and what doesn't, you can both incorporate and avoid those behaviors as appropriate. While you are listening to speeches, you can learn something about how to be a better speaker. As you listen, you may discover that one person with an enthusiastic delivery gets a strong positive reaction while another bores the audience with a dull, listless presentation. Take the experiences as messages not just about *those* speakers, but about yourself as a speaker as well. Let the best experiences inspire your own presentations. These experiences also help to build your skills as an evaluator of messages.

In addition to learning about strong or weak presentation techniques, you may gain ideas that you can use later in your presentations. For example, if Angela uses a quotation you enjoyed or thought was powerful, remember the source and go investigate it on your own. You may discover a new source of supporting material for your own presentations. If Thran has an interesting topic that catches your imagination, you may want to remember it so in another setting you can refer to those ideas to help make your own clear. Being inspired by other people is a constant source of information and a compliment to them. Use your listening time to constantly search for ideas that you can develop and then take in your own original directions.

Finally, listening responsibly can make you a more informed consumer. As we are bombarded with a constant flow of ideas and messages, the ability to listen critically becomes an important job of every receiver. One of the challenges of your lifetime is to take all the information that comes to you daily and make sense of it. Many people get overwhelmed and simply stop paying attention. They get into a habit of *not* listening—they avoid the news; they stop reading anything but material assigned; and they avoid magazines and newspapers with substantial or challenging content and style. Several commentators have identified this as part of the "dumbing down" of America (Hirsch, 1988). Fewer and fewer people get involved in running their lives; they fail to attend political forums; they avoid public lectures; they skip school board and city council meetings; and they decline to take part in voting and other expressions of opinion that count. These people can be called "listening dropouts" for they have failed to listen responsibly. At the other extreme, people trying to pay attention to everything do not act as critical consumers. A careful consumer selects information from the huge variety available on the basis of the quality it offers. Listening consumption is much like other forms of consumption—you want to get value for the time and effort invested. One way to get value for your effort is to put into practice the simple training from this chapter, sift out the valuable and relevant, and decide if the information or the message or the recreation gained from your time is worth it. Good consumers become *selective* consumers. Are three hours a day of soap operas worth that much of your recreational time? Create a listening budget in with a certain number of hours each week for informational listening, persuasive or motivational sources, and for recreational uses. You might even want to keep track of how much of each type you engage in for a week to see if your personal budget is getting you the most value.

Skill in Note Taking   Responsible listening can improve your competency as a skilled note taker. Focus on key ideas, and jot down information in a form that keeps ideas and relationships connected and in order. Follow an outline pattern in your note taking. The relationship of main ideas to subordinate ones needs to be clear when you review your notes. Keep main ideas to the left of your sheet of paper, and cluster related ideas under those by indenting to the right. When the speaker moves to a new main idea, put that key term to the left and create a pattern for your notes. Remember, you're not taking dictation; don't try to capture every word or attempt to write full sentences. Just include main ideas expressed as key words. When you apply what you learn about outlining and critical thinking skills, you will find yourself becoming an effective note taker as well. Taking good notes requires practice, but each time you put your ideas into a brief form, it will become progressively easier.

As a Speaker   You can help listeners enormously in several ways. In general, start by being clear in your own mind about the purpose and focus of your message. Think back to the barriers mentioned concerning source/sender, and think about how to make yourself clear to others. Then, build a clear message with a logical outline that develops a central thesis or main idea. Use transitions and restatement to assist listeners in moving through your presentation with you. To help them maintain attention, add interest by telling stories or providing examples that are meaningful and captivating to your listeners, as well as relevant to your purpose. Use a vocabulary that suits their level of experience and background. Make certain that you provide plenty of definitive information in the form of examples or similarities. Keep your voice loud and clear, and make eye contact around the room so that everyone will feel included. You can look for feedback from listeners who may express interest or puzzlement or agreement. If you decide to use visual aids, make them large, simple, and clearly directed to a main idea; make sure the visual information presents a clearer message than words alone. Public speaking training deals extensively with details about preparation and presentation of speeches for impact and clarity. Remember that good listening is a shared responsibility of the receivers and senders of messages.

LISTENING BEYOND THE CLASSROOM

On the job, in family interactions, and during the reception of constant media messages, your skills at effective listening are a valuable asset.

As a listener in society you will receive many messages about products, ideas, people, and policies that ask you to make a decision or a choice. Use the skills of good listening to make informed choices from among politics, services, and products that are competing for your attention. As a critical consumer of information, you can quickly identify slogans or catch phrases that lack substance and support. As a competent listener, you will not permit superficial, incomplete, or distorted messages to influence your behaviors or beliefs. When you practice active listening, you will be on the lookout for clear and detailed development of ideas, and demand convincing, comprehensive support for ideas. Active listening trains you to become a discriminating and intelligent consumer of all the information that comes your way.

▶ **IMPROVING COMPETENCY**

Listening Applications

Training in listening is designed to increase your listening options—to build your *repertoire* of knowledge and skills. From that increased repertoire, you can *select* the appropriate listening technique—probably that one called active listening. You can then *apply* the skill or technique with confidence that you have a good chance of improving your listening behavior. Finally, *review and evaluate* your experience to determine whether you have achieved improvement in your communication competency.

SUMMARY

Both the reasons to be a good listener and the skills that allow you to reach that goal were discussed in this chapter. Now you should be able to distinguish between the physical process of hearing and the activities involved in comprehensive listening. The four main principles—getting prepared, staying involved, avoiding snap judgments, and reviewing and evaluating afterward—were outlined. The common barriers to effective listening were related to the parts of the communication model presented in Chapter 2. Looking ahead, you saw that the methods of preparing and presenting speeches will help you develop further competencies in listening. Remember that listening probably occupies more of your time than all other communication activities combined; an investment of your time and energy into applying listening principles will pay handsome dividends for you every day.

Key Terms

listening, **36**
appreciation, **36**
empathic listening, **36**
comprehension, **36**
hearing, **37**

active listening, **38**
barriers, **40**
empathic listening, **43**
critical listening, **45**
feedback, **47**

EXERCISES

1. Compare listening to an event on the radio and watching the same event on television. For example, listen to a sports event, a major news event, or some other presentation that is simultaneously televised and broadcast on the radio. Turn off the sound on the television and turn on the radio. What does the radio announcer do differently from the television announcer? What are your reactions when you close your eyes and listen only to the radio?

2. Keep a listening log of the amount of time you spend in a typical day listening to the radio, in classes, on the job, and with friends. Do your percentages match the research discussed in this chapter? If they are different, can you explain why?

3. Sit in your room in silence for ten minutes, keeping your eyes closed and the lights out. Listen for the sounds around you. How many different sounds can you identify in that period of time? Include such sounds as other people's voices, vehicles, animals, television or radio broadcasts, creaks, and wind noises.

4. Count the number of advertisements you hear on the radio for one hour. Include public service announcements, political advertisements, and commercials. What similarities and differences do you notice? How do you explain these?

References

Barker, L., R. Edwards. C. Gaines, K. Gladney, and F. Holley. "An Investigation of Proportional Time Spent in Various Communication Activities by College Students." *Journal of Applied Communication Research* 8, (1981): 101.

Burmeister, David. "The Language of Deceit" in *Language and Public Policy.* Hugh Rank, editor. Urbana, IL: National Council of Teachers of English, 1974.

Caputo, J. S., H. C. Hazel, and C. McMahon. *Interpersonal Communication.* Boston: Allyn and Bacon, 1994: Chapter 8.

Coakley, C. and A. Wolvin. "Listening in the Educational Environment." *Listening in Everyday Life.* D. Borisoff and M. Purdy, Eds. Lanham: University Press of America, 1991.

Hirsch, E. D. *Cultural Literacy.* New York: Random House, 1988.

Pauk, Walter. *How to Study in College.* Boston: Houghton-Mifflin, 1989.

Postman, Neil. Interview, *U.S. News and World Report* (19 January 1981): 43.

Rowe, M. B. "Wait Time: Slowing Down May Be a Way of Speeding Up." *Journal of Teacher Education* (January/February 1986).

Steil, Lyman, Larry Barker and Kittie Wilson. *Effective Listening.* Reading: Addison-Wesley, 1983.

Sypher, Beverly D., Robert Brostrom and Joy H. Siebert. "Listening, Communication Abilities, and Success and Work." *Journal of Business Education,* 26 (1989), pp. 293–303.

Wolff, Florence I. and Nadine C. Marsnik. *Perceptive Listening,* 2nd ed., Ft. Worth: Harcourt Brace Jovanovich, 1992.

Wolvin, Andrew and Carolyn Coakley. "A Survey of the Status of Listening Training in Some Fortune 500 Corporations." *Communication Education,* 40 (1990), p. 153.

Wolvin, Andrew and Carolyn Coakley. *Listening,* 4th ed. Dubuqeue: Wm. C. Brown, 1992.

CHAPTER 4

Critical Thinking and Communication

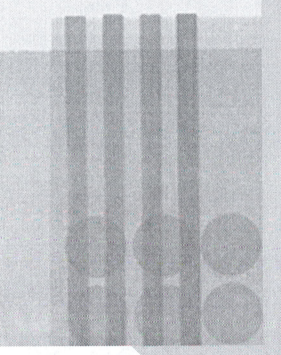

After reading this chapter you should be able to:

- Define the elements of *critical* and *thinking* as used in the term *critical thinking*
- Describe the processes of deductive and inductive reasoning
- Understand how the Toulmin model represents everyday thinking
- Use appropriate tests to evaluate information, sources, and supporting materials
- Apply critical thinking to your own decision-making processes
- Communicate the results of your critical thinking analysis in order to improve communication and thinking skills

If listening is our first communication event, then trying to make sense out of the sounds we hear follows naturally as the second event. When we focused effort, interpretation, feelings, and imagination on those sounds, and started to associate them with things, events, people, and later, ideas, we began the process of thinking. Thinking is the use of the mind to process information. One thesaurus lists the following as synonyms for "think":

consider	recollect	suppose
contemplate	remember	create
meditate	conclude	envision
ponder	judge	imagine
reflect	presume	invent
recall	reason	conceive

Each of these terms also has a list of synonyms, so you can see that thinking involves a variety of meanings and associations. Like emotion and intuition, thinking is part of our human makeup, and we more or less do it all the time, with greater or lesser efficiency and precision. Improving the quality of our information processing, or thinking, is not a matter of luck or chance, but in fact is a learnable skill. The term used in most academic settings to describe this enhanced ability is *critical thinking*. Let's take a moment first to define this skill, then to look at its components and how they affect our ability to make quality decisions. Finally, let us see how we use reasoning as a mental habit to increase our communication competency.

CRITICAL THINKING DEFINED

You get a good idea about the *thinking* part of the term from the list of synonyms, but you also need to focus on our use of the term *critical*. The word *critical* can be used in a variety of ways, many of them with unpleasant connotations: *acute, dangerous, grave, grievous, serious, crucial, decisive, important, momentous, pivotal, derogatory, disparaging, faultfinding, finicky, picky, analytical, discriminating, judging.*

It is important to consider your associations with the term *critical*. Teachers in many colleges and universities have found resistance to courses or lessons in critical thinking because many people associate the negatives of *faultfinding* or *derogatory* practices with the skills of critical thinking. Yes, you may become expert at finding weaknesses in much of the communication you encounter, but that is not a goal of the process so much as it is a reflection on the sad state of so much communication.

A critical thinker will be skilled in serious, crucial, decisive, important, pivotal, analytical, discriminating, judging, thinking. Some of that thinking may produce positive evaluations, and some of it may produce negative evaluations. Critical thinking will help you judge the accuracy of statements and the soundness of the reasons that lead you and others to conclusions and to actions. It will help you interpret complex ideas, appraise the evidence offered in support of arguments or claims, and make a distinction between the reasonable and the unreasonable (Ruggerio, 1990).

Thus, critical thinking forms a complement to other ways of gathering and using information, such as your experience, intuition, and feelings.

These abilities are important in many ways, not the least of which is in your schoolwork. Drawing conclusions from information involves much more than simply summarizing, repeating, or rephrasing it. Your training in critical thinking should equip you to *evaluate* the information that comes at you through careful *analysis* of the information—its form, content, sources, bases, biases, assumptions, methods, implications, applications, and limitations.

IMPROVING COMPETENCY

Creativity, the Workforce, and the Classroom

Observe your classes. What is the climate in the room regarding the asking of questions? Are questions and challenges encouraged, discouraged, or ignored? Can you find a relationship between the size of the class and the instructor's tolerance for questions?

One of the criticisms of business and industry in this country is that they lack imagination to solve problems or to create new products. Do you think this criticism is justified? If so, could there be a link between the way students are taught in school and the quality of the workforce? How many questions are asked on average in your classes? The imaginative use of questions can begin in the home and school. Building your questioning skills so they reflect critical and creative processes can be an important part of your communication competency.

Thinking critically does not come automatically, and in fact, may be discouraged at many times in your life by influential people around you. For example, students who constantly challenge assumptions can be annoying and take up a lot of time in the classroom. Children who constantly ask "Why?" of their parents can become tiresome. So, when people discourage the habits of questioning and examining for the sake of expediency, they run the risk of extinguishing skills that will be needed later on.

Critical thinking skills are also important beyond the classroom as you make important decisions affecting your life. In her book, *Reasoning and Communication*, Josina Makau underscores both the skills and their value:

> These skills include the abilities to ask relevant questions, find, evaluate and effectively use relevant information, draw reasonable inferences and evaluate inferences. Proficient critical thinkers share at least several basic characteristics. They are committed to careful decision-making. They make effective use of freedom of choice in their personal and professional lives. And they understand that exercising our liberties requires the development and use of critical thinking skills. (Makau, 1990)

Critical thinking becomes a lifelong skill, to be used in the way you look at the world and evaluate the information you get every day. It should become a habit—a habit of mind—that enhances your ability to live successfully.

Critical thinking is the process of finding, interpreting, integrating and evaluating information. At its base is the concept that all evaluation is dependent on a series of other judgments, reports, abstractions, perceptions, inferences, and predictions. For example, if you were asked, "Who is the best singer in the world?" the immediate temptation is to begin tossing out names based on feelings or associations you already have in your mind. A better approach is to look for some systematic method by which we can judge. A good start would be: "It all depends on what is meant by 'best.'"

The answers to even the most subjective sounding questions, such as the one above, are based on some assumption or criteria. Whether that basis is sound can be evaluated according to standards of critical thinking, and thus its reasonableness can be established. Applying the skills of critical thinking can help you make better use of information so that you can improve your reasoning and thereby improve the quality of the decisions you make daily. Before we apply these skills, let us first define the ways reasoning can be approached.

APPROACHES TO REASONING

The formal study of **reasoning** is several thousand years old and was one of the subjects included in many of the early Greek texts on rhetoric used in early Greek schools. As philosophy and rhetoric interacted in the early days, one concern common to both was the use, or lack thereof, of logic in thinking and speaking. Formal approaches to thinking and speaking were guided by the principles of *deduction* while the less formal conclusions were obtained by a reasoning process called *induction*. We will examine both of these forms and conclude this section with a modern method for examining the reasoning process proposed by contemporary philosopher and rhetorician, Stephen Toulmin.

Deduction

Early in the teachings of the ancient rhetoricians and philosophers, the formal processes of reasoning were placed into structures and rules, which were called **deduction.** Careful systems were devised to lead thinkers, speakers, and listeners from *premises* to *conclusions.* The standard form was the **syllogism,** which consists of three parts: the major premise, the minor premise, and the conclusion.

The major **premise** usually expresses some main idea, universal law or principle. The minor premise connects some specific example to one part of that main idea. The conclusion makes a connection to the other part of the main idea through a logical link.

You probably are familiar with the classic example:

Major premise: All men are mortal.
Minor premise: Socrates is a man.
Conclusion: Therefore, Socrates is mortal.

This is a good example because it is short, it is based on sound premises, and it exactly follows both the form and the rules for a syllogism.

The Story of Communication
Tension with Western Logic

THE CONCERN FOR LOGIC and reason is especially strong in Western European traditions and cultures. They followed the Greek and Roman models that emphasized the mental, knowable, factual base of learning, often called "Aristotelian thinking." While this base has led to many material advances, other cultures have emphasized feelings or intuition or insight.

Many societies struggle with the tension between too much emphasis on one model or the other, while some try to blend elements of both. In materialistic societies like the United States, you will find from time to time the appearance of counterculture movements, such as the hippies of the late 1960s and early 1970s and the New Age adherents in the late 1980s and 1990s. In societies with more spiritual emphasis (e.g., Native American, religious communities, and Afrocentric traditions), there are struggles over whether or how much to accept the material approach, and how much rational thought should influence personal, social, and cultural development.

The Western mode has tended to dominate in the United States and elsewhere, but it has not done so without causing stress and tension. Your own communication style and preferences reflect degrees of influence from this variety of modes.

Unfortunately, people reason in many ways that look and sound like correct syllogisms, but are not. These errors are called **fallacies.** Under certain circumstances, there may be a fallacy in the previous example:

All men are mortal.

Socrates is mortal.

Therefore: Socrates is a man.

Actually, Socrates may be my pet goldfish; he may be mortal, but not be a man! Watch for incorrect assumptions.

What went wrong with our reasoning here? The major premise is the same in both cases, and the premise is true. The minor premise in both cases may also be true, yet the conclusion in the second example does not necessarily follow and may be false. The problem is in the format, that is, the order of these sentences.

Look at this example:

Socrates is a man.

Socrates is a mortal.

Therefore: All men are mortal.

The statements are all *true,* but not logically *valid.* You cannot make the claim that all men are mortal based on the one example of Socrates.

Let's take a closer look at the two components used in analyzing deduction—the **truth,** or accuracy, of the premises, and the **validity,** or rule-following of the format. It is important to get beyond the *appearance* of logic by testing ideas and arguments that are expressed in logical form. Many people are persuaded by just the *resemblance* to logic. As rhetorical scholar, Jesse Delia (1970) pointed out,

Since form conveys reason directly to the mind of the receiver, an argument cogently laid down according to the rules of logical form inherently has the power to... persuade.

You receive a flood of information every day, often put into logical forms, which asks you to buy, believe, behave, or vote in a certain way. Knowing about the forms of logic will enable you to analyze it.

Truth   The truth of the premises is usually easy to test, but often difficult to see. Three questions help to determine the truth of premises: Are they based on what is known? How was that knowledge derived? How is the knowledge expressed?

First, the premises must be founded on accurate observations and reporting of information. The data can be tested by rules of information accuracy. For example, is the major premise the result of carefully observed and tested examples? Or is it rather the impression of an observer? Is it the result of untested tradition or uninformed bias? There are several ways to examine the accuracy of the premises. Does the statement or claim made in the premise agree with general knowledge? That is, does it seem, on its face, to agree with generally accepted ideas? Or does the statement or claim call for special or expert knowledge? The premise, "All men are mortal," fits very well with what we generally know. However, if the major premise is, "All recombinant dynacarbo nucleic modules are the result of meta-thermal hydrosis," you would probably want to ask an expert in biochemistry (who would tell you that the statement, though perhaps sounding somewhat impressive, is meaningless).

Since major premises are usually the result of analysis of many specific instances, you can evaluate the soundness of the statement by looking next at how it was derived. Was the **evidence** on which it is based both sufficient and representative enough to justify the statement? The fact that everybody who has ever lived has also died (there are no recorded cases to the contrary) gives us plenty of justification to warrant the "All men are mortal" conclusion. How about "Bodybuilders eat sushi" as a premise? At first, you might reject it as unsupported, but suppose you know four competitive muscle-builders and each one of them eats Japanese rice topped with raw fish? You might feel justified in your statement, but it would not pass an objective test of sufficient and representative data.

Many of our cultural premises and values or **assumptions** can be subjected to the same test. "Honesty is the best policy" or "Men are better drivers than women" or "Mexican food is spicy" are similar in that they have no known sample or data behind them. They are generalities without support, yet are believed by many on the simple basis that they are repeated often. Check the underlying support, if any, of the premises of any statement that passes as a rule. Many elegant, perfectly formed and articulately expressed arguments actually begin with a false premise.

In addition to lacking a valid premise, an argument might not be expressed completely. Some part of it could be (and often is) left out, with the assumption that the listener will supply it mentally. Aristotle called this partial syllogism an **enthymeme**. He pointed out that most arguments and public presentations omitted premises or conclusions that the speaker thought the audience would think of themselves. For example, take any correct syllogism and block out one of the three parts. You can probably supply the missing part needed to complete the connections. Missing parts are possible danger points because there is always a chance that the audience will fill in that part in a manner you had not intended. More examples of enthymemes will follow in the discussion of the Toulmin Model of reasoning.

DIVERSITY IN COMMUNICATION
Variety in Premises

Cultural premises in decision-making can vary to the point where people may talk past each other. In 1855, Native Americans and representatives of the United States Government met to work out a treaty in *Walla Walla*. Consider these excerpts from speeches presented at that meeting:

General Palmer: "I have made treaties with all the Indian tribes in the Willamette Valley, with all in the Umqua Valley, and all in the Rogue River and Shasta country. They have agreed to remove to such tracts as shall be selected for them. They have agreed to be friendly with the whites and all the other Indians. They have sold us all their country except the reservations. We have agreed to build them mills, blacksmith shops, wagon makers shops, to erect a tin shop and gun shop, to build a school house and hospital, to employ millers, mechanics, school teachers, doctors and farmers.... Do you want these things? Do you want a sawmill to saw the timber to build your houses? You have a few lodges now, how long will they last?.... The Buffalo were not as plenty as they were once. Where are they now? All gone.... If we make a treaty with you...you can rely on all its provisions being carried out strictly."

Chief Peo-Peo-Mox-Mox: "Why not speak tomorrow as well as today? We have listened to all you have to say, and we desire you should listen when any Indian speaks...[you] want an answer immediately, without giving them time to think.... In one day the Americans became as numerous as the grass. This I learned in California. I know that it is not right. Suppose you show me goods, shall I run up and take them? Goods and Earth are not equal. Goods are for using on the Earth. I do not know where they have given land for goods.... I do not wish you to reply today. Think over what I have said."

Young Chief: "We have been tiring one another for a long time. We did not know our hearts. We did not understand each other on both sides about this country. Your marking out the country is the reason it troubles me so and has made me sit here without saying anything.... The reason why we could not understand you was that you selected this country for us to live in without us having any voice in the matter. We will think slowly over the different streams that run through the country. We will expose the country and think over it slowly. I cannot take the whole country and throw it to you.... I think the land where my forefathers are buried should be mine; that is the place that I am speaking for. We will talk about it, we shall then know. My brothers, that is what I have to show you. That is the place I love, where we get our roots to live upon. The Salmon comes up the stream. That is all."

The Nez Percé War started twenty-two years later, 1877, as a result of an attempt to drive the tribe out of a large portion of the reservation guaranteed to them by this treaty. (McGlone and Fausti, 1972)

Truth has a second dimension—the language used may be unclear, have meanings that shift, or be *ambiguous*. The "recombinant dynanucleic" example above is filled with such problems. But you do not need bizarre words to be led astray. The very simplest of words can be used in a variety of ways, and such variety can create a problem in the premise. For example, consider the following syllogisms:

All men are created equal.
Women are not men.
Therefore: Women are not equal.

Good taste is hard to get.
Ice cream is good to taste.
Therefore: Ice cream is hard to get.

All dogs have fleas.
My used car is a real dog.
Therefore: My used car has fleas.

While these may be amusing, they reflect a real difficulty in creating sound premises. As a word shifts meaning, or has a meaning that is unclear, a conclusion may be drawn which many might be tempted to believe, but is nevertheless erroneous because of the use of ambiguous language. Is abortion murder? Is capital punishment murder? Is beef or pork meatpacking murder? Is polluting our environment murder? "It all depends," says the careful, critical thinker, "on what you mean by…."

The fallacy of *ambiguity* means that a word may reasonably have two (or more) distinct interpretations. A second fallacy is *equivocation*—using two senses of a term by starting with one, and then shifting to the next. The examples above show very clearly that "men" in the major premise is used as a generic term for "people." In the minor premise, the meaning clearly shifts to mean just the male of the species. The equivocation fallacy is seen with "good taste" and "dog" in the second and third examples.

Vagueness is a third fallacy of premises gone wrong, and it is often seen in such platitudes as "I will do only what is good for the country!" What does that mean? "I will stand up to the crooks and swindlers who have invaded our sacred halls of freedom and justice, and resist their efforts to bring down all that has made us great!" Meaning? Just what will you do, and how, and to whom? When words soar to high levels of abstraction, referring to concepts so broad that they have no concrete referents, you are probably witnessing the vagueness fallacy. The danger in critical thinking is that the major premise is supposed to sound like a general or universal principle, so how can you tell whether it is sound? Go back to the principle of testing or verifying with facts or examples.

Finally, *obscuration* is a term used to describe the use of unusual or highly technical words, technical *sounding* words, jargon that is specific to a group of insiders, or highly complex and convoluted sentence structures. Our statement concerning "metathermal hydrosis" is an attempt to obscure the message by hiding behind complexity. You can detect and guard against this fallacy by breaking down a complex message into small, simple parts and examining each part for definitions, specificity, and concreteness.

Examining premises means you test them for the truth they contain. Truth is measured by these criteria: (1) What is known, (2) How it was derived, and (3) How it was expressed.

When you are satisfied with the truth of the statements, you move to the next step in testing deductive syllogisms: examining the process used to link the ideas of the premises to the conclusion. That process determines the validity of the deductive logic that is used to reach the conclusion of the syllogism.

Validity   In formal logic, a deduction is not valid if the conclusion of an argument is false and the premises are true. If, in fact, the premises are true, and the conclusion is false, then the logical process used to reach that conclusion is invalid.

For example, the conclusion "Socrates is a man" was quite possibly false, since Socrates could have been the name of my goldfish. Even though the premises were both true, they did not *necessarily* lead to a true conclusion because something was wrong with the deductive reasoning process. We mixed up or reversed or inverted the statements so that, while still true independently, they no longer connected correctly to lead us to a single, necessary, true conclusion.

Remember, truth involves the evaluation of each statement by itself, whereas validity involves the evaluation of the connections drawn from combining the statements. There are many rules of deductive validity for there are several kinds of deductive syllogisms.

One test is that the general subject or condition of the major premise must appear as the "result" in the minor premise and that the predicate of the major premise must also be the predicate of the conclusion. For example,

All dogs have ears.

John has ears.

Therefore: John is a dog.

This syllogism violates this rule, for the subject of the major premise is dogs which is connected to the predicate term *ears*. The result or predicate of the minor premise must link to the *subject* of the major premise—*dogs*, not *ears*. With this beginning, only a conclusion about ears is possible to meet the second requirement that the predicate term of the major premise is the same as the predicate term of the conclusion.

All dogs have ears.

John is a dog.

Therefore: John has ears.

This form is now valid because the term dog has been properly placed as the connector term in the predicate part of the minor premise. Is it true? Check John

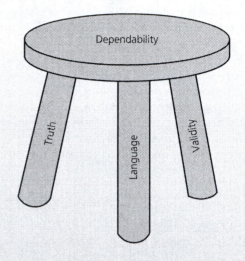

Would you stand on a two-legged stool?

for canine qualities. If indeed John is your pet collie, he has ears. If he is not your collie but your hamster, the logic still may be valid and the conclusion may be true, but the minor premise is not true. It is however possible that John is identical to his friend Socrates, and both are swimming in the goldfish bowl. Check truth, check the language, and then check validity. You need all three to draw conclusions that are absolutely dependable (Reinard, 1991).

But what if you cannot investigate all the conditions necessary for deduction to work, and you are not interested in absolute dependability, but just good, strong *probability*? The kind of reasoning that helps you decide the likelihood or probability of your conclusions being true is *induction*.

Induction

Induction is the way most of us think. It is the drawing of conclusions based on a review of the evidence. Induction does not tell us what *is* true, but what is likely to be true based upon the weight of the evidence. Whereas deduction is concerned with what is true and valid, induction deals with what is probable.

Determining what is probable involves evaluating the evidence or support behind a conclusion. Are elephants gray? How do you know? Or, better yet, why do you believe elephants are gray? You could answer this simple question about elephant coloring by stating that every elephant you've ever seen is gray; every photograph of elephants you've seen shows them gray; you've heard of no other color associated with elephants; and therefore, "Elephants are gray."

In this example, you can see the elements of induction. A number of examples or *samples,* are examined; they are combined by something they have in common; and they lead to a conclusion that seems to be acceptable.

As is true for deductive reasoning, there are some accepted rules for good inductive reasoning. These rules are related to the quality of the evidence and the process used to link them to the conclusion. There are three rules to apply when evaluating the supporting evidence.

The Sample Must Be Known   This rule might seem simple, but many conclusions, especially ones held dearly and passionately, often lack any supporting data about a sample. "She's the most wonderful girl in the world." "The Dodgers are the all time greatest!" "Republicans are rich." "Democrats are big spenders." The list could go on. Most of these statements are based on some sort of *assumed* or *implied* evidence, and you could probably make up samples that could lead you to the conclusion expressed. You could, for example, offer comparisons of the favorite female's qualities with others and conclude that she is indeed "wonderful." Or, you might list the accomplishments and statistics of the Brooklyn / Los Angeles baseball franchise and conclude they are impressive. If you have met or heard of several identified Republicans, all of whom appear to be well off, we can draw a conclusion. Likewise, if the voting record of a number of Democratic politicians reveals they support big budgets, we may feel that we have support for the conclusion.

On the other hand, you may be guilty of believing unsupported conclusions when you simply repeat what you have heard before, trusting in some sort of "logic of longevity"—thinking that if a statement has been around for a while and repeated, it must be true. The first step, then, is to look for the sample—is there one present, or is it implied? Asking people who make conclusions to reveal their evidence is often the best clue as to how sound their reasoning is. After you establish the existence of a body of evidence, the evidence can be analyzed further.

The Sample Must Be Sufficient   At this step in the analysis of evidence, you ask whether *enough* information has been gathered to make certain that the conclusion is sound. How many people are included in the comparison? How many years of baseball need to be examined? How many Republicans or Democrats need to be in the sample? The answer is not always the same, but there must be enough evidence to give you a *reliable* picture of the event. In induction, conclusions will almost always be drawn on incomplete evidence. You cannot survey every Republican, or have the Dodgers come out in first place in every possible measure of greatness. What you can do is guard against the limited sample that is too small to be useful.

The Sample Must Be Representative   By asking, "Is the sample representative?" you examine the supporting evidence to see whether it is *typical* based on a fair cross-section of the total group. For example, you might take a random sample of one hundred students and ask for their grades to determine the projected "average GPA" of your school. If you took your sample from 10 to 11 AM on Tuesday, you would miss those students who are on campus only in the evening. If you got your sample from the room where the Honor Society holds its annual installation ceremony, the responses may not be typical of students in general.

An often-stated rule of representativeness is that every member of the base group must have an equal chance of being selected for the sample. Advances in the scientific identification of target respondents have enabled professional samplers—pollsters—to be very specific and very accurate in their sampling measures. For example, the Gallup Poll, one of the most famous and often used of our national survey organizations, only contacts about 1400 people in each survey, yet it can accurately identify what 250,000,000 people think. By making absolutely certain that the sample is representative, the organization achieves reliability within 3 percentage points. Often, its results are even more accurate than that.

Make certain that your evidence is soundly based on a full cross-section of the entire possible base. You should ask others how, where, and when their evidence was gathered. Keep in mind that people may change their responses over time. In presidential elections, polling is done weekly to detect trends or changes because, on important issues, people may change their opinions. Over a period of just ten years, the proportion of incoming freshman who smoked cigarettes dropped from 48 percent to fewer than 5 percent. Obviously any conclusions about college students and tobacco must be based on the most current information.

Later in this chapter you will read about *informed decision-making*, and further guides for evaluating information, sources, and supporting materials. For now, remember that when reasoning inductively you must evaluate the likelihood or strength of a claim or conclusion and that evaluation must begin with a look at the information that leads to the conclusion.

Once you are satisfied with the evidence, you can construct a logical format for induction similar to the syllogism used in deduction. It might look like this:

Person A lived and then died.
Person B lived and then died.
Person C lived and then died.
Person D lived and then died.
Persons E and 7 billion others also died.
Therefore: People are mortal—they die.

Notice that in induction, a general conclusion comes from a series of observations. Clearly, the number and accuracy of your observations will determine the believability of your conclusion. Thus, induction takes specific examples or instances, connects them with a common factor, and draws a conclusion based on the connection. The example takes everyone who has ever lived, connected them with the common factor of death, and then drew the conclusion. Following the rules expressed above, we had a known, sufficient, and representative sample. It wasn't necessary to research every person who was ever born, simply because the evidence is universal. But, what about Republicans? Sushi eaters? Mexican food? Chemistry instructors? Can these rules still apply? The answer is that they do and the guidelines for evaluating them will be discussed in the final section of this chapter.

It is evident that induction and deduction are related though different. What they have in common is the general rule or conclusion. Deduction begins with general principles, and induction ends with them. In fact, induction is the process

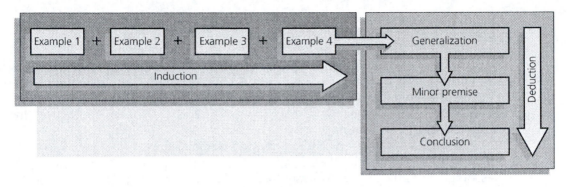

Induction and deduction connect with generalizations.

that supplies deduction with its major premises. The two processes are connected at the point of **generalizations.** In the syllogism about Socrates, induction and deduction intersect at the generalization "All men are mortal."

The truth of that major premise was discovered through the processes of induction, and now it can be applied with great certainty to any particular person we meet. We must, of course, follow the rules. One way to look at the rules of logic was introduced in 1958 by Stephen Toulmin, and it comprises a third way to engage in formal critical thinking.

The Toulmin Model

Because so much attention was paid to very complicated systems for the development of logic and mathematics they became difficult to use in ordinary thinking situations. Stephen Toulmin devised a system to examine the way he observed most people thinking (Toulmin, 1958). This system is often called the **Toulmin Model** and it consists of three main elements: The grounds (Toulmin et al., 1978), the warrant, and the claim. The **grounds** (or data) are the pieces of information we think about or collect that relate to a topic; the **claim** is the conclusion we draw when we look at the information; and the **warrant** is the connecting principle that allows us to link the information to conclusions. This model is illustrated:

These three elements are the basis for drawing conclusions about the world. In some ways, the warrants exist before the other two elements in the habits and manners you use to organize and connect information. Warrants are the general approaches or rules you use to guide your thinking processes. They are often derived from our values and beliefs about the way the world works, and we probably put them into practice automatically and without thinking.

When you draw a conclusion in a statement such as "I can't go to the movies tonight; I have a mid-term tomorrow in my Critical Thinking class," your listeners will take the grounds (mid-term exam) and connect them logically to your claim (can't go to movies) by filling in the implied *because* between the two. They will supply the warrant (one should stay home and study the night before a test) without anyone ever mentioning it. It is an assumed, trustworthy rule understood by anyone going to school. The warrant is the reason to believe that grounds justify the claim.

Sometimes, however, people supply a warrant different from your own, and you may be puzzled by the conclusion they draw from the same grounds. For example, they may have a warrant that says, "You should relax before a big test." It that case, they would insist that you join them for an evening out, while you would insist on staying home. Both of you would wind up thinking that the other person's behavior is strange. An important part of critical thinking is to recognize the assumptions—the unstated warrants—that operate in all of us.

Notice that the warrant is much like the generalizations used to begin the deductive syllogism or to conclude the inductive chain. Thus, you could easily show the following:

People with examinations the next day should not go out the night before.

Sue has an examination tomorrow.

Therefore: Sue should not go out tonight.

The usefulness of the Toulmin Model is that people seldom talk in syllogisms. They make statements, sometimes offer grounds for those statements and that is all. They are often unaware of their reasoning, and rarely express their underlying logic. The Toulmin Model, even in this basic form, guides our attention to the elements that operate each time we communicate reasons for taking an action or reaching a conclusion. Even in the following brief interchange, you can fill in the missing elements once you know how to look for them.

"Hi, Sue. We're going to the movies, want to join us?"

"Sorry, mid-term tomorrow."

The rest of the group nods with understanding in response to this enthymeme and continues on. Reasoning clearly exists without formal syllogisms.

On the other hand, you must exercise caution in assuming warrants. If you were to say, "Let's study for the critical thinking mid-term and invite Brad to join us," and your friend replied, "Not Brad, he's a Gamma Alpha Gamma!" some kind of warrant would be operating. It may be that the members of that fraternity have a reputation for being poor study partners, or that they have a dance scheduled for the same time. One way to discover the unstated warrants is to ask, "What does being in Gamma have to do with studying for the test?" Once you discover the missing warrant, you need to evaluate the warrant's trustworthiness to be applied as a rule.

You do this evaluation much the same way you evaluate any generalization. (This evaluation process can also be applied to the other two sections of the basic model to provide a more complete picture of the reasoning process.)

The first step of evaluation is to look for **support,** or backing. The warrant is the place to begin, but you can also look for backing for the grounds as well. If you were examining the warrant in the case of Sue, you might ask for backing such as, "Do you really need to study more than the seventeen hours you've already put in during the past three days?" You could seek support for the grounds by asking, "Was that mid-term rescheduled for next week?" In the case of Brad, you could look for support in the warrant (Gammas are poor study partners) by finding out what the sample was, how recent, representative, sufficient, and so on. Stereotyping is one especially limiting and usually unfair form of unexpressed or unsupported warrant. One of the dangers of using enthymemes in communication is that listeners can fill in a missing logical link with stereotypical and other kinds of illogical thinking.

A second way to test the logic of statements is to look for **rebuttal** materials. A rebuttal considers exceptions or unusual circumstances that might apply in a particular instance. For example, perhaps the movie is short, or a once-in-a-lifetime chance to meet the star, or Sue is already assured of an "A" in the course, or Brad might be the top student in the class. Any number of individual circumstances can and often do call our grounds or our warrants into question. The Toulmin Model asks us to examine possible rebuttal information.

Finally, we apply **qualifiers** or reservations to the claim to show how strong or confident we are in our conclusions. When you say you are *probably* going to pass the test, or *possibly* going to pass the test; you are expressing two very different degrees of confidence in your claim of being able to score sufficiently well on the exam. We hear this type of qualifier all the time, especially in such daily items as the weather report. If the TV weather forecast says there is a 20 percent chance of rain, do you pack an umbrella? How about a 50 percent chance? A 90 percent chance? These percentages are qualifiers to a claim that it will rain. We react differently to the claim depending on its strength and the reliability of the previous forecasts.

Given the importance of evaluating all statements for their logic, we can add the elements of evaluation to the basic Toulmin Model. An expanded Toulmin diagram would look like (Toulmin et al., 1978):

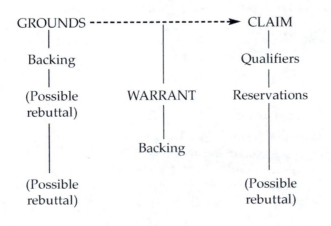

Once all the elements are in place, they may appear complicated, but nearly every conversational claim and every formal conclusion can be analyzed by using these elements. Importantly, these elements remind us where to look for missing parts of our reasoning, or what else needs to be expressed in other people's statements so their conclusions can be trusted. Get into the habit of asking for backing, seeking the grounds, expressing warrants, and examining qualifiers and potential rebuttals in your own statements. These are good mental habits, and the mind that does not accept a simple grounds-to-claim statement is well on its way to being a critically thinking mind.

People who understand the basic logical relationships involved in reasoning truthfully and validly from generalities (deduction), in creating reliable generalities (induction), and in testing reasoning in everyday communication (using the Toulmin Model) will make better decisions.

INFORMED DECISION-MAKING

We all make decisions, virtually minute by minute. Some are so common and made so often that we no longer even think about them as decisions. "Shall I have a cup of coffee with breakfast?" is a good example of such a decision. Others are so weighty and consequential that we may agonize for days or months over them. "Shall I apply to a college far away, even though the person I love most in the world is staying behind?" is a question involving a serious decision. Making quality decisions is a goal of critical thinking, even if the decision is not one of action but only of judgment, such as "Who *is* the best singer in the world?"

To make decision-making a manageable process, look at the bases for your decisions and the likely consequences they may have.

Evaluating information, sources, supporting materials, and probable outcomes requires a usable evaluation system. This system is based on specific *criteria*, and can be divided into four areas of **decision-making** that we discuss next.

When you ask, "What do you mean by the 'best' singer?" you are asking for **criteria**—a measuring system to define the term *best*. Without criteria, no informed decision is possible. The criteria we use, however, are often unexpressed, assumed, unknown, or hidden. Here is where critical thinking comes into play. By demanding that criteria be expressed, we, as decision-makers, can become aware of the forces that drive decisions. We can examine them, evaluate them, and clarify or modify them as appropriate. Let's look at each of the four parts of informed decision-making.

Evaluating Information

Information is data we get through our senses or manufacture in our minds. As the previous chapter pointed out, much of your knowledge about the world comes to you through listening. Good, critical listening helps you to retain and evaluate information. You can listen for information, for empathy, for recreation, and for evaluation. These types of listening are not mutually exclusive; you can be doing

The Story of Communication
What Criteria Are Appropriate?

IF YOU CAN JUDGE the "best" singer by world records, Leontyne Price holds the record for longest standing ovation—forty-three minutes. The group Abba's record albums outsold the Beatles; Barry Manilow has more Grammy Awards than Bob Dylan; and Barbra Streisand holds the record for the most money for a concert, even though Nana Mouskouri has sold more records. Who is the best singer in the world?

several at once. When evaluating information from a critical thinking perspective, examine four areas: premises, consistency, completeness, and coherence.

Each of these elements is important but *premise,* the most significant in terms of evaluation, is perhaps the most difficult of the elements. **Premises,** are the general statements that precede conclusions. These premises are called "warrants" in the Toulmin system. A critical thinker will attempt to discover these premises in any communication event. The criteria for sound premises are fairly simple to express: they must be based on known, sufficient, and representative facts. A well-expressed idea based on a faulty premise is still faulty at its core. Likewise, a soundly based claim may have shortcomings in the way it is expressed, but still be sound.

To meet the condition of **consistency**, the information must have the same meaning both in the known world and within itself. For example, in the known world (external consistency), studying for midterm exams is a consistently reliable way to pass them. However, if Sue has never before studied when she said she was staying home for that purpose, we may suspect her premises are not consistent with her behavior. External consistency means that warrants, grounds, conclusions, and premises are based on reliable information. Internal consistency exists when information applies in a similar manner in similar circumstances. The language must be consistent—not shifting its meaning midstream. Definitions must remain the same throughout the reasoning process.

Sufficiency or **completeness** requires that you be accountable for your information. Are your samples or data missing key elements? Have you met the test of representativeness? Are key parts of the reasoning process skipped or omitted? Check especially for the warrants, or underlying premises, to make certain they are clear and explicit, not implied or left to inference. Can you account for any contradictory evidence? How do you explain data that go against your conclusion? People who find just what they were hoping to find, and then stop investigating often overlook the requirement of completeness.

Coherence is the last guidepost to good decision-making. Be sure to evaluate the care and precision used to express messages. Do the premises, the data, and the conclusions all relate to an underlying concept? Can you follow the development of ideas? Is there a pattern or sequence that builds logically from one step to the next? Or is there a scattering of thoughts, irrelevant information and asides mixed in with the other data? Coherent expression communicates a clear goal and is perceived by listeners and readers as a sign of both the intelligence and the logical force of the ideas. Therefore, it is important to keep your ideas focused, on topic, and linked clearly.

Evaluating Sources

Your reputation is important because it tells others around you how to relate to you. In the same way, so is the reputation of the sources of the information you use to draw your conclusions about the world. Did you get your information from *Time* magazine or from a clerk in a store? From the *California Law Review* or from your instructor? Any source of information can be evaluated by standard tests, and those tests generally involve reputation.

For example, *Time* magazine is known and respected for being honest in its research and truthful in its reporting. The magazine certainly has an editorial bias, but when you encounter a statistic from *Time*, you can be certain that it was checked before it was published.

However, any conclusions the editorial writers drew from those statistics should be evaluated as opinion—informed, educated opinion, yes, but the opinion does not have the same level of reliability as the statistic. Likewise, when your friends recommend a movie, a restaurant, an instructor, a date, or a book, you need to evaluate the reliability of their previous recommendations and respond accordingly. Have they the same tastes in film, food, faculty, and fiction as you do? If they've been reliable in the past, then you can trust them again. Generally, the more permanent the source, the more reliable the information. Textbooks and encyclopedias tend to be around for a long time and make good references (in an uncensored society). Supermarket checkstand tabloids are out to make sales based on sensational stories and may need to be examined carefully before accepting their unusual, eye-catching claims.

Look for qualifications and expertise in your evaluation of sources. Does a Ph.D. degree in chemistry qualify someone to give medical advice? Tax advice? Baseball advice? Make certain that the expert is in the right field. Tests for evaluating information can also be adapted here. Are the premises clearly stated and in agreement with what your other knowledge about the world? Are they consistent with the knowledge of other experts? With the same expert's body of work? Is the information complete—that is, are your sources telling you the whole story? Finally, is the information coherent? Does it make sense when you read or hear it?

Evaluating Supporting Materials

The test of recency of information is especially important when you evaluate supporting materials. Time changes data. What was true about a certain place, or people, or event a few years ago may no longer be true today. Think how significantly our view of our society and security issues changed after the terrorist attacks on New York's World Trade Center and the Pentagon. You may have an excellent textbook, written by an outstanding professor in the proper field, but if it is about Middle East politics, or the Soviet Union, you had better check the date

Often thought of as the great thinker of the last century, Einstein knew the power of creative and critical thinking.

it is about Middle East politics, or the Soviet Union, you had better check the date of publication. Even maps become incorrect in a short span of time. To the four previously discussed criteria: premises, consistent, complete, and coherent, we now add a fifth (**current**) for evaluating information. A simple conclusion about a restaurant may be incorrect if the chef left between the time your friend went there and you received the recommendation.

Critical and Creative Thinking

Although you may be tempted to view critical and creative thinking separately, they actually complement each other. Intuition and **creativity** can help you discover premises and warrants although wild creativity can lead down unproductive routes if there is no evaluation of the ideas at some point.

Brainstorming is a good exercise for demonstrating the reciprocal activities of creativity and criticism. Brainstorming has two phrases. In the first, a group of people comes up with ideas. They do so without restrictions or evaluation. In about ten minutes or once they have generated several ideas, they stop and move to phase two. In this phase, the group examines the ideas for their ability to solve a problem or their practical use.

Creativity and critical thinking can work hand-in-hand to improve your thinking skills. Consider this passage from *The Wizard of Oz* (Baum, 1956):

> "I don't know enough," replied the Scarecrow cheerfully. "My head is stuffed with straw, you know, and that is why I am going to Oz to ask him for some brains."
>
> "Oh, I see," said the Tin Woodsman. "But after all, brains are not the best thing in the world."
>
> "Have you any?" inquired the Scarecrow.
>
> "No, my head is quite empty," answered the Woodsman. "But once I had brains, and a heart also. So, having tried them both, I should much rather have a heart."

When you use both critical and creative thinking, you access the dimensions of both knowledge and feeling. Remember, knowledge and feeling are two of the three competencies of communication mentioned earlier.

TECHNOLOGY AND COMMUNICATION
Where Do Our Inventions Come From?

Albert Einstein, one of the smartest people we know of, once said, "Imagination is more important than knowledge." In helping to provide modern society with some of its greatest advances, Einstein knew the value of applying a creative mind to questions of science and technology. Critical thinking coupled with imaginative applications have helped us apply Einstein's ideas and principles to develop incredible technological creativity.

Critical Thinking Competency and Communication

Critical thinking can help you select from alternatives. The purpose of critical thinking is to expand your *repertoire* of choices so you can make intelligent *selections*. You face a multitude of everyday choices and by making those selections with a critical and creative mind, you can materially increase of the quality of your life. *Evaluating* the grounds for your decisions, their underlying assumptions, their consequences, any qualifiers or reservations you may find, and the quality of any supporting information is the essence of critical thinking and can become an excellent habit of mind.

This brief introduction is only that—a place for you to learn about the main elements you can use to make sense out of all the information you encounter daily. To sift through the enormous flow of data to which you are subjected every day requires vigorous effort. This effort is made easier with tools that help you to divide the information into manageable units. The deductive and inductive patterns show you how generalities are used to produce premises and conclusions about the world. The Toulmin system is an especially clear and useful way to categorize parts of the reasoning process to help you sort out and test the logic operating in your life.

SUMMARY

The process known as critical thinking is defined as the way we process information so that reasoning guides our mind. To think critically, we must find, analyze, interpret, and apply information in such a way that we can rely on our conclusions. Although the rules for deduction and induction could fill entire textbooks, they are based primarily on the ideas of creating generalizations (induction) or taking generalizations and applying them to specific cases (deduction). When you check for the truth of statements, find out how the information was derived, and examine the process by which each step was taken; then you will have begun to apply the rules of logic to the way you process information.

In short, the use of critical thinking in informed decision-making involves the evaluation of information, sources, and supporting materials so that your decisions have a strong base in which you can feel confident. Critical thinking is an old study, founded in logic, with applications to every decision you make, every day. When you combine critical thinking with creativity and feeling, you make good use of both your brain and your heart.

Key Terms

reasoning, **56**
deduction, **56**
premise, **56**
syllogism, **56**
fallacies, **57**
truth, **57**
validity, **57**
evidence, **58**
assumptions, **58**
enthymeme, **58**
induction, **62**
Toulmin Model, **65**
grounds, **65**
claim, **65**

warrant, **65**
generalizations, **65**
support, **67**
rebuttal, **67**
qualifiers, **67**
criteria, **68**
decision-making, **68**
premises, **69**
consistency, **69**
completeness, **69**
coherence, **69**
current, **71**
creativity, **71**

▶ EXERCISES

1. Clip an advertisement for any product from your favorite magazine. Try to identify the elements that serve as the major premise, the minor premise, and the conclusion. Some of these elements may not be expressed (enthymemes), so you may need to provide them in your own words. Bring your advertisement to class and share your analysis.

2. Search the newspapers for a report from one of the major polling firms—Gallup, Roper, Field, or another. What information does the article give you about the poll? Do you find polls credible? Why or why not?

3. Examine a letter to the editor or an editorial in a local newspaper or your campus paper. Apply the Toulmin Model to the information presented. Try to identify the data, warrants, claims, backing, reservations, and any qualifiers. Does your analysis help you to decide whether to support the point of the letter or editorial?

4. Review a recent disagreement you had with a friend. Can you identify any warrants that may have been involved?

References

Baum, L. Frank. *The Wizard of Oz.* New York: Grosset and Dunlap, 1956: 41.

Delia, Jesse G. "The Logic Fallacy, Cognitive Theory, and the Enthymeme." *Quarterly Journal of Speech* LVI (April 1970): 141.

Makau, Josina M. *Reasoning and Communication: Thinking Critically About Arguments.* Belmont, CA: Wadsworth, 1990: 4.

McGlone, Edward L., and Remo P. Fausti. *Introductory Readings in Oral Communication.* Menlo Park, CA: Cummings Publishing, 1972: 312–319.

Reinard, John C. "Structural Tools for Testing Arguments," in *Foundations of Argument.* Dubuque, IA: Wm. C. Brown, 1991.

Ruggerio, Vincent Ryan. *Beyond Feelings: A Guide to Critical Thinking*, 3rd ed. Mountain View, CA: Mayfield Publishing Company, 1990: 14.

Toulmin, Stephen E. *The Uses of Argument.* Cambridge: Cambridge University Press, 1958.

Toulmin, Stephen E., Richard D. Rieke, and Allan Janik. *Introduction to Reasoning.* New York: Macmillan, 1978.

CHAPTER 5

What We Know About Nonverbal Communication

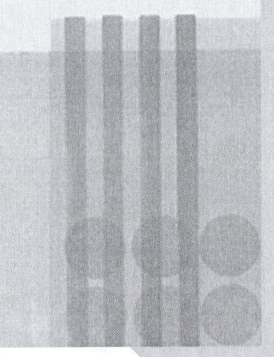

After reading this chapter, you should be able to:

- Understand the important role of nonverbal communication in your daily experience
- Describe some of the contexts and rules that govern nonverbal communication behavior and our understanding of that behavior
- Define the concepts of paralanguage, movement, objects, space, and time, and the senses as they function in nonverbal communication
- Feel competent to improve your nonverbal decoding and encoding skills

Y ou may already know that nonverbal communication generally means communication without words. It can *involve* words, such as when you use voice inflection to color the meaning of your message. Nonverbal communication also includes the use of gestures or movements, and the way people use objects and personal appearance to communicate. Your nonverbal communication can be filled with purpose and the desire to send a message, or it might be accidental and unintentional. Whatever the mode or the meaning you select, nonverbal communication is a powerful part of your communication ability. Let us look at the definition of nonverbal communication and then examine the impact it has on your overall communication. We will also consider some contexts and rules for nonverbal communication, the types of behaviors we use, and finally how you can improve your ability to communicate nonverbally.

A DEFINITION OF NONVERBAL COMMUNICATION

Nonverbal communication is the transmission of information from senders to receivers when the dominant meaning is not conveyed by the use of words. Another way to put it is that nonverbal communication is your use of interacting sets of visual, vocal, and invisible communication systems to convey and interpret meaning (Leathers, 1992). It includes several major categories: *paralanguage or vocalics, pace or proxemics, objects or artifacts, posture and movement, time, and the senses.*

Vocalics is the use of the volume, tone, rate, pitch, and quality of your voice that gives dimension and meaning to your words. Since you use your voice to "surround" the words you speak, this part of nonverbal communication is also called *paralanguage*. For example, you raise your pitch at the end of a sentence.

Proxemics is the use of space to communicate. For example, you may feel uncomfortable if someone sits right next to you in the library when the whole table is empty.

Artifacts are those objects—clothing, jewelry, even an automobile—that relay a message about you. Do you wear three earrings through your pierced ears? Seven? Do you wear one in your nostril? People will sense a message about you if you do.

Movement includes your posture and gestures and facial expressions and eye contact. When you wave, smile, gaze at someone, or slump at your desk, you are using movement, and that movement communicates.

The way you use **time**, or *chronemics,* can communicate attitude or status. Are you showing respect by being early to an appointment with the job interview, or lack of respect by showing up a half-hour late to your study group meeting?

Finally, messages can be sent through the five **senses**—including taste, touch, and smell.

These elements constitute the basic components of nonverbal communication, and when you use them to enhance your communication behaviors, they can have significant impact on your total message.

THE IMPACT OF NONVERBAL COMMUNICATION

You might smile when you read the next paragraph. You might frown or even shake your head in disbelief, or nod in agreement. You could tap the page with your pencil in recognition of the truth of the material. Someone watching you could probably tell by those actions just what your response to the message is. That is because nonverbal communication has a powerful impact on your total communication process. Some early estimates about the impact of nonverbal communication ranged from about sixty-five to ninety-three percent of the overall meaning of any message (Mehrabian, 1968); subsequent research suggested that closer to one third is derived from nonverbal information (Birdwhistell, 1970). In a project that examined twenty-three studies of nonverbal communication, more recent research suggests that about two thirds of the meaning of messages is communicated nonverbally (Philpott, 1992). If those estimates are even close, they show the importance of nonverbal communicative behaviors.

> **IMPROVING COMPETENCY**
> ## An Hour of Silence
>
> Can you keep totally silent for one hour? Try it, and keep track of how you manage to respond to other people. Keep track of your observations of how much information is being exchanged without the use of words. Do you think you could go through an entire day of your regular schedule without speaking?

Whereas you may have spent ten to fourteen years studying writing and reading skills, and perhaps a few short lessons on listening and public speaking, you probably have not had any formal instruction in the skills of nonverbal communication. Yet you do it, usually well, and nearly constantly. How is this so? Is it a natural, inborn ability? Is it something you just picked up along the way? Researchers who have studied these questions have concluded that humans *instinctively* want to communicate, both verbally and nonverbally. The distinctive *symbol codes* we use in our culture are specifically learned. Generally, we learn by imitation and reinforcement at first, then by formal practice and instruction later. Nonverbal communication is similar to our use of words in that both are governed by specific forms, functions, and rules that help to create clear meanings. These rules vary by group and culture, as do our verbal practices. Let us consider some of the principles involved in using nonverbal communication.

NONVERBAL COMMUNICATION CONTEXTS AND RULES

Functions

You use nonverbal behaviors to communicate in a variety of situations. Sometimes you wave instead of saying hello. At other times you point in order to clarify the direction you are talking about, or raise your hand in class to be called on, or smile when you see someone do a good job. Each of these actions illustrates one of six **functions of nonverbal communication** behaviors: (1) substituting, (2) reinforcing, (3) regulating, (4) contradicting, (5) managing impressions, and (6) establishing relationships.

Waving or nodding instead of talking illustrates the *substituting function*. Here, the movement has replaced or substituted for a word. Replacement can range from the easy examples above to more complex functions, such as the movements ground personnel use at airports to signal pilots as they guide airplanes to their proper spots at the gate. You can learn complete languages that use only movements such as the sign language developed and used by Native Americans in the Great Plains, or the popular American Sign Language taught on many campuses and used by millions of hearing-impaired people every day. In sign languages, the simple movements and gestures of everyday life, such as waving, are the foundation of more complex movements used to build whole sentences and communicate sophisticated concepts.

In addition to using nonverbal communication substitutes for words, you communicate nonverbally to *reinforce* or complement your verbal sounds. When you point to clarify your meaning, or nod your head while you say, "Yes, of course, I see what you mean," or pound the table in anger with your fist, you are reinforcing your message and complementing your words.

CRITICAL THINKING IN COMMUNICATION
American Sign Language

In the late 1800s, a French priest, Abbé Sicard, developed what we now know as American Sign Language. Many of the signs he created were based on Wild West views of the United States that seem funny to us today. For example, the sign for the United States is made by putting the fingers of both hands together so they alternate. This action was designed to simulate the wall of a log cabin.

The system was not always based on logic. Another example for a sign developed without the use of critical thinking is the sign for the thick red tomato sauce you put on your hamburgers and hot dogs and French fries. The sign originally had two parts. The first part used both little fingers to make a "mustache" motion and is the sign for the four-legged, feline animal, cat. The second part of the sign consisted of pointing with the index finger, to indicate "up." The relationship of these signs to the tomato sauce—ketchup or catsup was that it *sounds* like those two signs when those two signs are spoken. Remember, this is a system for *deaf* people! Now, however, the sign has changed and consists of making a fist with one hand, then pounding the fist with the flat of your other hand twice. Try it, and you'll see that the new sign is much more logical.

Gestures have meaning within a cultural context.

If you want to join a conversation, you use nonverbal signals to indicate your interest. Such movements *regulate* the flow of interaction. In class, you use a formal motion to get the instructor's permission to speak—raising your hand. In ordinary small group conversations, people who want to join in usually nod, raise their eyebrows a bit, begin to open their mouths slightly, and breathe in as they sense the other person coming to a pause. Sometimes we raise and lightly tap a pencil or pen to signal that we desire to begin speaking. Or, if you are speaking, you may put your hand up slightly from the table, with palm facing the other person to "hold" them for a moment while you conclude an idea.

If you want to *contradict* your verbal message, you can easily do so by displaying an opposite nonverbal behavior. For example, if you want to relay the message that you do not like a certain food, you might choose *vocalic* sarcasm as your strategy. Thus you could say, "This turnip is really wonderful," while you used your voice to stress and roll the words, *really* and *wonderful* and place an elongated and exaggerated stress on the *won* syllable. At the same time you would crinkle up your nose, and perhaps use your thumb and index finger to pinch your nostrils together. The message is accurate only if the receiver also knows the nonverbal information in your paralanguage and facial gestures because the words alone give information that opposes your intended message.

Deceiving another person with your nonverbal messages is another form of contradiction. For example, you may be bored on a date or in a class, but you do not want to communicate this feeling. So you pretend—you simulate interest by keeping eye contact, nodding, and sometimes smiling, none of which are truthful messages about your feelings. Much research has been done on **deception** in nonverbal communication, from the cues we all use in social situations, to the efforts criminals employ to deceive their victims and police investigators (Hocking and Leathers, 1980; Leathers, 1992). In their studies, Leathers and Hocking have looked at eye contact and hand-to-face gestures as clues to deception. The size of the pupil of the eye can also reveal heightened anxiety or interest or arousal, as can measurements of the electro-conductivity of the skin, which is measured by "lie-detectors."

A fifth dimension of nonverbal communication is *impression management*, that is creating and controlling the way other people perceive you. You arrange your hair a certain way; you speak with a chosen pitch or tone of voice; or you have a particular car or dog or bicycle or wristwatch or ring or shoe or eyeglasses that represents *you* to the rest of the world. You spend much time in selecting the right outfit for a job interview, or for a lunch with the parents of someone you're dating.

In each of these situations you attempt to construct a message about you based on the impression these items and behaviors may make on the intended audience. When you listen to others, respond to them, wait for them to finish (or cut them off mid-sentence), you are creating an impression. Sensitive nonverbal communicators make sure the impression their listeners receive is the same as the one they intended to send. On the other hand, you probably have met people who seem too loud or too pushy, or stand too close, or lean into a group and interrupt. These people are likely violating social norms for acceptable nonverbal behavior and they are not managing their impressions well. Later, this chapter will offer some suggestions for improving nonverbal communication.

Finally, you can use nonverbal messages to establish or reveal a *relationship*. The simple gold band on the ring finger of your left hand is one way to communicate a relationship using an object. Standing at the head of a table around which others are seated communicates a relationship through posture and proxemics. A police officer in uniform has a clear relationship to a traffic accident. In a clinic, people wearing white jackets and stethoscopes communicate to us about their relationship to medicine. Whether you touch someone else, and how, when, and where you touch communicate information about the relationship.

TECHNOLOGY AND COMMUNICATION

From GSRs to Videotape

The use of scientific instruments to help record and measure nonverbal communication took a leap forward when psychologists discovered that the ability of people's skin to conduct electricity changes with their emotional states as do the heart and breathing rates for most people. Researchers devised machines to record all of these changes, and then attached the machines to people undergoing questions. For many people, the galvanic skin response (or GSR) machine was able to indicate when they were truthful and when they were not. More recently, inventors of machines that can measure tiny changes in vocal stress patterns and video cameras that can record the pupil dilation of your eyes have made similar claims. Both are thought to be uncontrollable consciously and both are thought to reveal truthfulness.

Rules

The six functions of nonverbal communication can be conveyed in a variety of ways and with a variety of outcomes, but there are some rules or principles that apply to all areas.

First, because everything about you—looks, dress, action, and inaction—can be interpreted, you are continuously communicating. Even if you close the door and turn off the light to avoid your friends, that is a message they are quite capable of understanding. You can be sleeping in the library, and everyone who walks by you will get some impression of who and what you are. If you have an early morning or late afternoon class and doze off, you will be communicating something to the instructor. Communication instructors often state this rule, "You cannot *not* communicate." Even without other people present, you communicate with yourself in dreams and thinking. So, through nonverbal communication, you are always communicating.

Next, nonverbal communication is often *ambiguous*. By themselves, gestures, movements, objects, and so on, may tell you only part of the story. You need to see the context, the relationship, the accompanying verbal behavior (if any) and responses. Students yawn in class sometimes because they're bored, sometimes because they ate a big lunch and are sleepy, and sometimes because they stayed up all night studying for an exam. Any of these is perfectly plausible, and each might call for a different response.

Or you may see someone gazing out a window. They could be daydreaming, avoiding someone, conducting a bird-watching session, or evaluating the possibility of snow over the weekend. Unfortunately, we may attach implied meanings that turn out to be erroneous. Although you can make a tentative conclusion about the nonverbal meaning, keep it tentative until you get more information from the situation or other clues about the message. Someone standing by the curb, backpack filled with books, in front of campus, facing oncoming traffic with their thumb extended provides a clear context, but not just from the thumb. All the factors together help to alleviate the ambiguity.

My son was involved in track in eighth grade, and I watched from the stands as he ran in the 100 meter finals in a large meet. The finish was very close, but he looked as though he might have won. A teacher who was helping record the official times knew where I was sitting, and after several moments of huddling by the officials, she leaned out of the circle, made eye contact with me, smiled, and held up two fingers. "Well," I said to my wife, "second place at the county finals is pretty good!" A few moments later they announced him as the *first* place winner, and the same teacher again smiled and again flashed her two fingers in the air—for the victory sign! The moral of the story is to be careful of the potential for ambiguity in nonverbal communication.

Third, remember that all communication, including nonverbal communication, exists in a culture. You learn a set of gestures, movements, habits, styles of dress, and so on within a cultural setting and that may not be even close to the set someone else has learned. Especially bothersome for international travelers are the gestures used to substitute for or accompany verbal expression. You might

DIVERSITY IN COMMUNICATION
Signs in Europe

I traveled with a group of U.S. college students in Europe for several months and we attended a soccer game in London, with the home team fans. We thought we'd be amiable and root for them as well. When they finally scored, one of my more enthusiastic students jumped up and put his fingers in his mouth and whistled loudly and continuously. The local fans looked at him with ugly, menacing expressions as I tried to quiet him immediately. Whistling like that in Europe is the equivalent of booing in the United States.

This same student went with a few companions to a small tavern in Greece, where he ordered and ate a fine meal. When the waiter asked in very limited English if they liked the food, my student gave the supposedly universal sign for "OK"—index finger touching the thumb to make a circle with the rest of the fingers flared out and a slight back and forth motion. This sign, unfortunately, is *not* universally positive. In fact, it is often interpreted in Mediterranean areas as something obscene and vulgar. My student was promptly punched by the offended waiter, and tossed out of the café. Thanks to these encounters, he slowly began to learn the lesson about cultural context and ambiguity; nonverbal signals are not universal!

point to clarify what you mean in our culture, but the movement offends people in other cultures. Anyone who has traveled will tell you stories of mix-ups and even altercations following a culturally improper use of nonverbal indicators. In the United States, we whistle to cheer on our teams at sporting events, whereas in many places in Europe, whistling is derisive.

Finally, nonverbal communication is probably best used to express attitudes, feelings, and relationships. The couple walking down the hall hand-in-hand is a clear example of expressing relationship. Whether you talk to someone while facing them, or facing away, standing up or sitting down, or even *if* you address that person at all, indicates much about the feelings or the relationship that might be involved. The surprised look on your face, or the deep frown, or the warm embrace are good examples of this use of interpreting nonverbal communication.

Now that we have taken a look at the uses and contexts for nonverbal communication, let's examine the actual types that you use to follow these patterns.

TYPES OF NONVERBAL COMMUNICATION

There are many ways to classify all possible nonverbal behaviors and objects, but the following elements, defined at the beginning of the chapter, seem to cover most situations: paralanguage, posture, movement, objects, space and time, and the senses—especially touch, smell, and taste.

Paralanguage

When you use your vocal apparatus to surround your words with color, tone, inflection—or even pauses, mumbles, or noises—you are using **paralanguage**. Sometimes called *vocalics*, this use of your voice is one of the most common aspects of nonverbal communication. Every time you ask a question with a rising inflection at the end of the sentence, you are employing vocalics to make your meaning clear. Every time you use the same rising inflection at the end of a declarative sentence, you let your listeners know that you may not be sure of your information.

Sometimes you say "hmmm" when thinking about an answer to a tough question. The "ums" and "ers" that many people put between words to give them time to think are examples of paralanguage. Even "okay" and "you know" when used as fillers have ceased to be words and have become just part of the noise stream.

The volume, rate, pitch, and tone of your voice can all be varied to create meanings. You can substitute for words, as when you make the sound "huh" with a rising inflection instead of saying "What?" or you can intensify your meaning by shouting or whispering. You may communicate a friendly or intimate relationship by adopting a warm tone, or you can shift into a shrill or clipped vocal pattern to suggest a hostile relationship. Sarcasm is an obvious way to use this nonverbal category to contradict your verbal message. Saying, "I had a really wonderful time on our date tonight," while giving a prolonged stress on the word "really" gives a contradictory message to the words, but one that is clear nevertheless.

Posture

You may not be directed to "Sit up straight!" just for your health; the speaker may have thought your slouching posture communicated a lack of interest or respect. Lounging back in your chair during a job interview, with your body leaning away from your interviewer will probably not help your prospects of getting the job. In public speaking situations, some speakers lean on the lectern, a posture that may communicate sloppiness or lack of dynamism or interest. Thus, you can use posture to reinforce or contradict your verbal message, to communicate its own message in place of words, or to control an impression or indicate a relationship. You sit closer to those you like, as you have probably noticed. You stand at the head of the table when you are in charge of the meeting. Posture can be used in all of these ways. But remember, the message conveyed by posture may also be ambiguous. The person slumping in the chair may really have had a great time and like you very much, but they are exhausted from studying all the night. As in other areas of communication, be sure to consider all the information before drawing absolute conclusions.

Movement

Included in the category of movement are the general motions such as walking, as well as the specific gestures associated with animated communication. Sometimes called *kinesics*, the study of movement is a rich area of investigation by communication scholars because of the great variety of possible kinesic combinations. When you stride confidently along the sidewalk you communicate to onlookers a sense of strength and deliberateness. On the other hand, slouching while walking—head down and taking small steps may communicate weakness, passivity, or fear. People who work in the field of assertiveness training, especially those who teach others to avoid assault, say that attackers often are drawn to potential victims by their seemingly weak posture and movement behaviors.

Gestures are an entire sub-set of behaviors involving movement. Some are cultural indicators and are specific to any group—for example, those of the student traveler mentioned earlier. Others may be connected to a job or occupation, as in the signals used at airports, or hand signals used on noisy construction sites. Every day you may be using gestures constantly and without much thought—wrinkling your nose when discussing something unpleasant or shrugging your shoulders when a friend asks for your opinion and you're not at all sure you have one. Platform speakers often use gestures to punctuate their words. In a review of research done on gestures, thousands of gestures and combinations of gestures were catalogued from a variety of studies (Burgoon and Saine, 1978).

Facial expressions constitute yet another set of movements which have rich meanings: the face is usually the first place listeners look to discover the total meaning of the message (Keman et al., 1972; Berry, 1990). Think of your facial expressions as gestures with which you can produce thousands of possible combinations. Most of the research on the communicative power of the face has been done with the communication of emotion. In fact, Charles Darwin wrote one of the earliest published works dealing with facial expressions in 1872! (Darwin, 1872).

More recently, the *Facial Meaning Sensitivity Test* was developed by Dale Leathers to determine the accuracy with which people can guess the emotions of someone else through facial expression alone (Leathers and Emigh, 1980). Leathers found five areas of meaning associated with facial expressions: (1) *evaluation*—we communicate pleasant or unpleasant and good or bad reactions; (2) *interest*—we tell others if we are bored or attentive; (3) *intensity*—we show the degree of our interest, boredom, disgust, or liking by our facial expressions; (4) *control*—whether we are in control of ourselves—our emotions and feelings—is communicated by our faces; and (5) *understanding*—we let others know whether we find their messages clear or confusing. Several expressions were almost always agreed upon, but others were more ambiguous (Motley and Camden, 1988). Again, the clearest communication occurs when you know the context, see the face, and hear the accompanying words. Given all of this information, a frown might be interpreted as an indication of anger or disappointment or thoughtfulness. It depends on the combination of information.

Objects

Objects are the things you have around you, that you wear or even those you drive or ride on. Jewelry, clothing, eyeglasses; even your pen or pencil can have communicative significance.

The Story of Communication
Woody Guthrie's Lyrics

WOODY GUTHRIE WROTE "This Land Is Your Land" and hundreds of other songs about people's experiences during the Great Depression of the 1930s. In one song, "Pretty Boy Floyd," he describes a bank robber in Oklahoma who was reputed to have given the money he stole to poor farmers. In the last line of the song Guthrie says , "Some robbers use guns, others use fountain pens." How can someone rob you with a fountain pen? Who used a fountain pen in the 1930s? Guthrie takes a simple object to communicate a whole picture of the banking business.

These objects exist in a cultural setting; a certain type of hat may mean nothing to you, but in another place it may indicate marital status or occupation. A uniform is an obvious example of an object that helps us distinguish between the police officer, firefighter, Marine, and tennis player. There are places you cannot go unless you wear the right uniform—such as restaurants which insist on coat and tie for men, skirts or dresses for women. Attention to clothes changes with the fashions and cultures of the times but the nearly worldwide influence of United States' culture has made blue jeans an international costume.

Objects symbolize certain jobs or characteristics. In filmmaking, for example, the director or writer may use an object to tell the audience about a character's interests, values, background, or job. What does it tell us if the heroine drives around in a jeep? Or a Porsche? Or takes the bus? Or is in a wheelchair? Or rides a ten-speed racing bike or an old balloon tire clunker with a wicker basket on the handlebars? All these variations are choices to be made so that the audience will have some information about the person being portrayed. Nonverbal communication discloses information about self-concept, expectations, and experiences.

When you go to a job interview, it is wise to consider the nonverbal power of objects and find out what the dress code or other standards are for the prospective place of employment. A corner hotdog stand employer will not require you to wear a business outfit to the job, but will probably be impressed if you wear neat, clean, casual clothes—not shorts and a tank top.

Space and Time

In all cultures definitions of space and time communicate much about relationships and status. If you have the largest office in the building all to yourself, and others are crowded—for example, four or five people in a same size or smaller room—you can be sure that the status and power implications are clear to everyone. Often called *proxemics*, the study of how space communicates has been the subject of much research. You already know that you move closer to people you like, and that you feel uncomfortable if you are sitting in the library at a large empty table, and someone sits directly next to you. On the other hand, if that last open seat is at a very crowded table, you feel far less discomfort.

The use of proxemics varies by culture and context.

Again, context and culture determine our use of space. North Americans have a personal "space bubble" that surrounds them to a distance of about twenty-four to thirty inches during normal conversations. Latin American, Mediterranean, and Arab people have a much smaller "bubble" and feel uncomfortable if you keep a larger distance from them while talking one-to-one. You may feel invaded by their bubble size; they may feel rejected by yours.

Time is another nonverbal area where we communicate relationships and controls. Suppose you are trying to petition the dean of your school to exempt you from a certain required class because you already know much about the subject. You set up an appointment for 3:00 P.M. What time should you arrive at the Dean's office? In typical college culture, the Dean has higher status than you, has power over your request, and is probably older and better educated than you are. Also, you are the one seeking the appointment. You need to arrive a few minutes *before* 3:00 p.m.; getting there at 2:50 or 2:55 is fine. Arriving at 2:40 is too soon and may seem pushy. However, arriving even at 3:02 may be seen as rude or insincere. Now, how about the Dean's arrival time for the same appointment? Is 3:05 acceptable? Even 3:10 is probably fine. If the Dean arrives after 3:15, some quick apology may be offered: "Sorry I kept you waiting, come on in." If it's after 3:20, you may get a brief explanation to accompany the apology: "Sorry I kept you waiting—I was on the phone." How long would you wait? This scenario demonstrates one function of time in our communication activities. Culture plays a big part in how we use time to communicate. Some places—generally in southern or equatorial climates—seem to have far broader and more flexible definitions of being "on time," while those from Northern European cultures have a more exact standard. While traveling in the former Soviet Union several years ago, our group needed to be reminded that when the tour bus guide said the bus was leaving at 10:00 AM, that meant that at 9:57 the bus started and people buckled up. The door closed two minutes later and the bus left the curb as the second hand swept past the 12 position—at exactly 10:00. Several members of our group would leave their hotel rooms at 9:57 AM and arrive four minutes later to find only exhaust fumes. What *just on time* means in Madrid is *late* in New York and *early* in Bangkok.

Time and space are two fascinating areas of research and study, and the interesting variations among cultures are important for you to understand if you are to become adept at nonverbal communication.

The Senses

Your five senses—taste, touch, smell, sound, and sight—are the avenues by which messages come to you. Most nonverbal messages arrive at your brain's message center through your eyes or ears. Others come to you through the sense of taste, such as when you discover food that is going bad, or through your sense of smell, such as when you discover a fire by smelling smoke.

Advertisers know the power of sensory messages. They appeal to taste in food and drink commercials. Perfumers are selling not just the smell, but the feelings and emotions they can conjure up with their product. Has anyone ever shaken hands with you so that you feel pain? Ever had a gentle pat on the back or a warm hug? Those gestures are some of the ways touch gives and receives messages.

There has been a good deal of investigation into extrasensory perception (ESP), but the results are more intriguing than certain. Some people claim to be able to read cards face down, or get impressions from other people or objects over long distances. Certainly, you have heard that police investigators occasionally consult psychics to help find missing persons. This area is the subject of ongoing studies all over the world, but trying to observe ESP is complex. Control of experiments and agreement of definitions are difficult to develop, given the unseen nature of the phenomenon. However, it is an area we may read more about in the future.

IMPROVING NONVERBAL COMMUNICATION COMPETENCY

Becoming aware of the ways you communicate nonverbally and knowing that different people have different ways of using *their* nonverbal communication is the best first step to improving your abilities. Self-awareness can be developed simply by getting into the habit of monitoring your behavior and taking note of your postures, movements, and objects. You may want to get some outside assistance by asking friends for feedback or even arranging for someone to videotape you in action during a conversation or making a speech, or as you participate in a group. All these activities will provide you with increased sensitivity to your own and to others' repertoire of nonverbal interactions.

Once you develop awareness, you might try to expand your repertoire of nonverbal activities. You can expand your ability to accurately decode the messages of others by expanding your own vocabulary for sending messages. There are ranges of behaviors to be explored that can add depth to your abilities if you learn them and practice them in your own communication.

Finally, remember that good communication focuses on the receiver of the message. If you become self-aware, then aware of others, and try to stretch your own abilities, you will have many choices from which to create clear messages for your listeners. You can implement these choices by sending appropriate signals that amplify or intensify your verbal messages. You can also look to your listeners and read their nonverbal messages to evaluate your performance and then adapt your messages. A powerful tool, nonverbal communication is an essential part of overall communication. Your school may even offer an entire course in this area.

SUMMARY

The impact of nonverbal communication is at least as significant as verbal communication and accounts for much of the research in the field of communication. Like its counterpart, nonverbal communication is subject to certain principles. It is always present, is usually ambiguous when used by itself, exists briefly in time and space, and is probably best used in conjunction with verbal symbols.

You can study your own use of postures, gestures, facial expressions, voice inflections, objects, space, and time, and you can study the information you take in through your five senses. You may even be capable of sending or receiving information through means, such as ESP, which are not yet fully understood. Improve your communication skills by remembering the four areas of communication competency: repertoire, selection, presentation, and evaluation. Being aware of yourself, others, culture, and context builds your repertoire. Analyzing your behavior helps you to select appropriate nonverbal messages. Receiving feedback helps you to evaluate your style and effectiveness, and to change them if necessary. So apply your knowledge and expand it in order to become an effective communicator.

Key Terms

nonverbal communication, **76**
vocalics, **76**
proxemics, **76**
artifacts, **76**
movement, **76**
time, **76**

senses, **76**
functions of nonverbal
  communication, **78**
deception, **78**
paralanguage, **83**

▶ **EXERCISES**

1. An interesting way to study nonverbal communication is to watch a television comedy show without the sound. Can you follow the plot and anticipate the next action? One of the great geniuses of comedic movement was Lucille Ball. If you can spend some time watching "I Love Lucy" reruns, you will have the chance to see a real master at work.

2. Spend one hour or one day without speaking. Keep a log of the ways you were or were not able to communicate clearly to others. What strategies and inventions did you use to keep your messages flowing clearly?

3. Sometimes, you may see students wearing blindfolds and being guided by others around campus. These students are participating in a blindwalk, sometimes known as a trustwalk, because the blindfolded person really needs to trust his or her partner to make it work. If you feel comfortable about trying this experiment, do it with special emphasis on both partners being quiet the entire time, except for minimal directions such as "We're coming to a stair step now." If you do not have a way to do this at school, blindfold yourself at home and try getting around in a very familiar space without your vision. Listen for sounds, be aware of smells, touch surfaces, and so on, all of which can help you determine where you are.

4. Pair off with a partner in class or a friend outside of class and conduct a nonverbal audit of each other's appearance. Start with objects, such as jewelry and clothing. List what your partner is wearing and what messages you infer from these objects.

5. Learn the letters of the finger-spelling alphabet used by deaf people. Pair off with a partner and conduct a brief conversation using only finger spelling. Pay attention to other nonverbal communication systems as well, especially the facial expressions that accompany the finger spelling. Do you see why finger spelling alone would not suffice for a sign language?

References

Berry, D. S. "What Can a Moving Face Tell Us?" *Journal of Personality and Social Psychology 58* (1990).

Birdwhistell, R. L. *Kinesics and Context.* Philadelphia: University of Pennsylvania Press, 1970.

Burgoon, Judee K., and Thomas Saine. *The Unspoken Dialogue.* Boston: Houghton Mifflin, 1978, 54.

Darwin, Charles. *The Expression of Emotions in Man and Animals.* London: Murray, 1872.

Gunkel, David. "Rethinking Virtual Reality: Simulations and the Deconstruction of the Image." *Critical Studies in Media Communication 17,* 1 (March 2000).

Hocking, J. E. and Dale G. Leathers. "Nonverbal Indicators of Deception: A New Theoretical Perspective." *Communication Monographs 47* (1980): 119–131.

Keman, P. W., V. Friesen, and P. Ellsworth. *Emotion is the Human Face: Guidelines for Research and an Integration of Findings.* New York: Pergamon Press, 1972.

Leathers, D. G. *Nonverbal Communication Systems.* Boston: Allyn and Bacon, 1976.

Leathers, D. G. *Successful Nonverbal Communication,* 2nd ed. New York: MacMillan, 1992.

Leathers, D. G., and T .H. Emigh. "Decoding Facial Expressions: A New Test with Decoding Norms." *Quarterly Journal of Speech 66* (1980).

Mehrabian, Albert. "Communication Without Words." *Psychology Today 2* (1968).

Motley, Michael and C. T. Camden. "Facial Expression of Emotion: A Comparison of Posed Expressions Versus Spontaneous Expressions in an Interpersonal Communication Setting." *Western Journal of Speech Communication 552* (Winter 1988).

Park, Hee Sun, and Timothy R. Levine. "A Probability Model of Accuracy in Deception Detection Experiments." *Communication Monographs 68,* 2 (June 2001).

Philpott, J. S. *The relative contribution to meaning of verbal and nonverbal channels of communication...a metaanalysis.* Unpublished master's thesis, University of Nebraska, 1983, as cited in Leathers, D. G., *Successful Nonverbal Communication,* 2nd ed., New York: Macmillan, 1992.

What We Know About Verbal Communication

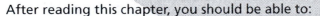

After reading this chapter, you should be able to:

- Understand how your use of symbols creates your communication environment
- Describe the process we go through from childhood onward to acquire and enhance our language skills
- Identify the similarities and differences between written and spoken communication
- Sense the appropriateness of a variety of types of English, and be aware of how language can be misused to attack others
- Feel confident in using your forms of English in a variety of situations
- Improve your skills in understanding and using language

We have finally arrived at the subject of language—often the first thing people think about when discussing communication. From the previous chapters, you have learned that language is only a part of a much larger communication process. Before you first acquired language and learned to use it effectively, a great deal had to happen. You needed to be able to hear and think, to receive and process information. Once you made sense of the sounds around you, you begin to imitate these sounds to get reactions, solve problems, or simply to enjoy making the sounds. Let us begin with a look at symbols, the basic building blocks of language.

SYMBOLS, UTTERANCES, AND MEANINGS

Your communication self—the listener, the thinker, and the person aware of nonverbal communication—has many of the tools you need to be effective in a variety of situations. Even though you spend most of your communication time listening and thinking, your most frequent interactions with others will probably focus on verbal messages. However, those messages will be carried on both the nonverbal and verbal channels. In the previous chapter, you learned about nonverbal communication. Now it is time to look closely at another component: verbal communication.

The way we use words—verbal communication—is one of the distinguishing characteristics of our species. We are able to turn our reactions to the world around us into symbols. These symbols are neither the things themselves nor are they our reactions. Rather they represent the physical aspects of the world and our own responses to them.

Like nonverbal systems, verbal communication is fraught with confusion and misunderstanding caused by mismatches between the messages people think they have sent and the messages people think they have received. Language is complex, and the processes we use to guide and build our use of it depend on understanding its nature. Let's first turn to learning about the symbolic nature of language, and how the sounds we utter take on meanings for us and for others.

Language as Symbol

A **symbol** is something that stands for something else; in our minds, it replaces what it stands for in a form of shorthand. For example, in our culture, a square, block red cross on a white background is a symbol for "medical services" in general, and the Red Cross organization in particular. It is seen on emergency vehicles, on hospital ships, and on the uniform of disaster relief workers. A red octagon, on the other hand, is the color and shape of a stop sign. The letters that spell "dog" have nothing in common with the shaggy canine creature on our doorstep. The word is merely a symbol for that animal and a multitude of similar animals.

The very letters we use to write in English are arbitrary. Anyone who has studied Russian, Hebrew, Japanese, or Greek realizes that the sounds we make when we see our symbols, are made by other people when they see other symbols. Even though there may be general agreement among speakers of the same language about the meanings attached to symbols, they may make different connections when responding to a certain symbol. The dictionary effectively records the general meanings speakers of a language may have for certain symbol combinations but it cannot tell us exactly what one individual's meaning is. If you look up the symbol combination c–a–t in a dictionary, you will get several general meanings, but there will be no picture of "Fluffy," the pet you have had for ten years. The difference between a general dictionary definition—**denotation**—and the specific associations and reactions you may have—**connotation**, is one source of confusion in verbal communication. It can also be a source of enrichment for symbolizing ideas. For example, if you wanted to create a romantic setting for a novel, would you be more likely to place the story in New Orleans or in Cleveland? Lots of people in Cleveland fall in love and have romantic relationships, but the sound of bayous, charm of Creole-accented conversation, and the smell of Cajun cooking all combine to suggest a New Orleans setting. Of course, you may well try to place a warmly romantic story in Cleveland, but most people's connotations of Cleveland do not include romance, a fact that must be considered when deciding on the setting for a story. These examples are broadly drawn, for we probably have connotations for most of the words we use. *Home, car, Mom, job,* even *bread* probably have a wide variety of connotations among your classmates.

Differences in background and experience create differences in the reactions people have to words. If you have eaten only the mild Cantonese version of Chinese food, you will tend to think of Chinese food as mild and slightly exotic. If the only Chinese food you've ever had is the extremely spicy, mouth-searing Hunan variety, your connotation of Chinese food will be quite different. The denotation of *Chinese food* is the commonly used, dictionary meaning. The connotation of *Chinese food* is your feeling about or personal reaction to those words.

People have always been interested in their own use of symbols and in the development of written and spoken symbols to represent and communicate about their world and experiences. In our time, two notable writers—Alfred Korzybski and S. I. Hayakawa—have been identified with this field of study (Korzybski, 1933; Hayakawa, 1990). Their writings have concerned the way people use and misuse language.

Korzybski and Hayakawa felt our misuse of symbols is partly responsible for many social ills. They stressed that "the symbol is not the thing." By this, they meant that symbols are representational and artificial and not worth fighting over. Our words, as Hayakawa pointed out, are like maps to a territory, but they are not the territory itself. In one example they found a state senator who blocked a bill in the legislature because it used a socially impolite term—"venereal disease." They argued that it was much sounder to attack the disease. They urged that we look at the reality, not at the symbol. They believed that if we could change the way we react to symbols, especially those of language, we could improve our orientation to reality and get to work solving the problem instead of arguing over what to call the problem. Their study and philosophy is called **general semantics** and is related to the study of how meanings and symbols interact.

In addition to *semantics*, the study of meanings and words, we can look at **phonologics**, the study of meaning and sound, and *syntactics*, the study of meaning and forms. These methods of looking at how we use symbols and signs are known as **semiotics**. Let's examine semiotics by focusing on each of its three parts as identified.

Semiotics

Semantics   The way we attach meanings to our words is known as **semantics** and users of words follow rules of semantics to put meaning into what they say. Users of words often give those words their meaning. For example, you and your friends may have a special term for taking a break or eating a certain food. The dictionary is not likely to have it listed, yet the meaning of the term is perfectly clear to you—the users. Often, children will make up a language or a code, perhaps to fool their parents or other children. These special codes underline the principle that *use creates meaning*.

The advice, "Look it up in the dictionary," is only good if the user of the term you don't understand was using its general application, the one found in the dictionary.

A few words about "word books" may be in order here. Dictionaries function like history books in that they record the way speakers and writers have used a word in the past. However, they cannot tell you what a particular speaker may mean if that speaker is departing from past usage. The job of dictionary writers is to review a wide variety of sources to find out how people are using words, and then to record and tabulate the results. If a word is no longer in use by anybody, then dictionary writers drop it from the current list, perhaps marking it "archaic." On the other hand, if the writers discover a word in wide usage that has not previously appeared, they add it.

TECHNOLOGY AND COMMUNICATION
Webster's Contributions

The widespread use of books did not develop until relatively recently in our history. The combination of printing technology and wide distribution of printed materials made it necessary for some standards, such as standards of spelling and grammar, to be established.

Noah Webster (1758–1843), for whom *Webster's Dictionary* was named, was concerned about the lack of standardization of American English in both grammar and spelling. Of his several books, the *American Dictionary of the English Language* was the first to be issued, in 1828, and has been reissued and updated for over 170 years now. A new edition is due out shortly and it will be available in hard-copy format as well as CD format. An on-line format is not far behind.

Webster thought his work would do much more than foster good spelling. He also thought that he would increase patriotism and improve morals through better communication, which was made possible then by improved printing technology as it is now due to the rapid development of the electronic media.

Every time a new edition of the dictionary comes out there are newspaper articles about the number of "new" words in it. Most of these new words are well-known to readers of newspapers because they have been in use for several years before being entered in the new edition of the dictionary. Some words are transitory, perhaps associated with a fad, and don't last long enough to be included in the dictionary. Others catch on and become permanent terminology. For example, before 1960, virtually no dictionary listed "countdown" as a word, yet it is now widely used and appears in every edition. "Compact disc," "microprocessor," and "byte" appear in current dictionary editions, but not in many before 1985. However, the absence of a word from dictionaries does not mean that it is not a perfectly good, communicative word. It only means that the dictionaries are slow to record word history. The best way to clear up doubts or confusion about the meaning of a word is to ask the word's users. Do you remember the scene from *Through the Looking-Glass* by Lewis Carroll (1949)?

> "I don't know what you mean by 'glory,'" Alice said.
>
> Humpty-Dumpty smiled contemptuously. "Of course you don't—till I tell you. I meant, 'there's a nice knock-down argument for you!'"
>
> "But 'glory' doesn't mean 'a nice knock-down argument,'" Alice objected.
>
> "When *I* use a word," Humpty-Dumpty said, in a rather scornful tone, "it means just what I choose it to mean—neither more nor less."
>
> "The question is," said Alice, "whether you *can* make words mean so many different things."
>
> "The question is," said Humpty-Dumpty, "which is to be master—that's all."

Which is to be master—you or the word? Semantics tells us that we control both our meanings and our reactions to the words around us. But mastering the meanings of our language system also means being familiar with other ways our symbols create meanings—sounds and structures.

Phonologics   The way a word sounds is one way we give it meaning. There are combinations of sounds that clarify meanings, and there are others that create only nonsense. From its sound, we recognize that the word "train" is different from "drain" even though the sounds of *t* and *d* are *nearly* identical. The phonemes, or sounds, change just slightly and the meaning changes completely.

Through sound, you provide not only differences in meanings, but information about yourself. Are you from Brooklyn? Atlanta? Fort Worth? Calcutta? Edinburgh? We all can say the same words, but slight variations in accent give listeners much information. Sounds govern our meanings, since written language is our ancestors' record of the sounds they made. Sometimes the original spellings remain, but over the years, sounds may change—as in the word "subtle." Say it and you will not hear the *b* pronounced. The rules that tell us how the sounds of words affect their meaning are one more part of the whole symbolic process.

Syntax   Finally, meaning comes from **syntax,** the rules of order of a language. You can probably guess the meaning of the sentence: "Dog, a large one there down the road coming is." You also know exactly how to change it to make it conform to the rules for English language sentence structure. Yet a word order close to this one would be preferred for speakers of Japanese or Hungarian. Sometimes a writer or speaker will deliberately invert word order or sentence structures to make his or her use of syntax stand apart from normal structures. Dylan Thomas, a master of the English language, began an essay as follows (1954):

> Across the United States of America, from New York to California and back, glazed, again, for many months of the year there streams and sings for its heady supper a dazed and prejudiced procession of European lecturers, scholars, sociologists, economists, writers, authorities on this and that and even, in theory, on the United States of America.

This sentence stretches our ability to follow its syntax, and is typical of Thomas's writing in both his prose and poetry. We recognize that the syntax is unusual, and perhaps we look more deeply into the meaning than we might have if he had used simpler patterns. There is always the chance, however, that the reader will give up on complex syntax, and there will be no communication at all. That is why it is wise to follow the rules of syntax for general audiences until they are committed to following you. Audiences expect you to follow these rules, and a barrier may arise if you don't meet their expectations. To gain mastery, you should follow the understood rules of definition, sound, and structure in your language.

Robert Zimmerman, born in 1941 in Hibbing, Minnesota, was a great admirer of the Welsh writer, Dylan Thomas. As a young man, Zimmerman also began to write, especially poetry used for dozens of powerful song lyrics. He was a composer as well; guitar and harmonica were his favorite instruments. Although he lacked a musically trained voice, he sang and recorded hundreds of his own songs, comprising dozens of albums. He influenced other singers and writers who also began responding to the incisive and creative communication of his material. Virtually every major rock, pop, or folk artist since the '60s has felt his influence. He was nearly killed in a motorcycle accident, and took over a year to recover to the point where he could once again lift a guitar. After more than twenty Gold Albums on his own and numerous awards, he now lives on the beach in Malibu, California under the name Bob Dylan.

The language that you use, and the language of everyone else, follow the understood rules of definitions, sounds, and structures. One of the universal connections of all people is that we have the capacity of language, and we acquire and use language—all languages—in the same manner.

ACQUIRING LANGUAGE SKILLS

When you first listened to the sounds of others around you, your brain had the capacity and the impulse to sort through these noises, to recognize patterns and to begin to attach meanings to those patterns. You had the phonological ability to make every sound of every language spoken on earth. If by some chance you were whisked away as an infant and reared in a Nepalese family, you would speak Nepali without any hesitation or a trace of an accent. It's just as we grow and acquire language, we drop those sounds not used or needed and concentrate

DIVERSITY IN COMMUNICATION

One Hundred Sounds

The International Phonetic Alphabet (IPA) is a widely used system of recording the sounds of spoken languages. First codified about 1889, it attempts to include a symbol representing every sound used in every language. Nearly one hundred such symbols are commonly in use. Only about fifty of the symbols are used to represent the sounds used by American English speakers. As you travel around the world, you will find that some of these sounds also exist in other languages; others are added and others are dropped as speakers either use or don't use certain positions of the teeth, tongue, lips, palate, and throat areas. The rich diversity of thousands of languages around the world tells us that while we may be diverse, we are also unified in the human family by our linguistic capabilities.

on the ones we hear around us. Sometimes the skill is very difficult to regain later, as when, in high school, you try to learn to roll your *r*'s softly in French class. The French *r* comes from the back of the tongue, a place not used in English pronunciation. In the southern tip of Africa the Xsosa people make a sound by closing the top of their throats and releasing quickly on a breath to create a pop or click represented by the English alphabet letter *x*. Thus, in order to say the name of the language, Xsosa, you need to be able to make this sound.

More important than the ability to make the right noises associated with any language is the aptitude to make sense out of those noises. Our primary language center, located in the left hemisphere of the brain just above the ear, is capable of organizing these sounds into meanings. However, the brain is a complex organism and researchers have discovered that other areas of the brain can also interact to make sense out of language. If damaged, parts of the brain will cease their functions, but sometimes other parts can, independently or through training, take over the functions of the damaged part. Much research is being done on this subject, and each year, a better and better understanding of these interactions emerges. Later, you will read about how children develop language skills, but for now, you can see that you have acquired them through living and responding to the world around you.

Your culture is also an important factor in determining your language processes. Much research has been done on the way we think compared to the way speakers of other languages think. There is a theory, called the **Sapir-Whorf Hypothesis,** that explains differences among cultures by looking at the linguistic patterns of the different languages. Simply stated, this theory says that you think within the linguistic patterns and boundaries of your language. Your vocabulary and your language structure determine what you think about, and how you think about it. For example, some Native American languages (especially Hopi and Navajo, which Whorf studied extensively) talk about *processes* in the world rather than events. Thus, you would discuss *dining* rather than *dinner* or *singing* rather

The Story of Communication
Shakespeare's Sonnet 18

Shall I compare thee to a summer's day?
Thou art more lovely and more temperate.
Rough winds do shake the darling buds of May
And summer's lease hath all too short a day.
Sometime too hot the eye of heaven shines,
And often is his gold complexion dimmed.
And every fair from fair sometime declines,
By chance or nature's changing course untrimmed.
But thy eternal summer shall not fade,
Nor lose possession of that fair thou owest.
Nor Death brag thou wander'st in his shade
When in eternal lines to time thou grow'st.
    So long as men can breathe, or eyes can see,
    So long lives this, and this give life to thee.

than *a song*, and so on. This dynamic flow of language is related to their patterns of thinking about the processes of the world. On the other hand, English places much emphasis on names and nouns to represent events, and may be said to be more static in orientation.

Language is a miracle in the sense that it can help us—our thoughts and ideas and feelings—travel across time, space, and culture. Why do people carve initials in a tree, or spray "Phil Loves Elisa" on a rock, or mark up walls of highways? They know that others, coming after, can read these symbols and thus the originator is, in a sense, still there—captured and frozen in time. Long after Phil and Elisa may have gone their separate ways, other people will still know about them and their relationship. You have the ability to learn from Socrates, long after he died, simply because others (mostly Plato and Aristotle) took the time to *write* about Socrates. Then others put Plato and Aristotle into an accessible form. Because you have language, you can share in the sagas and stories of Native Americans or Vikings who lived a thousand years ago. At the end of one of his Sonnets, Shakespeare wrote, "So long lives this, this gives life to thee," meaning that while there is still someone around to read about his loved one, she remains "alive" in our minds. You can send your thoughts and ideas around the world for less than the cost of a gallon of gas because you have language; you can write, and someone else on the receiving end can read. Remember from Chapter 1 that one of Western Civilization's greatest moments came in 1799 when Napoleon's army dug up a large stone tablet in Egypt, now called the **Rosetta Stone**. Inscribed in it was a message written in three languages—Greek, Egyptian, and hieroglyph. Until then, the writings of Egypt were not understood and this great African civilization was known only through its objects, paintings, and the writings of others. When we finally unlocked the key to their language, thousands of messages became available to us, and history filled in several thousand years of blank pages.

Your ability to use language is special and important. That is why there are communication classes to help you understand, appreciate, and enhance your abilities. The ability to learn about language does not stop in childhood, and if you wish, you may keep building language skills as long as you live.

SPEAKING AND WRITING

There is a direct relationship between speaking and writing. You first listened, then thought, then spoke, and then wrote. The symbols you use to write were created in an attempt to "capture" the sounds of spoken language. An example is the use of the article *a* before any word that doesn't start with a vowel. *A book* is fine, but *a umbrella* is not. Why not? Because *a umbrella* is harder to say than *an umbrella*. Notice that it is not harder to write; in fact it is a bit shorter. It would be more economical to use *a* all the time but our speech patterns came first, and we retain in rules for writing the same rules we developed in speaking.

There are some differences, however, in *style.* Written communication can be more complex than oral communication for several reasons. Readers have the opportunity to go back over written materials. You can put down a book, go get a drink of water, check your mail, grab a snack, and then pick up right where you left off, or any other place you like. When listening to a conversation, you have no such ability. If you get up and leave for a few moments, you cannot rewind the conversation back to where you left it. Therefore, written communication style can be more complex, have longer sentences, and summarize less than oral communication. The aware public speaker knows that you cannot simply read an essay and expect an audience to follow as if they had a copy in hand. A speech is not an "essay on legs" as one writer once commented. It is different because it *needs* to be different. A good way to think about the relationship between speaking and writing is to see them as complementary functions. Being skilled at one can help you be skilled at the other, but the skills are not interchangeable.

USE AND MISUSE OF LANGUAGE

Language is a powerful tool; it can help to guide us to new achievements or it can damage and degrade. As poet Robert Frost once said, "The first tool I stepped on turned into a weapon." The tool doesn't care how you use it. You can cut wheat or kill a person with the same scythe. Anyone who has seen any of the "chainsaw" genre of films is familiar with this tool/weapon dichotomy. You live in an English-speaking culture and at the moment, you are involved in higher education—a sub-culture within the mainstream one. In this environment, certain kinds of language use are dominant and expected. In other times and settings, other forms of English may be expected.

Mainstream American English

Mainstream American English is the language we all hear on the network news and national television programs. It is the common language of commerce, government, entertainment, and business. When new arrivals come to this country, one of the first steps they must take to integrate into the culture is to learn at least the basics of this language. Some may live in an ethnic community where the native language is spoken in every store and home, but, historically, European-based neighborhoods seldom last more than one or two generations beyond the original families (Gans, 1979). The native speakers die or move on and their grandchildren pick up the mainstream language.

Where there has been an enforced separation of neighborhoods, usually consisting of people from non-European backgrounds, group patterns may persist longer, and be carried from one ethnically similar neighborhood to another. Communities comprised almost entirely of African Americans or Puerto Ricans or Chinese or Latinos are still the norm in most large cities and are exceptions to the "scatter" pattern noted earlier. Most people in these communities have bilingual capabilities—they understand and can use Mainstream American English, but often communicate in other forms of English with friends, family, and local businesses. The language patterns of these people are reinforced by those around them, so they persist, yet it is likely that with the influence of schools geared toward Mainstream American English and the television, they will diminish over the coming years unless a strong force keeps them in use.

Mainstream American English is the form this book uses, and it is a bit different from other forms of English, such as those used in England, Ireland, South Africa, India, or Scotland. A wonderful television program, *The Story of English*, took viewers around the world to trace how English, in its many forms, has become the world language. Interestingly, the words of many of the persons interviewed had to be displayed as subtitles on the screen in order for Americans to comprehend them. English varies in spelling, pronunciation, vocabulary, and syntax, and you do not need to travel overseas to experience this for many forms of English are used here in the United States.

Variety in American English

Black English is probably the most notable and widespread variation on American English. With popular African American musicians leading the way, people outside the Black culture are often given a glimpse of this form of the language. Black English is much more complex than a simple shift in vocabulary, or the rhymed lyrics of a rap artist. Its grammar rules form a logical system independent of Mainstream English, and Black English has at least two major forms (Jenkins, 1982). It developed over several centuries in African American communities, and persists today because those communities stayed intact. One scholar described it as "an Africanized form of English reflecting Black America's linguistic-cultural African heritage and the conditions of servitude, oppression and life in America..." (Smitherman, 1972). That description emphasizes the growth of Black English in the context of African American history. For example, linguists can trace patterns, vocabulary, and styles in Black English to similar patterns and styles in the West African languages spoken by the ancestors of modern Black Americans (Hecht, Collier, Ribeau, 1993). Black English will likely continue for three reasons, contends Dr. Shirley Weber, African American Studies scholar. First, because Blacks experience the world differently from other groups (Covin,

1990), their language reflects and communicates that different experience. Secondly, Black English is a common element that binds African American people together, even though they may live in different areas or find themselves in different social or economic situations. Finally, Black English can be seen as a political statement that reflects connections with and pride about a shared African heritage (Weber, 1991).

Another variety of English includes those forms associated with Hispanic cultures. This blend of languages is sometimes called *Spanglish* (Castro, 1988). This form uses both syntax and vocabulary related to English and Spanish, and serves the functions of community identity and solidarity as well as group communication. Whether it will persist as long as Black English and develop an enduring linguistic identity remains to be seen. If social forces change so that these groups no longer experience a markedly different experience from the mainstream culture, the reasons to maintain a separate linguistic identity will also begin to disappear (DeVos and Romanucci-Ross, 1982).

Professional, Personal, and Popular Codes

Certain forms of English are associated with individuals by virtue of their occupations, interests, or relationships to current events in popular culture, and are commonly called *jargon*. For example, there is a medi-speak which uses medical terms and shorthand, and computer-speak which everyone inside the computer

CRITICAL THINKING IN COMMUNICATION
Computer History

In 1965, computers worked with vacuum tubes, and those simple machines were housed in large rooms or sometimes took up entire floors of buildings. They processed much faster than a human could, and a time of several hours to process a batch of data was considered good. Data were recorded on three-by-seven inch punch cards that had hundreds of places for small, rectangular holes to be punched out by machine. These holes were read by the computer to process data.

At that time, Charles Thacker, a senior at the University of California, Berkeley, envisioned a computer "the size of a college notebook binder." People laughed—it was impossible to comprehend such a bizarre vision. Thacker went to work for Xerox and later became an independent professional.

The introduction of the personal computer in the late 1970s, and the now widespread presence of the laptop computer have made Thacker's vision part of our daily reality. For his part in developing the computer revolution, Thacker was inducted into the National Academy of Science in 1996. Incidentally, the tabletop PC you use at home or school can do hundreds of times more operations than the room-size computers of 1965, and at a fraction of the time and cost. As a result of combining the analytical and logical processes of critical thinking with a creative vision, the way we communicate has changed forever (Chesebro and Bonsall, 1988).

community understands. A few years ago, only a few people knew the terms *CPU, motherboard, byte,* or *mouse* in this context. They are now commonly known because of the widespread use of computers, yet some terms are still the province of the experts and hackers.

You may share a personal code with a few members of your family based on common experiences or traditions. It might be quite simple. For instance, when my cousin Candace and I were about twelve years old, we went to another cousin's wedding celebration. Being mischievous, we tried to sneak sips of champagne from other guests' glasses without being caught, and set a record of four consecutive sips. Ever since that day, whenever we think someone is drinking too much, all we do is say "Four" (or hold up four fingers) to the other and the meaning is perfectly clear to us.

Popular codes stem from music, television shows and personalities, and popular movies. Terms from the 1960s surf culture, such as "fuzz" to mean police have largely disappeared, and only a few leftovers from the hippie era still say "Groovy!" with any regularity. Current listeners to Simon and Garfunkel are sometimes amused to hear the words to the "59th Street Bridge Song"—"feelin' groovy!" The Valley Girl talk of the late 1970s and early 1980s was, in turn, replaced by modern surf terms such as "tubular" and "barney," neither of which are heard much anymore. Some terms have staying power and enter the mainstream language; others, called *neologisms,* are current and reveal their users to be part of some popular movement of the moment. They can be both fun and useful and they keep the language vibrant and colorful.

Linguistic Oppression

One of the more controversial aspects of language is its association with stereotypes and insults, or **linguistic oppression.** Racism, sexism, ageism, handicapism, and other areas of offensive discrimination are all associated with actions, attitudes, and, especially language. The intention of the user is an important factor in determining meaning; it is considered offensive if a man calls a woman "girl," but within the African American community, women call each other "girl" with affection. Persons who are part of the reference group may be able to use terms within the community with less offense, or even with affection. Used by outsiders to attack, these terms are offensive; used by insiders, the intended meaning may be just the opposite.

These labels have of course changed over the years; one of the most notable modifications relating to Black Americans. Already popular, the term, "African American" has been overtaking "Black" as the preferred expression. We have come in less than fifty years from "polite" terms of "colored" to "Negro" to "Black" to "African American" so the process seems to be well established (Hecht, Collier and Ribeau, 1993). Older people are not so much "elderly" these days as "seniors" or "senior citizens." The "Senior Center" in town is a place where people over the age of sixty go to participate in a variety of activities. The context tells us it is a different kind of senior than someone in the last year of high school or college. Our study of semantics shows how words develop meanings as people use them. Both the intention of the user and the way you react to and apply words are involved in this active process. When you remember to supply a context to your communication, you help listeners understand your dynamic use of language.

Linguistic oppression is a topic felt deeply by many who are on the receiving end of such deliberate attacks through language. The whole issue of *hate speech* concerns the language of attack, and the issue of the right to free speech is sometimes in conflict with the right to be protected from attack. *Speech codes* on many campuses are an attempt to guide behavior and protect people from language used to attack or belittle. Some communication texts, such as this one, attempt to address the

IMPROVING COMPETENCY
Attacks on Self-Concept

One activity suggested by law professor Geoff Cowan is to write down an incident where you felt humiliated or abused by the use of hate speech. Try it. Search your memory for a time that may still be painful to recall. Was there an incident in which you were called a pejorative name? Were you put down by someone? Almost anyone can be a target and victim of language on the attack. If you are like most of the people in Professor Cowan's audiences, you will recall an incident where words were aimed at you on a personal level—perhaps by someone you knew. He uses the example of his brother who suffered from severe acne as a teenager in an exclusive prep school. Because he was Jewish and in a decided minority at the school, his brother was sometimes attacked with the words "kike" or "Jew." While certainly hurtful in both intent and effect, these insults did not remain as memorable as when he was taunted with the words "pimple face."

issue directly in a way to help people learn about the negative effects of such hate speech. Some communication classrooms use discussions, exercises, or simulations to accomplish the same goals (Jensen, 1993). Being labeled a certain way can both communicate contempt for the target and reveal attitudes of the speaker. Another difficulty is that people sense put-downs and may, if they hear them often enough, begin to incorporate the connotations of the term into their own self-concept. Thus, women who are referred to as "girls" may develop an immature affect, believing they are dependent and incompetent. While it is true that words are only symbols and are not reality—I can address you as "Your Majesty" but that will not make you ruler—they nevertheless have the powerful ability to influence our construction of our own realities. The Sapir-Whorf Hypothesis gives support to the idea that linguistic oppression, especially in the labeling of distinct groups within a culture, can be harmful. Many Native Americans remember being forbidden to speak any language other than English at reservation schools. The implication was that their native tongues were not valuable or important. American tourists are criticized for expecting people in other countries to speak English. When these kinds of messages come from powerful sources, they can affect the development of positive self-worth.

Be careful of your choices of words, for they can have tremendous impact on those who react to words in forming self-concept. In reality, that means almost all of us. Whether we like it or not, most of us are not so sophisticated that we realize that words are just the noises of other people. People are hurt by rude remarks, and one way to break out of this cycle of attack is to understand that certain labels can have an oppressive effect on those being labeled.

Magic, Taboo, and Ritual

Other important functions of our verbal code are expressive—that is, they provide us with some psychological release.

Magic   In the earliest times, our ancestors thought that language was a gift from the gods, or otherwise divinely inspired. The *Book of John* in the Christian Bible begins, "In the beginning was the Word," and equates Jesus with *the Word*. The use of special prayers and ritualistic chants has been with humans longer than recorded time. *Casting a spell* means to make something happen by saying it. Magic ranges from simply wishing—"I *will* get taller! I *will* get taller!"—to complex voodoo curses that make their believers sick. By saying these words, a special process is invoked—**magic**! Our relationship to the magic power of words is so strong that many people will not wish aloud, and thus break the spell. Or, a person may express a hope about a potential loss or danger—as in, "I'll pick you up tomorrow if the car doesn't break down—knock on wood!" Expressing this magic idea needs to be reinforced by a magic act—knocking on a handy wooden object. Likewise, a person standing in line to board an airplane simply doesn't say aloud, "Gee, I hope the plane doesn't crash!" Even the "Gee" is a magic shorthand for "Jesus," used to avoid violating an injunction about "using the Lord's name in vain."

Taboo   That ancient Commandment,"Thou shalt not take the Name of the Lord in Vain," is one of our earliest records of **taboo**, or words that are forbidden. The ancient Hebrews would neither write nor pronounce "Yahweh" (later, "Jehovah") which is said to be God's personal name. Instead they used substitute words, or *euphemisms,* to discuss their deity. To this day, many strictly observant Jews will not write the word "god" but will leave out a letter, as in "g–d," so as not to violate this taboo. The development of "gosh darn" and "gee whiz" were responses to the prohibition against forbidden uses of religious names in Christian culture.

The power of words to live beyond their utterance is recorded in the *Book of Matthew* as well: "For I say unto you that every idle word which you shall speak you will give account of on the day of Judgment. For by thy words shalt thou be justified, and by thy words shalt thou be condemned." (*Matthew* 12, 36–37.)

We also include forbidden subjects, such as sex, death, and bodily functions in our taboo list. Certain words are seen as crude and vulgar, others as acceptable or polite, even when in reality what the words refer to is identical. Anatomy is a favorite target for taboo, especially when the part may have sexual connotations. The Victorians were famous for **euphemisms**, and required polite people to avoid the words "leg" or "breast"; thus our chicken and turkey parts turned into "light meat" and "dark meat" and table legs got covered with long cloths. To *sleep with* someone is a euphemism going back centuries to describe not really sleeping at all. You can probably list a dozen ways to discuss *death* without mentioning the word itself. *Passed away* and *gone to heaven* have a gentle touch to them, while *kicked off* is a bit brusque. Nevertheless, we avoid the word in many social situations, especially when talking to someone who has recently had a death of a close friend or relative.

Taboo is valuable as an index of the comfort or importance a topic has to a person or a culture. The taboo words themselves change over time and what is not permissible in one place now may be common in a few years. Many of the terms of hate speech discussed above would not have been allowed in print a few years ago. New euphemisms are constantly taking the place of older ones as the older terms become so closely identified with the vulgar term that they too slide into the taboo area. Each culture has its own terms, and it is interesting to note that often the taboos are about the same subjects—religion, sex, death, and bodily functions. In Wichita, you may "need to use the bathroom" but in London, you visit the "loo." In Ohio, to avoid the subject of death, you might say your grandparent has "departed" while in Tokyo, to observe the same taboo, you may avoid the number four, pronounced *shi*, as it is also the sound for death. We react to these words because we have been *trained* to react to them. If someone swears in another language, you have virtually no response, even if you can translate the term. Only when we get inside our own culture and associations do we readily blush or become angry.

Ritual   **Ritual** is a formal cultural way of using language to convey a sense of power or mystical union. The Roman Catholic Church used to have its religious services in Latin as a way of demonstrating a link to previous ages. For Muslims

Ritual communication often involves special clothing, language, and movement.

gathered in prayer, the words of the service are repeated in a formal way, and creates a sense of unity among the participants. Your physiology changes in response to ritual use of language that is meaningful or important to you. Do you feel a swell of pride as *The Star-Spangled Banner* is sung at a Veteran's Day service? Do you join in the recitation of the *Pledge of Allegiance* and feel a union with others reciting the pledge? Does the *Battle Hymn of the Republic* or *We Shall Overcome* bring a lump to your throat, or a tingle at the back of your neck? If so, you are participating in a ritual response to words that link you to others engaging in the same activity. One of the interesting developments of our public culture in the past few decades has been the addition of Canadian baseball teams to the major leagues. Now, whenever Toronto or Montreal plays a game, two national anthems are sung or played. Future generations of American baseball fans may come to know "O, Canada!" as well as their own anthem. Repeating familiar words, especially those that may also carry mystical connotations, helps provide comfort and security and a sense of connection for those participating.

IMPROVING LINGUISTIC COMPETENCY

Before you can begin to improve your linguistic competency, you must be aware of the components of the communication process, understand their relationship to the rest of the process, and understand how to use them. As with any other skill, virtually no one is perfect and virtually everyone can use some refinement.

The first step is to understand that words are symbols, arbitrary and abstract. They represent things, ideas, and responses, but they are not realities in themselves beyond their existence as sound waves or ink and paper. We need to understand that they are wonderful aspects of our humanity, but only those who use them and react to them give them meaning. The development of meaning is always dynamic—meaning may change with different speakers, writers, situations, contexts, of time frames. An understanding of language is the beginning of mastery.

Second, an expanded awareness and understanding of word usage should lead you to expand your repertoire. Gather a larger vocabulary by reading widely, learning additional languages, and looking up words you encounter. Ask people to explain their use of terms. Remember, a better question than "What does that word mean?" would be "What do *you* mean when you use that word?" An expanding vocabulary can be obtained by keeping your awareness level high as you read books, newspapers, and magazines. Listen to films and music closely for new terms or expressions. You may even want to buy one of those "new word a day" calendars to enlarge your repertoire of words. With a greater vocabulary comes the possibility of greater precision in your communication.

The end result of enlarging your vocabulary is an increase in your options—an expanded repertoire. Instead of using a general term to convey an idea, you can select from a variety of terms to find the one that best communicates your meaning. You can help your listeners come nearer to understanding you if you can select words that they can interpret more precisely than generic terms. "I got a lot of stuff at the store" probably leaves your listeners little more than informed of your return from shopping. "I bought a dozen kiwis at the Import Grocery" is more precise and informative. Some people take vocabulary-building courses, and they can be an excellent start for you if you wish. Others work on self-oriented games or processes such as writing down unfamiliar words, or solving word quizzes in magazines and newspapers.

Language can be inspiring to us; it can be depressing to us. Our ability to use and control our communication rests greatly upon our verbal skill.

SUMMARY

Since words are such an important part of your educational experience and will continue to be a part of your future interactions in career, social, and recreational settings, it is important to know how words function as symbols in our world. Our language is a means of controlling our environment and it develops the same way in all of us, regardless of place of birth. The language you learned is simply an accident of where and to whom you were born. Your language probably helps shape your thought process, and skillful users of language can expand their options for describing their world and for interacting with others.

English comes in many forms, all useful at times to their speakers. Accents, regionalisms, and cultural variations of English can help identify individuals' backgrounds, provide a sense of connectedness within a group, or simply create variety in the communication setting. Sometimes language can be psychologically oppressing and can, in turn, create physiological reactions in us.

With attention and effort, we can continue to develop our use of language; then we will be able to draw from a continually expanding verbal reservoir that will enrich our future interactions. We can be better listeners as well as better speakers, writers, and thinkers if we improve our language skills.

Key Terms

symbol, **92**
denotation, **93**
connotation, **93**
general semantics, **93**
phonologics, **94**
semiotics, **94**
semantics, **94**
syntax, **95**

Sapir-Whorf Hypothesis, **97**
mainstream American English, **99**
Black English, **100**
linguistic oppression, **102**
magic, **104**
taboo, **104**
euphemisms, **104**
ritual, **105**

EXERCISES

1. At the front of most major dictionaries is an introduction that may discuss the history of English, language in general, and the processes used to compile this particular edition. Select two dictionaries and read their introductions. Take notes, and be prepared to present a short report or participate in a group discussion about the material.

2. Make up a nonsense word to replace a common word, such as "pencil." Now create four sentences that use the nonsense word and give these sentences to a partner from class. Try to figure out the definitions of one another's words.

3. In a popular game called "Dictionary," one person finds an obscure word in the dictionary and then asks the other players to each write out a short definition that they invent for that word. The leader then reads all the definitions aloud, including the first one from the dictionary and the players try to guess which is correct. This game, now sold under the name "Balderdash™," can give you insights into how definitions are created. Try playing either version of this game with friends or classmates.

4. Buy yourself a "Word a Day" calendar and use it!

5. Buy a popular newspaper or magazine written by and for an ethnic group different from your own. Pick out vocabulary or syntax that is unfamiliar to you and bring these examples to class to share with other students. How can you determine the meaning of unfamiliar material?

6. Make a list of *your* taboo terms—you may do this mentally if writing them out violates your behavior codes. To what subjects are the first five related? Where did the words on this list come from?

References

Castro, Janice. "Spanglish Spoken Here." *Time* (July 11, 1988).

Chesebro, J. and D. G. Bonsall. *Computer-Mediated Communication*. Tuscaloosa: University of Alabama Press, 1989.

Covin, D. "Afrocentricity in O Movimento Negro Unificado." *Journal of Black Studies* 21 (1990): 126–146.

De Vos, G. A., and L. Romanucci-Ross, Eds. *Ethnic Identity: Cultural Continuities and Change*. Chicago: University of Chicago Press, 1982.

Gans, H. J. "Symbolic Ethnicity: The Future of Ethnic Groups and Cultures in America." *Ethnic and Racial Studies* 2 (1979).

Hayakawa, S. I. *Language and Thought in Action*. New York: Harcourt, Brace, 1990.

Hecht, Michael, Mary Jane Collier, and Sidney Ribeau. *African American Communication*. Newbury Park: Sage Publications, 1993.

Jenkins, A. H. *The Psychology of the Afro-American: A Humanistic Approach*. Elmsford, NY: Pergamon, 1982.

Jensen, M. D. "Developing Ways to Confront Hateful Speech." *The Speech Communication Teacher* 8, 1 (Fall 1993).

Korzybski, A. *Science and Sanity: An Introduction to Non-Aristotlean Systems and General Semantics*. Lancaster, PA: Science Press, 1933.

Smitherman, G. *Talkin' and Testifyin'*. Boston: Houghton Mifflin, 1972: 2.

Thomas, Dylan. "A Visit to America." *Quite Early One Morning*. New York: New Directions, 1954.

Weber, S. "The Need to Be: The Socio-Cultural Significance of Black Language," in L. Samovar and R. Porter, *Intercultural Communication: A Reader,* 6th ed. Belmont, CA: Wadsworth, 1991: 282.

CHAPTER 7

Intrapersonal Communication

After reading this chapter, you should be able to:

- Understand how communication within yourself affects your self-concept and the way you communicate with others
- Describe the role of experiences in the development of self
- Define values, attitudes, and beliefs
- Explain the differences between functional and dysfunctional communication systems
- Take steps toward improving self-communication competency

Communication is part of your social self. Because we are using a *person-centered* definition of communication and not one related to machine or animal communication, it is important to see how the personal self is at the heart of all communication interactions. You think, you listen, you respond, and you speak from your self-perspective. You need to look to the self—*your* self—to understand the key to any communication event.

A DEFINITION

Intrapersonal communication is communicating within yourself. You engage in intrapersonal communication when you are thinking, daydreaming, studying, creating, contemplating, or dreaming.

You are both the source and the destination of this type of communication. You use your brain wave as a channel and the outcomes are thoughts or ideas, sometimes decisions, and sometimes actions or behaviors. You still communicate within a context or environment. Your language and other social considerations shape that environment.

If the Sapir-Whorf Hypothesis discussed in the preceding chapter is true, then your thoughts are formed, shaped, organized, and expressed in the language(s) you speak. You sequence your ideas and decisions in certain ways that are parallel to the way your primary language is structured. For example, in Japan, students who engage in high school and college debates do so in English because Japanese does not lend itself to direct clash and counter-argument the way English does. In other words, you think of ideas and relationships in a linguistic

DIVERSITY IN COMMUNICATION
Culture and Self

How you think about yourself is influenced greatly by your culture and its linguistic patterns. For example, the practice of name usage is different in different places around the world. In the United States, we usually give our names by stating our personal name first, then our family name: "Hi, I'm Ray Zeuschner." This pattern is opposite that found elsewhere—in Japan, China, and Hungary, for example—the family name is usually given first, followed by your personal name: "Hi, I'm Zeuschner Ray." Some scholars attribute this pattern to the importance placed either on the individual or on the family. In some places, it is important to establish your family affiliation first because your identity and meaning as an individual are secondary and follow from your connection and identification with your family. These patterns may be reflected in your intrapersonal communications as well, as you place yourself in a cultural context.

Similarly, if asked to introduce yourself in a two-minute speech to your classmates, would you begin with your physical attributes or your major? Hometown or religion? Family details, parents' occupations, class level? Hobbies? Awards? These choices may reveal how your culture influences you to think about your self.

context. If you are bilingual or multilingual, you may be able to shift from one pattern to another, and have a real intrapersonal advantage because you have a variety of perspectives to use as you approach ideas, problems, and creative thought.

DEVELOPMENT OF INTRAPERSONAL COMMUNICATION

At the center of your self are your experiences, self-concept, values, and perceptions. These elements have come to you from just being alive, or from messages you have been sent by others, or those you have sent to yourself. Together, they form the well of experience that you draw upon for your thoughts and messages. Each of these sources of your intrapersonal communication can be examined in order to better understand how you have become the type of communicator you are.

Experiences

You have selected some experiences; others were given to you. As a small child, you may have chosen some toys to play with and ignored others. At the same time, someone else put that selection of toys in your reach, chose to talk to you or read to you, put you in front of the TV, or left you alone. As you grew, the number of choices you had to make increased, and the opportunity for self-directed experience expanded greatly. You may have tried playing a musical instrument, or gone skindiving, or tried to ski or bungee jump or surf or play chess.

Each of these choices has given you experience, and one of the challenges of attending school is finding and selecting new experiences. For instance, have you become involved in a club or activity as means of enhancing your life experiences? Perhaps you do some sort of volunteer work set up through your college. You may take a course as a means of trying new or potentially difficult experiences. Travel is a method to expand your perspectives. Many schools offer a variety of international study and travel opportunities.

Of course, not all experiences turn out to be terrific. Nevertheless, you can learn from those as well, for they broaden your range of options—they increase your repertoire of communication experiences and choices. This increase in your repertoire is the first dimension of communication competence. The accumulation of a variety of experiences builds your intrapersonal communication repertoire by adding depth and variety to your storehouse of ideas.

Self-Concept

Your **self-concept** is what you believe about yourself. It is your impression, opinion, attitude and description regarding yourself. Your self-concept includes your physical, mental, and emotional makeup. Self-concept is the way you identify yourself. All of these factors affect your overall self-concept and contribute to the formation of your personality and communication style.

Although a complete discussion of personality is better left to the psychologists, there are some inescapable connections between your personality and your communication. Let's start with the social self—the way to see yourself in *relation* to others. This part of your personality is your communication self because communication is the means you use to create a relationship to others (Fine and Kleinman, 1983). As you look at communication within yourself, it is important to examine that process and what it produces.

Your self-concept may flow from many sources. You have a sense of your body, your talents, your roles, and your expectations. You have emotions, self-appraisal, and reflection, predictions and apprehensions. Each of these forms a portion of your view of yourself.

Body Image

You may be familiar with the way some psychologists used to divide people into three general categories based on body type—the *ectomorph* is thin and lean; the *mesomorph* is athletic and muscular; and the *endomorph* is soft and round.

These categories may also be part of our image of our own bodies—even if that image is not accurate. We may wish to be thin and perceive ourselves to be overweight. The U.S. ideal of a slender, healthy, slightly tanned, and blond young athlete is an image projected relentlessly in advertising and in films, but it is only a subjective view created by current social norms. The paintings of Michelangelo, DaVinci, and Rubens done hundreds of years ago show plump, dark-haired, pale-skinned nudes. Those artists were not painting some unusual image of beauty, but rather were reflecting the idealized social image of women in their time. They would probably find our current image too scrawny and unappealing. Social norms, therefore, define body image and are reinforced or rejected by our family and friends.

A major problem among young American women, especially those of college age, is their feeling of inadequacy related to body image. This feeling may lead to pressure to change and can cause anorexia or bulimia, two eating disorders associated with negative body image. Young men also are faced with stereotypes about strength, hair, height, and other physical attributes.

Body image, therefore, is the way we perceive ourselves in relation to the social standards of our culture. Body image, in turn, may influence our communication patterns. If you think you are far from the ideal, you may become reluctant to participate in class or to stick out in a crowd by expressing your opinion. You might become withdrawn or defensive, both of which modify your attempts to send messages to others and affect your interpretation of messages you get from others.

Personal Attributes

Your *talents* are an important part of your objective and subjective selves. You may have hidden talents, but you may be unaware of them because your self-concept does not yet acknowledge them. For example, I had a difficult time with arith-

TECHNOLOGY AND COMMUNICATION
Feedback Affects Self-Concept

Two tools that can help you improve the accuracy of your self-perception are audio and videotape. Remember the first time you heard your voice recorded—or, worse, *saw* yourself on videotape? These experiences can be unsettling because the feedback we get from these machines may not match the self-perception we had. Usually, the machines are more accurate. With repeated exposure to this feedback, you can begin to develop a realistic self-perception. I know one person who had thought she was tall because in the early elementary grades she was much taller than the other children in her class. Her growth also stopped early, and she remained 5'3" from the time she was about ten years old. Only when, as an adult, she saw herself in a videotape, lined up with a crowd of her friends did she exclaim, "I'm the shortest one in our group!"— a fact that everyone else in the group already knew.

The feedback that widespread access to technology makes possible may or may not be pleasant news to you, but it will likely be accurate.

metic, so I assumed I was not talented in math in general. In graduate school, I needed to take statistics, and found to my surprise that not only did it make sense to me, but I actually liked it. My self-concept changed as a result of that experience.

Often, self-concept formation comes early in our experiences, so we may prematurely and incorrectly label ourselves. When we are young, we are simply not as talented, intelligent, or competent as when we get older. A self-concept can and should change to meet the realistic changes of our lives. As we find and explore previously unknown talents and abilities, we can enlarge our sense of competency in a variety of areas—everything from public speaking to statistics.

Social Roles

The **social roles** you find yourself in may be varied. You are a student, a child, a friend, a volleyball player, a pianist, a poker player, a cousin, a hospital volunteer, and a salesclerk. Each of these roles is a real part of you—even though the word *role* sometimes means "something artificial." Here, the roles you play are those normally associated with different aspects of your life.

The roles we have are sometimes *assigned to* us and sometimes *adopted by* us. For example, when you go for a job interview, your role is to be a polite listener, interested responder and discreet questioner. You would be out of role if you appeared dressed in casual beach clothes, or made demands on the interviewer.

Most of the roles we follow are those we see in the models around us—that is, those that social values and customs tell us are appropriate. One of the strongest models we have is from our own parents. A parental role you assume and play out may be a repetition of one you observed in a parent of your own. Or you might form that role by watching popular television, or emulating one in a novel such as the father in *To Kill a Mockingbird* or the mother in the book *Sounder*.

We play these roles through our communication behaviors. If we follow the Bill Cosby parent model, we are thoughtful listeners with ready answers. Or we may be like the aggressive poker players who try to deceive others with their non-verbal communication—especially facial expressions. We may be knowledgeable and deferential salesclerks, attentive and responsive students, and modest concert performers, depending on how influential our models have been and how much self-appraisal of these behaviors we have done. Our communication in these contexts tells others what we perceive our role to be.

Of course, your roles can, and do, change. For example, you went through a series of roles as a child. At an early stage you were compliant with your parents' requests. You may have gone through a rebellious stage in your early teen years, but now are likely to be functioning on an adult-to-adult basis with your parents. Or, you may have started out as a temporary salesclerk, but now are moving up to a shift supervisor role. With your change in role comes change in communication. Researchers on personal identity have concluded, "Thus, identity is formed and shaped through social interaction. Once formed, identity influences the flow of social behaviors and continues to be influenced by social interaction" (Hecht et al., 1993, p. 47).

Your perception of yourself, and the social expectations of the various roles you play throughout the day will determine your communication patterns and behaviors. You will communicate from a self-perception and, at the same time, you will create an impression—someone else's perception of you. How well you meet the social expectations of your roles will determine other people's evaluation of you as a student, parent, salesclerk, or child. The evaluation of good or bad is determined by how closely your behaviors match the idealized expectations of those who observe your behaviors. You could, of course, become adept at playing the role of a bad student, but for now we mean how close you come to the positive ideals for that role. Both the communication you send and the way that others perceive communication is based on a broad *social* sense of what is proper in any given role. These expectations are part of our social value system and create powerful pressures on your communication.

Values, Attitudes, and Beliefs

You might use those three terms interchangeably in conversation, but in communication and psychology, they usually have three distinct meanings. *Values* are broad, life-orienting, social principles that are shared by large groups of people, such as nations or civilizations; *attitudes* are the more focused interpretations of values applied to your own circumstances; and *beliefs* are the specific applications of your values and attitudes. Let's examine each of these concepts in relationship to intrapersonal communication.

These three aspects of yourself are especially important because they influence the way you see not only yourself, but also everything else around you.

Values   Your **values** provide you with a general orientation about the *right/wrong* aspects of your ideas and thoughts and actions. Values are broad, "approach-to-life" concepts which are usually formed early in life and are heavily influenced by

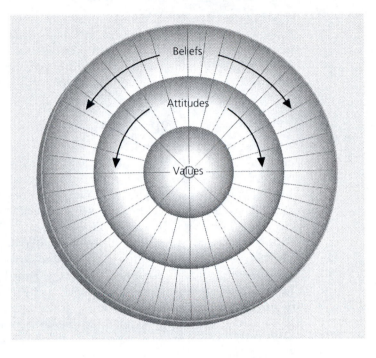

Your core values lead to many attitudes that are the basis for a multitude of beliefs.

family. For example, you may think that education is an important part of life. Your family and closest friends are also likely to value education. In fact, you may find it difficult to remain in a relationship for long with anyone whose core values are very different from yours. Although your values can and do change over time, they are likely to change slowly, for values tend to be enduring.

Attitudes   **Attitudes** are the ideals that stem from your values and that you apply to life situations. They also affect the way you take in information from the outside world and give meaning to your experiences. Moreover, you constantly alter and may explore your attitudes, but always as expressions of your values. For example, following from your general value that education is good, you may decide to enroll in college. You may also think that paying taxes for good public schools is the proper thing to do. Your value—the goodness of education—orients your thinking to evaluate college education in a positive way, and to be generally in favor of financial support for educational purposes. However, each time you encounter an issue involving education, your opinion will depend on the specific circumstance. Should private companies support public education? Should taxes support private schools? Your responses to these very specific areas come under the heading of *beliefs*.

Beliefs   **Beliefs** are the smallest units of these three concepts, and you have many more of them than you have of either values or attitudes. Continuing on with our example, you may *value* education, have a favorable *attitude* toward college in general, but *believe* that school X is better than school Y. Or you may believe that majoring in sociology is better than majoring in mathematics. You may be in favor of tax money for education but believe that a particular bond issue in your town is not needed at a particular time. When you apply your values and attitudes to single cases, you are dealing with beliefs. The beliefs that you express are the specific, case-by-case operation of your core values and long-term attitudes.

Perception and Self-Concept

Your values, attitudes, and beliefs affect the way you perceive the world. These aspects of your thinking constitute a sort of camera lens through which you view others as well as the events around you. These views of the outside world are called your **perceptions.** The way you view yourself is your *self-concept.* Perception and self-concept are so closely intertwined that you can think of them as interacting constantly. What you think about yourself colors, shapes, and in some ways determines, what you see around you. Conversely, the information that you get from outside of yourself provides valuable feedback and helps you to create an image of who you are. Sometimes, however, people disregard feedback that doesn't fit their self-concepts. For example, your self-concept may be that you are a wonderful cook, so every slightly positive comment anyone may make about your skill in the kitchen is taken as support for that notion. Any disparaging remarks, on the other hand, you dismiss, filter out; if you think about them at all, you interpret them as signs of jealousy or humor or as just plain wrong.

Your perception of yourself may be accurate or may be distorted. The *real* you may be different from your *perceived* you. For example, you may have had a terrible experience in a public speaking situation early in your life, and thus you have created the self-concept *poor speaker.* The reality may be that you are quite competent as a public speaker, but your memory of that one experience prevents you from viewing yourself objectively. This memory may become a self-fulfilling prophecy that causes you to do poorly in situations where you might have succeeded. In some cases, people fail to give themselves credit where it is due and others overrate their talents. You may know people who insist on singing because they believe they have beautiful voices when, in reality, they are constantly off-key, harsh, or both.

Expectations

Your self-concept and your perceptions also affect the expectations that you have of yourself. Expectations are those future-oriented messages you send to yourself about what you *ought* to do. Some writers refer to these expectations as *life-scripts*—that is, well-developed, long-term roles you follow. Your script predicts what you will do; it may be given to you early in your life or you may develop it yourself.

For example, if you come from a family where traditional sex-roles are important and are reinforced by your parents, they may have always communicated a future vision for you: "When you grow up and become a mommy, you can take your children to the park while daddy is at work." Without directly ordering you to follow those patterns, the messages take on a scripting process by determining what long-term expectations you'll have for yourself. On the other hand, your family may have sent you messages such as: "When you grow up to be a woman, you might like being an attorney or a physician. How would you like to be a firefighter and ride in a shiny red fire engine?"

Expectations can exert very powerful forces on your self-concept. Even now, as you go through college, you may be evaluating some of these expectations. Are they ones you accept? Or have they just been there forever, without your examination? Perhaps there are roles you would like to create for yourself. If so, you are thinking about what we call *self-fulfilling prophecies.*

> ▶ **IMPROVING COMPETENCY**
> ## Self-Fulfilling Prophecy
>
> Try writing down a list of the prophecies you think you have heard in your family regarding your career. Can you list those from each parent, or those from other figures in your past—perhaps instructors or friends? How many of the prophecies on your list have you examined consciously? Do you simply accept them? If you feel comfortable doing so, share your list with a classmate. What similarities and what differences do you notice?

Self-Fulfilling Prophecies

Prophecies are messages about what you expect. Moreover, you can affect whether or not they come true. For example, you may convince yourself that you will do poorly on an exam and, when the results come back, you may indeed have done poorly. Since attitude can affect outcome, you can also create a positive outcome.

The field of sports psychology is filled with positive expectation training for athletes. For example, athletes use *visualization* to create positive images of themselves in performance—mental images that help them practice and reach the prophesied level of performance. Positive visualization is used in many areas of performance—speaking, singing, business management, and sports.

If a instructor tells you, "I'm sure you'll never get this material," that instructor is suggesting a negative expectation. Some people have a self-concept that is highly susceptible to such suggestions and they may wither under such a comment. Another person with a strong self-concept will react differently and may suggest a counter prophecy by saying, "Oh, yeah? I can pass any test you can make up!" While the strong response is a sign of positive imagery, the student who says it still needs to counter the perception of the instructor by actually passing the test.

> # The Story of Communication
> ## *The Power of Imagination*
>
> THE WORLD'S GREATEST DIVER of the past fifty years, Greg Louganis, was featured on the cover of *Sports Illustrated* after he won the 1988 Olympics. When asked about his training, he said that the most important part of it was going home, sitting quietly in his room with his eyes closed, and *mentally* rehearsing every dive until he could do it perfectly—in his head. This practice session would last twenty or thirty minutes a day and it was one he never skipped.

THOUGHTS, FEELINGS, AND DREAMS

Thinking, feeling, and dreaming are important parts of your self-concept, your communication self. You respond to an array of factors within your mind. You have values, attitudes, beliefs, images, roles, and expectations. You have a reservoir of talents and abilities, but an awareness of only some of them. You process information only partially because your perceptions are limited by your thinking style and your physical ability to handle information. You are also limited by the psychological filters and screens you learned about in Chapter 3—the barriers that come between incoming information and your reception of it. The extent to which each of these barriers influences individual people varies but each barrier is at work in all of us.

Thinking Styles

Much work in educational research has been done recently on *cognitive style*—the way you typically receive and process information. You may be primarily a visual learner—that is, you attend to and best comprehend information you can see. People who prefer this style like to diagram, outline, sketch, and read. You might be a verbal learner, someone who is most responsive to auditory information. If so, you may prefer to listen to descriptions, sounds, or impressions. Some people learn by physically doing something—that is the kinesthetic style. When you communicate intrapersonally, do you doodle or sketch? You might have a visual or a kinesthetic learning style. Do you mumble aloud or even shout at yourself? If you are alone and you hit your finger while hammering, do you comment out loud, exclaiming, "Ow! That was really dumb!" If so, you might have a verbal cognitive style.

The manner in which you communicate to yourself may provide clues to the cognitive style you prefer. In trying to improve instruction, many instructors are now looking at cognitive styles—their own and those of their students. If a n instructor is primarily providing information in one style, that message may be lost on students who are primarily working in the other style. Good teaching, like good communication, requires an ability to recognize and function in a variety of styles. An aware instructor may try to communicate important points in a variety of ways. An aware student, who is not easily following or comprehending a certain instructor, should try to get help from someone who communicates in a more compatible style than the instructor uses. Perhaps a mismatch in cognitive styles is responsible for the gap in communication.

In addition to the critical thinking approach described in Chapter 4, you can also approach the subject of thinking from an intrapersonal communication perspective. Three functions of thinking have been identified—to interpret, to solve problems, and to create (Jabusch and Littlejohn, 1981).

Interpretation   When you are thinking to interpret, you are communicating with yourself to classify, group, or cluster information coming in through your senses in a logical way. You may make broad categories of connections, such as when people compare Chinese food with Japanese food and say, "They're really about the same, right?" Wrong, actually, but they are both Asian, both use rice, so for many people with limited experiences, these two items are sufficient for them to create a single concept—Asian food—and then cluster or classify many items within this single concept. Another way we use interpretation is to reason from one idea or bit of information to conclusions about that information. The syllogism and Toulmin systems described in Chapter 4 were examples of this part of your thinking processes.

Problem Solving   If you communicate within yourself to solve problems, you probably begin with a few ideas and balance potential outcomes with desired benefits. You are engaging in reflective thinking as you decide which class to take next term, or whether to change your major. When you finish reflecting, you may take the next step: planning. With this type of self-communication, you plot out a strategy, make a list or create a sequence of ideas, think about them, and evaluate their likelihood of getting you to the desired goal.

Creativity   The final area of thinking—creativity—may be the most fun to do, and most difficult to describe. When you brainstorm by letting your mind wander around a certain point, idea, or problem, you are tapping the creative dimension of your intrapersonal communication processes. Sometimes you will have an "instant insight" into the problem or idea. Called by many investigators the *"Aha!" phenomenon,* it refers to the experience of getting an idea "out of the blue." Actually, the idea or solution is probably a product of the creative connections your thought processes make when you switch from the focused, step-by-step orientation of interpretation or problem-solving and move, instead, into a free-flowing associational mode of thinking.

Much of the time, unfortunately, you are not called upon to be creative in the school setting. The emphasis there is placed on the more routine methods of learning terms, concepts, and facts. Traditional American public education has not paid enough attention to developing the creative ability of students but changes are emerging. For example, many high schools now require some form of creative arts class for graduation. Being able to shift gears appropriately between your potential intrapersonal communication styles—to interpret, solve problems, and be creative—is a valuable communication skill. Some courses can help you to develop that ability and to realize your potential for rich, intrapersonal communication.

Physical Limitations

Each channel of communication has a finite capacity to carry information and can be blocked by such conditions as deafness and blindness. The notion of **channel capacity** means that you can only process a certain amount of information before you reach overload. You probably have been to a party or a crowded room with many people talking—loud music, visual distraction of people moving in and out of your sight lines, dancing in one area, and eating in another. In that setting it is difficult to remain focused on someone talking to you. Your channel capacity for active listening is close to or at its maximum.

After the party, you might be at home, sitting alone quietly. But you may be worried about a test coming up the next day, a problem with your roommate that needs settling, bills that are due in the next few days, an important date coming up with someone you hope turns out to be special, and a phone call you haven't yet returned. Now you are trying to read this chapter and remember all about intrapersonal communication. But are you really reading this chapter? Your internal channel is overloaded. Go pay a few bills, get your problem with your roommate straightened out, return that important call, and then come back and finish reading. You didn't clear out *all* of the competing information but enough so that you now have the capacity to read these words. Recognizing overload is a helpful skill in that it can let you know when you are getting close to breaking down. Breakdowns can lead to fatigue, lack of concentration, depression, or mental illness.

Finally, we all use psychological *filters and screens* to let some information in and keep the rest out. These filters may come from our values, as when we pay more attention to advertisements for products or candidates or speakers we like. Filters may come from previous experiences, fears, or expectations. Our self-concept may prevent us from hearing negative feedback from a friend or may allow us to hear *only* negative feedback. When our ego, emotions, or fears are involved

CRITICAL THINKING IN COMMUNICATION
Filters and Screens

One of the basic elements of critical thinking is to gather complete, relevant information or data. As your data pool grows, you have more ways to look at and process information.

At a convention of educators in Los Angeles, I heard one highly placed, well-educated official of the United States Department of Education suggest that the way to solve discipline and drug abuse problems in the public schools was to have "Dad lay down the law" more, while "Mom could visit the school, volunteer her time, and read to the children more at night." However, many of the homes to which children return every day have only one parent, who was likely to work several jobs. Visiting the school and reading more at night are simply not options enjoyed by these single parents. Yet the government official spoke as if the traditional nuclear family, with a strong father to enforce rules, and a housewife mother with plenty of time to volunteer in the schools was the norm in Los Angeles—or any major city for that matter.

Perceptual screens and filters are at work in everyone. Critical thinkers are aware of that fact and attempt to gather as much information as possible, even if it is unpleasant and contradictory to what they would like to believe.

in a communication transaction, our filters and screens work overtime. In a way, filters are part of our ego defense system. They help us to protect our self-concept and, as such, perform a kind of survival function for us. On the other hand, they also inhibit honest feedback we may need to help us change in a positive direction. For example, there is a famous story of the French Queen, Marie Antoinette, who said, "Let them eat cake!" when she was told the people of Paris had no bread to eat. Because of the way she filtered information, she had no idea that people could be living in such poverty that, when they ran out of one kind of food, they could not simply switch to another as she would have done. The extreme form of using filters as a defense mechanism can be called *denial*. This term describes behaviors in which people refuse to recognize, deal with, or even see an event that is too painful, horrible, or threatening. Survivors of various types of abuse often protect themselves by shutting out any aspect of the abusive behavior.

FUNCTIONAL AND DYSFUNCTIONAL COMMUNICATION SYSTEMS

One of the first signs you may have about how someone is feeling is that their communication undergoes changes that reflect these emotions. Obvious examples are a constantly downcast face or expression and a voice consistently low in tone and slow of pace. Someone with a habitually self-effacing style who avoids contact may be experiencing stress on his or her mental health.

Communication and Mental Health

The internal communication system is your own private monitor of your mental health. When your internal messages get scrambled, when you cannot make sense out of the data you get from the outside world, when your conclusions are consistently refuted—these may be signs that your mental health is at risk. One of the symptoms of the mental illness schizophrenia is hearing imaginary voices. People suffering from schizophrenia are obviously not functioning as realistic communicators. One way to approach the treatment of mental illness is to see its communication related attributes. Autism is a mental illness that precludes interaction or communication with stimuli outside of the self. The

The Story of Communication
Autistic Savants

YOU MAY HAVE SEEN the film *Rain Man* in which Dustin Hoffman plays an autistic savant—someone who has very low interpersonal communication abilities, yet fantastic mental abilities in other areas. Not all people with autism have these abilities, but a few do, and their stories fascinate professional communication researchers as well as the general public. In this film, the character Raymond actually functioned beyond the level of most autistic people but, through Hoffman's powerful performance, viewers had a glimpse of the intrapersonal communication these people experience.

image of the child, rocking alone in a corner, is a good representation of autism—a condition of total, exclusive self-communication. Autism is intrapersonal communication carried to the extreme of excluding any other source but self.

Is mental health the same as *not* being mentally ill? In other words, if you are open to messages from outside yourself and are in touch with reality enough to know you are a college student and not the monarch of France, are you mentally healthy? Positive intrapersonal communication goes beyond just the absence of problems—it means that you are improving your internal message sending and responding so that you reach *optimal* levels of functioning. You can be adequate and still have room for improvement. A positive ability to communicate well within yourself leads to a positive mental outlook. Self-fulfilling prophecies become important in this context. If you send yourself positive messages about yourself, you can guide your behaviors toward matching the messages.

Communication and Achievement

As previously noted, athletes the world over practice positive imaging to become better at their sport. If you repeat a message over and over, it becomes part of your subconscious—almost an automatic source of internal messages. You can use this intrapersonal communication strategy as well to enhance your mental well-being and your levels of accomplishment. For example, some Olympic weightlifters were told the weight on the barbells was an amount they had already lifted successfully several times. In actuality, the amount was greater than they had ever lifted before. Because they *thought* they could, they did in fact lift the heavier amount. Later, they were given the same barbells to lift, but told the real weight. They failed to lift the weight because they thought they would fail.

Clearly, optimal intrapersonal communication functioning needs to be a product of both your skills and your attitudes. When you examine your attitudes, adjust them to reflect a positive mental outlook. Recall that in Chapter 2 you learned about communication apprehension (CA). One of the strategies for dealing with apprehension is to change your vision of yourself. You learned that you can reduce your level of anxiety and thereby increase your level of performance—a good example of making important mental adjustments.

People with CA are often painfully aware of that fact and their awareness may lead them to have low self-esteem. They may feel inadequate and their internal messages are those of incompetence and lack of personal worth. Again, both mental health and achievement are negatively affected for persons with high levels of CA. You probably experience some anxiety or tension before giving a speech or going to an important interview. While those sensations are perfectly normal and universal, even those levels of apprehension may affect you slightly in the form of negative communicative outcomes. You may have increased dysfluencies ("ums" and "uhs") during a job interview or you may lose your train of thought during a speech. These minor dysfunctions create a negative impression on your listeners and they can also reinforce a negative self-image. For those reasons, it is important to work on improving intrapersonal communication.

IMPROVING SELF-COMMUNICATION COMPETENCY

You have already taken an important first step toward developing optimal intrapersonal communication abilities by learning about yourself and the factors that make up your values, your perceptions, and your internal message systems. Remember the four areas of communication competency—repertoire, selection, implementation, and evaluation. Each of these can be developed as you enhance your intrapersonal communication abilities.

You can expand your repertoire by understanding a variety of ways to process information. You can try to see new perspectives, take another point of view, and question your repeated use of strategies that do not seem to get the results you wish.

After you expand the number of ways you can receive and process information, you can experiment by selecting different methods, as appropriate. After analyzing a situation and remembering past responses, you may elect to withhold quick judgments of information, or you may try to evaluate a comment from several viewpoints before you react. You may experiment by shifting from one thinking pattern, such as problem solving, to another one, such as creativity.

Putting these insights into practice will allow you to implement different skills. Try a new way of reacting. For example, respond from your rational self rather than your emotional self next time you think you are being slighted. Conversely, try reacting with your feelings when faced with a tough problem that defies logical solution.

Finally, take careful note of how these new strategies are working or are failing in a given situation. Evaluate your success and make any adjustments needed. The important thing is to keep trying; keep evaluating until you sense improvement in your intrapersonal communication skills.

SUMMARY

You are a social being, and the basis for your interactions in the social world is your self. You have inside you a variety of values, attitudes, and beliefs that shape the way you think, the way you process information internally, and the way you send messages out to the rest of the world. Your perceptions are both the product of your internal communication and a screen through which information must pass to become meaningful to you. Both your thoughts and feelings are important to becoming an integrated communicator. The messages you send and receive about yourself create your self-concept; they lead you to positive feelings and enhanced abilities or they may be negative and damage your self-worth. Your ability to communicate well internally affects your ability to communicate with the world around you. You can unlock much potential for success if you first develop and expand your intrapersonal communication skills. Overcoming the negative effects of severe communication apprehension is one positive, proactive step you can take on the road to optimal communication experiences.

Key Terms

intrapersonal communication, **110**
self-concept, **111**
body image, **112**
social roles, **113**
values, **114**

attitudes, **115**
beliefs, **115**
perceptions, **116**
channel capacity, **119**

EXERCISES

1. Can you list the five or ten most important values you hold? Make such a list and then test your values against your actions. Do you behave in ways consistent with those values? What circumstances cause you to modify or add qualifiers or reservations to your values?

2. Take five minutes to create an idealized vision of yourself. What do you look like? What talents do you possess? In what circumstances do you live? Now, select one aspect from your vision that you think is possible to realize in the next few weeks or months. What steps would you have to take in order to bring it about?

3. Ask a friend to describe three things about you in writing, such as height, personality traits, or likes/dislikes. At the same time, write down your own description of the same three items. Now reverse roles and do the same for your friend. Compare your notes and see how close your descriptions match your friend's.

4. Describe to a classmate one special activity or interaction you had with a parent that you think was worthwhile and you would like to do as well if you were a parent. Is there one action you would do differently? Compare notes with your classmate to see if there are similarities.

References

Braithwaite, Dawn O., Loreen N. Olson, Tamara D. Golish, Charles Soukup, and Paul Turman. "'Becoming a Family': Developmental Process Represented in Blended Family Discourse." *Journal of Applied Communication Research* 29, 3 (August 2001).

Fine, G. A. and S. Kleinman. "Network and Meaning: An Interactionist Approach to Structure." *Symbolic Interaction* 6 (1983).

Hecht, M. L., M. J. Collier, and S. A. Ribeau. *African American Communication.* Newbury Park, CA: Sage, 1993.

Jabusch, D. M. and S. W. Littlejohn. *Elements of Speech Communication.* Boston: Houghton Mifflin, 1981: 74–86.

Interpersonal Communication

After reading this chapter, you should be able to:

- Define interpersonal communication and describe its relationship to affection, inclusion, and control needs
- Describe communication and relationship development
- Feel confidence in your everyday interpersonal interactions
- Understand communication climates and conflict
- Develop conflict management strategies
- Improve your interpersonal skills

The social self meets another self as you take your internal messages and send them out. When you turn from thinking, dreaming, and other internal forms of communication, it's time to step out, face the world, and connect with other people. Just as you move from dreams when you get up each morning and begin your daily interactions with others, this chapter moves from the intra-personal world of thoughts to the interpersonal world of interaction. Of course, you never leave the self behind, just as you can recall your dreams during the day. For the purpose of breaking down the study of communication into manageable units, we divide this book into chapters, but all the elements of communication are constantly present and constantly interacting—listening and thinking, verbal and nonverbal, and intrapersonal and interpersonal. We look in this chapter at what happens when you take your self out for a walk and it meets another self.

DEFINITION OF INTERPERSONAL COMMUNICATION

Simply put, **interpersonal communication** is a communication transaction involving two or more people. This chapter emphasizes the one-to-one setting in transitory and long-term interactions. The general definition of interpersonal communication encompasses much of our communication and includes the rich interaction that takes place in the socially meaningful pair. When you buy gas and give the clerk your money, you engage in an interpersonal exchange, but it is not the meaningful relationship you have with close friends or even other members of this class. A useful distinction can be made between the brief transaction com-munication of the sales exchange and the *personal* relationship that builds over time and involves your thoughts and feelings beyond a superficial level. Therefore, a full definition of *interpersonal communication* is communication trans-actions between individuals in a personal relationship.

Personal relationships are part of our daily lives. They affect us constantly and in meaningful ways. As interpersonal communication researcher, Stephen Duck (1985) put it, "People's lives are fabricated in and by their relationships with other people. Our greatest moments of joy and sorrow are founded in relation-ships." The values and attitudes that were discussed in the previous chapter were developed in our relationships with others. Self-concept is derived largely from the messages we received in interpersonal settings.

These messages are part of the interaction—the give-and-take—of a personal setting. These messages can be intense largely because they are so direct and focused. There is just you and one other, or perhaps two others, involved. The message cannot get lost in a noisy crowd; the feedback is immediate and clearly directed.

There are, however, some risks in this type of communication because of the private setting. What we talk about in these situations is often ourselves and our immediate relationships. We discuss things we think about, feel, worry about, and that are important to us. Good interpersonal communication also includes dis-cussing things important to the relationship. All of these topics come under the

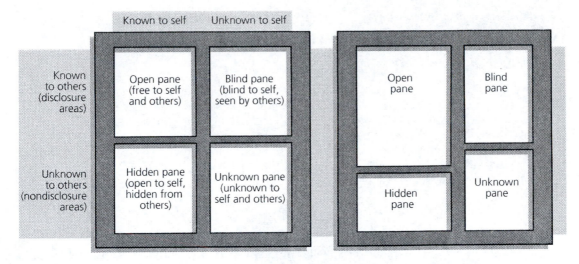

The Johari Window is a way of looking at your self-disclosure and self-knowledge.

heading of self-disclosure. When you talk about things that others are not likely to know about you without directly asking you, you are engaging in self-disclosure.

The Johari Window

One useful model for thinking about self-disclosure is the **Johari Window** (Luft, 1969). The Johari Window is a diagram that represents your self, how much you know about yourself, and how much others know about you. Four possible combinations of knowledge about yourself are illustrated in the diagram: (1) What you and others know about you, (2) What you know but nobody else knows, (3) What others know about you that you do not know, and (4) What about you that is known to neither yourself nor others. These four types of public and private knowledge are represented by the four quadrants of the diagram, which looks somewhat like a window with four panes of glass. Moreover, the term *window*—that is, a place for looking out and looking in—is especially appropriate for the interpersonal communication context. Let us look at each quadrant of the window and see how these possibilities operate in communication involving self-disclosure.

Things everybody knows about you would fall into the quadrant called the *open* pane. Your physical appearance, gender, hair color, occupation, and perhaps your general economic condition can all be inferred by anyone who observes you or listens to your spontaneous conversation during your public moments.

The *hidden* area covers those things that you know about yourself but you conceal from others. You may have secret fantasies, or aspects of your past or your personality, you wish to keep private. You may have habits you conceal or food dislikes or even a secret ambition that no one else gets to know. Even in very close, long-term, personal relationships, you may still keep some information in this quadrant.

The Story of Communication
The Origin of Johari

WHEN YOU FIRST SAW the term, *Johari Window* what did you think about the term *Johari*? Is it a town in Pakistan where this idea was born? Is it the name of the Japanese communication scholar who developed it? Is it an exotic animal from Bali or a rare wood from India? Many students guess these and other answers. The second idea comes closest to the truth. The window is associated with Professors Luft and Ingram who devised the concept. "Luft-Ingram Window" didn't seem very interesting to them, so they playfully combined their first names—Joseph and Harry—to form *Johari*.

The area which represents things others know about you, yet remain unknown to you is called the *blind* pane. You may have heard it said that someone has a "blind spot" about a certain issue or person. This expression means the person simply does not recognize in himself or herself something that is obvious to others. Your self-concept may let you think you are taller than you really are, or you may not believe you have a good voice, but others like it. You may have a talent for doing a particular job, building relationships, or solving problems that others recognize in you, yet you may be unaware of these qualities. Or, the blind spot may be the opposite—we give ourselves credit for having a great sense of humor yet others never laugh at our jokes.

Finally, there are probably things about you that are as yet undiscovered by anyone. You may have a talent for harmonica playing but you have never tried it. You may have likes or dislikes that have never been tested and thus are part of the *unknown* pane. If you have not thought about, read about, heard about, or tried something, you simply have no exposure or information to guide you in self-knowledge about that thing. Since we cannot know everything, or try everything, we are bound to have some unexplored territory in our selves.

The processes of interpersonal communication often deal with the areas (panes) described above. For example, you might try out opinions or ideas on your friends to develop them or modify them. If these ideas were previously hidden from others, then the hidden pane of your self gets a little smaller and the open area gets a little larger. The Johari Window is an easy sort of shorthand to describe how we act in interpersonal settings. Some of us have large open areas; others have larger hidden or blind areas. The process of interpersonal communication, if it is authentic, inevitably involves enlarging the open area, and making some combination of the others smaller.

What motivates us to indulge in this type of communication? Looking at our interpersonal needs—that is, those needs that can only be met through interaction with others—provides one explanation. These interpersonal requirements have been classified as *Affection-Inclusion-Control* needs and have been the subject of study by researcher William Schutz (Schutz, 1958).

Inclusion, Affection, and Control Needs

One of the ways we use communication is to express and receive *affection*. Schutz contends that a basic component of the human makeup is the need for affection and we fulfill that need with our interpersonal relationships. The range of our emotions goes beyond affection, of course, but the positive regard, or affection, we get from others is a central and motivating force behind our interpersonal interactions.

> ### IMPROVING COMPETENCY
> ## Check Your Perception with a Friend
>
> Try filling out your own personal Johari Window. How much area do you allot to each section? Next, ask a trusted friend or two to make up a Johari Window diagram about how they perceive you. Do the diagrams come close? If not, what significant differences do you find? How can you explain these differences?

You will find **affection** in many situations and dimensions. You can have an affectionate regard for family members and loved ones. Another dimension of affection is for close friends, such as roommates or team members. You may find affection with some associates at work or fellow members of organizations or clubs. Most important in your life will likely be a relationship with a significant other person in a long-term interaction.

The messages you send and receive which exhibit warmth, support, respect, genuine interest, and empathy are all mechanisms to communicate affection and to help you meet this need. The reciprocal nature of interpersonal communication is most important in affectionate relationships. If you have ever been in a one-way relationship, you know how frustrating and ultimately unsatisfying that can be. The need to give and receive affection seems to be a central, motivating force in our lives, and affection is most likely to be found through interpersonal communication.

Schutz describes **inclusion** needs as the desire to be part of the events and interactions around us. The person who wants to be asked along on every outing or short trip to the store is exhibiting this need, albeit excessively. When we join groups or clubs, we see the tremendous pressures this need to belong can exert on people. The need to belong is one of the strongest motivating factors that encourages membership in gangs. In the interpersonal realm, wanting to be noticed by others and included in their relationship is an expression of the need for inclusion.

Finally, **control** needs are those that make us want to feel secure and safe in our surroundings. We want to have power over our environment, ourselves, and other people. We feel that structures, systems, and rules are in place to give us a sense of security. On one level, this need for control may express itself as the ability to influence another person—to have someone listen to our opinion and react to in a significant way. On another level, the need for control may involve dominating another through manipulation or bullying tactics. Emotional blackmail, another example of excessive control needs, begins for many people at an early age with the playground message: "Let me have that or I won't be your friend!" This type of message is a control strategy and uses our needs for affection and inclusion as the tools of control.

Each of these needs is part of the dynamics of interpersonal interaction and drives us to engage in relationships in order to be fulfilled. Next, we will see that our communication develops over a regular pattern during the course of a relationship. That pattern has come under increasing scrutiny by experts in the field of relational communication.

COMMUNICATION AND RELATIONSHIP DEVELOPMENT

You are a social being, which means you exist partly in terms of your relationships with other social beings. As you move through your life, you experience various stages. We are infants, children, adolescents, young adults, middle-aged, and senior citizens. In much the same way that life stages follow a predictable course, **relationship development** has typical patterns that can be described and understood.

Although each relationship has its own unique aspects, there are general patterns that seem to be consistent no matter what the setting. Communication scholar Mark Knapp has studied these patterns and has identified ten stages in relationship process from beginning to end (Knapp, 1984). The coming together stages include initiating, experimenting, intensifying, integrating, and bonding. When a relationship begins to come apart, it also goes through five stages: differentiation, circumscribing, stagnating, avoiding, and terminating. While other scholars' research brings up questions about Knapp's descriptions (Baxter and Wilmot, 1983), his terminology provides a useful reference point for identifying and examining different parts of an interpersonal relationship. Each of these stages is discussed here as a way of viewing the communication changes people go through as relationships grow and decline. Your interactions may or may not follow this pattern exactly, but this information may help you to understand what is happening in your relationships.

Coming Together

The first stage, *initiating,* is filled with communication data. You may have heard that you "never get a second chance to make a first impression." That observation stresses the important interaction that takes place upon initial meeting. Your first contact allows you to form an immediate, complex, and lasting impression. You make an evaluation of the person's potential for future relationship development, and you may also draw a host of other conclusions about his or her intelligence, interests, economic status, and so on. Be aware that the other person is doing exactly the same thing when meeting and observing *you.*

The other person's physical aspects are easiest to observe and the attention and effort we put into our appearances reflects our understanding of this fact. During this stage, you make contact, say hello, and engage in conversation about impersonal matters you may have in common—the class you have together, the concert you are both attending, the restaurant, the day or event you are currently experiencing, or, if all else fails, the weather. This stage may take a few minutes or a few weeks.

When you have sufficient information and responses from the other person to enlarge the channel for communication, you are ready to move to the next step: *experimenting*. In this stage, you make an effort to continue the interaction and to include other topics of a more specific and perhaps more personal nature. You might engage in an evaluation of the event or class. You venture opinions on different types of foods or restaurants or movies.

This experimenting can involve a wide variety of topics. Much of the information you would include in the open pane of your personal Johari Window would form the communication at this stage of a relationship.

Notice that a relationship moves from one stage to the next only if both parties continue the pattern. If the other person ignores you or keeps the subjects of conversation to weather and other impersonal topics, then you are getting a signal that the relationship is still in the initiating stage. It is likely that you have been in a situation where someone initiated contact with you, but you had no interest in further development so you tried to find a way to discourage the sharing of personal information. You can do this through not responding; through responding in short, neutral, and noncommittal tones; by not volunteering information about yourself; and, when pressed, by declining to respond or responding at the most general level. If you wish to be direct you tell the other person that you are not interested. You may try a combination of strategies—for instance, being indirect at first and then becoming more direct if your first responses do not succeed. Suppose someone at a party wants to initiate a relationship faster than you do. She may ask, "So, where do you live?" You might respond, "Around campus." The person may persist, "Really? So do I! What street?" You could continue to avoid the question by keeping to the same level as the previous answer, "Well, let's just say close enough to walk." You have given a clear signal of disinterest, and you hope the other person is sensitive enough to understand the full meaning of your response. If she is not, and continues on, "So, tell me your address," you may need to reply, "Excuse me, I'm going to try some of the snacks," and walk away from the person.

Stage three, *intensifying*, assumes that both parties are mutually interested in developing the relationship further based on the information and responses that occurred during the experimenting stage. One of the main indications that this stage has begun is the amount of time you spend in each other's company. In potentially romantic relationships, you begin dating. Going to places you discovered were of mutual interest in your experimenting conversations is one dating idea. Virtually all of the open information in each one's Johari Window is known to the other and you begin to disclose to each other some of the topics reserved in the hidden pane. You may even offer each other some feedback about information observed in your blind panes. At this point, the feedback about your blind panes is likely to focus on the positive attributes you see in each other, and less likely to involve a criticism.

This pattern is especially likely in a developing romantic relationship. Physical contact becomes more likely and frequent. In friendship relationships there may be borrowing and using personal items, such as an article of clothing, music items, and money. As the relationship develops, a series of mutual experiences accumulates. A mutual code, such as a set of shorthand references to events only the pair understands, emerges. Perhaps they were eating out together and the cashier dropped their check and exclaimed in an unusual voice, "Excuse me, I'm *so* clumsy!" From then on, whenever anyone drops something, one will start the sentence, "Excuse me…." The other, perhaps mimicking the unusual voice of the cashier, will finish, "…I'm *so* clumsy!" after which both parties laugh hysterically, leaving others in the room wondering about the reference. Signs of such communication interactions will strongly indicate that a relationship has moved into the intensifying phase.

If both parties find interpersonal needs met with this relationship and they feel comfortable enough, they may move to the next step, *integrating*. At this stage, they are together often enough that their friends and associates begin expecting to see both people together rather than separately. Mutual friends feel they can inquire about the absent one with the expectation that the present one will know the answer. Meanwhile, the partners divulge more and more private information to each other and develop a strong mutual trust. They may freely use each other's personal items without always asking permission first. They may make commitments for each other on the assumption that they know each other's schedule and likely response. People will ask one of them about the other's tastes, preferences, and opinions. If Pat and Chris are very good friends, you could ask Pat, "Do you think Chris would be interested in going out with my roommate?" People both perceive and treat the relationship as a unit. Inviting one to a party means inviting both. If they are in a romantic relationship, they will be treated as a couple; in strong friendships, they will be treated as best friends.

In your lifetime, you will probably have only a few such relationships—perhaps with members of your family, school friends, or a marriage partner. Your personal Johari Window for these people has a large open pane because of the extensive communication you have with these people. Any negative information from your blind pane can now be shared as well in the form of feedback from them. Their personalities may be different from yours, but they likely share and respect substantially the same values and enduring outlooks on the world that you do.

The final stage in developing a close relationship is called *bonding*. This type of formal coming together may be exemplified, at one level, by agreeing to rent an apartment or lease a house together. Initiation ceremonies in sororities and fraternities also contain elements of formal bonding. At another level, in romantic relationships, there may be an engagement announcement, or a joining together in household or financial matters in a public and formal way.

Marriage constitutes our most formal bonding activity in interpersonal relationships. At this stage, communication patterns between the two members of the relationship are fully integrated and intense. The marriage partners are a formal unit, and even people who barely know them will be able to ascertain the status of the relationship and treat the pair as a unit. Their Johari Windows will continue to change in the same direction as before, with the open pane growing and the other three diminishing correspondingly. You are a unique and complex individual; although it could take a lifetime for a partner to get to know everything about you, the direction in a continuing bonded relationship is always to create larger and larger open areas. One of the factors that may, in fact, contribute to a stable, long-term bonded relationship is the sense of continual growth in knowledge—both of the self and of the other.

Not all relationships go through all five of the coming together stages; in fact, very few get past stage one. Most people have just a few relationships that make it to the bonding level. Knapp indicates that each step follows and builds upon the previous ones. A relationship may even reverse direction or terminate. Depending on several factors, including the type of relationship (romantic or friendship) as well as the uniqueness and flexibility of the communication, the reversal or termination may take several forms (Baxter, 1983). Knapp believes that when a relationship begins to deteriorate, there are five levels it can go through. This perspective can provide a useful way to talk about your relationships.

Coming Apart

Knapp calls the first stage of coming apart *differentiation.* This phase of the relationship mirrors the initiating stage, but instead of focusing on what the two people involved have in common, this stage is characterized by the communication of differences. Conversation begins to be dominated by what one partner does, likes, thinks about, admires, or tolerates that is *different from* what the other partner does, likes, thinks about, admires, or tolerates. "Chinese food again! I never did care for it." Or, "Do we always have to listen to your CDs? I much prefer something else." If the communication pattern goes beyond simply acknowledging or pointing out the differences, then conflict is the likely result. You may have visited friends who are in this stage and found yourself in the middle of such conflict. They may even ask you to side with one or the other or to arbitrate the conflict. In romantic relationships, stress is placed on the communication when the initial positive regard they had for each other is replaced by mutual identification of differences. They may begin encoding messages that discuss the other in the third person when they both are still in the room, such as, "Did you see what he does? Leaves his dirty dishes right there all day, as if I were his mother." Differentiating messages lead to hostile and defensive behavior, and the Johari Window begins to revert to earlier configurations of a smaller open pane and a larger hidden pane.

The next stage is called *circumscribing* and can be identified by the message patterns evident in the relationship. Instead of taking a telephone message for each other, they simply tell a caller to call back and speak directly to the absent partner. They deal in matters of less substance and avoid issues of personal importance. Requests for information or assistance become routine and brief. If there is a strong desire to continue the relationship, then conversations may turn toward the state of the relationship itself.

If friends or roommates are having this conflict, an honest and frank discussion may clear up the problem and return the relationship back to a positive mode. A third party may need to assist, or the two persons involved may be able to work on the relationship together. Obviously, if one party does not wish to continue the relationship, any attempts to focus on improvement will be met by an attitude of neutrality and minimal response. It is also possible that focusing on the relationship will bring out further dissatisfaction. Additional areas of discontent may be revealed, and old problems may be revived so that renewed conflict ensues. In couple communication, focusing on the relationship may deepen the difficulty rather than solving it. If there is a desire to maintain the association, then a professional third party, such as a qualified counselor or therapist, may be needed. Such a person can teach the couple alternative ways of managing conflict so that it is resolved and not simply deferred, only to return repeatedly in new rounds of circumscribed communication and resulting conflict.

While they are in this stage, and even if they are actively involved in a counseling program, the partners in the relationship will likely still be perceived as a viable pair by others and will continue to do the things together that they have been used to doing.

By the time a relationship reaches stage three, *stagnating*, it is well on its way to coming apart. Silence is the hallmark of this communication pattern. Brief exchanges of a necessary nature—"Please hand me the bread" or, "It's time to pay the rent; I'd like your half today or tomorrow," may be typical. A neutral, flat feeling describes the interaction. You might think that this is a short stage, but some couples fall into this pattern and remain in it for years. Sometimes, religious belief concerning marriage, restrictions on financing, housing needs, children, social pressures, or other factors may keep the couple together to create an appearance of the relationship as it existed in earlier stages. But for the two people involved, stagnation is clear.

Overt unpleasantness in virtually every interaction indicates stage four, *avoidance*. It is annoying to be around each other; perhaps hostility is in the tone of voice and direct antagonism permeates the interaction. In a friendship situation, the parties avoid seeing each other, and perhaps one makes a direct request to discontinue the interaction. Couples will come and go without acknowledgment, eat and sleep at different times, watch television in different rooms, and so on. Roommates may alter their patterns so as not to be around each other, choosing to stay late at the library to study, or spending more time in friends' apartments. If there is a time dimension to the relationship as there is with school roommates who are nearing the end of a term, preparations begin for termination of the relationship. New roommates are sought; new places to live are explored without the other being involved. In other circumstances, where no obvious or natural break occurs, then the final stage, *termination*, occurs.

In *termination*, Knapp has identified three distinct message types that can be expected as the relationship comes to a formal end (Knapp et al., 1973). Partners signal this stage by summarizing the relationship: "Well, we sure had some good times at first, didn't we?" Or, "Well, this semester together has had its ups and downs." Much like the conclusion of a speech, the summary tells the receiver that the interaction is coming to closure. Next come statements telling the other that interaction will be limited or stopped. You might say something like, "We just can't see each other again," or, "We'd better limit ourselves to just finishing English class and not get together anymore outside of class." You could, of course, be more restrictive with a message such as, "Don't ever call me again!" In the final message form of terminating a relationship, you point out what you would like any future relationship to be like. It could range from, "I still like working with you, so I hope we can get together on some projects in the future," to, "I hope I never see your face again!" In a school setting, you may likely run into the person again inadvertently, so such total termination may be impossible to maintain. Likewise, in a marriage with children, unless one partner will never again be involved with the lives of the children, interaction is almost impossible to avoid. There will be graduations, weddings, birthdays, and other events of the lives of the children where both parents are likely to be present. So, even if the termination comes under painful and angry circumstances, the partners may agree to try to avoid further stress on the children through some sort of contract. One of them might say, "Since we'll probably see each other at events for our children, I hope we can be cordial to each other." Ending a relationship is never easy, but communication scholars have found that we learn and use certain patterns or strategies (Baxter, 1982) that should help us understand the ending process and assist us in going through its stages.

This approach to understanding relationships is useful in helping us understand our interactions, but you should realize that not all relationships follow such a steady or predictable path. Your particular relationship may follow variations on these stages depending upon the choices and events unique to your life. What researchers select to observe in any relationship may vary, and thus their results may show a variety of trajectories for any specific interaction (Duck and Miell, 1984). So use these patterns as a guide to what often happens, and what is likely to happen, in relationships, but take care to allow for your own individual applications.

Everyday Interpersonal Interactions

Needless to say, most of your interpersonal communication will not travel the road of full relationship development and decline. In an everyday situation, you may have a brief initiating interaction and then move on your way with hardly another thought about the event. However, your important relationships take up significant amounts of time and go through at least some of the stages of relationship development. When this happens, you are likely to take the attitudes, values, and beliefs of your self further into the relationship. Because we all have slightly different values, attitudes, and beliefs, there is the potential for conflict. The longer and more intense your relationship, the greater you reveal your hidden self. With increased interaction involving personal and private matters, there is a greater chance of running into conflict with the other person's self. This conflict may have both positive and negative effects. Because they are such a constant factor in everyone's lives, conflict and interpersonal communication deserve greater attention.

COMMUNICATION CLIMATE AND CONFLICT

What factors contribute to a positive, sustained communication interaction? What helps a relationship stay on track or go sour? Communication scholars have looked at these important questions, and the answers to them can help make our relationships work better.

Think about the relationships you have. Some are pleasant; some are uncomfortable. You may be very offended if someone signs you up for an activity without asking you first. Or it may bother you when someone expresses his or her ideas so forcefully that they leave you no opportunity to express your opinions. You may be irked by people who always seem to be talking about their exploits—adventures in which they always perform better than anyone else. You may go to a party where you don't know anyone, and other guests ignore you as if you didn't exist. Each of these situations helps to create a *negative climate*—a feeling or tone that you respond to with dislike. Maybe you become a bit rude or touchy, and snap back at others, or put a sarcastic tone into *your* voice. Perhaps *you* are one of the people who does the ignoring, the one-upmanship, or the expressing of opinions with absolute certainty. In any case, communication researchers have given much time and attention to the establishment and maintenance of **communication climate**—and they have some good insights for you!

Jack Gibb developed the most prevalent descriptions of the communication climates that help or hurt relationships. In the process of observing small group dynamics, he created six categories of behaviors and identified a *defensive* and *a supportive* style of communicating for each category (Gibb, 1961). Like Knapp, Gibb may be simplifying and idealizing the situation (Eadie, 1982), but his model still provides a useful approach to understanding communication climate, the way conflict arises, and how to avoid or solve conflicts.

The Gibb Climate Factors are as follows:

Supportive Behaviors	*Defensive Behaviors*
Description	Evaluation
Equality	Superiority
Problem orientation	Control
Spontaneity	Strategy
Empathy	Neutrality
Provisionalism	Certainty

Gibb contends that each of these behaviors helps to establish and maintain a communication climate—a general sense or tone in the interaction. Some people call this sense or tone the *communication environment*. Next, we'll examine in detail each of Gibb's styles—*supportiveness* and *defensiveness*—to better understand how we create and perpetuate certain tones in our interactions.

Supportiveness

The six behaviors of a **supportive communication** climate help to maintain an open, inviting, encouraging, accepting, and continuing communication atmosphere. Each of these is easily recognizable.

Description is the habit of talking about the observable world rather than the inferred world. You talk about what you see, not about what you think might be behind what you see. Consider a situation in which your roommate comes in and slams down his book. A descriptive comment might be, "That was pretty intense. I do that when I'm upset or angry." The statement does not fill in a reason or a guess as to the cause or motive; it just describes the observed behavior and invites further clarification.

Equality means that you view the other person in a relationship as being on the same level as you, neither superior nor inferior, and that you communicate such feelings authentically. You would ask this person, "Can I help?" as an expression of cooperation. You would not say, "Here, let me do it for you," nor would you offer to take on a task beyond the level of the other. Equality cannot reflect an absolute sameness in talent or ability, but it does imply a regard for the other as being worthy and deserving respect.

Problem orientation requires us to look at the situation as an event to be dealt with in a satisfactory way. Otherwise, the interaction may become a contest over who is in control or whose solution is adopted, regardless of whether it can solve the original problem. Thus, people fight over solutions to problems not to identify the best one, but to get recognition for having had the winning idea. When one partner in a relationship drops a bowl of spaghetti sauce on the kitchen floor, a problem orientation response is to look for a mop, not spend time berating the other for being clumsy. People who engage in problem-oriented behavior look to the value of the idea itself and pay little regard to the source. The best solution to a problem can come from an unpleasant braggart; who supplies the idea should not matter. Try to get past the person and focus on the worth of the idea. A positive communication climate will be one of the results.

Spontaneity means that you are neither calculating nor manipulative in your communication and that you react authentically to people and situations. You don't hold back to calculate a response but are honest in your reactions. Someone who is spontaneous communicates that he or she is open, trusting, and self-confident. You may be thinking about all the times when you need to be less than authentic in order to be socially correct. For example, if your aunt wore a new perfume that she loved but reminded you of month-old decayed lilies, you might say, "It reminds me of garden flowers!" In other words, your social self contains a certain measure of tact and sensitivity that prevents you from offending other people. A balance between always saying just what you think without hesitation and never venturing an honest opinion is the goal of spontaneity in communication.

Empathy means that you share a common core of feelings with the other person. You give the other person positive regard, and you identify with the other person's emotional state. Having empathy means that you understand a situation from the other person's point of view. Even when the other person's point of view is not exactly the same as your own, you are nevertheless capable of looking at a situation from his or her perspective. This involves "getting into the other person's shoes" and seeing from his or her viewpoint. Sympathy may consist of simply offering a pat on the back or saying, "That's too bad." Empathy takes more effort, and the effort itself is felt by the other person as genuine support and caring rather than impartial concern offered out of courtesy or social obligation. When you make the effort to create empathy, you show that you value the other person, respect his or her feelings, and acknowledge that person's worth.

Finally, *provisionalism* helps to create a supportive climate by indicating your willingness to wait. You take time to consider your responses in order to make them appropriate. You wait to hear all perspectives or to listen to your partner explain a different idea or approach before insisting that your solution is the best. You wait before making a quick judgment so you can check the details and make certain you have the necessary information. An open mind helps you to look at a situation in different ways, to respect other people's approaches, and to let go of your own idea or method if a better one comes along. If you are always sure that you are right, you spend your time and energy defending your ideas—perhaps without listening very well to others. When you start defending, they start defending, and the climate shifts from one of support to one of argumentative, nonproductive bickering.

The six communication behaviors—*description, equality, problem orientation, spontaneity, empathy, and provisionalism*—that foster a supportive communication climate allow authentic interpersonal communication to take place. When you use the positive actions associated with these styles, you have direct influence in creating a positive communication climate. However, you are probably also aware of the times, perhaps even daily, when your relationships are not characterized by supportive communication. At those times, you may experience what Gibb describes as a defensive climate.

CRITICAL THINKING IN COMMUNICATION
Think Before You React: Provisionalism

The critical thinker is trained to seek out supporting data before accepting ideas. If you let critical thinking become a habit of mind, then you will apply this skill to your interpersonal conversations and interactions as well as your more formal communications. The habit of waiting before reacting buys you the time to engage in some critical thinking. Is an idea consistent with what is known? Is it consistent with previous information from this source? Making assessments of information is easier and more accurate when you give yourself a little time to think about the information—to check the data and make logical connections between what is known and what is *assumed* to be known. What inferences can you draw that are warranted? Which ones are not? The mind of a critical thinker is continually on the alert to such questions, even in conversations—and such alertness requires a provisional acceptance of information.

Defensiveness

Defensive communication climates are characterized by six counterparts to the six supportive communication behaviors just discussed. These defensive behaviors are all too common in most people's interpersonal communication. Knowing what they are helps us recognize when and why defensiveness comes into play. Suggestions for managing conflict and improving interpersonal skills will follow the brief descriptions of the six defensive behaviors presented below.

Evaluation, the first characteristic of defensive climates, is ubiquitous. Your instructors grade you; your friends evaluate your housekeeping skills; and your peers ask you how you did on a test. Your parents want you to stand up straight and eat right; your boss does a performance appraisal; and the coach of your softball team yells at you for striking out or flubbing a play. Any judgment, direct or implied, negative or positive, comes under the heading of evaluation and leads to a defensive climate. *Description*, the counterpart to evaluation, is found in supportive climates. Description balances evaluation by objectively focusing on observed actions without attaching value judgments to the communication.

The defensive counterpart to equality is *superiority*, a common communication style. When someone says, "Here, let me show you how that's supposed to be done!" that person is communicating a tone of superiority. The defensive response is often silence, withdrawal from communication interaction, resentment, or possibly counterattack. When your self-esteem is threatened, you normally make the effort to protect yourself and a defensive climate results.

Superiority messages can be verbal or nonverbal, as when someone grimaces when you say you are cooking your famous lasagna for dinner or when friends roll their eyes in response to your offer to work on a project. Often, there are perfectly valid grounds to feel superior to someone—you are a better basketball player; you do better in mathematics; you play the piano very well; or you are very good at repairing cars. People do vary in their skills, development, and ability. But when that fact dominates the message, a defensive climate is created.

Equality, on the other hand, is the willingness to accept another person on their own terms, at whatever level they may be. Equality also recognizes that people change, grow, and develop; the other person may need some space and time to expand his or her talents. Superiority in a message suppresses other people's potential by diverting their energy away from positive growth to negative defensiveness. You may remember having to remind your parents that you have moved past a former, no longer appropriate stage of development. They may nevertheless insist on acting in a superior way, giving unasked for advice about choices you make. This parental superiority may last long past adolescence—perhaps even as long as the parties are alive. No matter when superiority makes its way into a conversation, expect a defensive climate as the result.

Control creates defensiveness by communicating to the other individual that you know how they ought to behave, think, or feel. Even an innocent-sounding remark such as, "I know you're going to love this movie!" can communicate a control message. Control is seen in our daily messages that start with phrases such as, "You should...," "What you need is...," or perhaps, "You'd better (not)..."

Warnings, threats, orders, directions, commands, guidance, suggestions, and rec-ommendations are all likely to be perceived as control messages by the receiving party, and they may invite a defensive reaction. What can you do, then, if you *are* the instructor or boss, to avoid the defensive reaction? It is a difficult situation since your role requires you to exert control in many situations while, at the same time, you may still wish to foster a supportive atmosphere. There are ways to combine authority and supportiveness in your communication.

Adopting a mutual problem-solving approach to issues such as classroom behavior or job performance is a useful approach to counter potential defensive-ness. For example, in a noisy classroom, the instructor may say, "There is too much noise for people to work. Can we work quietly for fifteen minutes and then have discussion? Or do we need to have the discussion before we can work on the problems? What can we do together to get the noise down?" The tools of active listening that were explained in Chapter 3 can also help to create a climate of mutual problem solving.

If you engage in *strategy*, others will feel that your messages are accompanied by an unstated or ulterior motive. People will begin to see you as not being forth-right, and they will lose trust in you. They will begin putting their defenses in place to protect themselves from the threat of being manipulated by you.

One of the temptations for engaging in strategic behavior is that it often works. You can often achieve a short-term goal or quick gain by less than honest or devious behavior. The reason that the gain is usually short term is that people discover the manipulation. Trust is destroyed and usually the relationship with it. Manipulation can take the form of giving out dishonest messages, withholding information, making up stories, planning in advance with someone to ambush a third party, sending incomplete or distorted messages, and just plain lying. If you have ever trusted someone and then been lied to, you know how hard it is to regain that trust. Using strategy in your communication is a surefire way to cre-ate a defensive climate in any relationship, and the closer the relationship, the more severe the effect. To prevent strategy from becoming part of your commu-nication style, remember the positive effects that come from spontaneity, and keep your communication authentic.

Neutrality is just what it sounds like—"I really don't care, one way or the other." Neutrality distances one person from another with an *impersonal* aura of detachment and lack of involvement. If you receive neutral responses to your messages, you are likely to feel that the other person is cold, uncaring, and lack-ing feeling or appreciation for you. Some people believe that anger is a better response than neutrality in a relationship because at least it reveals involvement and interaction. The worst response in a relationship may be indifference, because it indicates that there is no sharing or commonality in feelings or perspectives.

Finally, Gibb observed that *certainty* is associated with creating a defensive interpersonal climate. In contrast to provisionalism, certainty allows little or no room for open exchange or considering alternatives. If you are in a relationship with someone who is always certain about his or her opinions, ideas, tastes, sug-gestions, and demands, you may begin to think of that person as closed minded, bigoted, or egotistical. Certainty can be associated with both superiority and evaluation. People who express certainty in their communication often refuse to recognize their own mistakes; instead, they rationalize them, blame others for them, or ignore them altogether.

The problems for those in relationships with people who take a position of certainty are that they may feel worthless; they may fail to trust their own opinions or values; and they may be reluctant to express their own ideas until after they have heard the person with certainty speak. Then they can agree with the partner and avoid upsetting him or her. This situation creates a waste of human potential, since only one perspective is used in examining ideas or problems and, as a result, the pool of ideas in the relationship gets smaller. If a relationship is in the early stages of development and one person is especially eager to please the other, a situation can be set up in which certainty becomes a dominant style, and a pattern may be set up that inevitably leads to a defensive communication climate.

The six pairs of behaviors that help to create supportive or defensive climates can and do affect your life in every interpersonal communication situation. Sometimes, a relationship may be shortlived and there will not be much consequence from establishing one climate or the other, but even in a brief sales interaction, climate could be an important factor. Suppose you were shopping for shoes, and the salesperson continually brought you shoes you didn't like or were too expensive for your budget, and kept insisting, "You really should get these." You might buy from this person, but it is more likely you would not; in fact, you would probably not return to that store again.

It is important to establish enduring supportive climates in family settings, long-term friendships, professional relationships, and affectional relationships. However, a supportive climate does not imply the absence of conflict. Conflict is inevitable in every relationship where you honestly communicate. Since we are all different and have a variety of likes and dislikes, we will experience many conflicts throughout our relationships. How we handle them can make the difference between a relationship that continues and grows, and one that declines and terminates. Therefore, knowing how to manage conflict is an important skill.

CONFLICT MANAGEMENT

What is *conflict*? Conflict can be a disagreement or an argument, perhaps a fight, a battle, or even a war. These situations all have elements in common. Communication writers Joyce Frost and William Wilmot have defined conflict based on four characteristics that can appear in conflicts ranging from the smallest disagreement—for example, the mix-up of your food order in the school cafeteria—to major international confrontations. The four elements are included in the following definition: Conflict is an expressed struggle between at least two interdependent parties who perceive incompatible goals, scarce resources, and interference from the other party in achieving their goals (Hocker and Wilmot, 1985). The first part of the definition refers to the *expression* of struggle, and that involves communication. Maybe you asked for a cheeseburger and the server brought you cheesecake. So you try to send it back, but the server refused because then he'd have to pay for it out of his paycheck. Or maybe Israel and the Palestinians both express claims on the same territory. In both cases, an expression of the conflict is communicated so that both sides know about it.

The definition of conflict also states that the parties must be *interdependent*, or somehow linked together in the situation. In the first case, the server is the connection between your food and you. In the second case, both the Israelis and the Palestinians occupy the same geographical space and have vital interests that are dependent on its control and use.

Third, the definition requires that the goals of each party in the conflict be seen as *incompatible*. If the server is asked to pay for the mistakenly ordered cake, there will be conflict. Both the Israelis and the Palestinians express the position that the other must be excluded from certain places or roles.

Finally, the element of *interference* from the other party comes into play when your goal of eating a quick lunch is delayed or even obstructed because the wrong order was delivered. The current Middle East conflict has raged for fifty years over troops, occupation, and aggression, so neither side has achieved its long-term goals.

Conflict Is Inevitable

As you experience more interpersonal relationships, you will experience different forms or levels of conflict. Conflicts can be as simple as a disagreement about which television program to watch or as complex and replete with lifelong implications as the decisions surrounding career choice, who to marry, where to live, and raising children. Since conflict is built in to any meaningful interpersonal relationship, learning how to manage that conflict constructively can have lifelong beneficial effects. There are limits to time, money, patience, resources, energy, abilities, interests, enthusiasms, and desires. These limits stem from the variety of personalities discussed in Chapter 7; when these limitations or differences enter into our relationships, as they do whenever one person meets another, conflicts will arise. Sometimes a problem may seem internal; you keep it to yourself and stew over it in your own mind without involving the other person directly. That does not mean that there is no conflict. It only means that the problem has very little chance of being solved. If it takes two people to create the conflict, then two people are probably needed to manage it effectively. Keeping your conflicts internalized may put enough stress on your mind and body that illness will result. Thus conflict still is expressed, but without much opportunity for resolution. Learning to manage your conflicts means learning to involve others. If you manage conflict well, you may even find that it benefits your personal development.

Conflict Can Be Constructive

We are often reluctant to engage in conflicts. Cultural norms may lead us to resist conflict, or we may believe that a relationship will be threatened if there is any expression of negative feelings. Actually, positive uses of conflict can unburden a relationship of barriers that prevent the people in it from growing closer. At

DIVERSITY IN COMMUNICATION
Conversation Styles

Communication patterns of African Americans differ from those of Anglo-Americans and one interesting place to see these differences is in conversation between these two groups. In one extensive study African Americans were asked about their conversations with Anglo-Americans. The research found several factors that contributed to satisfying or unsatisfying interactions. Primarily, African Americans felt these conversations could be improved if *they* were more active in managing the interaction and in asserting their point of view. They suggested that their Anglo-American partners could improve the quality of the conversations by being more open-minded. The study quotes one African American male as saying:

> Blacks and Whites may come away with different meanings from a conversation because concepts aren't defined in the same way. The members of the ethnic groups tend to think in a different manner. Most times Blacks don't get a lot from conversations with Whites, so when it occurs, it is highly valued—like the gates opening.

Open and honest conversations were seen as rare (Hecht, Ribeau, and Alberts, 1989). Perhaps one way to manage communication between diverse groups of people is to follow the advice given here—be more open, effective at conversation management, and honest in asserting your ideas.

worst, the conflict can reveal problems that need to be resolved; if the conflict is irresolvable, we have the choice of terminating the relationship or changing our attitudes or values. Conflict, therefore, is useful in interpersonal growth and in personal development. The creative energy that can come from exploring, expressing, and resolving conflicts can be channeled toward improving self-esteem, increasing social skills, widening a repertoire of communication abilities, and improving relationships. For all these constructive outcomes to occur, effective conflict management must become a regular practice.

Process of Conflict Management

There are several ways to keep conflict constructive. Unfortunately, in the middle of a conflict, these methods may be forgotten, lost, and unused. Keeping them in mind may be the hardest part of the process. In many ways, good conflict is similar to good listening, and the four areas of active listening presented in Chapter 3 are parallel to the four aspects of constructive conflict.

Be Prepared   Being prepared is your first responsibility in constructive conflict management. Think about what the conflict is *really* about and then focus on that item. If it is only about your partner's constant reluctance to wash the dirty dishes, go into the conflict with that as your focal point. Be careful not to expand the conflict by introducing other topics until you are at the point of saying, "So everything you do shows how you don't care!" Such a conflict is a conflict out of control. On the other hand, if the *real* conflict isn't about dirty dishes at all but a deep resent-ment over feeling ignored or unappreciated, then make *that* your theme. Good preparation also means looking at your available strategies and selecting the ones most appropriate for your purpose. If you are relying on the conflict to strength-en your interpersonal relationship, then be careful to avoid attacking and wound-ing the other person so that the relationship doesn't begin to reverse direction toward termination. Review the supportive climates, especially focusing on *description*.

Be Involved   Be an active participant in the conflict. Withdrawal and avoidance are two strategies that prevent conflicts from being resolved. Be clear about your own thoughts and feelings. Other people do not force them on you; you are responsible for them. If you use the word *I* more than the word *you*, you are com-municating that you are involved as one of the participants. Keeping your mes-sages direct and staying on the issue by making specific observations will help the conflict move toward resolution.

Withhold the Quick Retorts   As tempting as it may be to respond with a quick retort, try to restrain yourself. When the other party hits you with an unfair state-ment and you think of a quick comeback—perhaps a sarcastic play on words—try to hold off for a moment. Remember, you are partially responsible for creat-ing the communication climate. If you want your conflict to have a positive out-come, withholding the quick retort can help you avoid introducing a new subject or creating a climate that just leads to further conflict.

Review or Summarize   When you feel the situation has been thoroughly dis-cussed and you are reaching closure, it is a good idea to summarize the discus-sion in descriptive terms. "So, I think the dishes shouldn't be a problem to me anymore now that I understand you will get to them a bit sooner, and you know how leaving them when you go out of the apartment annoys me. Thanks for lis-tening to me and I appreciate your willingness to do them before you leave in the morning." A good summary can identify the problem and restate whatever reso-lution is created. It may be that the conflict cannot be resolved in one session. A good summary would be, "It's time for me to go to class, and we still haven't resolved the dishes problem. Could we get together between 3 and 5 this after-noon and pick up with your point about time being too short after breakfast?" That message brings the session to a close, if not the conflict. It does, however, avoid simply letting the conflict stop without resolution. In international affairs, negotiators will often take breaks in their sessions, sometimes for many weeks or months, in order to consider their goals and determine how to proceed next.

The best-selling book, *Getting to Yes*, offers four strategies for managing con-flict constructively. The researchers were part of a group called the Harvard Negotiation Project which looked at all sorts of negotiation and bargaining situa-tions—from deciding which movie for a couple to see to international conflicts such as the Arab/Israeli situation. Former President Jimmy Carter has maintained his international profile as a skilled negotiator using this approach. The four steps are as follows (Fisher and Ury, 1986):

1. Separate the people from the problem.
2. Focus on interests, not positions.
3. Generate a variety of options before coming to a decision.
4. Develop an objective standard to judge the result.

The first step involves keeping your focus on the event or problem and not attacking or diminishing the other party's interests, motives, or personal attributes. Rather than worrying about who wins, be concerned with what is gained. The second step advises that you focus on interests and avoid announcing a bottom line. Instead, think about what you are trying to gain. If a fair settlement is your goal, then be careful to have in mind a full idea of what *fair* means, not just a single position. The third step involves developing or enlarging the number and variety of alternatives. Some aspects of the conflict may be more important to you than others. By creating a large number of choices, you increase the chance of giving alternate perspectives to your conflict resolution; also, a large number of sub issues may help break down large and complex problems. Finally, insist on objective criteria to evaluate the final product or solution. This advice is also found in Chapter 4 on critical thinking. Asking the parties in a conflict to define in objective or measurable terms what the result should look like will help both parties to recognize a settlement. You might use the *Blue Book* price in negotiating over the cost of a used car, or you could settle on equal amounts of time spent on household chores. Try to develop objective criteria to measure your settlement before you try to identify that settlement.

Regardless of which approach you choose, practice will help you become better at managing the conflicts that are inevitable in your relationships. In turn, better conflict management will help you to improve your interpersonal relationships.

TECHNOLOGY AND COMMUNICATION
Light Up a Liar

You can purchase various devices to attach to your telephone that claim to tell you whether the person at the other end is telling the truth or lying. I frequently see these devices advertised in airline magazines. They are electronic measurement systems that detect slight changes in the tension level of the voice. The human ear cannot detect such changes, but they can be monitored by these instruments. The devices often use red, yellow, and green lights to indicate the likelihood that the other person is telling the truth.

Negotiations in business take on new dimensions if the other side hears you say, "That's the highest offer I can make!" and the red light comes on to indicate that it is not. These devices are extensions of the old "lie detectors" (polygraphs) which measured the electrical conductivity of the skin, heart rate, breathing, and muscle tension in an attempt to discover whether the subject was telling the truth. Our advancing technology is often applied to areas of interpersonal importance and truth telling is one such area.

IMPROVING INTERPERSONAL SKILLS

All the ideas of this chapter taken together give you only a start in improving your interpersonal relationships. You can take entire courses, probably at your college, that focus exclusively on interpersonal communication. There are several guidelines, however, that you can begin to use right now to improve the quality of your interpersonal communication.

Be Assertive

Being assertive means that you are willing to communicate. The passive, withdrawn, inactive person will not elicit much response from others, so to get interaction from others, you must first interact! Notice that *assertive* is not the same as *aggressive*—pushing yourself on to other people, interrupting others, and telling strangers intimate details of your life story at great length. These behaviors are all associated with the over-personal behaviors Schutz described in his work on *Inclusion-Affection-Control*. Being assertive also means being responsible. This means you acknowledge that you are an independent person and take responsibility for your own ideas, your own thoughts, and your own feelings. You are responsible for communicating according to the social and cultural norms and expectations that help people feel comfortable and in control.

Be Considerate

You need to be aware of the other person as another complete person. Other people have their own backgrounds, personalities, and experiences that they bring to the relationship. If you try to practice *empathy*, you will find yourself becoming more aware of another individual's qualities. Then you will find more ways of communicating with that person.

Listen

The act of listening seems deceptively easy to perform; you can immediately use the skills of active listening that are described in Chapter 3 to help improve your interpersonal relationships. If you have already started putting them into practice, you probably have noticed an increase in both your understanding of others and your ability to send and receive messages with accuracy and clarity. You can listen actively to others' words and nonverbal messages so that your feedback becomes more accurate and appropriate.

Develop Language Skills

Keeping in mind the information from Chapter 6 about the variety, richness, and problems associated with our use of language, you can be on the lookout for your own uses of abstractions (or snarl words), jargon, or clichés as well as for the many other habits of language that interfere with building clear communication.

Be Supportive

Putting all the qualities of supportive communication into an ongoing communication style can be challenging but, with the help of self-reminders and practice, it is within your reach. Large doses of good-natured humor can go a long way toward energizing your efforts. Once you are in the habit of approaching others with warm, positive regard, you will remember to check the communication climate in which you find yourself and change it, if necessary, by your actions.

At the heart of all good interpersonal communication is the positive regard you give to others. It is based on an authentic commitment to communicate well because you believe the other person is genuinely worthwhile. That attitude may not be easy to maintain with everyone, but people who have it seem to be the best at interpersonal communication and they, in turn, are warmly regarded by others.

Finally, try to apply either of the conflict management approaches outlined above. The first set may be easier at first because it parallels active listening and the two skills reinforce one another. For formal situations, the Harvard Negotiation Project method may provide you with a more sophisticated approach; you might want to get the book, *Getting to Yes*, and become fully informed about this system.

SUMMARY

Interpersonal communication is a topic so vast that many of the following chapters will continue to explore its various details and settings. The general principles outlined here serve as guidelines for your continued interactions with others. Your needs for affection, inclusion, and control are present in a one-to-one relationship, in small groups, interviews, families, and even in public life. Your life will probably follow, at least to some degree, the patterns of relationship development and relationship deterioration. You probably recognized yourself in some of the examples showing how people get to know each other and how they break off relationships.

If you can carry the practice of supportive communication into your personal life, you will find your interpersonal climate improving and providing you with greater satisfaction. Supportiveness helps open clear channels of communication; defensiveness closes them down. Even though conflict is probably woven into our very nature, there are ways to manage it so that problems are resolved with minimum damage to the relationship and to the self-concepts of the persons involved. Constructive conflict is helpful in friendships, on the job, and in romantic relationships. The ideas regarding conflict and conflict management are many, the behaviors complex, and the rewards rich and plentiful. Begin today to apply these skills and reap the benefits they offer.

Key Terms

interpersonal communication, **126**
Johari Window, **127**
affection, **129**
inclusion, **129**
control, **129**

relationship development, **130**
communication climate, **136**
supportive communication, **137**
defensive communication, **139**

EXERCISES

1. Keep a journal for one full day of your interpersonal interactions. Record when you felt your values, attitudes, or beliefs were similar to and different from the people with whom you interacted. Note one or two examples of these values, attitudes, or beliefs.

2. List the interpersonal activities you engage in that fulfill your inclusion needs, your affection needs, and your control needs. Which activities relate to more than one of these at the same time? Which activities are unsatisfying because they fail to meet these needs and which meet these needs to a greater extent than you really like? Which activities do you feel you are likely to remain doing for a long period of time?

3. Pick three relationships in which you are an active participant and indicate which stage of development you are in for each one. What do you predict will happen next in each one of these? What behaviors can you specifically identify which confirm your placement of a relationship in any particular stage?

4. Keep track of the defensive messages you receive for one day. Record how you were able to respond—either defensively or supportively. Share these reactions with your class and ask if they have suggestions on how to alter the climate for any one of these interactions.

5. Describe a recent event of interpersonal conflict. Write a script of the interaction as it occurred. Now write a second script of how you could have applied principles of conflict management to create a better process. Do you feel comfortable enough to share these two scripts with the other person involved in the conflict?

References

Baxter, L. "Strategies for Ending Relationships: Two Studies." *Western Journal of Speech Communication 46,* 3 (1982).

Baxter, L. and W. Wilmot. "Communication Characteristics of Relationships with Differential Growth Rates." *Communication Monographs* 50 (1983).

Baxter, L. "Relationship Disengagement: An Examination of the Reversal Hypothesis." *Western Journal of Speech Communication 47,* 2 (1983).

Duck, Stephen. "Social and Personal Relationships" in *Handbook of Interpersonal Communication,* M. L. Knapp and G. R. Miller, Eds., Beverly Hills, CA: Sage, 1985.

Duck, Stephen and Miell, D. E. "Towards a Comprehension of Friendship Development and Breakdown," in *The Social Dimension: European Perspectives on Social Psychology,* H. Tajfel, C. Fraser, and J. Jaspars, Eds., Cambridge: Cambridge University Press, 1984.

Eadie, W. "Defensive Communication Revisited: A Critical Examination of Gibb's Theory." *Southern Speech Communication Journal* 47 (1982).

Fisher, R. and W. Ury. *Getting to Yes.* Boston: Houghton Mifflin, 1986.

Gibb, J. "Defensive Communication." *Journal of Communication* 11 (1961).

Hecht, M., S. Ribeau, and J. K. Alberts. "An Afro-American Perspective on Interethnic Communication." *Communication Monographs* 56, (December 1989):385.

Hocker, J. L. and W. Wilmot. *Interpersonal Conflict.* Dubuque, IA: Wm. C. Brown, 1985:22–29.

Knapp, M. L., R. P. Hart, G. W. Friedrich, and G. M. Schulman. "The Rhetoric of Goodbye: Verbal and Nonverbal Correlates of Human Leave-Taking." *Speech Monographs* 40 (August 1973).

Knapp, M. L. *Interpersonal Communication and Human Relationships.* Boston: Allyn and Bacon, 1984.

Knapp, M. L. and Gerald Miller. *Handbook of Interpersonal Communication.* Beverly Hills, CA: Sage Publications, 1985.

Koper, Randall J. and Marjorie A. Jaasma. "Interpersonal Style: Are Human Social Orientations Guided by Generalized Interpersonal Needs?" *Communication Reports* 14, 2 (Summer 2001).

Luft, Joe. *Of Human Interaction.* Palo Alto, CA: National Press, 1969.

McKinney, Bruce E., Lynne Kelly, and Robert Duran. "The Relationship Between Conflict Message Styles and Dimensions of Communication Competence." *Communication Reports* 10, 2 (Spring 1997).

Schutz, W. *FIRO: A Three Dimensional Theory of Interpersonal Behavior.* New York: Holt, Rinehart and Winston, 1958.

CHAPTER 9

Interviewing

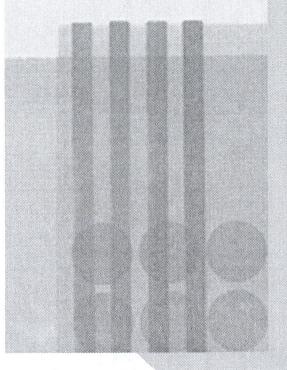

After reading this chapter, you should be able to:

- Understand the three common types of interviews
- Follow the steps of preparing for and participating in interviews
- Explain where and why interviews are an important part of interpersonal communication
- Feel more confident when being interviewed and conducting interviews
- Be at ease during a sales presentation
- Evaluate your interview experiences to improve them in the future

A graduating senior is seated in the office of the Personnel Director of a large and impressive company.

"First, tell me a little about yourself," begins the Director.

"Well, I like sports," replies the senior.

"Oh? Any in particular?"

"Most of them."

"I see. How about some of your school activities. I see on your resumé that you were in the Wilderness Club. What was that like?"

"Fun."

"Just what was fun about that group?"

"Everything."

"OK. Let's see, I notice that you wrote that you'd like a job in management. That's pretty broad. Any aspect of management that you'd like to focus on or took courses in?"

"Not really."

A specialized form of interpersonal communication is the focused and purposeful exchange of questions and answers—the interview. There are many types of interviews, with the job interview being one everyone will experience. Performing well in an interview takes skill and, as you can see from the responses of the senior in the example above, our friend has yet to acquire it. Because interviewing occurs in a variety of situations—many of them having lifelong consequences—gaining knowledge and skills about interviewing is worth your time and energy.

We start with a definition of interviewing, then examine the various types of interviews with a focus on three of the most common ones, and finally look at a variety of ways you can become skillful at both being interviewed and conducting an interview. Let's begin with a definition of the interview and take a look at the variety of interview situations that communication scholars have identified.

DEFINING THE INTERVIEW

The definition of an interview incorporates several different characteristics. First, there are usually just two parties involved in an **interview**—the person being interviewed and one other party. At times there may be several people on an interview team and one person being interviewed, but the idea of *two parties* being involved remains the same; one primarily asks the questions and one primarily gives the answers. The second element that defines interviews is questions. There are many questions asked in interviews, and most of them are asked by one party and directed at the other. As in most other communication situations, there is a purpose to an interview that both parties know and understand. So, the interview situation can be defined as *specialized two-party communication primarily involving questions and answers directed at a preplanned objective*. The objective determines the type of interview. Let's now examine some interview objectives.

TYPES OF INTERVIEWS

In their extensive work on interviewing, Charles J. Stewart and William B. Cash, Jr. defined several important types of interviews (Stewart and Cash, 1985). Some of these types can easily be considered together; for example, information giving and information gathering can be combined into information interviews. Five such distinct areas emerge, representing each of the primary interview situations (Skopec, 1986). This chapter will briefly examine each type and then identify three common techniques which you will find useful when you interview another person. Finally, you will learn how to create a resumé and increase your interviewing competency.

Information Interviews

In the exchange that takes place in an information interview, one person is the source of information for another, as is the case when you see your academic advisor or begin orientation for a new job.

In the information-giving format, one person may be new to the situation whereas the other person is an expert who provides information that will help acquaint the first person with a particular subject. In the interview, the expert usually structures the communication situation, but the new person might do most of the questioning. The expert may be training you to operate a machine, follow a procedure, fill out a class schedule, or find your way around a building or the campus. Situations in which you can ask questions of another person are information-giving interviews.

The *information-gathering* format is a common type of interview through which you might gain information from an expert. However, the expert does not give you prepared orientation materials. You are the one who structures the communication. Journalists who interview people for news stories are gathering information (Biagi, 1986). Interviewing a faculty member on your campus for information while doing research for a speech is another example. Another common example is a survey or poll, whether it is conducted in person or on the telephone. You might be asked to sample a new product and then answer questions about your reactions. A police detective questioning a witness to an accident or associates of a suspect is also engaging in information gathering.

Selection Interviews

The purpose of selection interviews is the screening of individuals for hire, admission, awards, placement, or any other kind of sorting. The selection interview takes place in many settings besides the job application setting. You might be interviewed to join a club, to get a scholarship, or to be chosen by potential roommates. However, it is the job interview that students usually think of when they think about interviewing. Many campuses make interview training services available to students so they can practice, often with videotape, in order to enhance their effectiveness during screening or selection interviews. Specific advice that addresses the job interview situation is presented in the second half of this chapter.

Most of us hold between three and eight different jobs during a working career—a figure that does not include the part-time jobs held during summers or while we are in school. If you have already been employed, you realize that every new job entails a job interview. These interviews are generally divided into two stages: screening interviews that reduce a large number of applicants to a few and final selection interviews in which those few are again interviewed and a single person is chosen. Stewart and Cash (1985) distinguish between the two types, referring to them as *screening* and *determination interviews.*

The person or group making the choice determines the structure of these interviews, and the questions are directed to the applicant or nominee. Whenever you seek a job, a college president is hired, or an admiral is up for promotion, a selection interview process is involved.

Appraisal Interviews

Appraisal interviews can involve problems of the interviewee's behavior. Sometimes, an instructor or employer will say, "Please see me…," and you know that person probably wants to see you about a problem with your work. This type of interview is sometimes called *a performance review,* an *evaluation interview,* or a *counseling interview.* You might be called in for something as simple as correcting a minor behavior or for something as serious as being fired or expelled. In a formal situation, rules or regulations are probably involved such as employer regulations or company polices. At school, this interview might involve a course deadline or performance level in a class. It could also involve something more serious, such as a school regulation which you have violated. This type of interview is very difficult for both parties.

A somewhat tricky situation involves the two parties in roles that are reversed from those in the previous examples. Typically, the party who is not in charge is there to complain about something. You may recognize this form if you have ever interviewed an instructor about a grade on your paper or exam. You may have felt there were problems with the class or an assignment or an evaluation—problems that came from the instructor. In such situations, you need to express your complaint to the instructor, and that may be a difficult thing to do. On the job, an employee may seek redress from a supervisor or there may be a formal grievance procedure that begins with the employee first interviewing the supervisor about the problem. Schools have formal procedures that allow you to express a complaint about an instructor but the first step is almost always to discuss the problem with the instructor involved.

Problem Solving and Counseling

The *problem-solving interview* is a situation in which both parties share in both the problem and the solution. The problem is not that you are about to be fired or that you are about to file a formal grievance against an instructor. The problem must be *mutual* and both parties must have a stake in the solution. The interview in this case focuses on what each party can contribute toward identifying the elements of the problem and what each can contribute toward finding and implementing a solution. Some clear decision should emerge as a result of the interview. A successful problem-solving interview will likely follow these steps: identifying the problem, defining it, identifying potential solutions, selecting criteria for evaluating the solutions, choosing a solution, and acting on it. Small groups that meet to solve problems also use these steps.

On the *counseling* side, you may be the one who initiates the process. Perhaps you are having a personal problem or difficulties in a relationship, or you might need help in deciding on a career or some other personal choice. You, rather than the other person, would then seek the interview. The problem may still be difficult to discuss, but the choice remains with you as to the course of action to follow.

Sales and Persuasion Interviews

The final category of interview listed by Stewart and Cash is the frequently encountered persuasion interview. Often, it is a sales presentation; you may get involved in these several times a week. If a friend tries to convince you to try a new class, change your major, or buy a used CD player, you are in a persuasive interview situation. The more obvious of these situations include someone coming to your door to sell you a product, service, or solicit a donation; telephone calls can serve these same purposes. When you visit a used car lot or stop in an electronics store to look around, you can expect someone to begin a persuasive interview with you: "Can I help you folks today? The model you're looking at is on sale this week, and the reviews it gets are terrific. Would you like a demonstration?" These questions and statements are typical of a persuasive interview. Of course, you can always walk away, close the door, or hang up the phone; that way, you can retain some control over the interview. Skilled persuaders, however, always seek to keep the communication flowing and connected. They do so by asking you simple questions and eliciting easy responses to engage you in their communication process.

You may expect to engage in all of these various types of interviews over a lifetime. You will find that interviews of the same type differ a bit because of the personalities and circumstances involved. Recall from

IMPROVING COMPETENCY
Entertainment Interviews

Watch any of the interview shows on television tonight—Jay Leno, David Letterman, or Conan O'Brien. These are good examples of a format in which there is one guest and one interviewer. Which of the types of interview is exemplified by the show? What key factors determine the best type of interview for television? Look at the kinds of questions that the host asks, and note those that seem preplanned and those that seem to be spontaneous reactions to the guest's responses. As you watch these programs, think about the standards for a good interview that we set in this culture.

Chapter 8 that the interpersonal communication situation builds on the interactions between the people involved. Both the close give-and-take of friends and the intimate conversations of couples can benefit from some guidelines for improvement. Interviews can be improved by preparing for them in advance. We now look at some common interview techniques that apply to all types of interviews and show how they can be used to build interviewing competency.

INTERVIEWING ANOTHER PERSON

The methods for successfully interviewing another person are similar to those used in active listening. To review, recall the four steps of active listening. The first step for good interviewing is to *be prepared*. You might need to do some general background reading first, or you may wish to find out something about the person you are about to interview. Students working on the college newspaper or majoring in our department sometimes interview me. Usually, they are doing a profile of faculty members, and the student conducting the interview will often ask me questions that are answered easily by other sources. For example, they often ask, "Where did you get your degrees?" This information is both in the university catalogue and in a handout available at the department office. By preparing ahead of time, the interviewer could skip these questions and ask more interesting or conversational ones. For example, they could ask me to compare and contrast my experiences at one college with those at another. I would also be impressed with their preparation. Prepare a variety of questions in advance so that you have a plan and a direction for the interview. Various types of questions are described later in this chapter.

Stay involved by listening and reacting to the answers to your questions so that a genuine dialogue develops. You may mentally be getting ready for the next question and miss an important idea that the interviewee is expressing. Staying involved also means keeping careful notes of both the questions and the answers. A good record will help you later when you write up the interview.

By *keeping an open mind,* you should be able to listen to answers that you might not have been expecting. Sometimes, a student hopes that I will say one thing in an interview, but instead I say something else. I then read about the interview in the next day's student newspaper and wonder why he or she didn't listen more carefully.

Review your notes immediately after the interview, filling in the blanks you may have left while talking with the other person. You may have written down key words that are intended to remind you later of a complete idea; get back to those words while the ideas are still fresh. You may be like many others and write a partial note or comment that has a very clear meaning at the time but, a few days later, you cannot recall the meaning. For example, you may have a telephone number written in your handwriting on a pad in your house or dorm, but have no idea whose name goes with the number. When this happens to me, I am tempted to call the number and say, "Hello, do you know me?" but I never do. To avoid this problem with your interview notes, go back over them as soon as you can, and fill in the details while your memory of the interview is still fresh.

STRUCTURE AND SEQUENCE

It is important to keep the information-gathering focus of your interview in mind and not invade a subject's privacy. It is in the correct format of an interview to have some getting-acquainted, personal exchanges. You might already have gathered some personal information on the interviewee; however, there is a difference between *personal* and *private* information. You can create a barrier to effective communication if you appear to be seeking private information. Defensiveness on the part of your subject can only lead to less sharing of information. Your subject will be much more cooperative and will provide you with more information if you are nonthreatening and sensitive to obvious social and cultural limits on questions. If you are courteous and respectful, you will create a favorable impression on your interviewee.

When you are planning an interview, it is a good idea to consider the *types* of questions you are going to ask, not just the questions themselves. Variety in your question types can keep the interview fresh and dynamic. There are two major types of questions: *directive* and *nondirective*.

Directive questions are those that require a clear answer, such as, "What were the dates of your stay in France?" Directive questions force the interviewee to give a specific answer and do not seek reaction or elaboration.

Nondirective questions, on the other hand, allow the respondent to structure the content and the tone of the answer. For example, the interviewer might say, "I see you spent nearly two years in France. What were the most vivid impressions you have of that time?" This gives the subject an opportunity to structure the answer. Notice that directive and nondirective questions are not different because one is specific and one is general; specific information is requested in both examples. The main difference is in the latitude the respondent is given to structure the

DIVERSITY IN COMMUNICATION

Skilled Communicators Can Reach a Diverse Audience

Two of the most popular interview hosts in recent television programming are Oprah Winfrey and Montel Williams. Some of their appeal comes from the fact that they have guests who are interesting to a wide variety of people. Some of it may be because they make an effort to be inclusive of different perspectives and ideas in their questions. Both of these hosts often refer to the experience of being African Americans in the United States, and they are both active in African American organizations and associations. They seem to be able to identify strongly with their home culture and to communicate clearly and positively with a broad spectrum of people as well. It might be worthwhile for you to observe and analyze how their communication skills contribute to this ability.

answer and fill in detail. The interviewer could say instead, "So, tell me about your time in France." Here the inquiry is both general and nondirective.

A good interviewer usually tries to provide variety in the types of questions asked, leaving some questions very open and using others to focus the interview or to gain a specific answer to a particular question.

Remember to wait and listen for the respondent to reply completely. The full answer may contain information you may need to use in later questions. If your time is limited—and it usually is for both you and your interviewee—you may need to move the interview along. If you are spending too much time on the friendly, introductory questions and missing the point of the interview, you may need to encourage your subject politely to move along. A good transition may be, "Let's turn now to your work on French politics. That's the theme of my term paper and I'm really interested in your research."

Finally, you may find yourself in a situation in which you must gather information to use when introducing your interviewee to a group. It is, of course, necessary to gather biographical information about the subject, but try to go beyond names, dates, and places where the subject lived or worked. Be attentive to the whole person and include in your introduction some of the impressions you gathered about the individual. That kind of information will help to fill out and add life to what otherwise could be merely a recital of fairly dull statistics.

By following these suggestions, you can make the information-gathering interview a productive interaction. When you put these suggestions into practice, you build on your knowledge of personal communication principles.

In addition to conducting interviews for the purpose of gathering information, you will most likely be interviewed as part of the job-selection process, to provide information to others, and as a receiver of persuasive messages. Next, you'll learn how to handle job or selection interviews.

The interview is an important part of most careers.

BEING INTERVIEWED

In terms of life experiences, the job interview may be one of the more important communication events you have. Even if you are the subject of only an information-gathering interview, you will want to present yourself and your ideas in the clearest and best possible light. The suggestions that follow parallel those of being a good interviewer and can be divided into three steps: (1) Preparation for the interview, (2) Responses during the interview, and (3) Follow-up after the interview.

Preparation for the Interview

Getting yourself ready to be interviewed means putting your information in order. Most job or other selection interviewers will want to know about your background, education, interests, and activities. They often will ask about these topics during the interview, and usually they will require some written information from you before the interview itself. You need to prepare a short summary of your background and put it into a form the interviewer can use. The most common form is resumé, sometimes called a *vita.* This summary should be brief, rarely more than one or two pages long. Some people, particularly as they accumulate years of experiences and a variety of training and education, prepare a complete version and a brief version. An interviewer who wants more details later can request the complete version. Initially, however, the short resumé is the most valuable. There are many slight variations in resumés (Bostwich, 1985), but a typical resumé might look like the sample on page 160.

This sample resumé lists a variety of items in a specific order. When writing your resumé, first list your name, address and contact information, then emphasize your educational and training background. Use clear headings and put the information into block form, not in sentences or paragraphs. The block format is designed to give the reader a quick, clear, and complete picture of you and it stresses relevant, job-related information.

It is important for you to realize that this is a formal piece of communication and that it is usually the first impression of you that the interviewer gets. People often seek professional advice in preparing a resumé. Your campus probably has a placement service or counseling center where other samples are available for your use and where someone can help to proofread your resumé.

Notice that only certain information is given under personal data. Federal law recognizes that your race, age, sex, marital status, religious affiliation, cultural background, and so on are almost always irrelevant to employment. Indeed, your performance on the job is not related to those things, so it is almost always illegal for an interviewer to inquire about them and unnecessary for you to volunteer information about them. However, after you are hired, an employer will sometimes need to know about your dependents for insurance purposes, or your age to fulfill bonding or licensing requirements, or to plan for your retirement. Hard fought battles over civil rights during the past forty years have made only

Jonathan A. Smith
7865 Green Meadow Lane
Anytown, TX 50554
(616–888–5555)

Employment Objective:
To gain an introductory position in management of a medium-sized company, eventually moving into personnel administration.

Educational Background:

Central Texas University Parkfield, Texas	2000–2003	BA: Business Management Minor: Communication
Llano Community College Llano, Texas	1998–2000	AA: Psychology
U.S. Army Technical School Ft. Lewis, New Jersey	1995–98	Data Processing
Anytown High School Anytown, Texas	1991–95	General Education

Employment Background

Bank of Parkfield 234 Main Street Parkfield, Texas	1999–present (part-time)	Teller
Llano College Bookstore Llano Community College Llano, Texas	1998–99 (part-time)	Assistant Manager
U.S. Army—Ft. Rollins Central Motor Pool	1995–97	Dispatcher
Anytown Electric Repair 342 West Elm Street Anytown, Texas	1994 (Summer) 1993 (Summer)	Sales Clerk Stockroom/Janitor

Activities/Personal Data

Parkfield United Way	2001	Funding Coordinator
Anytown Community Action	1998	Youth Activities Director

Hobbies include water-skiing, backpacking, singing with a country-pop band, and volunteering as a reader for the blind.

References are available upon request from each employer listed.

The Story of Communication
Equal Employment Opportunity

UP UNTIL THE 1960s, the content of questions asked in job interviews was up to the questioner. With the passing of certain notable legislation—that is, the Equal Employment Act of 1963, the Civil Rights Act of 1964, the Age Discrimination Employment Act of 1967, and the Equal Employment Opportunity Act of 1972—employers were prohibited from inquiring about personal information that was deemed irrelevant to the job but possibly related to the applicant's ethnic, religious, political, or other characteristics that are immaterial to performing a job. More recently, the Americans With Disabilities Act expanded on these other laws to include disabled persons. This aspect of our communication content, then, is subject to regulation by the government. The purpose of this regulation is to protect people from prejudice and discrimination. Some factors, such as race, ethnicity of your last name, age, and gender, often are self-evident, so employers can still use that information if they desire to. However, they would be open to charges of unfair discrimination in hiring if any pattern or consistent behavior against certain individuals or groups became evident.

job-related items required on a formal resumé and in an interview. Other details can be saved for informal conversation after you are hired and if you wish to expand your Johari Window once you are on the job.

Part of your preparation should involve a little research about the prospective interviewer's organization. If you are applying for the Martha M. Holgate Memorial Scholarship, you might find out who she was and why a scholarship was named for her *before* you go to the interview. If you are applying to ACME Tools, Inc., you can read copies of the company's annual report or find out about the company from the local Chamber of Commerce or other business associations. Having a little background can help you to answer common questions, such as "What is it about ACME that inspired you to apply here?" You could answer, "I really don't know anything about ACME," or you could say, "I like the way your production has been expanding by sixteen to twenty percent over the past five years and am especially intrigued by your new operations in Japan and Singapore." You can figure out which answer is more likely to land you the job.

Responses During the Interview

Speaking of good answers, your responses during the interview are the major determinant of the success of your interview.

Your communication, as you know, has both nonverbal and verbal aspects to it. Effective nonverbal communication during an interview can increase your communicative ability and the overall impression that you make. Begin by dressing appropriately. For your interview with the loading dock supervisor at a local bakery, you probably would not wear a business suit; your clean jeans and clean pullover are acceptable. However, if you interview for a job as a bank teller, you might visit the bank beforehand to see what the employees are wearing. In any case, make sure you are appropriately attired for the message you wish to convey. A prospective employer who sees that you are sensitive to every aspect of the nonverbal communication situation will get a good impression about your awareness in general. If you are not certain what to wear, a low-key approach is best. Try to avoid the latest in trendy fashions and flashy jewelry. Your interviewer will be distracted from your good qualities if your clothing is "shouting" while you two are talking.

While presenting your answers, try to maintain an energetic, friendly, and relaxed nonverbal presentation. Keep good eye contact so that you can discern any nonverbal cues from your questioner that tell you how your answers are being received. Project energy in your voice and facial expression, and balance this energy with a body posture that is at ease. This particular combination will create an impression of confidence and interest. If you show nervousness or fidget with a pencil, ring, or other item, your listener will be distracted from the content of your message. It may be difficult to control your nervous energy but by being aware of unwanted nonverbal signals, you may be able to stop them. The techniques for controlling the effects of communication anxiety will be useful in the interview situation; deep breathing for several minutes before the start of the interview may be just what you need. It may be difficult to control your nervous energy, but if you are aware of your nonverbal signals, you may be able to stop tapping your pencil or twisting the ring on your finger.

As for your verbal messages, recall the advice that was given earlier about listening in an information-gathering interview when you are the interviewer. Use the same skills when you are the one being interviewed. Most interviewers will give you clues about what they are seeking in the way they phrase their questions, and you can infer a great deal of information from a question by listening carefully. For example, the interviewer might say, "Your experience has been in banking, but our need is for someone who is more people-oriented than money related. Do you think you have more than money skills?" Rather than answering with a simple "Yes," try to respond to the question's implicit message: Your primary experience is not seen as relevant. You might elaborate by saying, "Yes, I do think I have people skills. My position at the bank involved handling large sums of money, but it also involved customer contact. As a teller, my first priority was to make clients feel welcome and comfortable before I concerned myself with their money. I felt really good some days when people would wait until my window was available because they enjoyed interacting with me." This answer is not too long, yet it addresses the underlying concern in the question by connecting your experiences with the needs and concerns of the interviewer. A good listener will respond to both the question's content and *intent*.

Another important factor in effective listening and responding is to make certain that you are answering the question that was asked, not the question you *wish* you had been asked or were hoping would be asked or were afraid would be asked. Don't over answer the question by digressing into long stories or examples.

Try to balance being complete with being concise. As you formulate complete answers, make certain that you cover the item completely, then stop. The interviewer has probably planned to cover several areas in a set amount of time. If you

TECHNOLOGY AND COMMUNICATION
Police Interviews

One specialized interview is that conducted by police investigators with suspects in a crime. Police are on the alert for deception in this situation, and many agencies have turned to technology to assist them in detecting deceptive answers (Hocking and Leathers, 1980, Hocking et al., 1979). One device they use is a camera that focuses on the suspect's eyes and records the amount of pupil dilation that occurs during questions. When people are trying to deceive, their eye pupils change size briefly and in tiny amounts. Advanced camera technology can record these changes and assist investigators in detecting deceitful communication.

take too long for any single answer, the interviewer will have less information to remember you by and to use in your evaluation. You can apply your nonverbal sensitivity to gauging feedback from your questioner. If the interviewer makes comments such as, "OK," "Ah, I see," and "Umm, that was interesting," he or she may be signaling that it is time to move on. You can always try to check directly if you are not sure. In the sample answer about your people skills in the bank, you could give your one example, and then say, "There were other aspects of my work that helped me learn about and use people skills. Would you like another example?" If the interviewer is genuinely interested in more information, he or she can say so. If not, the interviewer can move along with a response such as, "Well, yes, if we have time later. Right now, I wanted to ask you about your community activities." Finding the right balance between completeness and brevity is not always easy, but if you keep it in mind during the interview, you will probably come close.

Many applicants take brief notes during the interview so they can ask questions about the job or the company that they could not find the answers to during their preparation. Keep your note taking to a minimum and do not write more than one or two items at a time; otherwise, you risk taking your attention from the interviewer. Asking a few questions that you could not anticipate before the interview can show you are responsive and attentive.

Most interviewers conclude by asking you if you have any questions. Time may be short, so have a few in mind. You may have formulated some questions before. If you have them with you, you can show the interviewer that you know how to prepare ahead of time and that you can anticipate future concerns. Try to keep these questions brief, and restrict them to areas you could not find out about in another, easier way. You could ask about any job-related expectations that were not completely clear from the job posting or advertisement. You might ask when a final decision will be made, or you could reverse roles and ask the interviewer whether there is any additional information or work samples he or she might want from you. Be careful of the time; there might be another interview scheduled right after yours.

Sometimes, interviewers will ask you if you would like to have something to drink. While the interviewer may be sincerely trying to make you feel comfortable,

CRITICAL THINKING IN COMMUNICATION
Interviewing Skills

You can use your skills at evaluating communication options to help you decide how much of an answer is enough and what the intent of the question is. I was once on an interviewing committee that had allotted about thirty minutes for each candidate. There were seven or eight questions that we wanted to cover for each of the eight finalists. One person, in response to a general warm-up question, proceeded to give us his life history, talking for nearly twenty-five minutes before we were able to make him stop. Needless to say, the other questions remained unanswered, and the candidate was not hired. Had he used his critical thinking skills, he would have analyzed the situation, gauged the first question to be an ice-breaker, and given it just a few moments, thereby allowing the team to set the direction of the interview. By dominating the time, he showed his inability to assess the goal of the interview and thus called into question his critical thinking skills in general.

you would probably be wise to decline. A cup of hot coffee or a cold glass of water is just one more thing to juggle or spill or cough on. Even the most graceful person can accidentally knock over a glass under the stress of an interview. Dribbling coffee on yourself is bad; dumping it on the interviewer's desk is a disaster. Get a drink before or after the interview, but not during it. Smoking is increasingly frowned on in the workplace, so even if you are a smoker, do not smoke during the interview.

The interviewer will indicate that the interview is coming to an end by saying, "Well, that's all the questions I have for you. Can I answer any questions?" or, "Well, our time is just about up— is there anything we didn't cover?" Be certain to respond by honoring the signal and keeping your closing remarks or questions to a minimum. You might conclude with, "Thank you for taking time to see me. I enjoyed coming here and look forward to hearing from you when you make your decision."

These steps can help create a solid impression of you during the interview and will allow your best qualities to be communicated clearly to the other person. You might later complete the interview process with a short follow-up.

After the Interview

Once you have left the interview, recall and address any follow-up requested by the interviewer. Did the interviewer ask for a letter of reference? If so, contact that person immediately. Did the interviewer ask for a sample of your artwork? Send it the next day. In any case, always send a brief note of thanks that can also serve as an appropriate close to the interview process. You might wish to send something like the letter on page 165.

This letter reinforces your interest in the job and will help to create a favorable impression of you in the interviewer's mind. In the letter, you come across as both serious and enthusiastic and indicate that you have responded to the request for a reference made during the interview. On the other hand, if you are not interested in the job anymore, it is a good idea to write and tell that to the interviewer as well. While you don't need to indicate any particular reason for withdrawing your application, you should be polite and remember to thank the interviewer for his or

7865 Green Meadow Lane
Anytown, TX 50554
June 5, 2003

Ms. Susan Hernandez
Personnel Director
Easy Electronics
4455 Easy Street
Hometown, AZ

Dear Ms. Hernandez:

My visit to Easy Electronics yesterday was informative and pleasant due to the time and effort you gave to our interview. Thank you for making me feel welcome. I am convinced that I would enjoy working with your company if it turns out that I am offered the position of management trainee in your personnel department.

I have contacted Dr. Ralph Yamato, my advisor at Central Texas University, regarding the letter of reference you requested. He assures me that you will receive it next week. If there is anything else I can provide, please do not hesitate to call or write. You mentioned you will be making your selection by July 1, so I look forward to hearing from you around that time.

Thank you again for your time and for considering my application.

Cordially,

Jonathan A. Smith

her time. You might say, "I find that my plans have changed and therefore request that you withdraw my name from consideration." If you have already taken another job you could allude to it by saying, "I have just taken a position with another company in the area, but I wanted to tell you that I appreciated your time during our recent interview." Skip the details about the other job's higher wages, better benefits, and nicer work environment. Someday you may be back applying for another job with the first company and your impression should remain positive. It is also possible that the interviewer will get another job with another company and you'll run into him or her in that setting. In any event, leave a friendly, positive impression that shows you to be a responsible person.

The three areas of preparation—what to do before the interview, how to conduct yourself during the event, and how to follow up—are easy to remember if you place yourself in the position of the person doing the interviewing. Who would impress you? What behaviors would they show? What manner of preparation would communicate thoroughness and reliability to you? By adopting a little of their perspective, you can help remind yourself of these areas of preparation.

Interview Formats

As was previously discussed, the most common **interview format** is one-on-one—one person asking most of the questions and one other person providing most of the answers. At other times you might be part of an interview team on which several people share the role of the questioner and one other person is the **respondent**. In this case, you will need to be sensitive to sharing time with the other members of the panel. Perhaps you will meet ahead of time and agree upon different areas for each person to cover. You might even develop questions for each other and work out a turn sequence so that you know when it is your time to ask questions.

As a respondent to a panel interview, your tasks and goals are the same as they are for a one-on-one interview. However, you need to include all the panel members in your answers, and you need to keep track of everyone's nonverbal responses to you. A simple rule of thumb is to give the person who asked you a question about fifty percent of your eye contact and spread the other fifty percent among the remaining members of the panel. If there are only two questioners, give the one who asked the question about seventy-five percent of your direct response, and spend about twenty-five percent of the time talking to the other person. This division of your attention helps to create a sense of having a direct conversation with the main source of the immediate question but, at the same time, it does not ignore the fact that other people are conducting the interviews, are listening very carefully to your response, and are forming opinions and making judgments about you.

Some interviews follow what is called the *funnel format*, which is a technique in which the interviewer starts with very broad questions and then focuses on progressively more specific questions.

To start off on an easy and general note, an interviewer says something like, "Tell us why you decided to apply to ACME." The questions will then become increasingly specific and narrow, hence the term "funnel," and move to questions such as, "Would you be comfortable working with a shifting job assignment?" and then to questions such as, "How many out-of-town trips per month would you be willing to take?" The funnel format begins with nondirective type questions and moves to more directive ones.

Some interviews can also be described as directive or nondirective overall. A general interview with your professor about your ideas for a future career may be nondirective in total approach. Counseling interviews can have that dimension, allowing the respondent to structure the whole event. At other times, especially when there is limited time and the objective of the interview is to obtain answers to a specific set of questions, a directive tone may characterize the whole interaction.

IMPROVING INTERVIEW COMPETENCY

During your lifetime, you are likely to be both interviewer and interviewee. You can improve your competency in both areas by building on what you have

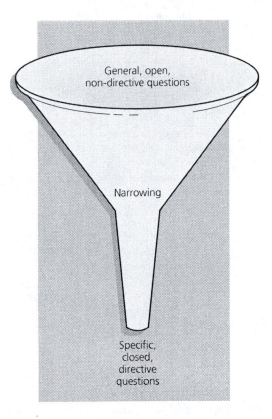

Interview questions generally follow a funnel pattern.

learned about communication competency in general. First, increase your background and knowledge about interviewing. That knowledge will provide you with a greater *repertoire* of types of questions and potential answers. When you analyze the situation from the perspective of both the questioner and the respondent, you can increase the skill and accuracy with which you *select* the right types of information to include on your resumé, in your answers and in your questions. When you think about and practice framing questions or giving simulated answers, you are rehearsing the *implementation* of your choices. Then you can implement again in the actual situation. Perhaps going through a mock interview with friends or with professionals available to you on your campus will give you practice in implementation. Finally, after practices or actual interviews, you can review and *evaluate* your choices. Sometimes you will also get feedback from your friends or others who have interviewed you. All of these steps contribute to your communication competency in interviewing—a significant activity in almost everyone's life.

In the interview at the opening of the chapter, the interviewer was trying to ask a variety of questions and also be open and encouraging. When you are the interviewee, interact with the tone, take the hints, and keep your messages clear and complete. Then, the interview might look something like this:

The graduating senior is seated in the office of the Personnel Director of a large and impressive company.

"First, tell me a little about yourself," begins the Director.

"Well, I like sports, was involved in clubs in school, and have been working part-time all four years of college, so there's quite a bit to talk about. Where would you like me to start?"

"How about sports? Any in particular?"

"I was in a softball league and play some basketball on weekends, but my favorite sport is one that not many people consider a sport—orienteering. I got involved in it after I joined the Wilderness Club. In fact, this year, I'm the coordinator."

"What about orienteering makes it attractive to you?"

"I like the challenge of being outdoors, working with a team, and facing the unknown—but with good preparation. I also get to know and work with a great group of people in an intense, focused, and personal contest. We divide up into teams; it's always fun to have a few new people as well as some experienced people on your team. Each event, win or lose, teaches me something about myself and about others."

"That sounds like a great activity. Can we look at your interest in management for few minutes? Any aspect of management experience or involvement you'd like to focus on in particular?"

"I took the standard courses, but I want to get involved in a career where I can use some of the approaches I'm learning from my orienteering experiences. I like teamwork, challenges, and a little risk. I'd be flexible about the specific assignment or division, but I like to keep some of these personal interests going in whatever position I'm in."

"OK. Let's talk a bit about your long-term goals."

Our senior is much better prepared to build from his experiences and ideas, and it is fairly certain that he has made a completely different impression this time.

SUMMARY

The three major interviewing activities are prior preparation, skillful conduct during the interview, and appropriate follow-up.

Preparation means doing some research about the subject. For example, if you are going to be the interviewer of applicants for a job, make certain you understand the job thoroughly. If your task is to interview people for an award, find out about the past history of the award and its requirements and intentions. If you have been sent materials beforehand, read them. Then you can focus your attention on the candidate during the interview. You can adapt and personalize your questions to the specific person and avoid the generic, uninteresting questions. By treating candidates as individuals, you can help put them at ease and elicit better answers from them.

Your conduct during the interview means more than just extending basic courtesy. As a trained communicator, you should also be able to apply the rules of active listening and give others the appropriate nonverbal communication they are seeking as feedback. Maintain eye contact with them, and keep note taking to a minimum. Try to create an open and encouraging atmosphere so that your respondents can express themselves clearly and completely. An open, encouraging attitude can assist the interviewee to provide the information you seek. Asking a variety of questions helps the interviewee provide a variety of responses.

As the person conducting the interview, try to keep the interview moving along. You may need transitions and connections to guide and direct the conversation if it veers off into a long discussion of a hobby you have in common or a recent vacation one of you enjoyed. You are responsible for setting both the tone and the pace of the communication. If you are on a strict time schedule, you might want to tell that to your interviewee. Sometimes job or selection interviews are deliberately structured to judge the candidates' capacity to handle stress, and may include tough questions. Otherwise, try to avoid making the interview difficult for the other person.

Following up after an interview can be accomplished with a letter, phone call, or personal visit.

If you follow these steps, keeping in mind both the interactive and directive nature of interviews, you can improve your competency in being interviewed and in conducting interviews. Your college may have workshops in interviewing, or you can take an entire course or read books dedicated to the interview situation. This introduction should be enough to get you started, but it is only a beginning. If you put these guidelines into practice and use them to build on your communication skills, then interviews will become a successful and rewarding part of your communication competency.

Key Terms

interview, **152**
directive questions, **157**
nondirective questions, **157**

resumé, **159**
interview format, **166**
respondent, **166**

EXERCISES

1. Make an appointment to interview the following people on your campus:

- A professor (not one of your instructors) who is an expert on a topic you will be researching for a class presentation

- A professional from your counseling center who advises students about career-interviewing skills

- One of your own instructors, but the interview should NOT be about class matters. Instead, make the interview about some aspect of your instructor's professional work, research interests, or recent publications.

In each case, follow the suggestions for conducting an interview. Compare the interviews by explaining how and why they were similar or different.

2. Get some sample resumés from your school's career center. There are a variety of ways to organize a resumé—chronologically, categorically, topically, etc. Which do you like the best? Why? Which do they recommend, if any? Why?

3. Pair off with a classmate, and interview that person for twenty minutes. Then reverse roles and become the one being interviewed. Did you learn anything from one role that can help you be more effective in the other role? Why does this switching seem to help?

4. Take a section of the "Help Wanted" ads from you local newspaper and try the same exercise in #3 above but, this time, play the role of the personnel director for a real job you find in the newspaper. Switch roles again and see if you can realistically create an interview that helps prepare you for a real job interview.

5. Prepare a resumé for #4 above, and bring it to class on the day of the interview. Help your partner by reviewing the one you receive when you are playing the personnel director. Listen carefully to any suggestions your partner may have about *your* resumé.

References

Biagi, Shirley. *Interviews That Work: A Practical Guide for Journalists.* Belmont, CA: Wadsworth, 1986.

Bostwich, B. E. *Resume Writing,* 3rd ed. New York: Wiley, 1985.

Hocking, J. E., J. Bauchner, E. P. Kaminski, and G. R. Miller. "Detecting Deceptive Communication from Verbal, Visual, and Paralinguistic Cues." *Human Communication Research VI* (1979).

Hocking, J. E. and D. G. Leathers. "Nonverbal Indicator of Deception: A New Theoretical Perspective." *Communication Monographs 47* (1980).

Park, Hee Sun and Timothy R. Levine. "A Probability Model of Accuracy in Deception Detection Experiments." *Communication Monographs 68,* 2 (June 2001).

Skopec, Eric W. *Situational Interviewing.* Waveland, IL: Prospect Press, 1986.

Stewart, C. J. and W. B. Cash. *Interviewing: Principles and Practices,* 4th ed. Dubuque, IA: Wm. C. Brown, 1985.

CHAPTER 10

Small-Group Communication

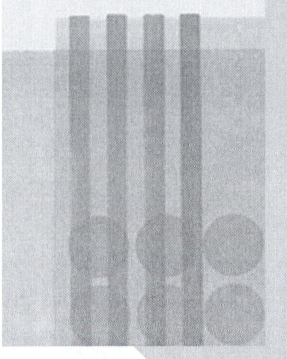

After reading this chapter, you should be able to:

- Describe the features of small group communication
- Describe the functions, types, and importance of small groups in your life
- Recognize the effects of personal influence and leadership in small groups
- Understand how small groups work together to build organizations
- Feel confidence in your ability to participate in member and leader roles in small groups

Most of the important decisions made about you have come from small groups. Most of the important influences that helped shape you have come from small groups. Most of the important activities you are involved in come through small groups.

Do you think that these statements are too bold? Think about the sheer number of rules and regulations that influence and govern your behavior. Speed limits, college admissions, and the amount of tax you pay on gasoline—all came about as a result of small group communication. Your family is a small group, and the way you functioned in that group when you were growing up and the way your family members treated you influenced the pattern of your development. In participating in most of the daily activities of your life—maintaining relationships with your family, a small circle of very close friends, a family of your own, a work group, or a career group—you act as a member of a small group (Rothwell, 1995).

You may make a few very important decisions on your own or with a significant other person, but most of your daily interactions with others will probably be in small group environments. Simply because you conduct so many of your activities in groups, it is important to know something about them, and to be good at working in them. If your experience is typical, you probably have been in some really good groups and some real disasters.

This chapter introduces you to some important aspects of small-group communication. It gives you an opportunity to learn a little about groups and to expand your own ability to make the groups you participate in more effective. Let's begin with a definition of small groups.

SMALL-GROUP COMMUNICATION

Several characteristics need to be present in small groups for them to be more than just a collection of individuals. In small-group **communication**, three or more individuals are involved in face-to-face interaction for a common purpose or goal. All of these factors need to be operating in order for true small-group interaction to take place.

Size

A small group must have a minimum of three people and up to about ten or twelve as a high-end limit. As you have already learned, only two people constitute a dyad or an interview. With three, there must be some sort of organization, pressures exist, and the interaction changes markedly from that of just two persons. The upper limit needs to be about ten or twelve, so that everyone can communicate with relative equality, ease, and directness. As you add people, you greatly increase the potential lines of communication until you are dealing with a huge number of potential interactions. The figure on the next page illustrates what happens when your small group grows.

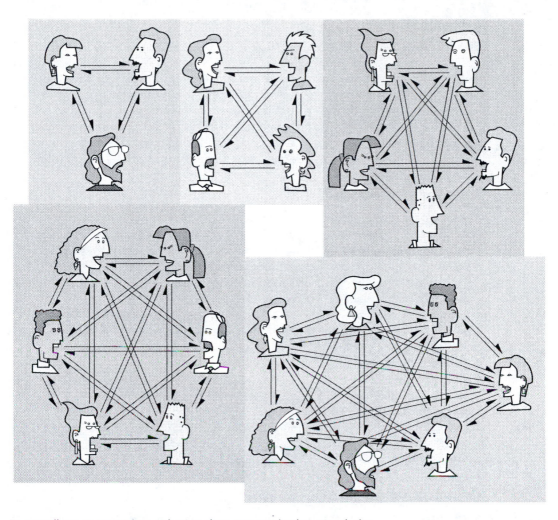

As a small group grows in number, so does communication complexity.

Have you ever noticed how, in groups more than ten, people will start little subconversations? They may turn to their neighbor and start a cross talk, or whisper a conversation while the rest of the group is focused on another speaker. This breakdown occurs because people want to be involved and, the more people in the group, the more difficult it is for everybody to have an opportunity to participate. The desire to communicate is still there, so people form small subunits out of the main group. The strain on the communication system increases with each additional person so that ten or twelve seems to be about the limit. Many people feel that between four and six is an ideal size because it permits a lot of ideas to flow but is still manageable in terms of opportunities to speak.

Interaction

The stress on the communication system that is generated by an increase in the number of participants is related to **interaction**, the second part of our definition of small group communication. As in any communication event, there must be senders and receivers in a small group. Here, those senders and receivers *influence* each other in an immediate sense. They have a full view of each other, so nonverbal messages can be processed at once, and they can hear each other easily, so verbal messages come through quickly and clearly. Taking turns, developing roles, and building a group relationship are the desired outcomes of small group discussion.

A Common Purpose

The group must interact about something, usually a common purpose or goal. This is the third major element in our definition of small group communication. The purpose or goal is usually what brings a group together in the first place and that holds it together in spite of tensions, conflicts, and strains.

Thus we can define a small group once again as a collection of three or more individuals, organized and interacting face-to-face for some common purpose. The exact number of members in a small group is not highly relevant relative to the other elements of interaction, organization, a common goal, and fairly equal access to the channels of communication. For example, an instructor lecturing to a room containing only four students does not constitute a small group because there is not much interaction during a lecture, nor is there equal sharing of the channels of communication. One person talks; the others listen and take notes. A common goal is missing as well. But when eight or ten people are focused on a common task, they are sensitive to each other so that everyone feels involved. There is equality and sharing, and they have the potential to become a successful small group with a **common goal**.

Organization

Most small groups are organized in some manner. An **organization** can be formed either with predetermined roles such as chairperson, secretary, and so on, or it can

DIVERSITY IN COMMUNICATION
Group Communication and Social Order

Among various cultures throughout world history, the wisdom of using small groups is evident. For example, the Jewish culture requires a *minyan*—a group of ten—in order to conduct certain types of religious meetings. The council of elders or chiefs of many Native American cultures vested power in a small group of leaders. Japanese culture still places great value on the collective wisdom of work groups and social groups. Western European governmental institutions developed councils of ministers, and churches established synods. Successful use of groups can create successful institutions.

evolve informally so that roles develop over time. For example, in one group, Anita might always start the discussion, Franco might bring the snacks, Art might keep good notes, and Willa might remind the group to keep focused and summarize the progress of the discussion.

These roles evolve from the group members' expectations and needs. At the same time, the mutual **influences** that they exert on each other eventually lead to the development of **group norms**. When people interact, they have certain expectations about how they should interact. Are group members expected to be on time for the group? Will they have an hour-long discussion and then take a break? Interrupt the discussion with witty remarks? Look to the oldest person for expert help? Norms are understandings about acceptable behavior in a particular group. In your classroom, one of the norms is that you raise your hand to get the instructor's attention and permission to talk. You may be a member of a small group that has norms about what you can and cannot do if you are to be perceived as a viable member of the group. Certain sororities may have a dress norm; a sports team may develop a celebration handshake or slap.

All of these norms develop as a result of the interaction within the group. Of course, different groups have different purposes and different ways of interacting. At the same time, most small groups can be categorized into one of three main types: a social group, a work group, or a decision-making group. Although each of these groups has all the elements mentioned in our definition, they are nevertheless unique in their focus and purpose.

TYPES OF SMALL GROUPS

The division of small groups by specific type or focus is common, and there are several ways to cluster them. For example, the group's reason for being together and staying together is an important characteristic and a good way to classify small groups. If being friends and interacting socially is your group's purpose, then you are interacting in a social group. If you have a task or job to do, then you would probably be classified as a member of a work group. If you are in a group whose goal is to come to some decision, then the development of that decision is your reason for being together, and you are in a decision-making group.

Each type of group is described in some detail to help you distinguish among them. Keep in mind that when a group's purpose changes, the group may shift from one type of group to another even though the group members remain the same. Distinctions among groups come from the groups' purposes and behaviors, not from the members themselves. Moreover, the same five people may move back and forth between types of groups in the same meeting. Observe group behavior for clues to the type of group you are in at any particular time.

Social Groups

Social groups include units such as families, roommates, or even a softball team. Throughout your life, you will find that there are structured times during which you engage in social interaction with others. Your family plans trips, vacations, meals, and conversation times. Your school has intramural sports, clubs, and outings. Your company sponsors annual picnics and a volleyball league. You may join a special type of social development group to learn about yourself, enhance your self-esteem, or confront and solve a personal problem. All these groups fulfill our need to interact with others. Do you recall the discussion of Schutz's inclusion, affection, and control needs in Chapter 8? Small groups provide us with the means to fulfill these needs. By creating social groups, we recognize the interactive dimension inherent in human behavior, and we sustain and support our psychological needs.

People form groups such as families, clubs, and teams to fulfill their social needs. We start out in life in a family, but we are so familiar with it that we might not think about it as one of the many forms of small groups. Recall from Chapter 7 the discussion of the many influences that helped to shape your self-concept. The effects of the family group can be long-lasting. There is much research about the special communication environment in the family group but, for now, think about a family as a small group that sees itself as a family.

Usually, this vision of a family involves a long-term commitment to the relationships within the family, even if those relationships are not always within the traditional family group of two parents and their children. It is becoming more and more common to consider as families groups that are not necessarily made up of a married couple and their children. Our definition of *family* might include a married couple, each of whom has brought children into the marriage, thus creating a blended family. It could also include a set of natural parents, their children, and adopted or foster children. Our definition also includes single parents with children and extended families having two or more generations of parents, children, uncles, aunts, cousins, and grandparents. Other family groups include people who are neither married nor related in any traditional sense, such as people living in communes and same-sex partners.

Each of these small groups acts as a **primary group**—one that is the major referent for its members, one in which its members share living and financial arrangements, and one that has certain characteristic and identifiable patterns of communication. These patterns flow out of the following characteristics: a long-term commitment, the ability to have and endure serious conflicts, a feeling of trust, and the development of roles and norms in the context of intimate and enduring relationships. A company or organization may form other social groups, such as teams or social committees.

As discussed earlier, people form and join groups to fulfill their social needs. We come from groups, live in groups, and organize our society around groups because we have social needs that only groups can provide. These needs include reference behavior, safety, solidarity, and esteem.

Reference Behavior   **Reference behavior** begins quite early in our lives. As babies, we constantly try to copy the behavior of the significant adults around us. Babies see their parents walking and using knives and forks to eat; they hear their parents talking. Babies respond by imitating those behaviors, and that is how they learn about the world and about their own capacities and abilities.

This same primary group—the family—also tells you about yourself. Your self-concept and personality are strongly influenced by your family's reactions to your behaviors. We also look to other groups, such as friends, fellow club members, or even gangs to show us how to behave. Peer pressure from these groups is so strong because our reference need is strong. Many college students enjoy clubs as a way of fitting into a new environment. Groups such as an intramural volleyball team, a fraternity, a debating team, and a concert committee are examples of referent groups. Sometimes reference power is so strong that people dress or talk alike. You can find this phenomenon in businesses that have a certain corporate look for all of their executives or in groups of friends who always go together to the same restaurant. In general, these behavior modifications help distinguish one group from another, one culture from another, one society from another. These differences are important because they provide us with some of the models and standards for our personal development and behaviors.

Safety and Solidarity Needs   It feels better to walk from the library to the parking lot late at night if there are other people walking that way as well. Even if you are not walking with them, it is comforting to be in the presence of others. Have you ever watched a horror movie on television by yourself? Wouldn't you have felt more comfortable if someone else had been around? There is a primitive instinct that reassures us of safety in numbers, and groups answer that need. **Safety and solidarity needs** can be met simply from being around other people.

It also feels good to be part of the crowd at a concert or stadium event. You identify with others in the crowd by wearing certain colors, T-shirts, or other emblems. In other words, you get a sense of solidarity from the group.

Unfortunately, this need for solidarity can go to an ugly extreme, as when groups get so large and out of control that people in the crowd take risks and engage in behaviors they would not even think of as individuals. In a phenomenon known as the *risky-shift*, people tend to shift their norms from a conservative risk level to a higher risk level when they are in a group. The same people would not make that shift when acting alone, but they lose their individual sense of responsibility in a group. The violent behavior of mobs is one example of this phenomenon.

Self-Esteem Needs   Groups can also be a place for us to meet our **self-esteem needs,** as we seek and gain approval from members of our groups. The roommates and friends who tell us we have done a good job when we get a high score on an exam and the award given to us by an organization for our outstanding performance are examples of how the need for esteem is satisfied in groups. Groups also provide us with recognition and reaffirm our sense of self-worth. In addition to your membership in work and school groups, you may also hold memberships in several social groups, ranging from clubs to volunteer groups to civic organizations. Personal development may come from therapy groups that help people overcome eating disorders, alcohol or other substance abuse, obesity, depression, or low self-esteem. Facing such problems with other people in a small group can be a highly effective way of treating them.

To summarize briefly, social groups are groups that provide interpersonal satisfaction through rewarding interactions. These groups provide us with references for our behavior and attitudes, may give us emotional support in times of stress, and often are the places where we find and build friendships. For most of us, the primary groups that are established in late adolescence consist of a few close friends from high school or college, a few work associates, and the members of our family. We may alter and modify these groups over time, as when we move to a new school, change jobs, or live in a different city. We can change location and still maintain contact with a few of our previous groups but with only a limited number of them. New groups and new friends will come into our lives.

The amount of influence that a group can exert on you depends on how much you value the approval of its members. Both on and off the job, you will value some groups more than others. Thus groups can affect your attitude and behavior to a greater or lesser degree. Social groups help to modify or reinforce our behavior, and they play an important part in many of our communications and in our day-to-day satisfaction with life.

Work Groups

In virtually every occupation, employees are placed together in units to accomplish their tasks. **Work groups** like this can also be found in classrooms. A project is due and a team of students works together to complete it. You might be a member of a civic club or other campus organization that has undertaken a project in which a group joins forces to get the job done.

Task Orientation   The notion of a task is what is important in all of these examples, and it binds the different settings described into the general category of work or task groups. These groups are different from social groups in that their goal is usually a visible, material product. In social groups, the *interaction* is the goal; in a work group, a *product* becomes the focus. The same elements of our original definition are still present, but the interaction centers on the accomplishment of a task, and the leadership centers on the skills and expertise of the members as they accomplish the task. While there may be personal dimensions to the interaction and while the group may work better if everyone feels included and liked, the interaction is determined by and focused on the product.

In a work setting, the implementation of an idea or plan is often turned over to a task force, or group, to complete, even if that group had little to do with generating the idea or plan. Businesses, therefore, are constantly trying to find ways to handle the problems that arise when there is a conflict between the group that came up with the idea or plan and the work group that must carry out the plan or idea. The work group may resent not being included in the early phases of the project, and the group's work may suffer as a consequence.

A work group must, first of all, organize its task. It must define the task and divide the work into logical job units. If you have ever worked on a group project in class, you know that it is important that each person have some clearly stated responsibility for a specific segment of the task. Otherwise, everybody tries to do

TECHNOLOGY AND COMMUNICATION

A Virtual Group?

With the widespread use of computer networking, some people hold simultaneous online conferences with others. By using speakerphones, several people can talk in the same telephone conversation. The development of fiberoptics for the transmission of sound and images has led to the virtual telephone, and the use of holographic projection makes it possible to beam the image of someone in a three-dimensional likeness. Current virtual reality game simulation centers place players in the center of interactive, wholly realistic situations. Will our idea of face-to-face interaction for small group communication change? Certainly, it is being expanded with the advances of technology.

everything, or many tasks are left undone or partially done because nobody had direct responsibility for them. Some tasks can be done cooperatively, some independently. For example, only one person needs to go to the library to look up dates or resources on a specific topic, but everyone should cooperate in planning the overall organization or format of the project.

Resource and Feedback Utilization   The wise work group will use the resources of the group members. If one person is an excellent typist but not a good proofreader, the group will divide the job so that all are responsible for parts of the task that they can accomplish realistically. A common practice in Japanese business settings is to have workers rotate through the jobs in a section of the company until, over time, they have tried every job in their area. Often, a worker excels in one area but not in others; the company can either provide that person with training or keep him or her on rotation until there is a comfortable fit between the person and a job. Even people who are very good at one job get rotated. In this way, they expand their knowledge and skill base and perhaps demonstrate that they are good candidates for advanced positions in the firm (Hatvany and Pucik, 1981).

Being open to change and feedback allows you to revise the task as necessary and to get constant updates on your progress. On the job, you might have a supervisor or manager who will help to establish a feedback loop for your group and who can help iron out many difficulties with the division of labor or establishing and meeting deadlines. A manager can be a resource for the group as well and will help you to understand that you are doing an important part of the task. Often, the success of one person depends on the success of the whole group and vice versa. The cooperative approach that most work projects demand makes it necessary for the group to understand how each member contributes to the completion of the goal.

As mentioned earlier, real groups are seldom completely task-oriented or socially oriented. Both group behaviors may be present. However, the social dimension of a work group can vary tremendously. A very concentrated project that has a high priority and little time to spare may have minimal social aspects to it. In a highly social group, the task almost becomes secondary.

Decision-Making Groups

A third type of group is characterized by a goal of reaching a decision at the completion of the group interaction. A city council or a student senate may be such a group because it does not produce a tangible product, nor is its purpose to develop social interaction.

Decision-making groups are brought together for the purpose of making a plan or decision about a task or policy question. You have already been in many decision-making groups. When your family has a conference to decide where to vacation, when you and your roommates meet to divide up household tasks, or when your club tries to find a way out of a financial crisis or to raise money, you are participating in a decision-making group.

These groups may be informal, and they may or may not have a designated leader. They meet to work out satisfactory solutions to problems of mutual concern. They may explore many ideas and alternatives before coming to a decision. There are probably hundreds of decision-making groups on your campus that plan concerts, decide on admission requirements, advise the president, revise course offerings, and evaluate the faculty for promotion. In business and industry, decision-making groups discuss the allotment of resources, union contract provisions, ways to develop new products, how to move the company into the future, and how to represent the employees' concerns to management.

Problem Solving   A special type of decision-making group is the **problem-solving group**. This group focuses on finding the best solution to a particular problem and on developing a plan of action for putting that solution into practice. If your group reaches the decision to select a particular student to receive the Outstanding Senior Award, then no plan is necessary. But if you want to solve the parking problem on campus or end the business recession, you need a complete plan.

There are specific steps to follow to create an effective, formal, decision-making or problem-solving group. First, the group must *define the problem.* This step is like creating a topic for an essay and is similar to the first step in the scientific method. Your group must also create and specify some *criteria* for judging the final outcome. "What are we looking for?" is a good question with which to start as you initiate your discussion about definitions and criteria. Developing a coherent system for evaluating your results will help you think about definitions and criteria.

When you begin, however, you may need to *brainstorm* for ideas, perspectives, and definitions. One problem with many decision-making groups is that the members stop brainstorming too soon. They take the first plausible definition of the problem and, in their eagerness to get on with the discussion, do not consider other possible definitions. Often, finding the best way to define the problem is part of the problem itself. For example, the county north of where I live was having problems with traffic congestion on a main highway. The decision makers used the most common perception to define the problem. They said, "The road is not big enough to handle these commuting cars every day." Predictably, the solution that they came up with was to widen the road. Suppose they had defined the problem by saying, "There are too many cars for this road." They might then have looked for solutions that decreased the number of cars, such as carpools, mass transit improvements, or a commuter rail system rather than increasing the number of road construction projects. The definition of the problem may, at the very first step of the project, actually predict and control the solution.

We have seen major changes of the definitions regarding nationwide decisions about energy. For many decades, we looked at our energy needs and decided that they were constantly in danger of not being met. We defined the energy problem solely as being one of not enough energy. The solution, therefore, was simply to get more of it. For years, that definition both predicted and controlled our approach to a comprehensive energy policy. In the 1960s and, more extensively, in the 1970s, policymakers and ordinary citizens began to rethink the problem. Some new definitions of the energy problem were generated. Inefficient use of the energy that we have could be said to be the real problem. This definition sparked a dramatic improvement in energy efficiency in everything from refrigerators to automobiles. Another way to define the problem was to say that dependence on the wrong sources of energy were also part of the problem. This definition led us to begin the exploration of solar, wind, geothermal, and other renewable sources of energy. The way we define a problem, and the way we *redefine* the problem over time, can be the breakthrough to finding solutions. In the section on improving your small group communication competency later in this chapter, some hints for good brainstorming are presented.

A good first step is to define the problem so that it is well thought out and well phrased. Taking the time to do this at the outset of your group's decision-making task can save you many difficulties later, in the discussion phase of the group's assignment. Work on getting a good definition of the problem and clear criteria for later use in evaluating the solution.

Second, now that you have a clear definition of the problem, take stock of *group resources*. Find out what expertise the members of your group have and what special abilities or backgrounds they have. You might discover a key person with talents or skills which, if used appropriately and effectively, will benefit the entire group.

Third, *create an agenda*. An agenda can be a complete plan of action or it can be the way you organize a meeting. By getting a plan in place, you can focus on the steps you need to take, and you can guard against skipping an important step. You might make an outline describing where and how the group is going to investigate the problem, the due dates and time frame for reporting information, and the dates and times of future meetings. You may also decide to break the problem down into small subunits so that your task will not appear to be so huge that it is overwhelming. After you have created the smaller topics, you can put them into a time frame to see how they fit and to decide which ones need be addressed first, which come second, and so forth. Feel free to try different orders of priority until you have an agenda that satisfies both the group's resources and its definition of the problem. The group needs to be assured that the agenda fits the group's purpose, time frame, and goals.

Fourth, once you have divided the decision-making process into parts that make sense, you need to *delegate the work*. For example, if there are several questions requiring some research, these questions can be handed out to various members for information gathering before the next meeting. If there are assignments that people can work on independently, they need clear instructions and a deadline. Other jobs, such as brainstorming or final voting, require that everyone work together.

Finally, *making a decision* combines the input that has been gathered from all sources—including appropriate results from the group's resources. At this point in the process, you might need to adjust your definition of the problem or your evaluation criteria on the basis of the inputs, so the group interaction is very important.

The group can come to a decision by using many methods. Sometimes, a vote is taken and the majority wins. At other times, it may be important for everyone to agree, so consensus will be reached by compromising or by merging ideas. Some groups allow just one person to make the decision. If that person has great expertise or power or is the one most affected by the decision, a group may want that individual to make the final decision. There are groups that cannot seem to come to a decision through discussion, so they average the suggestions offered. For example, you might need to decide how much to charge for admission to a concert. One way to decide is to add up all the suggested prices, find the average, and settle for that. Another way groups get out of a deadlock is to pick a decision at random. For example, drawing straws, tossing a coin, or pulling a name or number out of a hat are ways to let fate decide. The shortcoming of these methods is that they fail completely to take advantage of the intelligence, insight, hard work, and expertise of the group. They don't necessarily lead to hurt personal feelings, but they bypass the research the group has done, ignore the group's desires, and eschew human communication as the way to find the best solution or come to the best decision.

CRITICAL THINKING IN COMMUNICATION
Brainstorming

One way to develop your critical thinking skills is to engage in the process of brainstorming. In brainstorming, *creativity* is used to generate ideas and *judgment* is used to evaluate them. The critical thinking skills a group uses to create and apply appropriate criteria to the solutions resulting from group discussion will also help your group make better decisions throughout the decision-making process. You might be tempted to skip the critical thinking phase because of group pressure to conform, but it is important for any group to use critical thinking skills. This is especially true when the group is specifying the evaluation criteria it will apply to the solution *before* specific solutions are actually offered. Sometimes a brainstorming session on evaluation criteria at the very early stages of group interaction can help a decision-making group focus its energies and save its members from wandering off on tangents. A group may also decide to appoint a critical thinker, often called a devil's advocate or critical evaluator, whose job it is to hunt for and bring out any possible flaws or problems in the group's ideas. Although the role of devil's advocate is not a particularly enjoyable one for most people, it is not permanent, and it fulfills an important function; it brings the insights that can result from critical thinking into the decision-making process.

COMMUNICATION PATTERNS IN GROUPS

Communication interaction in small groups follows predictable patterns, or networks. When you look at the way messages go from one person to another in a group, you can observe some common lines or patterns of communication, also called **communication networks.**

An X pattern puts one person at the center of all messages, and everyone speaks to that person. This pattern is fairly formal and is used when a small group is holding its discussion in front of an audience, such as at a city council or board of supervisors' meeting. The X pattern may also be used if there is a great deal of interpersonal tension in the group; the chair serves as a neutral center.

A circle pattern is one in which each person talks only to one or two others. A group of roommates in which each person gets along with only two or three others or an office may have this pattern. In this pattern, not all members of the group communicate with each other. When they have one member in common to whom they all talk, they form a wheel pattern.

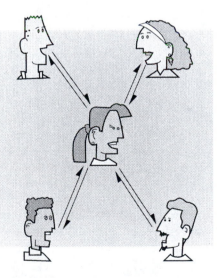

The person at the center of an X network can be a gatekeeper or a facilitator.

There is feedback in the circle network, but it can be delayed because it might not be direct.

The line network suffers from status, control, and feedback problems.

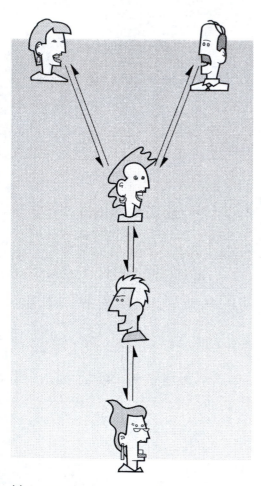

Many organizations have a Y network pattern.

The star network allows all members to communicate with each other.

The chain, or line, pattern does not involve a group. It is simply a line of communication links in which one person talks to one or two others. No connection is made to provide a return, as in the circle pattern.

A special type of chain is called the Y network. In this pattern, one person acts as a sort of center for three or four others. Everyone else gets farther away from the interaction as they chain out away from the center. Many business and other organizations have patterns like this, but it is very difficult for a small group to function adequately with a Y communication pattern.

The star network is the one that is used by most small groups that are communicating authentically. It is called the star because it is the best but also because it is represented by a pattern in which all members communicate with every member. Some writers call it the *all-channel network,* which certainly describes it. However, calling it *star* will remind you of how important it is for everyone in an effective small group to communicate directly with everyone else.

Please note that these diagrams do *not* represent seating arrangements; they represent message flow. If you are seated next to someone but speak only to the chairperson, you are in an X pattern of communication. On the other hand, where you sit is an important consideration and is covered in the next section.

ENVIRONMENTS

Much study has been done on the circumstances of small group meetings. Are the members seated in comfortable chairs? Can they see each other clearly? Is there a draft or noise? All these factors create an environment that can help or hurt group discussion. Think of the times you may have gotten together with others to study. Sometimes that worked well, but sometimes other people kept walking through the room, a television set was on in the next room, and the smell of pizza was coming down the hall. All of these intrusions from the environment can and do work against the effectiveness of a group session. Perhaps you had to sit on the floor because there were not enough chairs, or there was no table to write on, or the light was poor. These examples illustrate how important a good environment is to good group functioning.

With a little thought, you can plan an effective workspace to get the maximum benefit from group interaction. Perhaps you need to reserve a room in your apartment or in the library or the conference center. You can make certain that someone is responsible for answering the telephone during the session and for keeping other sounds away. Are you going to set a meeting for 5:30 in the afternoon? Think again, or be prepared for eating habits to interfere with your plans. Some campus groups always schedule their meetings for 12:00 noon. People are typically fifteen or twenty minutes late for these meetings because they have had to stand in line to get a sandwich. Then they bring the sandwich, a drink, and some chips to the meeting. Then they crunch, munch, and spill during the entire meeting. The focus of the group easily moves away from the topic and the task, and the groups that call these meetings regularly find low satisfaction and low productivity in their sessions.

If you pay attention to the environmental factors of time, space, setting, noise, and seating arrangements, you can enhance the value of the time you spend in groups. What you cannot influence to any great extent are the personal attributes members bring with them to every meeting. These attributes will be discussed shortly, but first let us look at the overall patterns that groups follow as they progress through a typical session.

PHASES OF GROUP DEVELOPMENT

The communication patterns of group development change according to four predictable **phases of group development**: orientation, conflict, consensus, and closure (Tubbs, 1995).

Orientation

The first phase of a group's interaction is called *orientation*. People get to know each other, get used to the setting, talk about the problem, look at the problem definitions, decide on appropriate evaluation criteria, and take stock of the resources and limitations of the group. Group members may assign, elect, or take on various roles, such as recording ideas, acting as moderator, or being in charge of social aspects of the group. Orientation, which can continue over several meetings, is a vital stage. If the group fails to take enough time to explore these areas, it runs the risk of skipping over a vital group resource or letting a job that is necessary for its work go unassigned. One of the most common reasons for a group's failure to create a positive outcome, and a common reason for members' dissatisfaction with the group process is a faulty orientation—an incomplete, rushed, first phase. Because members may be in a hurry, under some pressure to complete the project, or uninterested or distracted, your group may be tempted to run quickly through a superficial orientation. Take your time; good groundwork will help avoid problems later.

Conflict

Avoiding problems sometimes creates problems in phase two, which is called *conflict*. In U.S. culture, there is a tendency to avoid conflict. We are told, "Be polite! Don't argue!" Some personality types are very uncomfortable with any kind of conflict; in groups, these people exert pressure on the group to go along with whatever idea comes first, seems plausible, or is presented most forcefully. Be careful of group pressure to conform because it limits the use of group resources. Conflict is a necessary and valuable part of good group process. It helps with the evaluation of ideas so that the group comes to the best possible decision or outcome. To encourage healthy conflict in a group, consider the problems that may be associated with a suggestion and the positive and negative aspects of reaching a particular solution. Speak up about any concerns, reservations, or hesitations you may have, for example, about moving too fast. Others may have them too, and you can save your group problems in the decision stage if you voice your concerns *early* in the discussion.

Engaging in conflict is not easy, for there are tremendous pressures to conform. You may have heard of the famous study of small group pressures done by Solomon Asch (Asch, 1952). Asch hired a group of students to give wrong answers to a simple question. He then added a new person to the group, asked for the answer to his question, and observed whether the new person gave the obviously correct answer or conformed to the clearly wrong one given by the paid students. He put three lines on a blackboard labeled A, B, and C and then added another line nearby labeled X.

He asked each person to say out loud which line—A, B, or C—he or she thought was closest in length to line X. One after another, his paid students all said it was line A. When it was the new person's turn, he or she also said it was line A a significant number of times. Asch then brought in another new person. This time all his hired students said the answer was line C. The new person conformed and said that it was line C even though that was obviously the wrong answer. In fact, lines X and B were exactly the same length, but the pressure to conform was so great that many people simply would not go against the rest of the group. But, when Asch repeated the experiment, this time asking the people to *write* their answers silently, the unpaid subjects always wrote that the answer was line B. The incorrect answers were not a problem of eyesight, of confusing directions, or of distance from the board. They were merely a matter of not going against the group.

Conflict is an important phase because it helps group members avoid the pressures of conformity. Some groups even assign the role of critic, or devil's advocate, to a member. The role of the critic is to prevent quick unanimity in the group, which might short-circuit the critical thinking skills of its members.

On the other hand, too much conflict can also bog down a group. If the conflict is repetitive, personal, or focused on issues outside of the group goal or task, then it is time to leave it. By returning to the orientation phase for a while—reexamining the group's goals, definitions, resources, criteria, or the personal attributes of the members—it is possible to let go of an unproductive conflict.

Consensus

The third phase of group development is called *consensus.* This period brings the conflict phase to an end by having members begin to compromise, merge ideas,

Asch used this line diagram to test people's tendency to conform.

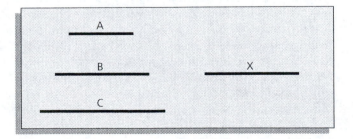

The Story of Communication
The Dangers of Groupthink

THE FREQUENT RESULT OF PRESSURE to conform is called *groupthink*, and there are numerous examples of this pressure resulting in bad decision making, even at the highest levels of government. One famous example happened during the 1961 Bay of Pigs invasion of Cuba by a small force of troops trained by the U.S. government. President Kennedy had a small group of advisors who relied on poor information and an exaggerated sense of their own superiority to make a decision to overthrow Fidel Castro's communist government in Cuba. No one wanted to appear to lack confidence in the information or the training, so there were no comments that were critical of the plan. This turned out to be total disaster. The failed attempt nearly brought the U.S. to a nuclear confrontation with the former Soviet Union, Cuba's main ally. The high status of the planners and the pressure of time prevented the group from engaging in the conflict phase; ideas were neither creatively formed nor critically examined. Peer pressure is not just a fact of life for junior high school gang recruits with low self-esteem. It happens among lawyers, teachers, government officials, physicians, and religious leaders. Just about everyone is subject to groupthink, and our history books are filled with examples of the resulting poor decisions.

and select from among the alternative ideas and solutions developed and debated during the conflict phase. "I agree with Phyllis's idea and think we could go with it and add Franco's suggestions for the deadline," is a statement that shows that the group is moving into this phase. Decisions are actually reached at this time, and people add their input to the final product. If there is a holdout who will not join the group norm, then it may be necessary to return briefly to conflict or even orientation. If that does not work, you may have to move to an alternative decision-making strategy, such as a majority vote.

Closure

Finally, *closure* is a short phase during which the final decision or product is brought forth, a restatement of the group goal and group consensus is made, and people reaffirm their support of the final decision. If any final, follow-through work needs to be done, it is assigned and accepted at this point.

A group may go through all of these phases each time it meets (Fisher, 1970) and, at the same time, have a long-term focus that carries through to each meeting. It is also possible to go through these phases for each item of business at a single, decision-making meeting. For example, your student senate or local city council may move through each of these four phases for every item on the agenda. Watch their communication behaviors, and you will be able to identify each phase easily. In your own small group discussions, remember that effective groups go through all four phases, and skipping or unnecessarily shortening any one, especially the first one, can lead to problems later.

PERSONAL INFLUENCES

Earlier chapters of this book discussed different aspects of communication and individual personalities. You may recall that some aspects of each person will always be evident in any group setting. Some of these attributes come about as a result of the small group interaction, while some are independent of the communication within the group.

Group-Related Influences

Those personality characteristics that develop from small group interaction include status and power. **Status** is the esteem or regard the members have for each other. It can come from previous success, reputation, or nonverbal communication signals that show wealth or experience. **Power** is related to status in that it is the ability to influence the group. For example, you can use your expertise to get the group to adopt your ideas. Or you may try using reference to others by saying, for example, "I know the boss really well." Some people, commonly in work settings, use rewards or punishments to influence the decisions and actions of others. Raises, bonuses, good grades or evaluations, and promotions are examples of rewards. Sometimes you may be an elected leader and therefore have legitimate power over the flow of information in your group. These personal variables can affect group dynamics—who sits where, who gets listened to or ignored, and who will help shape the final outcome of the group effort.

Independent Influences

The *personal influences* that are generally independent of the group interaction are usually those that the members had before they joined the group. A member's personality type is fairly constant; if you are an easygoing open-minded individual, you will most likely be that way in a group. We dread working in a group with someone who is bossy, pushy, demanding, or close-minded, because we know they will bring those qualities to the small group interaction.

Age, gender, and health can affect the way people function in a small group, yet they are not consequences of the group interaction and will remain constant after the group has finished its task. However, they do affect the way the group as a whole operates. If you are significantly older or younger than the rest of the members of your group, you may be more or less likely to be selected leader or more or less influential in the decision-making process. People tend to value experience, so if you are obviously younger than the rest of the group, you may find it difficult to have your ideas treated with the same intellectual weight as those of an older person. Even if your ideas have merit, they may be missed because of your young age. This problem is especially frustrating for young people recently out of college who enter a workplace filled with experienced employees. The existing group may be somewhat resistant to suggestions or ideas from new, younger personnel. For the same reason, a senior, not a sophomore, will probably head a sorority on campus.

While much progress in equality for women has been made in recent decades, our culture still shows a bias for giving leadership, influence, and power to males rather than females. This is similar to the way people from majority cultures have been favored over minorities. If you are female, your gender alone may influence a group to ask you to be the secretary for the group or to bring the refreshments, whereas you may be asked to chair the meeting if you are male. You may be utterly incompetent at a particular job and wonderful at another. Because stereotypes persist and are difficult to identify and overcome, the step of *identifying the group resources* is very important. An objective assessment of the talents that are available among the group members allows the group to use members' abilities realistically. In the same context, people with physical handicaps are often passed over because others are apparently reluctant to focus on their abilities rather than on their disabilities. People from minority races or cultures are also familiar with the reactions of others who ignore their potential out of prejudice.

You know intellectually that these factors influence our reactions, but so many of these reactions are subconsciously motivated. So you need to make certain you are conducting an objective analysis of peoples' talents. Monitoring your own communication behavior is the best way to develop sensitivity to the talents of people who are different from you.

LEADERSHIP INFLUENCES

When you think of small groups, you should automatically think about **leadership**. The two concepts seem to fit naturally together, and many people believe that one reason to teach about small group communication is to help students develop their leadership abilities. This perception is true to some extent but, unfortunately, many people think of leadership in terms of a single person *directing* a group, when leadership is better defined as *any behavior that influences the group*. We like to think of leadership in its positive sense; therefore good leadership behaviors are those that help the group to attain its goal. Bad leadership prevents or deters the group from achieving goals.

Leadership is the quality a group member needs to help the group meet task goals. Leadership also helps the group to meet social goals. Some people are good at influencing part of the group discussion, but others are not. For example, Todd reserved the room, set up the tables and chairs, and adjusted the thermostat but said very little during the discussion. Did Todd play a leadership role? How about Cora, who brought the encyclopedia and dictionaries that everyone used all evening? Then there was Maya, who called the meeting to order, and Greg, who brought chips and drinks and kept notes on what was said.

Each of these behaviors helped the group—influenced it for the better to accomplish its task. Some people would look just to the chairperson as having leadership, and they would miss all sorts of leadership activity going on in that particular small group. Influences can also be negative, as when Freida barges in late, asks the group to give her advice on purchasing a new car, then leaves without giving the group the piece of information on which they were counting. In this example, Freida has exerted a negative influence on the group's task.

There are four types of group leadership climates, or styles: authoritarian, democratic, laissez-faire, and abdicratic. *Authoritarian* leadership is characterized by the dominance of one person and the acceptance of that dominance by others. A single member can have complete influence over a group, and the group goes along with it. If the group is in an emergency situation, its members probably want an authoritarian figure who is also an expert in the work of the group. Fighting a fire, running an army or a police force, or meeting a midnight deadline for a project will most likely produce leadership in the authoritarian mode. The problem is that most members do not rate having an authority figure as being personally satisfying, so the group will probably lose some of its resources.

We value *democratic* leadership in our culture because it rates high in both utilization of group resources and member satisfaction. If time is not a big problem and members have an abundance of good input, then a sharing of power, decision by consensus, and consultation might be appropriate. Clubs often operate in a democratic mode, as do members of most voluntary associations.

You may remember *laissez-faire* leadership from your political science or history classes. It is characterized by a let-it-happen or hands-off style of leadership. Minimal direction is offered, and the group just finds its way without much of an agenda or deadline. A party is a good example of laissez-faire leadership. Some planning is necessary, but once the party is launched, no goal or task need drive the group. A laissez-faire approach might work well for social interactions, but what a disaster it would be for building a house, producing a car, or fighting a fire.

The fourth type of leadership is barely visible and occurs in those brief periods of time when everyone in the group actively rejects any leadership at all. It is called *abdicratic* leadership, and it is almost a contradiction in terms. Members are reluctant to take steps to influence the group, and the group quickly rejects any attempts that are made. The group is in a state of rebellion, and group disintegration is often quick to follow. In large societies, anarchy and revolution are the expression of this behavior. Curiously, the style of leadership that is most likely to follow the abdicratic style is the authoritarian style, bringing our styles around full circle. Imagine a study group in which the members start to wander off the topic, begin to play music, order out for pizza, drift to side conversations, and lose all focus. Someone may finally shout, "Let's get back to work!" and begin to turn off the music, put away the pizza, and try to take charge. This person may become an authoritarian leader. This is a good demonstration of how leadership styles can come around full circle.

OUTCOMES AND MEASUREMENT

Once you have settled on your group type, worked on creating an appropriate setting and leadership style, and taken into account all the personalities and resources in your group, you are ready to assess the **outcomes** of the interaction. How do you evaluate a group?

The easiest way to begin is to ask, "Did the group reach its goal?" If members set out to have a good party and did, then the group was successful. If the members set out to get good grades on an exam the next day but instead had a good party, then the group did not reach its goal.

Measurement of group outcomes can be done in many ways. If the group is a task group, then you can look solely at the product. Sometimes, you may wish to measure member satisfaction. Often, a combination of the two is helpful, because people who are enjoying the group experience are likely to facilitate a good outcome. If a group is well organized, uses group resources, and establishes effective communicative interaction, then its final outcome will be better than that of a group that fails to create such a positive communication climate.

In an interesting series of experiments, communication scholar Dale Leathers measured the communication processes of a number of small groups and then had independent raters assess the quality of the products these groups produced (Leathers, 1969). A consistent finding was that if the discussion process was disrupted or faulty in any way, then the product was judged to be inferior. This latter judgment came from people who had no knowledge of how the group had behaved; they saw only the final product. If you think that it does not matter how people are getting along and it matters only that the job gets done, Leathers' research could change your mind.

Group process, as differentiated from group outcome, can be measured by assessing the good communication skills and attributes you have learned about throughout this text. Clear use of language, respect for others' opinions, good use of evidence and logical thinking, attention to criteria and definitions, and equal opportunity to express opinions are among the important qualities to look for when evaluating small group communication processes.

ORGANIZATIONS: GROUPS WORKING TOGETHER

When a collection of groups works together within a large system, they are most likely part of an organization. Many of the characteristics of small groups—networks and patterns, personal influences, leadership, and outcomes—are also seen in the larger, multiple group system of the organization. Sometimes, the effect on the organization of one or more of these characteristics is magnified and becomes very powerful. For example, status in an organization can become so strong that it is intimidating. Suppose you were a production line employee at a large company and the senior vice-president in charge of production came walking through your department one day, unannounced. If she were to ask you how things were going, you might say that things were just fine, even if you had a complaint. Workers are more likely to make a complaint to an immediate supervisor and to increasingly distort their messages in a positive direction as the status of the recipients becomes higher and higher (Krivonos, 1976).

Communication in an organization takes time, and people at message intersections who have control over the flow of messages can become very powerful. For example, a secretary who gets all the messages and distributes all the memos can be an important person. By being at the crossroads—where information is exchanged—the secretary becomes very knowledgeable. People in this position are sometimes called *gatekeepers* because they can either let information pass through or hold it up. Message distortion is more likely to occur in an organization than in a small group for the obvious reason that, in a small group, there is immediate feedback to check information. In an organization, not only do delays distort information, but messages are filtered and screened by the people who receive them and then pass them along. If the message starts out from very high in the organization, it may become more and more negatively perceived as it travels downward. Rumor begins to color the message so that the message may be very different by the time it reaches the entire organization. Imagine a college president talking about impending budget cuts and saying, "We'll have to do more with less next year." If word spreads from one level down to the next, there may be rumors around campus of classes being canceled, salaries being cut, and people being laid off, all within days of the transmission of the original message.

Some organizations build in automatic correction mechanisms, such as bulletins, suggestion boxes, open meetings, and direct conversations to guard against and correct distorted messages. Yet distorted messages seem to be a fact of life for large organizations. Good communication tactics that counteract this phenomenon use the small group principles of feedback and response to help minimize the negative effects on messages due to the sheer size of the organization. For example, suppose a major corporation decides to expand its operations and build a new plant in another state. After hearing the news, someone might wonder aloud whether that means cutbacks or closing of existing plants. Pretty soon others are repeating that they heard from so-and-so that their jobs are being relocated. The rumor started on the basis of some factual information; then, as the information was passed along, it became distorted. Finally, a worker asks the area supervisor about the "impending layoff plan," which motivates the supervisor to ask top management for clarification. The next day, a bulletin comes from top management explaining that a new plant opening will not affect the operations of the existing facility.

A final effect is generated by the variables of competition and cooperation in large organizations. If resources and rewards are plentiful, it is fairly easy to get small groups within an organization to cooperate. However, as is more often the case, if resources are limited, there will be a competitive atmosphere in the organization. If held to an optimal level, competition can increase both motivation and loyalty to the small group. At its worst, it can lead to the deliberate spreading of misinformation, secrecy, suspicion, and even sabotage. A good management team is aware of the potential for communication conflicts in an organization and uses proven techniques of interpersonal and small group communication to moderate them.

IMPROVING SMALL-GROUP COMMUNICATION COMPETENCY

One way to increase your effectiveness as a small group participant is to understand the processes of small group interactions and the influences that help those processes to become effective. For example, a goal must be clearly defined for a group to reach it. If the goal for some people is social and the goal for others is to get some work done, you can help by initiating discussion about the purpose of the group so that the conflict has a chance to be resolved. Other problems can be avoided if the group recognizes that the most appropriate leadership style for situation A may be completely wrong for situation B. Can you move from a democratic to an authoritarian or laissez-faire style if that is what your group needs? By learning about the variety of group communication styles, you can increase your *repertoire* of communicative behaviors.

Selection of the most appropriate behavior from your repertoire is the second step to communication competency, and it is often a difficult one. For example, if you are involved in a strong disagreement, it may be hard to step back and analyze your own behavior to select a more appropriate behavior for that situation. If you have a personality clash, selecting a different style of group leadership may be a challenge. You may find it difficult to work with someone on decision-making criteria for the group if you have just gone through an extended conflict with that person. Selection can involve some experimentation as well. If you try one behavior and it does not work, analyze the situation again, go back to the alternatives you have learned about, and try another.

The process of analysis can involve the entire group. One useful method for generating possible solutions and then selecting from among them is called **brainstorming.** This method of small group communication is one you may know about, yet few groups use it when it is most needed or do it very well. The method is basic, and it has two phases. The first phase involves the generation of a large number of ideas as quickly as possible. During this period, any idea is acceptable, and no verbal or nonverbal criticism, especially any that is negative, is allowed. If someone tosses out an idea that you do not like, don't waste a moment thinking about it. Keep generating your own ideas or playing *off* their suggestions to come up with other ideas. Someone should be appointed to the job of recorder and should write down every idea mentioned—humorous, brilliant, bizarre, off-color, or nonsensical. The first phase must generate a large pool of ideas, and anything goes. Usually, between five and fifteen minutes are allotted for this phase. Do not be tempted to stop when there is a pause and give up by saying something like, "Well, I can't think of anything else; let's quit now." Give the group a set amount of time to brainstorm, and keep at it until that time is up. It is important that you avoid evaluating other people's ideas *and* that you avoid doing any self-criticism. For example, you might get a quick inspiration, then judge it yourself, decide that it sounds silly, and never mention it. Such internal censoring hurts the entire effort. You might be right; your idea might be silly but it could very well inspire someone else in the group to come up with a spin-off idea that exactly solves your group's problem. If you hold back, you markedly diminish the total resources of your group. Does this advice mean that you never evaluate? Not at all. *Evaluation* is the second step.

Once your group has generated a number of ideas and has written down all of them, it is time for an *evaluation* of those ideas. Sometimes a short break helps to keep the two phases—brainstorming and evaluation—separate. Now go back over the list of ideas. Usually people neither remember nor care who said what. They want to pick through the ideas and select those that seem to fit the group's goal. If you are following the five-step decision-making model outlined earlier, you will have a definition of the problem or some evaluation criteria to help sort out the various ideas and suggestions into those that correspond to the group's goal and those that do not. Brainstorming and evaluation can be excellent tools for generating and selecting the option that best fits your group's needs.

Once you have selected your plan or strategy, it is time for *implementation.* Putting into practice or applying the selected approach to the problem will require the cooperation of the whole group. The interaction and mutual dependence of small groups are controlling factors that require that the group work together. If you have taken care to carry out the brainstorming and the development of the evaluation criteria in a fair manner, you will have an easier time putting the group's choice into practice. Implementation may require that jobs be identified and assigned appropriately, an aspect of communication competency that is also covered in a five-part decision-making plan.

The *evaluation* aspect of communication competency can take place in small steps throughout the duration of the group's work. When you gather feedback and incorporate that feedback into the evolution of the group's activities, you are making use of the strategy of evaluation. Of course, there is

▶ IMPROVING COMPETENCY
Overcoming Stereotypes

Many small group members carry around stereotypes about what kind of person is good at a particular job or role. Such attitudes block small groups from achieving full potential. These stereotypes may be based on age, gender, race, ethnicity, level of education, or other factors. They may be those you have about other members, or they may even be about yourself. Remember, one of the primary suggestions in this chapter is to utilize the resources of your group, and these resources must be recognized before they can be effectively included in the group interaction. This may mean that you need to volunteer for a variety of jobs or take on role behaviors different from those you typically assume in a small group. Take time for job explorations. In addition to exploring your own talents, remember to check with other members about their talents, preferences, and experiences. Check your own assumptions about who knows the most about baseball or who can type fastest or who knows all the current television shows or who can repair computers. Work to include all of the group's resources as a way to make your group as effective as it can be.

always the final evaluation. Your group had a successful party, built a great car, or turned in a highly rated project for your class. You can also evaluate member satisfaction, the quality of the group's communication interactions, and the quality of the project's final outcome.

Any increase in your communication competency is a result of your being able to use evaluation as feedback. You will be able to identify ways to do things differently in your next small group. Moreover, you will have increased your repertoire of potential behaviors, and the decision-making process in your next group can begin on a stronger footing.

SUMMARY

Small groups are a fact of life and, in this chapter, we have barely scratched the surface of the many factors that go into successful small group interaction. Many schools have entire courses devoted to small group communication. Some courses focus on the skills that are needed to function well in small groups; others spend an entire term exploring the research that has been done on groups. You can begin immediately to improve your performance as a competent, small group communicator, and you can also work at developing various aspects of that ability throughout your life. Because small groups are such a common and important aspect of our lives, the time and effort you spend enhancing your abilities as an effective communicator will be well worthwhile.

Key Terms

small-group communication, **172**
interaction, **174**
common goal, **174**
organization, **174**
influence, **175**
group norms, **175**
social groups, **175**
primary group, **176**
reference behavior, **176**
safety and solidarity needs, **177**
self-esteem needs, **177**

work groups, **178**
decision-making groups, **180**
problem-solving group, **180**
communication networks, **183**
phases of group development, **186**
status, **189**
power, **189**
leadership, **190**
outcomes, **191**
measurement, **192**
brainstorming, **194**

EXERCISES

1. Make a list of the various groups in which you participate during a typical week. Identify those that are formal and those that are informal. Next, designate the ones that are primarily social, those that are task-oriented, and those that are focused on decision making. In how many groups do you participate in a week's time?

2. Consider the small groups that you identified in the first exercise. What roles do you play in each? Do you find yourself engaging in any leadership behaviors? What leadership styles—authoritarian, democratic, laissez-faire, or abdicratic—do you find in each of your groups? Do some styles seem more or less appropriate for a particular group than other styles? If so, why or why not?

3. Peer pressure is a force that often leads to conformity. What examples of peer pressure can you observe on a daily basis, either in yourself or in others?

4. The next time you are in a group, try to apply the five steps of problem solving. For example, it can be very stimulating to engage in brainstorming if, thanks to you, everyone is aware of the rules and follows them. Your continuing efforts with the remaining four steps can also help give your group focus and energy throughout their problem-solving discussions.

References

Asch, Solomon. *Social Psychology.* New York: Prentice-Hall, 1952: 450–501.

Fisher, B. Aubrey. "Decision Emergence: Phases in Group Decision Making." *Speech Monographs* 37 (1970): 53–66.

Gibson, Melissa K. and Michael J. Papa. "The Mud, the Blood, and the Beer Guys: Organizational Osmosis in Blue Collar Work Groups." *Journal of Applied Communication Research* 28, 1 (February 2000).

Hatvany, Nina and Vladimir Pucik. "Japanese Management Practices and Productivity." *Organizational Dynamics* (Spring 1981): 5–21.

Krivonos, Paul. "Distortion of Subordinate to Superior Communication." *Meeting of International Communication Association.* Portland, Oregon (1976).

Leathers, D. G. "Process Disruption and Measurement in Small Group Communication." *Quarterly Journal of Speech* 55 (1969): 287.

Rothwell, J. Dan. *In Mixed Company,* 2nd ed. New York: Harcourt, 1995.

Scott, Craig R. and Jolie C. Fontenot. "Multiple Identifications during Team Meetings: A Comparison of Conventional and Computer-Supported Interactions." *Communication Reports* 12, 2 (Summer 1999).

Tubbs, Stewart. *A Systems Approach to Small Group Interaction,* 5th ed. New York: McGraw-Hill, 1995.

Preparing Speeches

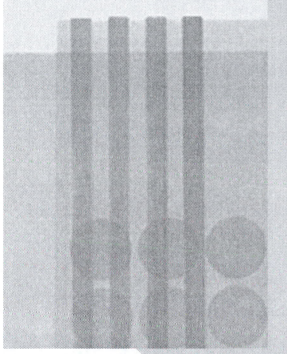

After reading this chapter, you should be able to:

- Understand and apply the principles for outlining and organizational development of speeches
- Describe and use techniques for analyzing an audience
- Identify and locate a variety of supporting material
- Feel competent to create and present a speech in public
- Have a commitment to communicating with your listeners
- Create an acceptable, formal speech outline

In preparing a public presentation, you need to consider many factors, including yourself, your listeners, your topic, the occasion, the setting, the amount of time you will have, and the purpose. Central to any message, however, is the necessity that it be clear. If you lack clarity, your message is likely to be misunderstood. The foundation of clarity is organization, and good organization will help you to accomplish all of your other goals.

After learning about organization, you will learn how to analyze your listeners so that you can adapt your message to them. Different types of supporting materials and how to find them are also covered in this chapter, but organizing your message is the starting point. Two approaches to help you with organization will be discussed: outlining principles and organizational development in speeches.

OUTLINING PRINCIPLES

This section reviews the outlining principles and techniques that you have been studying for many years in language arts classes. You are probably familiar with the major symbols that are used to organize an outline: Roman numerals, capital letters, Arabic numbers, lowercase letters, numbers in parentheses, and letters in parentheses. This system is universally used in outlines for both written and oral composition. These symbols have been developed over many years as a way to keep the sequence and relationships of ideas in order. Speaking well involves much more than just talking clearly. A coherent message is one that is carefully constructed and attentive to techniques of organization from the very beginning. When you have selected a particular type of speech and the appropriate thesis to go with it, an outline provides you with a complete structure to guide you in constructing a speech.

General Outlines

The outline format lends itself to a variety of purposes. For speeches, you can select from among several patterns of development, all of which fit into the same

CRITICAL THINKING IN COMMUNICATION
The Logical Structure of Outlines

One characteristic of an outline is that it is logical. If you place items in logical sequence and appropriate relationship to each other, you will be able to create an organized speech. The linking together of superior, coordinate, and subordinate ideas can help you to move from large subjects to specific, supporting materials. It helps to cluster ideas or examples because the items in these clusters will form the subdivisions of your speech outline. In the outline, place main ideas in superior position and details or explanations in subordinate position. The main ideas should fit together logically.

general outline structure. A simple outline that can be used in virtually any pub-lic-speaking situation has five main parts. Each of these parts is defined briefly; then some rules and guidelines for creating an outline are presented.

Sample Outline   A five-part speech outline looks like this:

I. **Introduction.** About ten percent of your time can be spent on the intro-duction. A brief story, an interesting example or statistic, a startling state-ment, a quotation, or an illustration can work well as an introduction.

II. **Thesis sentence.** This statement represents the main idea of your speech. It also expresses the central purpose of your speech.

III. **Body of the speech.** About eighty-five percent of your time will be spent on the body of the speech. A preview of the main ideas in the body of the speech can be a good transition from the thesis sentence to the body itself. The body of the speech usually has between two and five main subsections. This example has four main subdivisions.
   A. First main subdivision
      1. Supporting material for A
      2. Supporting material for A
   B. Second main subdivision
      1. Supporting material for B
      2. Supporting material for B
      3. Supporting material for B
   C. Third main subdivision
      1. Supporting material for C
      2. Supporting material for C
   D. Fourth main subdivision
      1. Supporting material for D
      2. Supporting material for D
      3. Supporting material for D

IV. **Conclusion.** About two to five percent of your time will be used for the conclusion. Include a brief review of A, B, C, and D; the thesis sentence; and the introduction.

V. **Sources/bibliography/references.** You may list sources alphabetically by author or in footnote order—the order in which they appear in your speech. You do not read this section aloud during your speech, but you may cite a specific source at the point in the speech when you are pre-senting information from that source. List your sources in a standard format.
   A. First source
   B. Second source
   C. Third source

Introduction and Thesis   The outline format presented here shows how you can link your ideas together. Each part has a function that relates to every other part. The introduction is where you capture the audience's attention so that your lis-teners will be ready to focus on your thesis sentence. You can take these moments—about ten percent of your total time for a short speech—to become comfortable with the situation and to let your audience become accustomed to looking at you and hearing your voice. You can also set the mood you want for your presentation. Will it be humorous or serious? Let your listeners clearly understand your mood from the beginning.

The **thesis sentence** is the main idea of your entire speech, but should you start with it? At the very beginning of a speech, the audience is often not quite focused on you; if you begin by saying, "Today, my speech is on…," they might miss your main idea. In addition, such an unimaginative and uninteresting opening will disappoint your listeners. Do not use your thesis sentence until after the introduction. Then make it simple and to the point. Everything else in the presentation is controlled by your thesis sentence. The introduction must lead up to it, and the body must explain and support it. The thesis sentence is the most important— but also the smallest—part of your speech.

Body and Supporting Materials   The **body** is where the speech takes shape and where you spend about eighty-five percent of your time. The body clarifies, explains, extends, defends, and supports your thesis sentence. Usually, the explanation of your thesis sentence can be broken down into two to five main subsections or subdivisions. Later in this chapter, you will see some examples of how to divide the body into logical patterns. For now, note that each subsection has specific supporting materials under it.

Supporting materials are the specific items that you use to illustrate or prove your point. They may be examples, statistics, short stories, illustrations, quotations, visual aids, or statements. Supporting materials can include personal experiences; case histories; results of opinion polls, research studies, or experiments; and materials from songs, literature, or poetry. One way to enrich your presentation is to use a variety of supporting materials. Different types of supporting material are explained in more detail later in the chapter.

Conclusion   The fourth subsection of the outline is the conclusion, which is a short review of the main subsections of the body (but not the specific supporting materials), the thesis sentence, and a reference to the opening material that you used in the introduction. The conclusion should be brief—about half as long as your introduction—and it should tell your listeners that you have come to a close.

Sources   Finally, you need a list of your sources—Part V in the sample outline. Sources can be a standard bibliography, a list of references, or footnotes like those you add to the end of a term paper. You need to credit the sources of your material to avoid a charge of plagiarism. Plagiarism means using someone else's ideas or words without giving that person credit. It is dishonest—a form of academic and intellectual theft—and a serious crime in any field. Certainly you need to use and probably depend on other people's work and ideas to create your own. By giving those sources credit, you acknowledge their contribution to your effort. In fact, you build your own credibility by making listeners aware of all the experts you have consulted. There are many reasons to make certain that you properly credit all work that is not your own.

There are several ways to acknowledge this credit. The Modern Language Association (MLA) format is the format that most colleges use. The MLA is a national group of English teachers, scholars, and others who are interested in the field of English. They publish the *MLA Handbook for Writers of Research Papers* (Gibaldi, 1999), which presents standard ways to cite sources for everything, from books, websites, and newspapers to interviews. The order of information for citations is usually author's name (last name first); the title of the article or book; the name of the larger work if the material is only one section of it; the publisher, city, date; and perhaps the page numbers. This is the format you have probably been using on every paper you have written since eighth grade. For this book, the citation would took like this:

> Zeuschner, Raymond. *Communicating Today: The Essentials*. Boston: Allyn and Bacon, 2003.

If you were using an article from a magazine or a journal, it would took like this:

> Rubin, Rebecca B. "Assessing Speaking and Listening Competence at the College Level: The Communication Competence Assessment Instrument." *Communication Education* 31 (January 1983): 19–33.

There are minor variations on these formats, but the important information is always present. You need to give listeners and readers enough information to easily locate the source. Although following the form makes your bibliography look correct, what is really important is that you credit all your sources in a clear and consistent way.

Subordination and Grouping

Among the rules to keep in mind as you create any outline for any message are the simple rules of subordination and grouping which can help you to create a logical structure. Always remember that your ideas exist in relationship to each other; in an outline, the more abstract or general main ideas are listed to the left and the smaller, detailed, supporting ideas are indented to the right. The *rule of subordination* tells you whether something should be labeled with a Roman numeral or a capital letter—that is, whether the item is a main idea or a supporting detail.

The *rule of grouping* tells you that all related ideas need to be in the same group. If a supporting detail relates directly to subdivision X, it needs to be in X's group. If it's not related to X, then it belongs to Y's group or Z's group. If it is not related to any of these, it belongs in yet another group or in a different outline.

Sample Outlines   The rule of grouping says that there must be a direct link among all the items in the group. At the beginning, the outline might look like this:

I. Main idea X
  A. First subordinate idea related to X
  B. Second subordinate idea related to X
II. Main idea Y
  A. First subordinate idea related to Y
  B. Second subordinate idea related to Y
  C. Third subordinate idea related to Y
  D. Fourth subordinate idea related to Y
III. Main idea Z
  A. First subordinate idea related to Z
  B. Second subordinate idea related to Z

The rules of subordination could continue further under X—A and B; or under Y—A, B, C, and D; or under Z—A and B, as follows:

I. Main idea X
  A. First subordinate idea related to X
  B. Second subordinate idea related to X
    1. First supporting material related to B
    2. Second supporting material related to B
II. Main idea Y
  A. First subordinate idea related to Y
  B. Second subordinate idea related to Y
  C. Third subordinate idea related to Y
    1. First supporting material related to C
    2. Second supporting material related to C
  D. Fourth subordinate idea related to Y
III. Main idea Z
  A. First subordinate idea related to Z
  B. Second subordinate idea related to Z

When an item is indented below another item, it must be related to the item directly above and must be of less importance, or subordinate to it. Keep the relationship of items in order. The main principles of outlining are at work. The most important, comprehensive ideas are flush left. Less important ideas, examples, illustrations, or research results that support the important ideas are indented. All similar or coordinate ideas must be in the same group.

Let us put these principles into a real-world outline. Look at the two examples below and determine which one follows these principles correctly and which does not.

Example A
I. Television shows and entertainment
  A. TV and music
    1. MTV
    2. *Great Performances*
    3. TNN

    B. TV and comedy
       1. *Tonight Show with Jay Leno*
       2. *Saturday Night Live*
       3. *Everybody Loves Raymond*
    C. Sports programs on TV
       1. *Monday Night Football*
       2. Olympic games
  II. Television shows and information
    A. News programs
       1. *The News Hour with Jim Lehrer*
       2. *Nightline*
       3. CNN—all-news format
    B. Special series
       1. *Nova*
       2. Jacques Cousteau specials
       3. National Geographic specials
         a. *Voyage of Columbus*
         b. *World of Antarctica*

Example B

   I. TV has comedy.
    A. Television entertains us.
    B. *The Tonight Show with Jay Leno* and *Saturday Night Live*
    C. *Everybody Loves Raymond*
  II. Television news informs us.
    A. Sports programs such as *Monday Night Football*
    B. Olympics every four years
    C. *The News Hour with Jim Lehrer*
  III. *Nova* and other PBS specials
    A. *The News Hour with Jim Lehrer*
    B. Jacques Cousteau specials
       a. Other specials are *National Geographic*
       b. *The Voyage of Columbus and Antarctica*
    C. *Nightline* is another good show.
    D. Specials and sports
       1. MTV has specials.

Even a quick glance will show that Example B is a hodgepodge of ideas. Not only do the ideas not follow the principle of subordination, but also the rule of grouping is ignored since many of the ideas do not belong together. Items related to sports are listed under both II and III; there does not appear to be any system at work. Which are the main ideas and which are subordinate? In Example A, the more abstract concepts—the ones that are comprehensive or "bigger"—are to the left while the specific examples are indented to the right.

Note that Example A is a clear illustration of the principles of outlining: The main ideas are flush left; symbols are used consistently; there is one single idea per

CRITICAL THINKING IN COMMUNICATION
Practicing Subordination

In any system of organization, including the college you attend, the same relationships are present. If you think of your entire school as your main idea, then what would constitute A, B, and C? Perhaps you would put the words Academic Affairs on your outline as A and then Student Activities as B. Facilities Operations might be C, and perhaps D would be Fiscal Affairs. You could then list Arabic numbers under each area so that, under A, academic departments become 1, 2, 3, and 4. Various student clubs and activities would be listed with Arabic numbers under B. Try filling out such an outline for your job, church, club, family, team, or city government, and you will see how patterns of organization are present in every aspect of our lives. Learning and applying the principles of outlining can help you to see, understand, and use the patterns that operate in our daily affairs.

item; and all items in one group are related to each other and to the main idea above them. Although both examples follow the rules for indenting, the use of numbers and letters is reversed in one section of Example B. Can you find the error? If you identified III, B as the problem and thought that the *a* and *b* should really be *1* and *2*, you understand how to use these principles. That example brings us to the next step in preparing a good outline: the consistent use of proper symbols.

Symbols

In preparing an outline for your speeches, use the standard outline symbol system. Remember to do the following: (1) Start with capital Roman numerals; (2) Alternate between numbers and letters; (3) Indent so that all similar letters and numbers are the same distance from the left-hand margin and are aligned with each other. These guidelines are illustrated below:

I. _____
   A. _____
   B. _____
      1. _____
      2. _____
      3. _____
   C. _____
   D. _____
      1. _____
      2. _____
         a. _____
         b. _____
   E. _____
      1. _____
         a. _____
         b. _____
         c. _____
      2. _____

Notice how each subsection is indented so that the relationships are clear. Main ideas contain subordinate materials. Thus E is superior to 1 and 2. Coordinate ideas are identifiable and are of equal importance. Which items are coordinate with E? If you think A, B, C, and D, you are right.

For most of your speeches, you will probably be able to express your ideas and their relationships by using just three or four levels of numbering. You may even stop at the Arabic numbers in a key idea outline.

Efficiency of Expression

Your main ideas should be expressed as simple, single ideas. You may use a full sentence or key words. Whichever you choose or your instructor assigns, be consistent throughout your preparation. Do not mix sentences or phrases in the same outline. Keep each line focused on one single idea. This guideline will help you decide to which group or cluster a particular item belongs. Try to avoid the use of the word *and* in your sentences or key ideas. That word may indicate that you have two ideas in one item. For example:

Wrong
    I. It's hard to raise guide dogs because of the time and attention and the strain it puts on the owners when you have to give them up.
      A. They take a lot of time away from other activities, and you need training to give them proper attention.
      B. It is difficult to give them up after you've raised them, so be prepared.

Instead, try being concise and simple. This second example correctly identifies three distinct areas of difficulty and keeps the sentences brief:

Right
    I. Raising guide dogs can be a difficult task.
      A. You need lots of time.
      B. You need special training.
      C. You need to be prepared to give them away.

TECHNOLOGY AND COMMUNICATION
Software Outlines

The importance of outlining can be measured by the development of software programs to help people in business develop outlines. Many of these software packages can help students as well. They provide a template that puts ideas into a format, automatically using the next correct symbol and providing the proper indentation. As you make internal changes and substitutions, the program automatically renumbers the subsequent material. However, responsibility for what goes into the outline still lies with the writer.

Outlining can be of real assistance to you in your speech preparation if you remember the five major parts of a speech, put your thoughts in order, and visualize the relationships among the parts. Make sure all parts connect to the thesis sentence.

In addition to using an outline for overall organization, there are a variety of ways to focus on the body of the speech and put it into a specific organizational pattern.

ORGANIZATIONAL PATTERNS

As you can probably sense, a good speech does not just come out of someone's mouth on the spur of the moment. Many excellent speakers appear smooth and spontaneous as a result of spending many hours thinking about their speech, researching ideas and supporting materials, trying out a variety of ways to organize the speech, and practicing until they are confident and comfortable. If you are going to achieve your purpose with your presentation, you should think carefully about your ideas and how each is related to the others. Examine your thesis sentence, and decide whether there are ways to break it down into a few subordinate ideas. For example, some topics can be thought of in terms of a sequence of steps or stages, each following the previous one in a logical or systematic order. Another common-sense pattern is to arrange subordinate ideas according to particular topics or divisions among the ideas. Finally, in persuasive communication, you may wish to put the body of your speech into a motivational pattern to move your listeners to agreement or action. Let us take a look at each of these **organizational development patterns**.

Sequential Patterns

If your topic has an obvious, step-by-step order or involves a series of ideas or events that move in a certain logical progression, you are dealing with sequence or the **sequential pattern.** There are four major sequential patterns: time, space, size, and importance.

The *time* sequence pattern is often called *chronological*, which means that you organize the A–B–C–D sections of the body of your presentation according to the relationship your ideas have over time. If you are discussing an event in the past—for example, an event leading up to World War I or the chronological events of your vacation trip—you start with the earliest events and finish with the most recent events. Many speakers find the past-present-future time pattern a convenient way to discuss items. If you use it, you'll find that the A–B–C parts of the outline are ready-made for you. In the A section, you will cluster the information about the topic's history and about the events that led up to the current situation. The B section will describe what is happening now. In the C section, you can speculate on what will be coming in the future. This pattern is popular because both the speaker and the audience can follow it and remember it with ease. Another use of the time sequence pattern is found in the process, or how-to, speech. Follow the steps above until you have completed your description of the process. Are you building a house? Preparing lasagna? Producing a play? The time sequence pattern may be perfect for your presentation.

A related pattern that works for some of the above topics involves *space*. For example, if your vacation started in Miami and you then went to Atlanta, then to New Orleans, and back to Miami, these events would be connected geographically—that is, in space—as well as in time. The spatial sequence pattern is easy to see in an outline that explains things that exist in the material world. For example, you could give a speech about the Hawaiian Islands from the perspective of time—early volcanic activity, the settling by Polynesians, the kingdom era, European arrivals, annexation to the United States, and statehood. Or you could discuss the fact that the islands start at Midway Island and end with the island of Hawaii. Your outline would then start with Midway Island and end with Hawaii. You could give a talk about your campus, starting at one end and moving in a spatial relationship from one building or section of campus to the next one that a person would come to if he or she were walking. Of course, you could also talk about the buildings according to the order in which they were built and then go back to chronological order. Do you want to discuss the solar system? Start with the sun and work your way out spatially until you reach Pluto.

The *size* sequence pattern is the third pattern, and it works well for a variety of topics. For example, your solar system speech may start with the sun, then move to Jupiter as the next largest celestial body, then Neptune, and so on until you get to Pluto, the smallest planet. Or you could reverse the order: Start with the smallest and move on to the largest. A speech on types of hawks, for example, might start with the smallest species, continue to the middle-sized birds, and end with a discussion about the largest member of the hawk family.

Finally, an *importance* sequence pattern could be used to discuss topics in which a judgment is made or criteria are used to evaluate ideas. If you were running a political campaign, you might start your speech with a time pattern or, if you had only a few minutes to explain a complex idea, you could order the body of your speech according to the importance of the items it contained. You could say, "The most important thing to do is…," and then, "The next most important thing is…," and then, "Finally, if you have the time or resources, consider…" In this way, your listeners would grasp the relative importance of each item.

As you can tell from these examples, a speech can be logically arranged in a number of ways, all of which make sequential sense. Your task is to select the sequential patterns that best suits you, your topic, your purpose, your research, your time frame, and your time.

Topical Patterns

If your ideas do not fit the sequence format very well, you might try the group of topical patterns as a framework for the body of your speech. **Topical patterns** are based on the way we break down or cluster ideas and topics into logical divisions. This pattern is called the topical pattern because it is useful when the subtopics of the thesis seem to flow naturally and logically from the subject of the thesis. The breakdown of the main ideas into subordinate ideas stems not from the relationship of those ideas in time or space but from the logical way they can be put together.

One of the most popular topical patterns is one that shows the relationship of *cause and effect*. This pattern asserts that event X was the cause of event Y. For example, the Hawaiian Islands were formed by a series of volcanic eruptions, so you could give a speech about the series of events that caused the islands to form. The factors that caused the earthquakes could be the subject of a cause-effect topical pattern. This can be a tricky pattern. One of the most common logical fallacies occurs because many events are related only in time, yet we make the faulty assumption that they also have a causal relationship. This fallacy is called *post hoc ergo propter hoc* (Latin meaning "after this, therefore because of this") or just the *post hoc* fallacy. The fallacy occurs because there is a similar pattern—a correlation—that sometimes looks like a cause-effect pattern but is not. For example, the failure to wear a seat belt is correlated with high death rates in motor vehicle accidents. The lack of a seat belt does not cause the accident, nor does it cause death. Smashing through a windshield or hitting the pavement with great force may cause death. However, the lack of a seat belt is connected, or correlated, with an increase in death rates in automobile accidents. Sometimes, correlation studies do show that one event might cause another. For example, all the studies of rates of cancer in smokers suggest that smokers have a much greater chance of getting lung cancer than nonsmokers. However, the fact that some people smoke and do not get lung cancer keeps this relationship from being, strictly speaking, a cause-effect relationship and places it in the category of a correlation. If you constantly miss class, will you get a low grade on the tests? Quite probably you will, but it is not certain that you will. However, it can be demonstrated that, as a group, students who skip class frequently have lower grades than students who attend class regularly. You, however, might be the exception; for example, if U.S. history is your hobby, you might be able to miss your U.S. history class and still do well on the tests. On the other hand, regular attendance correlates highly with good grades.

Parallel to the cause-effect pattern is the *problem-solution* pattern. In this pattern, the A section of the outline presents a particular problem, such as air pollution. The B section follows with ideas and suggestions for solving the problem. You will find the problem-solution format useful in giving persuasive speeches. Many policy decisions are made through problem-solution approaches. Watch television commercials, and you will see dozens of problem-solution presentations in an hour: "Do you have gray hair? Just use Young Forever Hair Cream." "How can you get rid of roaches in your kitchen? Easy, just buy Roach Bomb Spray!" "Are you tired of corruption in government? Vote for Zeuschner!" Examples of this format are everywhere.

Motivational Patterns

There are many explicitly persuasive patterns that speakers have used for centuries, and they belong in the **motivational pattern** group. Although each of the patterns previously discussed could probably be used to organize the body of a persuasive speech, motivational patterns have that application as their goal. One of the most widely used motivational patterns is called the *motivated sequence*. It was developed by speech teacher Alan H. Monroe over seventy years ago and has been popular ever since (Gronbeck et al., 1995). The five parts of this pattern are as follows:

1. *Attention:* Capture the attention of the audience and focus it on the topic.
2. *Need:* Present the problem so that the audience sees it as one that needs solving.
3. *Satisfaction:* Present the solution to the problem.
4. *Visualization:* Stimulate the audience's imagination by having its members think about the consequences of either adopting or not adopting the solution.
5. *Action:* Motivate your listeners to take some specific step to put the solution into operation.

Although Monroe and his later collaborators used this five-part process to describe many types of speeches, its effectiveness is clearest when the speaker asks the audience to take some action to solve the problem. In this format, your speech outline would have four parts to the body because the first step, *Attention,* would already be on your outline as I. *Introduction,* in the format presented at the beginning of this chapter. Then, under III. *Body of the Speech,* you would list A as the *Need* step, B as *Satisfaction,* C as *Visualization,* and D as *Action.*

You can also motivate your listeners by using a *benefits* pattern, a pattern that describes all the good things they will gain if they adopt your thesis. Or you might take the opposite view and show them the *costs* they would incur if they took another course of action. Or you might combine the two into a *cost-benefits* pattern that shows how much your suggestion costs and how much the alternatives would cost. Then you could compare the two on the basis of probable benefits.

From these organizational patterns—sequential, topical, and motivational— you can create the body of your speech so that it flows together in a logical order

The Story of Communication
Alan H. Monroe

ALAN H. MONROE was one of the important figures in the development of the field of speech communication. His textbook *Principles and Types of Speech*, published in 1935, was one of the early and most widely used books about public speaking. It included materials he had tested for nearly a decade in his own classes and in collaboration with scholars in psychology and business. He developed his organizational format largely on the basis of formats used in sales presentations. In 1940, while at Purdue University, he was president of the National Speech Communication Association. He taught and influenced an entire generation of scholars and practitioners in communication. With his use of social science approaches to a field then dominated by traditional rhetorical perspectives, he broke new ground for the discipline. Speech communication today continues to draw from a blend of the social sciences, the humanities, psychology, and rhetoric. Professor Monroe died in 1975.

that will make sense to you and your listeners. Your presentations will be clear and will have the impact that you intended on your audience. When your main topic and its subordinate ideas are related in terms of size or time, you will probably use a sequential pattern. If the relationship is more like a grouping or cluster, you may want a topical pattern. Finally, if you are trying to get your audience to do something, look to a motivational pattern to organize the body of your speech.

Each of these patterns is designed to help both parties in the communication transaction between you and your audience. To create a message that has both clarity and impact, you need to select a pattern that will enhance it. Communication in this setting takes place only if the audience gets the message that you intended, so make your message clear and strong by taking some time to think about the pattern that will best help you do that.

ANALYZING YOUR LISTENERS

A great deal was said in Chapter 3 about active listening from a receiver's point of view. In Chapter 7, you read about yourself as a processor of information. Now put those two ideas together, but see yourself as the sender of a message to a group of individuals who will listen to and process what you have to say. Once you are focused on the audience, you can begin the steps of audience analysis.

Aristotle's book *Rhetoric* devoted large sections to advice about how to approach a topic if older people or younger people were the audience. His reasoning was based on the values, attitudes, and beliefs that people bring with them when they are listening to a speaker. Values, attitudes, and beliefs as they relate to you personally are discussed in Chapter 7. Now it is time to think about how those aspects of your listeners might affect the way you create and deliver your presentation. The attitudes of the members of your audience will affect their ability to listen. If they are in a good mood, they will like you as a speaker; if they feel involved and connected to the topic, it will be easier for you to deliver your message (Lumsden and Lumsden, 1996).

Values are the social principles, goals, and standards—that members of your audience have in common. Their values determine the overall guidelines for their life patterns, and they are generally few in number. If you are speaking to a college group, you can guess that they value education. A group of owners of small businesses probably value hard work and independence. These values provide the framework or foundation for their feelings and attitudes.

Several major value systems in our society have been identified that can help you to adapt your message to your listeners. For example, the *Protestant-Puritan-Peasant* system is known for its emphasis on hard work, family, religion, and education. Incidentally, many more people than those who come from those three backgrounds hold these values. Jews, Catholics, Buddhists, and very wealthy people may also hold these fundamental values. Another type of value system is the *progressive* value system, which stresses newness, invention, development, and exploration. On the other hand, some people hold primarily to the *transcendental* value system, which places an emphasis on spiritual feelings, intuition, and getting away from materialistic ties. Some researchers have identified Native American value systems, Mormon value systems, and specific corporate value structures (Reike and Sillars, 1983). It's important to remember that your listeners will apply whatever seems to them to be a relevant value, attitude, or belief to the message they hear—your message. Therefore when you function as the primary sender of a message, you need to consider how to connect your values to those of the audience. Consider the people listening to you and how they will react to your message.

To speak effectively to your audience, you need to gather information about it and the situation in which you will be speaking. Recall that in earlier chapters, you learned about communication as an interactive process—a transaction between senders and receivers.

Analyzing the Occasion

When you consider your listeners, think about why they want to hear your speech. What event or purpose brings them together? Think about the degree of formality of the occasion. If the speech is a classroom assignment, then one style

DIVERSITY IN COMMUNICATION
Understanding Audience Diversity

Audiences come in all sizes and shapes, and that diversity challenges you to adapt appropriately to your listeners. Their age, gender, ethnic background, and other demographic factors can guide you to become a speaker who connects with the specific group of listeners you face. Be careful, however, of stereotyping. One student began her speech by saying, "Ladies, would you like to save money on your dresses, blouses, and skirts? I know I would—and I do by sewing many of my own clothes. So today I'll tell you about some simple sewing techniques you can use to make your own clothes and keep the ones you buy in good repair." Fourteen of the twenty-five people in the class were males. Does this mean that she picked the wrong topic? If you said yes, then you, too, are stereotyping. Are there good reasons why men should know some basic elements of clothing construction, maintenance, and repair? It seems to me that everyone could profit from this knowledge. In another class, a young man began his speech by telling "us guys" about automotive tune-ups and oil changes. Does this mean that women have nothing useful to learn about automobile maintenance and repair? Often, it is not the topic, but what we choose to do with the topic that adapts it to the diverse audiences who are likely to hear the speech. Even if you are one of only a few African Americans in a class, there are lots of reasons why your classmates should hear about the concerns and perspectives of your group. Likewise, age differences, gender, culture, and background can all be linked to members of a diverse audience as long as you take care to be inclusive, not exclusive. Find the common connections, concerns, interests or motivations, and then build on those in the development decisions you make as you create your speech.

of dress and presentation is appropriate. If it is a formal contest or the presentation of an award, a different mode of dress and style of presentation are called for. You may be giving a speech welcoming an important visitor to your business or school. Be aware that different occasions call for different norms of behavior. The joke that you have for the classroom may not be the right one to tell at a religious meeting in a mosque, temple, or church. Formal approaches may work at a business presentation in the main conference room of a major corporate headquarters but not at an outdoor pep rally.

Many of you reading this advice probably think that it is unnecessary and that you would certainly adapt appropriately. You would be surprised at the number of people who forget to do so. Speakers who fail to consider the different demands of various occasions fail to reach their audience. If you violate listeners' expectations associated with the occasion, they will stop paying careful attention to your message. In addition, you also need to think about the setting—that is, where you will be presenting your message.

Analyzing the Environment

Environmental factors in your presentation are one of the most important areas for analysis and attention. Location factors include the size of the setting. Will you be speaking in a small conference room or a large auditorium? Indoors or outdoors? Although this consideration usually relates to the size of the audience, it is not always the case. For example, you may be outside, but speaking to only twenty or thirty people. What if you are scheduled for a large convention hall or auditorium, and only thirty or forty people show up? You might consider stepping down from the platform, asking the audience to move to the first few rows, and increasing your interaction with them. You should also think about where to stand, where to put your chart or overhead projector, or even whether to use a chart if it is not visible to everyone in the audience. Other elements such as poor lighting, distracting views, windows, noise, drafts, and heating and air-conditioning vents must all be considered so that you can adjust your plans to the location or, if necessary, change the location.

Once you have become aware of your listeners' values, the occasion or context for your speech, and the setting in which you will give your presentation, you need to consider ways to support your message so that it is clear, relevant, and interesting. The way to do this is to add good supporting materials to a well-constructed outline.

USING SUPPORTING MATERIALS

Suppose that you have identified a topic that is suitable for you, the occasion, the audience, and the setting. Suppose that you have put together a tentative outline, complete with major parts and two to four major subdivisions. The next step is to find support for each of those subdivisions. You can provide interest and substance for your main ideas by including specific information about them. The following section presents the types of information to look for, and the section after that helps you to find some specific materials. There are three classes of information that can support your ideas: verbal, numerical, and visual (Zeuschner, 1994).

Verbal Supporting Materials

Specific pieces of information that can be conveyed only in words are called **verbal supporting materials**. You already use these supports every day whenever you explain or describe something to someone else. When you tell your friends on Monday morning that you had a great weekend, then tell them about the football game and party on Saturday, and finally give them details about the picnic on Sunday, you are using verbal supporting materials to amplify or describe your thesis—that is, that the weekend was great. In your speeches, you will probably use *short stories* or *anecdotes, definitions, descriptions, examples,* and *quotations* as verbal supporting materials.

Short stories are sometimes called anecdotes and can be an excellent way to support your ideas. If you can tell a vivid, clever, funny, or moving story, your audience will have a chance to identify with the story and remember your point. A good story for a speech should meet several criteria. It must clearly illustrate the point you wish to make, be complete so that your audience will understand the plot, and be appropriate to the situation. Do not tell a series of complex stories to an audience that is unfamiliar with your subject. Personal experiences are one type of story that, if used carefully, can both clarify ideas and show your connection with, your interest in, or your expertise in the topic. Keep off-color jokes out of a speech. Stories that are offensive because they mock gender, race, or age are sure to backfire. Your story must also be concise so that it does not take up too much time. If the story runs on and on, you risk having your audience forget the point. Remember that a story should not dominate the point, but support it. Remember that, in the standard outline, supporting materials are listed as 1 or 2, not A or B. This placement tells you that they are subordinate to the idea they support.

Definitions are sometimes very easy to find. Go to your dictionary and look up a term or concept. Sometimes you will find an encyclopedia or one of your textbooks to be helpful. If you cite your source for your audience when you present a definition, you will give it greater impact. Definitions are good supports because they usually come from a professional source. They are also short, relevant, and clearly written. Of course, you can always create your own definition and even use it to add an element of humor to your speech.

Descriptions are a combination of definitions and examples. When describing an object, an event, or even a feeling, give your listeners only relevant, specific, information so that they can picture what you are describing. If you tell them that the Empire State Building is really very big, you are not being very descriptive. However, if you describe the number of floors it has, what distance you can see from the top, and how many tons of steel and building materials it took to build it, you are approaching a good description. By using the elements of comparison and contrast, you can describe something in terms of its relationship to something else. If your listeners are in Chicago, then comparing the Empire State Building to the Sears Tower will help them to understand their comparable sizes. A miniature pony can be described as being similar in size to a golden retriever. The texture of a mango can be compared to that of a peach. Descriptions like these will help to enrich your speech and make it interesting for your audience. If you go into a point-by-point comparison, you are probably drawing an analogy. These extended comparisons often have a poetic or figurative element. You may recall from your English classes the uses of metaphor and simile as forms of comparison that are rich in expression and vivid in content. Each of these forms—analogy, metaphor, and simile—can be usefully included in your supporting materials.

Examples are detailed, specific instances of events, ideas, activities, or other items. If you have a story that is not long enough to have a plot, it is probably an example. You should provide enough detail in an example for the audience to appreciate and understand both your example and how it relates to the main idea it supports. If you are urging your classroom listeners to visit the campus counseling center, you might say: "Many services are available at the center. For example, you can get free aptitude testing and other testing for career guidance. They offer career-planning small groups and interest workshops all year. If you need someone to talk to about personal problems, someone on staff can help you immediately. Or the counseling center can refer you to a trained professional in one of many areas, including health. Staff members can even help you select a graduate school. These are just a few examples of the free services that are available at the counseling center." There is no plot, so this is not a story about the counseling center, but there are a number of clear, short specific items—examples—to support your idea.

Quotations allow you to use someone else's direct words to support your ideas. You may think of quotations as being the lofty or clever words of famous people. While those types of quotations are popular and insightful, try also to go beyond those standbys. Think about quoting a newspaper article, a poem, a line from a song, even your grandmother or your next-door neighbor. Quote the words of great authors or well-known speakers, but also quote many others to support your ideas as long as the quotations are clearly relevant to the topic and capture your listeners' attention. Make certain to credit the source of your quotation when you present it. Giving the source before you present a quotation helps the audience to focus its attention and realize that a shift in voice is coming up. Sometimes, for a surprise effect, you may want to wait until after the quotation to give the source. A favorite quotation that can be used with this surprise strategy tells about how young people these days are unruly, hard to teach, impolite, and academically ill prepared. The surprise comes when you tell your listeners that the author of the statement was Socrates, speaking 2400 years ago! Usually, however, you will increase audience attention if you present your source first.

As you have seen, verbal supporting materials are excellent ways to define, clarify, and add impact to your presentation. However, there are times when verbal supports do not meet your needs, perhaps because they do not fit the content or purpose of your main ideas. Another form of supporting materials—numbers— may be just what you need.

Numerical Supporting Materials

When you collect several individual examples into a single measurement, you are using numbers for statistical support. You would not talk about each baseball hit by a major-league player; you would give only his average. You cannot list every donation to a local blood bank, so you might say the following: "Last year, our local blood bank collected over 1200 pints of blood. That comes out to less than four pints a day. The need for blood transfusions was well over six per day. Clearly, we are failing to provide this blood bank with sufficient funds." Since you cannot detail all the examples of needed transfusions, you collect them into a statistical support—"six per day." You might select one powerful story to bring the statistical support "six per day" to life for your class, but the sheer volume of many examples will force you to collect material into numerical units. Although not as colorful as stories, statistics can often have a significant impact on your audience if you use them wisely. Since numbers are not as easily remembered as stories and examples are, your impact will be stronger if you use only a few numbers during a speech.

Any time that you use numbers to show relationships, you are in the area of **statistics.** In the blood bank example, if you had mentioned only the 1200 pints of blood collected by the local blood bank, your listeners would not have been able to relate the figure 1200 to anything meaningful. However, when you used that number to calculate a daily donation rate which you compared with a daily need rate, you were able to discuss the relationship of those two rates to each other. In other words, you were using statistics to increase the impact of your message on your listeners.

You are probably familiar with such basic statistical concepts as rounding off, averages, trends, and percentages. These concepts will be familiar to your audiences as well, so you should feel free to use them. If you are trained in more complex statistics and think that your audience would benefit from information about standard deviation, margin of error, or correlation coefficients, include that information as well. But do not assume that, because you know what these concepts mean, your listeners will as well. For most purposes, basic statistical relationships will tell your audience what it needs to know to understand your point. Remember to be accurate, clear, up-to-date, interesting, and relevant.

Visual Supporting Materials

Effective, total communication involves more than the sound channel; it includes the sense of sight as well. If you supplement the words you speak and the numbers you present with supporting materials that can be seen, you will increase the interest and clarity of your presentation for your audience. Using **visual aids** to support your ideas gives your listeners more ways in which to receive and understand your message, thus increasing your chances of success in transmitting your message. Using visual supporting materials also gives you an opportunity to add variety to your speech and to give your audience a break from listening to words.

As with any supporting materials, make certain that your visual aids are linked to your ideas by placing them on the outline as level 1 or 2 items. They should support, clarify, emphasize, define, or explain an idea better than words alone could possibly do. Sometimes, you might find an excellent photograph or object that has little to do with your main idea. Do not make the mistake of trying to use it. Make your visual supporting materials both relevant and uniquely valuable to your speech. For example, if you try to explain the beauty of the Grand Canyon without using a visual aid, you are probably making a mistake. If you want to explain the checks and balances of the federal government and show as your only visual aid a photograph of the White House, a drawing of George Washington, or a map of Washington, D.C., you are also making a poor choice.

There are several types of useful visual aids: *pictures, maps, diagrams, objects,* and *models*. You can also combine numbers and visual aids into *graphs* and *charts*.

Pictures and Maps   Pictures and photographs are the most popular visual aids. You can use anything that will illustrate an item in your speech—a photo of your car, the Eiffel Tower, your pet calf, or your apartment building. If professional photographs or pictures are not available, do not be afraid to make one yourself. You do not have to be an artist to create a reasonably clear line drawing or sketch. If it's the right size, is clearly drawn, and supports your idea well, do not worry about its aesthetic merit.

A picture can indeed be worth a thousand words. Try showing a photograph of the Yosemite Valley to an audience and then try matching it with a verbal description. Color, size, shape, scale, and setting are almost always easier to show than to tell about. How would you begin to describe the color purple when there are dozens of shades of purple? Bring in a sample of the shade you want to describe, and your description will be clear instantly. A description that is long, labored, and obscure in words can be quick, direct, and clear in a visual aid. Keep your visual supporting materials simple. (Remember the *KISS Principle—Keep It Simple, Sweetheart!*) Use visual support materials for one major item or theme at a time. Make sure that people at the back of the room can see them. Make them interesting and colorful. Do all of these things, and you will have effective visual supports.

Maps, too, can be useful and effective. If you buy a professional map from a bookstore, it will be neat and clearly drawn. However, it might be too small or overly detailed for your presentation, so you could try drawing one yourself. Keep it neat and simple and follow the suggestions for size, clarity, and color that were previously discussed. The location of Slovakia may be too difficult to explain, but a map segment of Eastern Europe with Slovakia shown in a bright color or darker shade of gray, could be very helpful to your audience. If you want to give the audience directions to your favorite eating spot, you can draw the directions on a large poster board, using a city map as your guide. A good map shows details and relationships more clearly and precisely than you can with words alone.

Objects and Models   Objects and models can also help you clarify your ideas if they are large enough to be seen by an audience. Do not ever bring a small object to class or to any other setting and say, "I hope everyone can see this." Hope? You

A map is an excellent
way to explain
location.

should know whether it is large enough because you were supposed to have checked it beforehand. Even worse is the speaker who says, "I'm sorry most of you can't see this." This statement tells your listeners that you know they cannot see the object, but you decided to use it anyway. Make certain that your object or model will be useful to your listeners so that they can experience it as support for your ideas. If it is not a good support, find something else to use. Show the types of rope used in sailing, bring in three different kinds of bicycle helmets, or make a three-foot tall scale model of the Empire State Building or the Eiffel Tower. Do not let yourself be caught in the position of not knowing whether your object or model is providing the support for your listeners that it should. Go to the back of the room before your speech, turn around, look at your object, and determine for yourself whether or not it can be seen from a distance.

Charts and Graphs   Combining supports by using charts, graphs, or diagrams can also be an effective way to supplement your communication. You could create a *chart* showing the steps of a process or the relationship of rising costs to

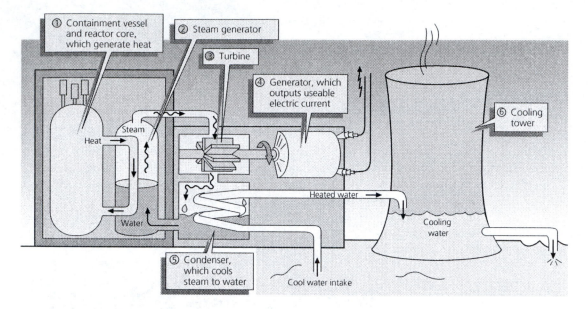

A schematic visual aid can help to explain how a complex process works.

declining profits. *Graphs* are an especially good way to show relationships among numbers. You might make some simple bar graphs to communicate the relative sizes of several numbers or amounts. Use different colors for different items and your audience will be able to find them easily as you discuss them. A line graph can show trends over time, such as tuition levels over the past twenty years at your school, the price of automobiles, or population changes. If time is an important part of your idea, then a line graph is a good supporting material to use. You might wish to compare the proportions of parts to a whole. In that case, use a pie graph. It can easily communicate that kind of relationship to your audience. A pie graph or chart illustrates the parts of a whole, and the relative sizes of all the parts equal the whole. Whether it is the distribution of your monthly expenses, the size of each department in a business, or the number of calories in each part of a balanced meal, a good-sized pie chart, with clear lines and a variety of colors, can do a great deal to support your idea.

In short, make sure that all of your visual aids are large enough to be seen; are easily made, handled, and presented; and are simple to operate. You probably should avoid electrical or mechanical devices that are subject to failure. Make certain that your visual aid is appropriate to both the audience and the setting. If you collect venomous snakes as a hobby and would like to bring them to your presentation on snakes, don't do it. Substitute a photograph for the real thing, and make your point that way. In the same vein, bringing in guns may be illegal but diagrams of guns are not. If you are discussing drought and famine, you might be tempted to bring in pictures of dying or dead children to emphasize your thesis but most people in your audience would be overwhelmed by such photographs and would probably stop paying attention to you. A student recently brought to class detailed photographs of an abortion in process to convince her listeners to oppose the procedure. The entire class avoided looking at her material, and two students left the room. So be careful about the appropriateness of your visual supports, especially in a situation where your audience is assigned to be there. Time is also a factor. Does your visual aid take ten or fifteen minutes to set up and then dismantle? Be aware of the time limits you will have to cope with in any setting. Remember, your visual aid is just like any other type of supporting material. It is a support for a subordinate idea. It is a third-level event, and the amount of time it should be allotted in your presentation should be proportionate.

Finally, passing around small objects or handouts to the audience can be distracting. It is better to enlarge one object so that everyone can see it at the same time. Then, you can control the time that it goes out of sight, and there will be no distractions in the audience while you are speaking. If there is something you really must give the members of the audience, hand it out at the end of the speech or presentation.

If you follow these guidelines, you can give a speech that has good supporting materials. The key to success is to make sure the materials are appropriate and have variety so that you can explain your ideas to your listeners in several different ways. Just how many of which type of support should you use? It all depends on you, your topic, your audience, and the situation. You can be sure, however, that a speech with a variety of supporting materials will go over better with an audience than a speech that is dominated by a single type of material. Keep variety in mind as you look for supporting materials. Where do you look for these supports? The next section will answer that question.

RESEARCHING YOUR IDEAS

Finding interesting and stimulating supporting materials is one of the best reasons to do research for your speech. As you learn more about your subject through research, you add depth and interest to your presentation. Sometimes, you may be speaking about a personal experience—for example, a trip from Miami to Atlanta to New Orleans. That does not exempt you from doing research. If you limit your speech to saying, "Well, then I went...," and "After that I went...," you will fail to provide either depth or variety to your listeners. Find out about the history of some of the places you visited. Quote from *Gone With the Wind*, get a map of the three areas from an auto club; use statistics about the populations of those cities. That type of supporting material will rescue your speech from being a self-centered, monotonous travelogue and turn it into a speech that is of keen interest to your listeners. Your presentation will be made more interesting by your personal touches, but they do not and cannot replace outside supporting materials culled from solid research.

So how and where do you find supporting materials? You can start with yourself, then talk to other people, and then research the print and non-print resources available to you.

Finding and Recording Information

You will have to do some exploration to find all the supports that were discussed earlier—short stories, statistics, visual aids, definitions, descriptions, comparisons, and contrasts. Once you have found this information, you must record it so that you can both remember it and properly credit it in your speech. How much information should you gather? A good rule of thumb is that you should collect two or three times as much information as you have time for in your speech. For example, if you have a four-to-six minute speech, you should collect about fifteen minutes' worth of supporting materials. That way you can go through your collection of stories, examples, statistics, and other materials to select the best ones for each subordinate idea. Evaluate each item for interest, clarity, and variety. Then choose only the items that give your presentation the most value. Otherwise, if you have only four minutes' worth of material, you will have to use it. It may be good, bad, weak, strong, clear, or unclear. It doesn't matter, you are stuck with it. So give yourself an opportunity to choose.

Using Personal Resources

Think of yourself as an expert in experiences—your experiences. You have visited different places, taken classes in many subjects, had hobbies and jobs, and read a small mountain of books and magazines. All of these experiences make you a resource. Consider the cartoons you have clipped out; the books you have read; and your photographs of favorite stars, sports figures or favorite vacation spots. Think about the variety of life experiences you have had, and use them as a starting point for gathering your supporting material.

Next, talk to some of the people you know. Interviews are an excellent way to gather quotations, and you have friends and associates who can lend their expertise to your speech if you ask them to do so. Your campus is filled with experts on hundreds of subjects, and most faculty members enjoy talking to students about their specialties. The main reason that students go to see instructors is to complain about a grade or ask about an assignment that the instructor thought had already been explained. What a pleasure it is for your instructors to have an intellectual discussion with someone who wants to know about their area of expertise. Remember to make an appointment and to prepare your questions in advance, as described in the section on interviews in Chapter 9.

Using Library Resources

When most people think about doing research, they think of printed materials. Books, magazines, newspapers, and other printed material are some of the best sources of supporting materials. The best place to find these items is, of course, a library. Learning how to use a library can be a great advantage to you in your college career as well as in preparing speeches.

Books are an easy and plentiful source of information. Keep track of what you read so that you can list it properly in your bibliography. Small three-by-five or four-by-six inch index cards are useful for this purpose. You can write down the important bibliographic information found on the copyright page of the book and still have plenty of room to note important information such as statistics, facts, or direct quotations. Perhaps the library still has a card catalogue—a large set of file drawers containing cards that list the books that are available. These cards are filed in three separate ways: by subject, by title, and by the author's last name. Most libraries have electronic catalogues that organize their listings in the same way—by author, title, and subject. When you begin your research, it may be a good idea to browse through the listings in the catalogue to get an overview of the holdings. Remember, books are always somewhat out of date, since they take at least a year and sometimes two to get from the author to the library. If an author has spent a year or more doing research, the information in the book may be at least two, and sometimes four or more, years old. For many items, this time gap will not matter, but if you plan to talk about current world events, unemployment rates, the cost of automobiles, or stock prices, books are not adequate. You will need current sources.

Newspapers and magazines can give you that information. Libraries subscribe to dozens of newspapers and magazines from all over the world. Magazines such as *Time, Newsweek,* and *U.S. News and World Report* are all well established and provide weekly coverage of important events. Of course, each has a particular perspective; nevertheless, they are well known for their accuracy. Other magazines may have a special interest, a particular political point of view, or a perspective from a different culture or country; all of these can give your speech both comprehensiveness and depth. Consult the *Readers' Guide to Periodical Literature* to locate the specific magazines that have the information you seek.

In addition, libraries collect booklets, documents, pamphlets, and flyers published on a variety of very specific topics. College libraries also collect professional journals in every subject taught on campus; they can be a source sophisticated and highly specialized information. Check the publication *Facts on File* for short articles about current research in a variety of fields. You might even call organizations with interests related to your topic and request some of their publications. Most organizations are happy to share their information and they usually enjoy helping students. Community action groups, local government, and utility companies are more places where you can get interesting print materials.

Non-print resources are increasingly important in a world of electronic information processing. Compact discs, videotapes, electronic data banks, and on-line services have augmented traditional sources such as films, tape, and records. If you are going to discuss the speeches of former presidents, you will get much more information about the topic from films and videotapes than if you simply read transcripts of the speeches. A speech on Native American literature would be somewhat impoverished unless you took the time to listen to some recordings of tribal storytellers. If you want to give something unique and memorable to your listeners, you need to look beyond ordinary sources of information. Most libraries have extensive indexes of nonprint resources including catalogues, references, and microfilm readers.

Using Internet Resources

Using electronic databases or searching the web will help you to combine the electronic format with traditional print media. Since these resources are on-line, they may be updated frequently—even daily—so they become a rich resource of current information. Your library or your own on-line service provider may give you access to several thousand separate periodicals. The *New York Times* and *The Wall Street Journal.*, are probably available via your computer browser. Web browser programs and search engines make using the Internet a useful part of your research. Remember, though, that much of the information your browser locates has not been verified. Just about anyone can post just about anything on a website, so be careful that it meets the tests for good information that were presented in Chapter 4. One further labor-saving advantage to your computer search is the ability to hook up to a printer; the printout will give you properly recorded information to include in your speech bibliography (Grice and Skinner, 1998).

Broadcast Media Resources

You can also collect supporting materials from television and radio. Did you recently watch a good program, see an important news broadcast, or listen to a song? Write down what you learn so it will be available to you for your speeches in the future. The average American household watches seven hours of television a day, so you have an opportunity to do research while you are being entertained. News broadcasts, documentaries, weather reports, sports programs, comedy series, and special programs are all potential sources for an example, a story, a funny description, a bold analogy, or a key fact. Intelligent and selective television viewing can produce excellent supporting materials.

Synthesizing Your Material

Once you have gathered your information, it is time to reconsider the basic speech outline discussed earlier in this chapter. To construct a speech that meets the goals of clarity and impact, you need to support your thesis and the main divisions of that thesis with materials that are lively, specific, colorful, memorable, relevant, and convincing. Your goal is to communicate a worthwhile message to your audience members so that they will both understand and remember what you said. The better the supporting materials you use, the more likely it is that you can achieve your intended results.

Consult your stack of index cards, and sort them into groups according to the divisions of the body of your speech (A, B, C, and so on). Some items may not be appropriate, in which case you can either adjust your ideas or put the items aside. A great story that does not fit in one place often can be used in another. The introduction of a speech, for example, is often a story, so you might create an introduction from the materials you have already gathered. If you have twice as much material as you need, review your speech outline; check all items for interest, variety, and impact; and then keep only the very best ones.

SUMMARY

Preparing speeches is like doing a term paper. You analyze your audience accurately and then engage in the research needed. You organize your speech by preparing an outline of major ideas and their supporting materials. You have to think about who your listeners are and how you want them to respond. Verbal supporting materials are the most commonly used, and they can be augmented with simple statistics and compelling visual aids. Finding these materials is the process of research, and you have a rich variety of ways to find the best material available. Once you have done all this, it is time to think about how to deliver those ideas and materials so they have an impact on your listeners.

The next chapter shows you the best way to prepare and practice so that you meet the goal of presenting a speech that is both clear and relevant.

Key Terms

thesis sentence, **202**
body, **202**
supporting materials, **202**
organizational development patterns, **208**
sequential pattern, **208**

topical patterns, **209**
motivational pattern, **210**
verbal supporting materials, **215**
statistics, **217**
visual aids, **217**

EXERCISES

1. Watch a frequently appearing commercial on television. Watch it several times so that you can verify your observations. Determine what pattern of organization is used in the commercial. You can probably identify a chronological or cause-effect pattern fairly easily. Are there any others? Bring a list of three or four differently organized commercials to class and compare them with those observed by your classmates. Did anyone use the same commercial but classify it as having a different pattern from yours? Why might this happen?

2. Create a keyword outline for an informative speech. Make certain that all five areas of a speech are included. Now use this same topic and thesis sentence but organize the body of the speech into a different format. Which format works better? Why?

3. Buy a packet of four-by-six inch note cards and have them with you when you go to the library; watch television; search the internet; and attend classes, lectures, or speeches. On these cards, write specific items you might use in a speech or presentation as they occur. For example, you might record an interesting anecdote, some compelling statistics, or a vivid example. Even if you are not planning to speak on the same subject as your example or statistic, you will find that items can often be transferred from one presentation to another. These cards will also help you to build a reserve of information to use if you are asked to give an impromptu speech.

4. Substitute a visual support for a verbal one. Can you show something better than you can tell it? Now do the reverse. Take something you think would make a good visual aid, and put the content into words. Is this item easier to say than it is to show? These tests can be done any time that you use supporting materials. Do them mentally to determine whether you should use a verbal or visual support.

References

Clark, Ruth Anne and David Jones. "A Comparison of Traditional and Online Formats in a Public Speaking Course." *Communication Education* 50, 2 (April 2001).

Downing, Joe and Cecile Garmon. "Teaching Students in the Basic Course How to Use Presentation Software." *Communication Education* 50, 3 (July 2001).

Grice, George L. and John F. Skinner. *Mastering Public Speaking*. Boston: Allyn and Bacon, 1998.

Gronbeck, Bruce E., R. E. McKerrow, A. H. Monroe, and D. Ehninger. *Principles and Types of Speech Communication*, 12th ed. New York: HarperCollins, 1995.

Lumsden, Gay and Donald Lumsden. *Communicating with Credibility and Confidence*. Belmont, CA: Wadsworth, 1996.

Gibaldi, Joseph, *MLA Handbook for Writers of Research Papers*, 5th ed., New York: Modern Language Association, 1999.

Reike, Richard and Malcolm Sillars. *Argumentation and the Decision-Making Process*. Glenview, IL: Scott Foresman, 1983.

Zeuschner, R. B. *Effective Public Speaking*. Dubuque: Kendall-Hunt, 1994.

CHAPTER 12

Presenting Speeches

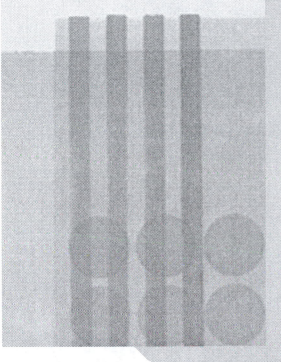

After reading this chapter, you should be able to:

- ● Know the four types of speech presentation styles, the causes of speech apprehension, and the standards for presenting and evaluating speeches
- ● Feel ready to give speeches to your classmates and other listeners
- ● Have control over your nervous energy
- ● Uphold ethical standards in communication
- ● Present an effective speech, and evaluate it and other speeches you hear

When you have done your research, gathered your supporting materials, put them in order, and developed your visual aids, then you will be ready to start practicing your presentation. No matter how much effort you put into research, outline construction, revision of your thesis sentence, and organization of the body of your speech, without an effective presentation your speech is not likely to have its desired effect. It is true that you must begin with substantial information on a worthwhile topic. But once your preparation is in place, it is time to make sure that your presentation does justice to all your work.

As noted several times earlier in this book, your presentation should clarify your ideas and give them impact. Speech delivery involves coordinating your voice and your body in a way that makes your message come alive for your audience. This chapter presents several styles you can use when delivering a speech, suggests ways to deal with the speech anxiety you probably will feel, and enhances your verbal and nonverbal presentation skills. Finally, you will learn about standards for evaluating speeches—your own as well as those you hear in class, in the community, and in the media. Let us begin with the four styles of presenting speeches.

TYPES OF PRESENTATIONS

For as long as there have been speakers, essentially four different types of **presentation styles** have been available: memorized, with a manuscript, extemporaneous, and impromptu. Your speech will fall into one of these styles of delivery every time you speak. Depending on the time and place, one type will be more appropriate than the others. Yet each one will be the right one at some particular time. The appropriateness, strengths, and weaknesses of each type will help you decide when to use and when to avoid a particular style. Your instructor may assign you one style for your classroom presentations but, outside of class, you will need to select the one you believe is most appropriate.

Memorized

A **memorized** presentation follows a word-for-word preparation. This process, although time-consuming and tiring, gives you the advantage of speaking without notes, of including every detail exactly as you planned, and of knowing precisely how long your speech will last. In a formal setting, and when you have only a few minutes to express your thoughts, this style of presentation may be just right. However, this style has one major drawback: You might forget part of your speech. As a result of the pressure that public communication can put on you, you may forget a line or a word. If you memorize the way most people do, you depend on one line following another, like the links of a chain. Each sentence ties you to the next. If your mind goes blank for a moment, you might forget not only a word or a line, but also all the lines that follow. If this happens, all the benefits of memorization evaporate along with the lost lines. You are now unable to speak. Now you need your notes, your timing is off, and you may skip ideas or materials on which you worked very hard. Unfortunately, many beginning speakers think that they must memorize to make a good impression. The more concerned and worried they are, the more they are tempted to try to control every second and every syllable of their presentation. Their very anxiety is their worst enemy. They forget their speech, and the disaster that they had nightmares about actually happens—caused by their own over-preparation. Memorized speeches are usually best left to very experienced speakers.

Another disadvantage of memorization is that all but the very best speakers tend to sound mechanical, stilted, and uninvolved when speaking from memory. Instead of establishing genuine rapport with their audiences, speakers who memorize often look and sound like robots, reciting lines with no direct connection to their listeners. If the audience does respond with some feedback, these speakers cannot adapt or respond to the audience, and communication interaction fails. The use of memory for most people is probably manageable if it is limited to very short speeches, such as a thank-you or a brief introduction in a very formal setting. Memorization probably will not be appropriate for most speeches or presentations you will give in your lifetime.

Manuscript

A speaker who delivers a speech from a **manuscript** usually writes out or types the speech word for word and then presents the speech by reading the manuscript. In the best manuscript delivery, speakers spend about ten to twenty percent of their time looking down at the script and eighty to ninety percent of the time looking at the audience to establish eye contact and direct interaction. The speaker must always focus on the audience and not on the manuscript. The advantage of speaking from a manuscript is that you have no fear of forgetting. In addition, you have control over what you say, and your timing will be very accurate.

You will usually see a manuscript delivery when you attend major events such as graduations, dedications, presidential addresses, public ceremonies, or religious services. Often, the delivery is very good, but sometimes it is not. One reason that people use manuscripts is to lend an elevated tone to the event by using polished vocabulary and sentence structure. With this kind of preparation, they can be sure that they will make no mistakes. Generally, a manuscript speaker does not sound as mechanical as a memorized speaker, but a manuscript can still create a barrier to good eye contact, and it does not allow for much adjustment to audience feedback. Reading from a manuscript lacks both spontaneity and immediacy, and it runs the risk of making the speaker sound flat, recycled, stale, or not directly connected to the listeners. Manuscript presentation is usually found in longer presentations— beyond eight or ten minutes—and when the ceremony itself or the accuracy of the information is the most important consideration.

Extemporaneous

An **extemporaneous speech** is the type you will give most often—both in the classroom and later in life. To deliver a good extemporaneous speech, you have to prepare and practice, but you must stop short of memorizing the words of your presentation or writing them out in sentences. Good extemporaneous speakers will carefully prepare a key idea or key word outline. They then memorize the outline but allow the exact words of the body to emerge spontaneously. They practice out loud many times; although the speech is very similar each time, it is never exactly the same. Moreover, they do not attempt to achieve exactness. If a phrase or a sentence reverses itself from one time to the next, that is permissible as long as the point of the topic or idea is clearly made each time.

The advantages of an outline to you as a speaker are many. Using an outline gives you a comprehensive plan, helps you to be comfortable with the materials, and ensures that you will have the results of your research and organization readily at hand. An outline also allows you to practice enough to know the length of your presentation. Finally, using an outline gives you the flexibility to be spontaneous and direct and to adapt to your audience immediately. You can remain conversational, thereby increasing audience attention and rapport. You can also create a sense of directness in your approach that helps give impact to your ideas. In virtually every situation, audiences prefer extemporaneous speeches, and they rate the speakers who give such speeches very highly.

There are, of course, some potential disadvantages to this type of presentation. You do not have exactness in your wording or your timing. You need to smooth out your phrasing; some speakers, especially if they are working in a second language, may not be as adept at spontaneity as others. However, because it is an appropriate type of presentation for so many settings, it is important for you to develop skills in extemporaneous speaking.

Impromptu

When you deliver a speech on only a few moments' notice, you are engaging in **impromptu** speaking. You may find yourself at a meeting and decide to speak about the issue under consideration. In your career, you may suddenly be asked by a visiting team to explain your section of the company. In class, you may be called on to provide a lengthy explanation of a point or a defense of a position. At a business conference, someone who has heard of your creative work may ask you to stand up and explain your latest project to a group or an assembly.

In each of these situations, you would not have prepared an outline or rehearsed your presentation. However, it is a mistake to call impromptu speeches unprepared speeches. In a very real sense, you are prepared—and in many ways. First, note that no one is asked to speak about something unless there is a reason or expectation that the person can do so. In class, you should know the material. In a meeting, you are there because of your interest. In work settings, you will find yourself explaining things that are directly related to your career. So you do have some research and some supporting materials that are with you always and everywhere: your experience, background, and knowledge. Moreover, this class and others have given you some preparation for organizing those experiences into a coherent speech. If you are asked five years from now to give an impromptu speech, you will already know that your speech should have an introduction, a clear thesis sentence, and a body organized into some pattern that has from two to five main divisions that relate to the thesis. You know right now that you need a quick review for the conclusion and supporting materials that are vivid, specific, and varied. You are already writing your future impromptu speeches. When the time comes, you will need only a few moments to jot down some notes so that you can quickly create a basic outline, fill in spaces, and be ready to give your speech. All of your

▶ IMPROVING COMPETENCY
Honing Your Presentation Skills

Try using the four different types of presentations as you speak in your classes, on the job, or in your community. You might read notes in one setting and make an impromptu speech in another. You could memorize a short presentation or try the extemporaneous method. By being aware of the four different types of delivery, and by putting them into practice, you will expand your range of abilities. What is more, you can start today.

earlier speeches will have given you practice in modulating your voice, making eye contact, creating transitions, and using good body language. Those skills will also be with you everywhere you go.

There are several advantages to being able to deliver an impromptu speech that will make your ideas more compelling than those of people who do not know how to make such speeches. Impromptu speeches are immediately adaptable to the situation and the audience, and they make it possible for the speaker to respond directly to any feedback from the audience. On the other hand, you may not remember to organize an outline, or your supporting materials might not be as strong or as varied as you would like. Your timing and phrasing might be off. Giving good impromptu speeches is a real challenge, but it can also be personally gratifying for the person who does it well.

You can evaluate and select from the four types of presentations according to the circumstances of your speech. No matter which type you select, you will most likely have one experience each and every time you present a speech: some nervousness.

■ DEALING WITH APPREHENSION

As mentioned in Chapter 2, the mere thought of giving a speech is enough to produce **speech apprehension** in most people (Richmond and McCroskey, 1995). This reaction is common and normal. The symptoms—tension, "butterflies," sweaty palms, tight and shallow breathing, and a lump in the throat—are felt by everyone. These symptoms are the standard physiological reactions to fear and stress. Like many other fears, this one can be managed and reduced.

It is important to know that any nervousness you have is natural and that, with preparation, you can respond to it so that it no longer hinders you when you are doing a presentation. You read about the source and effects of speech apprehension in Chapter 2, in which several approaches to the problem were recommended.

Apprehension may flow from one or more of three sources: excessive activation of your physical responses, inappropriate cognitive processing of the situation, or inadequate communication skills (Richmond and McCroskey, 1995). In this chapter, some very practical, specific suggestions are made that you can use when it is your turn to speak. Giving a speech puts a person in the spotlight and most people have a strong desire to appear competent in the eyes of others. If you have never had any training in giving speeches, you might be afraid of making mistakes and appearing to lack competence. If you have never learned how to drive a car, you should keep out of the driver's seat. However, once you take a driver-training course and gain a little experience, you still won't be an expert driver, but driving should no longer be such a formidable experience that you avoid it altogether. In the same way, preparing and presenting a speech, when you approach that task with some knowledge and experience, can develop your competence and your confidence.

The bottom line is: To appear credible, you should be credible. Many of the steps to gaining credibility have already been covered—select a substantial and worthwhile topic; give it the clear organization and preparation it deserves; provide yourself with significant supporting materials; and select a presentation type that is appropriate for both you and the situation. The last task of your preparation is to practice; while you practice your speech aloud, you can also practice some physiological and psychological exercises that can augment your total preparation.

Physiological Preparation

If you have excess energy, you can learn to use **physiological preparation** to reduce some of that energy. As you sit awaiting your turn to speak, you will probably experience your greatest level of anxiety. There are several physical exercises that you can practice ahead of time that will help train your muscles to relax. If you practice physiological preparation now, and then again as you practice your speech, you will have some excellent tools to help overcome the negative effects of your natural tension.

Correct Breathing   First of all, the best method that has been proven to counter excess tension involves breathing. In ancient cultures that taught us yoga and in modern Lamaze childbirth methods, correct breathing is at the heart of controlling and channeling energy. The importance of breath control is seen in sports, singing, exercise, acting, childbirth, and public speaking. These techniques can help you to gain control over your apprehension and ease the labor of presenting your ideas to others. These breathing techniques are easy to learn and easy to apply.

The basic exercise is to breathe slowly and regularly from your diaphragm. Yoga teachers point out that when you relax the center of your body, a calming feeling emanates through the rest of your body. By breathing regularly and slowly, in and out, while you practice your speech, you will develop a habit of relaxing that will help you while you are waiting for your turn to speak. By so doing, you will supply your brain with oxygen, keep your butterflies under control, and begin to calm your entire body. You can practice slow, regular, and deep breathing while you are rehearsing your speech.

Muscle Relaxation   Another physical exercise that you can practice, and then do while waiting for your turn to speak, is a tensing and relaxing of various muscles. Try this: Locate the calf muscle in your right leg. Now, keeping your thigh muscle relaxed, tense just the calf muscle. This exercise is not easy. Try to make the calf muscle tight; hold it for a count of ten; then relax. During this exercise, you should be breathing slowly. Now switch legs and repeat the exercise. Try the same exercise with the thigh muscles. Continue to breathe slowly. Now try tensing your forearm but leave your biceps relaxed. Breathe slowly.

You can do these exercises very subtly so that even if you are doing them on stage in front of an audience, no one will be aware of what you are doing. In fact, what you will be doing is using up some energy—skimming off some of the tension so that your muscles will be more relaxed. You will still have plenty of energy to give a dynamic presentation, but you will not have the shaky knees or the quivering hands of speakers who tense up and then hold onto that tension. You might try the exercise at home with any combination of muscles. Try selective tensing—hold for five deep breaths, and then relax. Airline passengers are often taught these and similar isometric exercises as a way of avoiding fatigue. If you are not on stage but in a fairly private setting, you can try shrugging your shoulders and rotating them forward and then backward. Another helpful exercise for reducing tension is to lower your head slowly until your chin rests on your chest. Then slowly rotate up one side, then down again, and slowly up the other side. A good, long yawn can help to relax the throat. You can even yawn on stage if you remember to keep your mouth closed. Try it now. Can you feel the stretch of your larynx? That stretch will relax your voice.

As you do the breathing exercises and the muscle-tensing and relaxing exercises, remember that you are in control. If you practice these exercises often, doing them in a slow and regular pattern, you can build your confidence. You will, of

The Story of Communication
Creative Visualization

A FEW YEARS AGO, the Public Broadcasting Service television stations ran a feature that described a basketball training camp experiment. The researchers divided students at the camp into three groups that were tested on their free-throw ability. The first group was thanked for its participation, sent home, and told to come back in a month. The second group was given four hours a day of instruction for four weeks and practice in free-throw technique. The third group was taken to a classroom, shown a film on perfect free-throw technique, and given instruction on positive visualization and self-imagery. For a month, these students sat in a quiet room for twenty minutes a day and imagined themselves shooting perfect free throws. At the end of the month, the first group had a ten percent decrease in average free-throw ability. The second group had a twenty-three percent increase in free throws. The third group had a twenty-one percent increase in free-throw ability. Although visualization was not as effective as the actual practice, the third group did improve significantly. This experiment demonstrates the power of visualization.

course, feel the direct, physical benefits immediately. When you go to your presentation, remember to start your deep breathing as you approach your position in front of the audience. Start your muscle tensing and relaxing as soon as you reach your seat. Getting in control of your physical reactions is a direct way to meet the challenge your physiology presents to you when you are under stress. Incidentally, people use these techniques in many different kinds of situations: taking a test, being interviewed, meeting a special person's parents, trying out for a team, or auditioning for a show. When you are in a situation in which you begin to feel the flight-or-fight reaction, counteract it immediately with the physiological responses described.

In some cases, the extremes of physiological reaction can be reduced effectively by a six-step process known as systematic desensitization (Wolpe, 1958). This process takes extremely anxious individuals through a series of imagined anxiety-producing situations in which they moved from low to high stress levels. Deep muscle relaxation training enabled the participants to master their anxiety at each level before moving to the next. This system has been widely applied (Hoffman and Sprague, 1982), and although why it works is not fully understood, we know that it does produce significant improvement for many people (Richmond and McCroskey, 1995).

Psychological Preparation

The second part of the communication apprehension reaction is psychological. Your mind is the place where the danger signals begin, so your mind is where you can work on countermeasures. Remember, in most presentation situations, it is appropriate to feel that the occasion is important, and you have every right to be concerned about your presentation and its outcome. However, in an effort not just to control the reaction, but to eliminate it altogether, many people wind themselves up even tighter and create exactly the opposite effect from the one that they intended. Acknowledge the importance of what you are doing, but remember that control of the reaction—not its elimination—is your goal. There are several steps you can take in **psychological preparation** to enlist your mind to help you deal with communication apprehension.

Familiarity   Become familiar with the situation. This means that you need to follow up on your analysis of the setting. If you take that advice, you are already on your way to having a positive frame of mind rather than an anxious frame of mind.

People dislike what is unfamiliar, so getting to know your setting is a big step toward psychological control. Your efforts to become familiar with your listeners—their backgrounds, values, and listening goals—will also help you to know what the situation requires and how to prepare for it. As you become familiar with the speaking environment and your intended audience, you will have fewer uncertainties and greater confidence.

Involvement   Be involved in your topic. This step helps you to focus on your topic and its importance to your listeners and therefore be less focused on yourself. Select

a topic that you care about. After you have expended energy on research and preparation, you will develop a psychological investment in the topic. As the ideas in
your presentation gain greater importance, your ego becomes less important. If you
have a strong desire to communicate to your audience about something you find
worthwhile and substantial, you will replace concern for your appearance or your
nervousness with concern for your message. If you are genuinely involved in your
ideas, your involvement and commitment to those ideas will show in your preparation, practice, and presentation. For that reason, you need to avoid a topic picked
out of a magazine the night before the presentation or recycled from a friend. Create
a sincere message, and your sincerity will be evident.

Concern   Show concern for your audience. After you have selected a good topic,
take the time to demonstrate that you also care about your listeners. Do you have a
sincere desire to communicate with them? Have you considered their reasons for
being in the audience? Have you approached the topic from their point of view? By
responding to these questions, you place the attention on your ideas and your audience rather than yourself. Focus on your listeners, and relate your speech to them.
In that way, your psychological commitment is to the ideas in your presentation
and to the receivers to whom you send those ideas, not to your own personal concerns. The message is communicated in collaboration with the audience or not at
all. Review Chapter 3 to gain a deeper appreciation of your listeners. Remember
that you are speaking not to a mirror but to real people. If you keep your listeners
uppermost in your mind, you will have less time to become overly concerned with
yourself. And don't forget to smile.

Imaging   Imagine yourself as a strong speaker. Do you recall the discussion about
how powerful self-concept messages can be? Use that knowledge to help you create an ideal speaker in your mind—in other words, you. Picture yourself doing a
good job. Imagine smiles on the faces of your listeners. Visualize your speech going
smoothly and ending at just the right time and in just the right way. Many people
dwell on negative thoughts when they are feeling apprehensive. They invest large
amounts of psychological capital in all the awful things they fear might happen. As
you learned in the chapter about intrapersonal communication, your internal messages are very powerful, but they are under your control. When you find your internal messages drifting toward negative thoughts, replace those thoughts with positive visualizations. Imagine yourself as a calm, energetic, and dynamic person who
thinks and speaks clearly. Imagine your audience's reactions as being positive—
nods of agreement, smiles at your ideas, and applause at the end of your presentation. Keep this image in your mind when you practice, while you wait your turn to
speak, and during your presentation. Positive visualization works for sports teams
and is exactly what getting "psyched up" for an event means. If you mentally predict success, it is more likely to come your way.

   You know enough about public speaking by now to realize that the best way
for physiological and psychological preparation to work is for them to work
together. The mind and the body are a team, not independent entities. When you
concentrate on your breathing, you will forget to get butterflies. In other words,

the human mind concentrates best on only one thing at a time. When you create a positive mental image, your physical energy is channeled into that image, and both your mind and your body help you to realize it. Teamwork between physical exercises and psychological responses can give you the focus and confidence you need to make the image a reality. You will find that you are able to control your public-speaking energy. You can then direct that energy into making yourself a skilled public speaker.

EFFECTIVE PUBLIC SPEAKING SKILLS

Once your preparation is strong and solid, you can pay attention to the presentation itself. The success of your delivery will depend on how effectively you use your voice and body to deliver your message with clarity and impact. There are five elements of **vocal delivery** that will be discussed next. Then, you'll learn how to use posture, movement, and gestures to enhance your message.

Verbal Skills

Because your listeners must be able to hear you, *volume* is the obvious first element of good vocal delivery. Speak loudly enough to be heard by every person in your audience. You may need to use a microphone if the room is especially large, so test the microphone for sound level and feedback—in advance, if possible—and then practice using it. In a classroom or business conference room, a microphone is not only inappropriate, it is unnecessary. For the majority of your speeches, you will be in front of a small or medium-sized group, and you will speak with a voice supported by good breathing from your deep-breathing routine.

You can find out whether the volume of your voice is adequate by practicing in the room in which you are going to speak and by having someone tell you how you sound. When you are actually giving your presentation, carefully observe your listeners. Do they relax and seem comfortable, or do they strain and lean forward to hear what you are saying? Keep in mind that a room full of people absorbs sound; do not practice in an empty room. Also, vary the sound of your voice. You can emphasize ideas by changing your volume, but do not be misguided into thinking that loud means important. Although we often raise our volume to emphasize an important idea, we also drop the volume very low to show the same thing. At a wedding, for example, the bride and groom speak at a very low volume when they say some of the most important words they will ever utter. Speak louder and then softer; it is the change in volume that alerts listeners that a change is taking place in the message.

Articulation and *pronunciation* are also important to your vocal delivery; they ensure that you are understood by your listeners, and they help build your credibility. The way you make your sounds should be clear, and your pronunciation should be within an acceptable range for your audience.

Articulation is the clear production of sounds that are crisp and distinct. It involves using your muscles and vocal structures as tools to produce clear and audible sounds. To develop articulation, you need to be able to hear yourself. Although that sounds like an easy task, it is actually somewhat difficult, at least at first. You are so used to the sound of your own voice that you might not be objective about the sounds you produce. Use a tape recorder. Then listen to your voice with a sensitive ear. Be especially sensitive to the final consonants *t* and *d*. Many people ignore them. Sometimes middle syllables are altered, as when people say "fas'nating" instead of "fascinating." Some people add syllables to words, as when someone says "orientate" when the correct word is *orient*, or "orientated" instead of the word *oriented*. As you work on developing sensitive self-feedback, your articulation will improve.

Sometimes people worry about pronunciation. Pronunciation is the use of clearly articulated sounds in any given word. You might try using a dictionary pronunciation guide at first; it will tell you how educated speakers of Mainstream English pronounce the word.

Your pronunciation can affect your credibility. Many listeners associate a level of competence with a certain pronunciation. If you have a strong regional accent, you may sometimes want to modify it when your audience is from a different region. In a well-known example, former President Kennedy was speaking to a group of ministers in Houston, far from his native Boston. In a recording of that speech, you can hear Kennedy modify at times his New England pronunciation of "Americur" to "America." Both Presidents Clinton and Bush softened their regional accents when speaking outside their native states.

Depending on the listeners, most regional and ethnic differences in pronunciation can be perfectly acceptable if the words are clearly articulated. If you have a regional color to your speech, there is no need to be overly concerned as long as your audience can follow you easily and feels that your speech is credible. Follow the generally accepted standards of educated people in your audience. Sometimes an accent can add interest or uniqueness to your presentation, and it may be a genuine part of you that you wish to retain, even when you are not dealing with listeners from the same cultural or regional background as you. Can your present listeners understand you? Does your credibility remain high? If so, don't feel that you must eliminate every trace of your background accent.

However, some accents do create an unfavorable impression if they are associated with substandard speech. Saying "gist" for the word *just* is an example of pronunciation that is often associated with a lack of education. Again your dictionary can help you with problems like this one. By following the standards of educated people in your community, you can be both faithful to your background and understood by your listeners.

Pitch is simply the musical note that your voice makes when it issues sound. You may have a high soprano voice, or you may be a deep bass. In any case, your voice has a range that is comfortable, and you have a typical pitch at which you usually speak. When people are tense, they tend to speak a note or two higher than their usual pitch. A closed-mouth yawn can help get you back to normal. If you feel that your pitch is too high in general, you can develop a lower voice by relaxing your throat and learning to speak in a lower relaxed tone. In a private setting, you might try to tilt your head back slightly and slowly gargle air; let your vocal bands relax and "flap" on the air stream. Lower tones also carry better than higher ones, so speaking in a low tone that is still within your normal range can help your voice to project farther out into the room.

Variety in pitch is also important. When you raise your pitch slightly at the end of an interrogative sentence, you are telling your listeners that your sentence is a question. You can also use the range of your voice to create interest and emphasis. A tape recorder can assist you in developing good variety in the pitch of your voice. Use it to learn how to enhance your message and to see what areas you need to work on if your voice seems to be stuck in a limited monotone.

Your *rate* of speech is how fast or slowly you speak. You have probably heard speakers who speed along so fast that you cannot follow them and others who drag on for so long that it seems to take them forever to get to the point. As is true for the other elements of vocal presentation, variety can be a key ingredient to your success as a speaker. Going fast sometimes and then slowing down adds interest to your speech, and you can also use this technique to emphasize key ideas for your audience.

Also related to rate of speech is silence, an important component of your speech. Pause at key places to emphasize ideas. For example, if you have an important word coming up, alert your listeners by pausing just before you say it. During the pause, gaze around the room at your audience to heighten the expectation. "And the winner is…!" is a perfect example of the use of a pause before a key idea to create an impact. After you have presented an important idea, you may want to pause to give the audience a moment to absorb or think about what you have just said. Try going through your speech to discover the impact that a well-chosen pause might have on your message.

The final element, *tone*, is the most difficult to vary. This aspect of your voice is also called quality, or timbre. The tone of your voice refers to those qualities that are unique in resonance and sound production. When Jim calls on the phone, you can distinguish his voice from Walt's voice. When you hear a note played on a clarinet, you can tell that it is not a violin even if it is playing the exact same note. The instruments may be played at the same volume, rate, and pitch, but tone is what distinguishes each instrument. Brothers or sisters may sound very much alike because they share many genes and have been raised in a similar environment. Therefore their vocal production and patterns may also be similar.

It is difficult to provide variety in your tone of voice and, unless your voice is at one extreme or another of the tonal scale, it is probably not very important to do so. However, if your voice is excessively nasal or so breathy that people think you are trying to imitate a movie star, you may wish to work on altering your tone production.

When is a person's tone of voice excessive? If your audience pays more attention to the tone of your voice than to your ideas, you are probably a candidate for tone modification. You can alter a nasal voice by learning how to close off the nasal passages and open your mouth and throat more. You can reduce a breathy voice by using less air in your vocal production and by forcing that air through a slightly smaller opening. Of course, you can have fun playing around with your tone production, and that may be one way to discover some tonal variety that you can use to your advantage in your presentation. If your tone production severely impairs clear communication with your listeners, you may need some sessions with a qualified speech therapist to develop some new habits of sound production.

All of these qualities of good vocal delivery can bring clarity and emphasis to your message. The use of volume, diction, pitch, rate, and tone can be enhanced by appropriate variety. You can increase your ability to discover and use this variety by careful self-monitoring, especially through tape-recorded practice.

Nonverbal Skills

Studies of speech communication have found that the use of both voice and body are very important in giving a speech. In one experiment, a trained actor presented a speech to several different audiences. Although the speech was the same on each occasion, in one half of the sessions he stood perfectly still and simply gave his speech. In the other half, he took a few steps from time to time and used a few arm, hand, and head movements. The responses to the speech were markedly different. The second group of listeners thought that the speaker was more intelligent than the first group did. They also thought that he was better looking and taller. Most importantly, though, is that after a month the second group remembered the content better than the first group did. Clearly, nonverbal communication that complements a verbal message appropriately can make that message more effective. Physical communication delivery has four major components: appearance, posture, movements, and facial expressions.

Appearance is the first thing your audience will notice about you, even in a classroom setting. It is said, "You never get a second chance to make a first impression." That first impression is always made by your appearance, and it can affect the way listeners will receive your complete message. Ask yourself what is generally expected or worn in similar circumstances, and let your answer be your guide. Is your speech a classroom speech? Are you going to be interviewed for a job or a scholarship? Will you be doing a reading at a religious service, or are you going to be a commencement speaker? Each of these settings probably has a standard of dress and grooming that is appropriate to it. Why should you be concerned with such a seemingly superficial concept as appearance? For the same reason that you would be concerned about your voice or a visual aid. If receivers pay more attention to those factors than they do to your message, they will miss the point of your communication. All the choices you make should enhance and highlight the content of your message. The great fashion designer and perfume manufacturer Coco Chanel was reputed to have said, "If they remember the dress and not the woman, they have remembered the wrong thing." On the days that you present a speech in class, you need not wear a business suit. But you can dress at the better end of the spectrum of what people normally wear to class. Caring about your appearance is one way to demonstrate care and respect for your topic, your ideas, your listeners, and yourself.

Posture refers to your overall stance, or how you hold yourself when speaking. Usually, listeners expect speakers to stand up straight—not slouch, lean on the lectern, or drape themselves across a chair or table. Your posture need not be

TECHNOLOGY AND COMMUNICATION
Honest Feedback

Videotaping your practices may be one way to get some direct feedback on your use of gestures, postures, and vocal variety. The widespread availability of video cameras and players makes this tool one to which you probably have easy access. Each year, the cost of these cameras and players comes down, and the quality and capabilities of the equipment go up. Technological advances will allow you to see yourself in slow motion, freeze the action, or fast-forward to get an exaggerated picture of yourself. About fifteen years ago, I began the practice of videotaping my students' speeches and letting them view the tape later, one at a time. Since that time, my students' abilities to present oral communication have improved beyond the levels they used to reach. Take advantage of this technology and use it to provide accurate feedback.

stiff and formal, but it should communicate alertness and energy. Posture also includes the way you position your body. You should turn from one side to another while speaking and eventually face all sections of the audience. In this way, you can vary your posture in a comfortable, useful way.

Movements are the many shifts, turns, and gestures you make while still maintaining overall posture. Appropriate movement that assists in the clear transmission of your message is not only desirable, it is essential. Some speakers seem to be in constant movement, which can be distracting to the audience. But a speaker standing perfectly still can be boring to the audience. Somewhere in between the two extremes is a level of movement that will both suit you and enhance your communication effectiveness. Speakers who engage in a moderate number of movements and gestures are rated by audiences as being more credible than those who do not move very much or those who are in almost constant motion. If you are showing your listeners a picture or a chart you may need to move so that they can see it properly.

Smaller movements are called **gestures** and include everything from slight hand movements and head nods to the expansive and descriptive shaping of space with your arms or perhaps your entire body. Most people think of gestures as hand movements because they are most common and most noticeable. You could, of course, lift your foot and point with your toe, but most people do not. Are you wondering what to do with your hands? Most people seem uncomfortable just letting them hang at their sides. Some people try clasping their hands behind their back, shoving them into their pockets, or folding them in front of the chest. These options severely restrict the opportunity to reinforce and complement your ideas with appropriate gestures. They may also influence you to hold onto tension. Gestures are best used when they are natural and spontaneous— just the way you would use them if you were sitting in your living room or at a lunch table talking with friends. A relaxed, natural animation helps the audience connect with the speaker and creates a friendly rapport. Videotaping your practice sessions is one way to get some direct feedback on your use of gestures.

Facial expressions include a raised eyebrow, a smile, a wink, a frown, or wide-eyed surprise. Research suggests that the face is the most powerful, non-verbal communicator because of the hundreds of possible combinations of expressions you can make with your facial muscles. You are also capable of recognizing and giving meaning to these combinations. Make certain that the message your face sends is consistent with the message of your speech. Have a friend help you videotape your speech. Then check it for clear and communicative facial expressions.

Eye contact is an important element in communication. Having good eye contact means that you look at your listeners almost all of the time, establishing a direct link between yourself and individual members of the audience. Many students find this contact difficult to establish and maintain. Some are reluctant to use eye contact because they start thinking about the person they are looking at instead of the idea they are speaking about. Other speakers may come from cultures or traditions in which direct eye contact is considered rude. In traditional Asian and African families, it is often a sign of respect to look away from the person you are addressing. Some families maintain these cultural norms through many generations. However, the mainstream American social norm is to establish direct eye contact with the audience when you are in a public-speaking situation.

It is difficult to think about your speech and simultaneously gaze around the room, looking at all the members of your audience. One common problem for classroom speakers is that they will find a friendly face and present most or all of the speech to that one person. Speakers are usually unaware that they are doing this. The best thing to do is to glance slowly around the room, looking directly at each person for only a brief moment and then moving on to the next person. Although some members of the audience may not be looking back at you at that precise moment, most of them will be, and you will make them feel included. You

DIVERSITY IN COMMUNICATION
The Emperor and the Messenger

In Kyoto, Japan, the imperial palace has a reception hall where messengers used to bring news and information to the emperor. A lowly messenger could not speak directly to the emperor, so three floor levels were built into the room. The messenger would kneel at the first level and present the message to the shogun, or intermediary, who sat at the second level, about ten feet away. The intermediary would then turn to the emperor, who sat at the third level (also about ten feet away) and repeat the message. The emperor probably heard every word the messenger said, since he was barely twenty feet away. Nevertheless, cultural communication norms had to be observed. Consequently the emperor showed no reaction, not even to terrible news, until the intermediary repeated it to him. The same process was reversed if the emperor had a return message. First he told it to the intermediary, who then told it to the messenger. The messenger, of course, could give no indication that he had heard a single word spoken by the emperor.

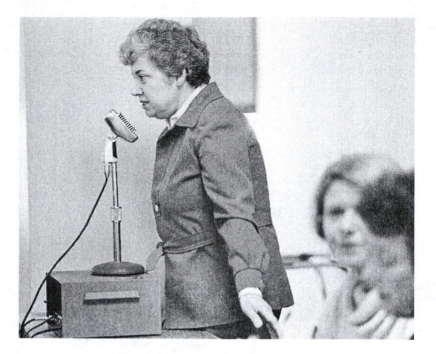

Presenting your opinion in public is part of good citizenship.

can also be reading their expressions and postures for feedback as you look around. Do you see some puzzled looks? Maybe you should explain your idea from a different angle. Do some people seem bored? Tell a lively story, change the volume of your voice, or make a dynamic movement. Eye contact makes the audience feel connected to the speaker and the speech. This connection is called rapport, and it is a strong factor in getting your message across. One way to create and maintain rapport is through direct, but passing, eye contact while speaking.

Verbal and nonverbal presentation skills are important because, together, they carry your complete message to your listeners. Good delivery enhances, but cannot replace, good content. The best speakers have both; they begin with a worthwhile message and then develop a good presentation. Each speaker will have some personal variations on the general suggestions presented here, so you can still demonstrate your individuality while working within this framework.

EVALUATING PUBLIC SPEECHES

Every time you give a speech in class or a presentation in public, you will be evaluated. You won't always get a written grade for your outline or your speech, but you can be sure that people will be forming evaluations of you and your message. Because evaluation is integral to any communication event, it is appropriate to look at how people judge the communication they receive. One way to **evaluate speeches** is to judge them according to standards of presentation, audience adaptation, and ethics.

Standards of Presentation

The presentation standards relate to the preparation and speaking skills you should exhibit in your speech. Whether you are listening to others speak or they are listening to you, the same criteria concerning topic, materials, organization, language, and delivery are evaluated.

The topic of a speech must have *significance*. This means that the topic itself must be worth the time and effort that you invest in preparing your speech. It must also be important enough to warrant your audience's attention. The topic should inspire new insights and perspectives in the listeners. It should not be trivial or superficial. The ideas you express should address what you assume to be the best aspects of your audience.

You should also enhance, illustrate, and focus your topic with *adequate* and *appropriate supporting materials*. The research sources and factual basis for the speech should be solid and very clearly presented. The supporting materials should contain material of real substance. A quick look at one issue of *Time* magazine is not adequate to support a speech on changing our policies in the Middle East. Moreover, personal experience should not be considered more than a place to begin. Even a presentation on your trip to the Grand Canyon could include some statistics about the canyon, a quotation from John Wesley Powell (the first explorer to travel the entire canyon by boat), a reference to a Havasupai legend, and a published interview with a ranger stationed there. Finally, the material must be appropriate for the maturity level of the audience, as well as for the setting, the occasion, and the time limits.

Your outline is the basic guideline for evaluating *clarity of organization*. Do you have clear and distinct subordinate ideas? Is the thesis clearly stated? Are there clear transitions that link major items together in a cohesive body? Remember, the body must have its own internal logic. Use one of the patterns suggested in the previous chapter to create a complete and comprehensive outline.

CRITICAL THINKING IN COMMUNICATION
Critical Message Reception

One of the positive aspects of being a critical thinker is that you automatically become a critical consumer of information. You call on this ability when you evaluate advertising, marketing, and other information that you receive. For example, you can use critical thinking skills to evaluate the speeches you hear in class or the advertising you see on television. As you read and gather information in support of your messages, keep in mind what you learned from evaluating the messages of others. You need to select from among many choices and options. Critical thinking helps you to compare your options and choose the best ones for the time, place, and circumstances of your communication. In short, applying critical-thinking skills will help you to listen more carefully to others and select more carefully for yourself.

Choice and fluency of language are two aspects of your delivery that go hand in hand. You should choose language that is vivid and at an appropriate level. Do you select words that both communicate and create interest? Are you using too abstract a vocabulary? Do you talk down to, or talk at, your listeners? Fluency concerns the ease with which your words flow. Do they flow smoothly, and are they presented in a tone and at a rate to which your audience can respond?

A final standard of delivery concerns the *use of voice and body*. This is what many people think of when they discuss presentation. Many beginning speakers focus almost exclusively on these aspects of their presentation. But these criteria represent only one of the five areas of evaluation. On the other hand, you do need to speak loudly and clearly and use movement, gestures, facial expressions, and eye contact to enhance your message.

Evaluating speeches according to these five standards will probably be sufficient for most presentations. However, if presentations were judged only by these standards, the judges would be lacking in terms of two very important, additional criteria—the adaptation of the speech to the audience, and the adherence of the speaker to ethical standards of communication.

Adaptation to the Audience

To meet the standard of adaptation to the audience, the speaker must demonstrate a clear attempt to select content that applies to the particular group that is listening to the presentation. Such aspects of the speech as level of interest, complexity of ideas, clarity of sentence structure, and type of visual aids are included in this standard. References to the immediate listeners—to their values and to their reasons for being present—are also included in this standard. In short, the question to be answered in evaluating presentations according to this standard is: What is the value of the information to the audience?

Standards of Ethics

An **ethical communication** must meet several tests. It must be *honest;* that is, you cannot lie to your listeners. You must make certain that what you purport to be true is, in fact, true. Some speakers depend on the statements of others. Then, when the statements turn out to be erroneous or faulty, they blame their sources. The responsibility for the content of a speech rests clearly and solely with the speaker. If the speaker depends on others' faulty research, it is the speaker who bears the fault. That is why it is so important to do wide-ranging research. Any unusual or inconsistent information will become noticeable to you when no other source confirms it.

Sometimes a speaker will invent a story to illustrate an idea. This type of invention is fine, as long as the speaker makes it clear to the listeners that the story is only a hypothetical support. Speakers usually let the audience know they are only telling a story when they say things like, "Let's imagine for a moment…," or, "Suppose that this happened to you…," or, "I once heard a story about a man who…." These phrases say very clearly that the information the audience is about to hear is fictional. Then you can be as creative as you wish. Otherwise, if you give your listeners the impression that what you are saying is true, it had better be true.

A second aspect of ethical communication follows from the first. That is, you must *credit your sources*. If you follow the five-part outline suggested in Chapter 11, you will include a bibliography in your own outline to document your research and give credit to the ideas that are not your own. But what about your audience? Since the spoken part of your presentation ends with the fourth section, the conclusion, you do not actually read your bibliography to your listeners. The way to include your citations is to work them into the flow of your speech. Instead of saying, "There were nearly 50,000 deaths on the highway last year due to drunk drivers," you might say, "According to the National Safety Council in their September report this year, there were nearly 50,000 deaths on the highway last year." This is a good citation, and it makes a strong impact. The audience will listen more carefully if you cite a respected authority. You do not need to include the complete citation, with page numbers, city of publication, and so on, but a reference to the source alone is sufficient to meet the ethical requirement that your listeners know where you got the information.

A third area of ethical consideration relates to the way in which the *audience is capable of using* the information. Sometimes it is ethical to deliver a certain message to one audience but unethical to deliver the same message to another group. For example, a high-power sales pitch for a set of expensive books is appropriate for a consumer who can afford them and who can benefit from them. A family that is struggling to pay the rent each month or has limited language skills would probably benefit from a gift of used books and information about free courses to improve their language skills. It would be unethical to try to pressure this family into a purchase. An ethical salesperson would give the first family a lively sales presentation and give the second family a list of places where they might find free reading material and language training.

Another way to evaluate the ethics of a message is according to its *completeness*. Not only must your message be true, supported, cited, and of value to the listeners, it must not deliberately leave out vital information. If a speaker tells you about a cure for cancer and fails to mention that it has been investigated and rejected by the American Medical Association, the speaker is being dishonest by giving you incomplete information.

To summarize, the distinguishing characteristics of speeches made by ethical speakers are truthfulness, completeness, fairness, and good documentation. Anything less would be judged as not meeting the minimum standards of communication ethics.

IMPROVING PUBLIC COMMUNICATION COMPETENCY

If you have ever admired speakers who exhibit excellent speaking abilities, you know that the first thing you notice about them is their **confidence**. The way to look confident is to *be* confident, and confidence can be achieved by following four distinct steps to improve your competency as a speaker (Zeuschner, 1994).

Know your subject well. If you have a comfortable feeling about your topic, you are well on your way to becoming a confident speaker. Of course, you need to select a topic that interests you or about which you already know something. Then you must spend time developing your knowledge and interest in the subject. If you consult many sources; if you interview or find published interviews of experts; and if you have personal connections to the topic, you will enjoy the confidence that comes from knowing your subject well.

Know your speech materials. Once you have gathered and reviewed your material, you should feel that you have a comprehensive selection of the best information available to you. Go through the research you have collected, and check the information for variety, interest, impact; make sure it is up-to-date. Have you tested your ideas for their relevance to the audience, the situation, and the time limits? Have you chosen an interesting story or quotation for your introduction? Do your visual supporting materials meet the criteria of clarity and impact? If so, you can feel secure with your materials.

Know your outline. This step requires that you fully understand and use the principles of outlining. Are all five parts of your outline distinctly labeled? Are the five parts clearly related to the thesis and to each other? Make certain that the body of the speech helps to explain, clarify, define, and defend the thesis. It should be broken into two to five main subdivisions based on a logical pattern. Try using a few different patterns until you are sure that you have the most appropriate one for you, your topic, and your audience. If your outline stands up under careful analysis and alternative outlines do not work as well, you can have confidence that you have selected the correct outline for your material. As you know, good organization is the foundation of good communication.

Finally, *practice*—and practice again. The best method for developing competency is, and always will be, practice. But it works only if you are practicing correctly. Go over your presentation enough times so that you feel sure that you know your speech. Say the words aloud six, eight, or ten times—until you can enunciate them clearly and naturally. Do not force yourself to repeat a sentence over and over again or to work toward perfection in your recitation. Try to achieve comfortable ease. It is the flow of your ideas that should be smooth. Your transitions should link one idea to the next. If you develop a direct, extemporaneous style, your speech will have slight variations each time you present it, yet the ideas will remain essentially the same. Knowing that you have the ability to present your speech comfortably will give you the confidence that is characteristic of a competent public speaker.

Developing these areas will increase your communication *repertoire,* giving you standards and criteria by which you can make appropriate *selections* from that repertoire. Practice in these activities and skills will enhance your *implementation.* Finally, the systems for *evaluation* presented above complete the competency cycle.

SUMMARY

You have great control over your ability to become a competent speaker. This competency is not something you have, but is something that you develop through effort. First, you need to develop a repertoire of delivery styles and types, organizational patterns, research strategies, supporting materials, and presentation skills. This will enable you to quickly and readily select the ones that are appropriate for you, your audience, your topic, and the occasion. Selection of a subject that is both important and interesting to you and your audience is the next step. Then you can implement your choice with materials that support, clarify, and give impact to your ideas. Furthermore, you will become more confident if you know that you have created an outline that fits a standard outline format and follows specific guidelines for good organization. Next, good speakers work at controlling excess energy, which is common to everyone. Not to be neglected in giving good speeches is the feedback from your instructors, friends, and even yourself with which you can evaluate both your own development as a speaker and that of others. Finally, you will gain a good deal of confidence if you give yourself sufficient time to practice your presentation until you know that you can deliver the ideas contained in your presentation with comfort and ease.

If you follow the steps suggested in this and other chapters, you will become like the vast majority of good speakers—a bit nervous on the inside, but also ready, willing, prepared, able, and confident when you appear before your audience.

Key Terms

presentation styles, **228**
memorized, **228**
manuscript, **229**
extemporaneous, **229**
impromptu, **230**
speech apprehension, **231**
physiological preparation, **232**
psychological preparation, **234**
vocal delivery, **236**

appearance, **239**
posture, **239**
movements, **240**
gestures, **241**
facial expression, **241**
eye contact, **241**
evaluating speeches, **244**
ethical communication, **244**
confidence, **245**

► EXERCISES

1. Describe specific examples of presentations that you have recently seen in which each of the four types of presentation was used appropriately by a speaker. For each example, describe the circumstances that made one type of presentation more appropriate than another. Can you think of a recent experience you had in which the speaker used an inappropriate style? What factors made the style seem wrong for the situation?

2. As you watch a sports program on television, identify some of the relaxation techniques used by the athletes that are similar to the ones you can use before a speech. Jot down some examples to share with the class. Look for deep breathing, head and neck movements, tensing and relaxing muscles, and eyes closed in concentration or visualization.

3. The next time that you are about to take a test, try the breathing exercises and the exercises in tensing and relaxing the muscles described in this chapter. Evaluate the effectiveness of the exercises after the test. Try to teach the exercises to someone else. Ask that person to apply them in a tense situation. Find out later whether the exercises helped to relieve the tension.

4. Listen to a speech on campus or in the community, and conduct an evaluation of the speech, just as your instructor does for your speeches in class. Rate the speaker according to the seven criteria presented in this chapter. Some elements of a presentation are easier to rate than others. Why? Share your evaluation with the class in an evaluation session.

5. Pair off with a member of the class and become that person's speech buddy. Agree to listen to your classmate's practice sessions in exchange for your classmate's doing the same for you. Then practice and practice again.

References

Behnke, Ralph R. and Chris R. Sawyer. "Public Speaking Arousal as a Function of Anticipatory and Autonomic Reactivity." *Communication Reports* 14, 2 (Summer 2001).

Dow, Bonnie. "Criticism and Authority in the Artistic Mode." *Western Journal of Communication* 65, 3 (Summer 2001).

Downing, Joe and Cecile Garmon. "Teaching Students in the Basic Course How to Use Presentation Software." *Communication Education* 50, 3 (July 2001).

Hoffman, J. and J. Sprague. "A Survey of Reticence Communication Apprehension Treatment Programs at U.S. Colleges and Universities." *Communication Education* 31 (1982): 185.

Jaasma, Marjorie A. "Classroom Communication Apprehension: Does Being Male or Female Make a Difference?" *Communication Reports* 10, 2 (Spring 1997).

Richmond, V. and J. C. McCroskey. *Communication: Apprehension, Avoidance and Effectiveness.* Scottsdale: Gorsuch Scarisbrick, 1995.

Wolpe, J. *Psychological Inhibition by Reciprocal Inhibition.* Stanford: Stanford University Press, 1958.

Zeuschner, R. B. *Effective Public Speaking.* Dubuque: Kendal-Hunt, 1994.

CHAPTER 13

Informing Others

After reading this chapter, you should be able to:

- Understand the purposes of informative speeches
- Use the different types and patterns of informative speeches
- Apply the standards that are used to evaluate informative speeches
- Be confident and willing to create your own informative speeches
- Present a short speech of definition, demonstration, or exposition
- Follow the steps for improving your informative speaking competency

One of the most common types of presentation or speech is one that informs the listeners. The speaker may be telling about a place or event, describing a person or a process, or shedding light on an invention or a hobby. When your listeners' goal is to gain information, you are probably giving an informative presentation. The goal of an informative speech is to leave your audience with more information than it had before your speech. Your listeners should walk away saying, "That was really interesting. I never knew that before!"

The key to their understanding an informative speech, or any speech, is the thesis sentence. When the thesis sentence states, "The microchip was developed in four distinct steps," listeners can tell that they are about to hear an informative speech. The body will probably be divided into four subdivisions, and it will most likely follow a chronological pattern of development. If your thesis sentence states, "Yellowstone is a great place to visit," your audience will again probably hear an informative speech, but this time it may follow a topical pattern. On the other hand, if you say to your audience, "There are four reasons why you should vote for Smith," you are making a persuasive speech. The difference between an informative and a persuasive thesis sentence is this: the first identifies a thing or an event as the subject of the sentence, while the second makes the listener the subject. The word *should* indicates persuasion. When you say, "I'm going to inform you why you should give blood," you are about to give a persuasive speech. Having the word *inform* in the thesis sentence is not sufficient, the intention of the speaker to influence you makes it persuasive. On the other hand, the goal of informative speeches is to convey information, and to do so clearly and accurately. The report on the speaking style of Sojourner Truth that appeared in an earlier chapter was an informative presentation, as would be, for example, a demonstration of pottery making.

DIVERSITY IN COMMUNICATION
Informative Systems

In some cultures, it is rude to be direct when asking for action or compliance. For example, an Asian speaker may present what appears to be neutral information to Europeans, yet it is really an indirect way of seeking compliance. Some writers believe that in the United States, some women's use of politeness in communication may seem to men to have informative functions. Some messages that women present in the form of questions may, in reality, be softened or polite forms of persuasion. For example, a woman who says, "Do you think it's time to go yet?" might not be looking for a "yes" or "no" response but instead be trying to influence the other party to hurry or to leave (Lakoff, 1979, 1990; Hoar, 1988).

By contrast, an American male might ask his female companion, "Do you want to make dinner tonight?" in an attempt to find out whether she has already planned a menu or whether he should go ahead with the one he planned. She might reply, "Okay, I will," treating the question as a request to make dinner even though she had not planned to and expressing compliance to his perceived request (Tannen, 1994).

When you are in a job setting, you may need to train a new group of employees, explain how a piece of equipment works, or clarify a new plan for organizing the work area. Your community life is also filled with informative presentations, such as the town meeting at which the new water plan is presented, or the city council meeting at which a person comes to explain the operations of a neighborhood crime watch.

The next section describes three kinds of informative presentations; all are applications of the patterns of organization covered in the previous chapter. This chapter concludes with a description of ways in which to use informative presentations and improve your competency as a speaker.

TYPES AND PURPOSES OF INFORMATIVE SPEAKING

There are different ways to categorize informative speeches, but the following three general categories are the most frequently used: speeches of definition, speeches of demonstration, and speeches of exposition. The differences among them are not great; in fact, you may notice a good deal of overlap.

Speeches of Definition

This type of informative presentation requires you to speak about an idea that is unfamiliar to your audience with the result that they understand something new. You need to divide the topic into logical units; describe the parts, aspects, or history of the concept; and give your listeners enough detail to fully comprehend the idea. Speeches of **definition** may be short and can be combined with others as a first step in a longer process. For example, you may be a member of a panel that is discussing an issue before an audience. The first speaker usually gives a speech of definition by defining the problem, describing the background, and clarifying the vocabulary or terms to be used in the rest of the discussion.

Defining ideas or concepts is not an easy task. A good speech of definition is concrete, rather than abstract; is specific, not general; and uses multiple approaches to making the idea clear. There are several steps that you can follow to create a good definition of an idea or concept for your audience. These steps can become the body of your speech.

As a first step, you might turn to a dictionary for help and present your listeners with definition(s) you find there. One way to work in some variety here is to use several different dictionaries. There are many specialized dictionaries, and even the popular, general ones may have slightly different, interesting ways to define the same term. You might begin with *Webster's New Collegiate Dictionary*, and then turn to the *Oxford Dictionary of the English Language.* Suppose you were talking about issues concerning the freedom of speech, and you wanted to explain the concept of libel. A general description would be adequate for a start, but you shouldn't stop there. You could then turn to *Black's Law Dictionary* or

Ballentine's Law Dictionary. You might find citations on the Lexus electronic search system to locate cases or rulings in the area of libel that contains statements that you could include in your definition.

A next step might be to discuss the origin of the term *libel.* In that case, you would present the etymology of the word, which means that you would discuss its origin, roots, history, or development. Because much of English vocabulary is derived from Latin and Greek—via the French of William the Conqueror—you may find yourself describing an ancient root for your audience, taking it apart, and delineating its meanings. If you are dealing with an idea or concept such as socialism, you could also research the origins, history, and evolution of the socialist movement.

One of the best ways to define any idea, word, or concept is by example. An example is a form of supporting material, and a speech of definition requires several clear, specific examples to help the members of the audience understand your point. If they are familiar with your examples, and if your examples are precise and clear, you will have made your subject understandable to them. For example, when telling your listeners about types of dogs, such as spaniels, retrievers, and shepherds, make certain that you provide an example or two of each. Let your audience know that cockers and springers are examples of spaniels, that goldens and labradors are types of retrievers, and that the Australians, Germans, and collies are examples of the shepherd group. Examples will make your presentation come alive.

If you tell your audience what something is not, you are defining by negation. For example, you might say to your listeners, "Let's talk about transportation for a minute. No, I'm not talking about fancy luxury cars. I'm not talking about all-terrain vehicles, nor am I interested in high-performance, two-passenger sporty models. I want to focus your attention on the economy transportation car." By eliminating some factors from your definition, you focus the attention of your audience on the definition of your topic. The problem with using this pattern for an entire speech is that you spend too much time on the areas in which you are not interested. This pattern can be useful if, for the sake of variety, you work it into a larger, positive speech of definition.

Finally, you can define something by providing additional words about it. This type of definition is called rhetorical and uses synonyms, rephrasing, or context to add clarity to your definition. For example, if you use a word that is unfamiliar to your listeners, you might give them some synonyms to help them understand the word's meaning. "The family was distraught—anxious, distressed, upset, and frantic—when their child got lost." Not only has your rhetorical technique helped anyone who did not know the meaning of the word *distraught*, but you have also reinforced the feeling and meaning of the term. Context refers to the setting, situation, or circumstances that may affect the meaning of a word. For example, the word *spare* in the context of bowling is very different from the word *spare* in the context of auto repair. A *citation* may be very desirable when it is from the Red Cross, very undesirable when it is from the police officer who has stopped your car, but desirable again when it is from the Chief of Police for valor.

The Story of Communication
The Evolution of Modern English

IF YOU LIVED IN LONDON in the year 1065, you would be speaking a form of Old German called Anglo-Saxon, and you might still be speaking a similar language today if William of Normandy's attack on England in 1066 had failed. William and his armies spoke Old French, which was derived from Latin. As was true of most conquerors, the Normans took all the good jobs—king, duke, and baron—and left Saxons to be servants and peasants. The official language of England for the next 400 years was French, and modern English grew out of a blending of Saxon syntax and French vocabulary. During those years, tension and strife was associated with the two languages. The tales of Robin Hood, for example, pit the oppressed Saxons—as represented by the Merry Men—against Norman officials—as symbolized by the Sheriff of Nottingham.

In England today, some family names are still strongly associated with the two cultures as are pronunciations used by different social classes and in different geographical locations. The United States, of course, also has linguistic stereotypes, as seen in relation to a variety of regional accents or dialects. In other countries, especially those having a conquered minority, language differences that reflect deep-seated nationalism can trigger persecution, punishment, and even war. The strife in many parts of the world is due to interethnic tensions and the desire of a national or ethnic group to have autonomy, including its own language. It took our English language ancestors about 400 years to blend their languages. When it comes to languages, the story of communication is still being written.

These approaches to speeches of definition can be used together; by using several forms for your ideas, you can be reasonably assured that your audience will understand your definition. A combination of approaches will also help you to create interest through variety. As noted above, a speech of definition can function as the first part of a longer speech. The definition clarifies your idea, and then the rest of the speech explains its details. For example, if your topic is nuclear energy, step one of your presentation might be to define the words fission and fusion. You would clarify those important terms by giving your listeners several approaches to their definitions.

Speeches of Demonstration

One popular informative speech, both in class and in your career, is the "how-to" presentation, or the speech of **demonstration**. Whenever you show your listeners a process, illustrate a technique, or teach them how to do something, you are giving a speech of demonstration. When you teach someone how to assemble a model, stand on a surfboard, play the guitar, perform CPR or tai chi, or even breathe deeply as a relaxation exercise, the demonstration speech is the form you will probably use. We learn most of our skills from watching others and then trying to imitate them. We watch someone riding a bicycle, and we attempt to copy the technique. Cooking, carpentry, calf roping, and calligraphy can be taught with a good demonstration.

There are several ways to create and present a strong demonstration. First, break down the process into smaller units that follow a logical order. A complex gymnastic routine will be easy to understand if each move is taken one at a time. The most intricate pattern—in music, lace, dance, macramé, or a computer program—can be made clear if its structure is identified and divided into smaller units. One of the great lessons in speaking (and living) is that when faced with a large event or problem, it helps to break it down into manageable units.

Next, arrange the units in logical order. Determine the appropriate sequence for your topic, and group the basic steps into that order. You will probably build from the simple to the complex. For example, when you talk about model airplanes, you might begin by demonstrating assembly of the fuselage, then the wings, and then the supporting struts.

Third, be sure that each step of the demonstration is connected by a clear transition. You must show your listeners how the links of your chain are joined together. Watch a cooking show or a demonstration of carpentry or plumbing on television. Each step of the process is clearly linked to the previous one. Professional demonstrators know that showing these connections is the best way to teach someone who does not understand a process enough that they can comprehend it clearly. In class, you might demonstrate a hobby or craft, an experimental procedure, or a design sequence. In a career setting, you may be asked to show others in your workplace how to do a certain procedure or how to accomplish a specific task. For example, you could be a training technician, showing others how to run a blueprint or loading machine or how to operate a computer terminal or a spreadsheet program. In many jobs, you could be called on to make a formal presentation to a group demonstrating one of your company's important procedures.

Usually, visual aids are a significant part of any demonstration. Recall that in Chapter 11 several guidelines were presented for the use of visual supporting materials. It would be wise to review these guidelines before preparing a speech of demonstration. Even if you know the topic very well, your audience does not. Competent speakers approach a demonstration not from their own expert perspective, but from the perspective of their listeners. Remember to present your demonstration so that everyone in the audience can see as well as hear the information at a pace that they can follow.

One of the interesting developments in the speech of demonstration is that demonstrations are now often electronically generated. With computer-generated visual aids, such as those created with an interactive laptop computer and a CD-ROM unit, many presenters now include computer graphics as part of their demonstrations. A lecture on Shakespeare's plays can now include a projected outline of the plot and a diagram of the relationships of the characters, followed by an actual video clip of a stage production to demonstrate these elements in action. A demonstration is another form of visual aid and should be indicated as such on your outline. The guidelines for those visual materials and demonstrations are the same. If you have access to a video camera, it will be beneficial for you to videotape your demonstration first, and then watch it from the perspective of an audience member.

Speeches of Exposition

While these speeches certainly may include elements of definition and perhaps of demonstration, they go beyond the limits of these forms to include additional explanation. They are also somewhat more complex in their subject matter and supporting materials.

If you are trying to explain surfing to your listeners, you might begin with some historical references to the Polynesians. Then you might show a diagram or photograph of a surfboard, demonstrate how to position your feet or hold your body, and then relate some personal experiences or stories about surfing competitions. The purpose of this speech goes beyond definition or demonstration though it includes elements of both. The goal of a speech of **exposition** is to explain completely some event, idea, or process. These speeches are most successful when you select a topic that is of interest to your audience and when there is a variety of vivid supporting materials.

When you make a **topic selection** for a speech of exposition, keep in mind that the information must be complete. Although you can never say everything about any topic, you can anticipate the major elements that listeners need to know and those that they will most likely want to know. If you limit your thesis sentence to a relatively narrow idea, you will be able to explore it in depth.

For example, investing in the stock market is too complex a topic for a five-minute speech, but you can break this general topic down and select one aspect of municipal bonds or how to invest on a college student's budget. These smaller topics will make it possible for you to present a complete explanation; general topics will not. In short, you'll reach your goal of creating understanding by keeping your topic clearly and narrowly focused and by following the guidelines discussed in earlier chapters for organizing and supporting speeches.

The speech of exposition may be the most frequently used presentation, so you should be thinking of ways to use definition and demonstration in combination to create a more effective speech. For example, you may wish to make the definition of your topic "A" in the body of your outline. You could then take some of the methods of definition described above and make those A.1 and A.2 headings; you might develop a demonstration and show some items as A.3. For the B heading, clarifying items become B.1, B.2, and so on. These could be mostly visual—maps, photographs, or other visual supporting materials. You could then finish the speech with a C heading which might cover developing the relevance of the topic to your audience. In that section, you could make connections between your explanation of the topic and the experience and values of your audience. The supporting materials for C (C.1, C.2, etc.) might consist of stories, examples, verbal illustrations, comparisons, contrasts, and perhaps a few more defining examples or even some additional visual aids.

To summarize, informative speeches are some of the most important and most frequent speaking experiences you will encounter. Both in class and on the job, you will need to explain ideas, interests, abilities, and duties—either your own or someone else's. Knowing how to prepare a complete explanation, enhanced by definitions and demonstrations, will enable you to present a well-prepared, clear expository speech.

PATTERNS OF INFORMATIVE SPEAKING

As you know, the goal of an informative speech is to convey information. Therefore, the presentation pattern that you select should help the audience to understand your material. This section traces the step-by-step development of an informative speech so that you can see how to construct such a speech yourself. The first three steps are (1) Select your topic, (2) Compose your thesis sentence, and (3) Develop your supporting materials.

Selecting your topic means to review the possible areas you could talk about and judge them on their suitability to the allotted time, the informative purpose, the audience, and you. The topic is usually a general idea that meets the following criteria: It is something you know about and that interests you, something that you can make interesting and relevant to your listeners', something you feel comfortable talking about, and something about which there is sufficient available information for you to develop a substantial and worthwhile message. If the topic is too broad in scope, select a subdivision of it.

Next, *compose your thesis sentence.* The key to creating a clear thesis sentence is to make it focused, simple, and comprehensive. Your entire speech is guided by your thesis sentence, so it is worth some time and effort to phrase it well. Suppose you have selected investing as your topic, and now it is time to narrow down this general idea. You consider your allotted time and the fact that the audience is composed of people who know very little about sophisticated investment strategies. You know that they have some knowledge of the stock market, and you guess that they would probably like to learn more about this aspect of investment. You create several tentative phrasings and finally settle on this one: "Stock market mutual funds are an easy way for people to begin investing."

Now you can turn to a consideration of an *appropriate outline format* and begin constructing your speech. Since you are not going to give a speech on the history of the stock market or the location of various parts of the stock exchange building, you reject both the chronological and spatial patterns and select a topical format instead. Your outline begins to take shape as follows:

    I. Introduction
   II. (*Thesis sentence*) Stock market mutual funds are an easy way for people to begin investing.
  III. (*Body [preview]*)
       A. Defining the stock market
       B. How the stock market works
       C. How small investors get started

You already know that IV will be your conclusion—a quick review of the main ideas A, B, and C; the thesis; and your introduction.

Notice that you do not yet have an introduction. Do not be concerned about that at this point. You can add it later. For now, just save some space for it, and continue to construct your speech.

The next step is to *gather your supporting materials*. If you follow the suggestions presented earlier, you will visit one or more libraries with a stack of four-by-six-inch index cards; you will arrange interviews with a few knowledgeable persons; you may browse the web under several key words; and you will take an inventory of the books and materials about your topic that you already possess.

After you have accumulated a variety of supporting materials, it is time to *sort them into groups* according to the A, B, and C subdivisions. Set aside any items that do not fit into those categories. A possible introduction may reside in that pile. With some work, your outline now looks like this one:

I. (*Introduction*) Short story about parents who started a small investment fund for children's college education.

II. (*Thesis sentence*) Stock market mutual funds are an easy way for people to begin investing.

III. (*Body [preview]*)
   A. Defining the stock market
      1. Quotation from *Merriam-Webster Dictionary*
      2. Description from *Investor's Encyclopedia*
      3. Interview with Brenda Hill, local stockbroker
   B. How the stock market works
      1. Visual aid flowchart of purchase/transaction
      2. Statistics on quantity of daily transactions
      3. Quotation from *Everybody's Business* (textbook)
      4. Graph of Dow Jones averages (ten-year trends)
   C. How small investors get started
      1. Types of investments (examples)
      2. Yield projection statistics
      3. How college students can benefit (graph of compounding effect)
      4. Quotation from Ramon Arguello, investment counselor in town

IV. (*Conclusion*) Brief review of A, B, C, thesis sentence, and introduction

V. Bibliography
      1. Source #1
      2. Source #2
      3. Source #3

Notice that this outline is simple. It states the key ideas and avoids any extraneous items. It does not elaborate on each item but simply identifies it. It provides variety in the supporting materials by beginning with a story and then incorporating a definition, three quotations, two statistics, three visual aids, and some descriptions. The speaker makes an effort in the outline to relate the material to the audience, probably a beginning public speaking class. Remember that the idea for the speech came out of an abstract and unwieldy topic—investing—and narrowed it down so that it could be discussed in an informative way in five to seven minutes. Notice also that it relies on specific supporting materials to clarify the meaning of the subdivisions of the body. You could take the same topic, and even the same thesis sentence, and create an entirely different speech. You might

CRITICAL THINKING IN COMMUNICATION
Structuring the Informative Speech

You can use your skill in examining ideas in a sequence to help you select an organizational framework for your speech. Keep in mind the post hoc fallacy while arranging your main ideas. The post hoc fallacy refers to the erroneous assumption that an event that follows another event must therefore be its result. Do the items that make up your topic follow a logical pattern in time, space, or structure? If they do, then your ability to apply inductive or deductive reasoning can help you to decide which pattern is most appropriate for your particular speech. Listeners like logic, too. If you create an organizational pattern that flows smoothly, your listeners' critical thinking abilities will be stimulated and will, in turn, help them to discover and remember your main ideas. When the time comes to present your speech, the clear pattern that you have organized will help you to remember the correct sequence of items, and it will help the audience to make the transitions from idea to idea with you. Critical thinking applications play an important part in your communication repertoire.

select another pattern or choose from your store of supporting materials seven or eight alternative items. The preceding example is only that—one example. How you would develop a similar topic depends on your personal perspective, creativity, and associations.

In general, an informative speech can follow a variety of organizational formats, and you should try out a few of them to get a feel for each type. An informative speech does not usually follow a problem-solution or motivational sequence. In your presentation, you are more likely to use a topical pattern (as was shown in the example), a chronological pattern, or a spatial pattern.

This discussion has taken you through the process of creating an informative speech. Try to follow the same steps as you create your own informative presentations. Remember that the basis for good communication is good organization, and the keyword outline is a good way to achieve that organization. Once you have your outline in order, consider it a preliminary draft of your speech. You can always change it, and it is much easier to change an outline than a manuscript. If you find new material that you think is better than the material you selected, just eliminate the old and insert the new. If you change your thinking about the subject, feel free to change the outline—that is, to rework the order, substitute new supporting materials for old ones, add or delete information, or make any other modifications you like. One of the best resources at your disposal is time. Give yourself enough time to create your outline; then put it away for a day or two. When you come back to it, you will have gained some perspective on it, and maybe some fresh ideas that will help you to improve it. Last-minute preparers do not give themselves this gift, and their speeches are weaker for it.

Once you are satisfied with your revision, it is time to begin practicing your presentation. Select a presentation style—probably extemporaneous—and copy your outline either on a single sheet of paper or on a few (three to seven) note cards. Limit your notes to the outline format you have already prepared. Many beginning speakers fall short at this point, and they attempt to write out their presentation on note cards, word for word. Unless the occasion calls for a manuscript speech, limit your notes to your outline. Then put into practice the ideas and guidelines from Chapter 12 to help you achieve clarity and impact in your speech.

EVALUATING INFORMATIVE SPEECHES

In addition to the criteria for evaluating speeches outlined in Chapter 12, you can examine your informative speech from three different points of view: (1) the listener's, (2) the speech critic's, and (3) the consumer's. To do this, you must consider what the goals of the speech are from each perspective.

Goals as a Listener

As a listener, you will be seeking particular information from speakers. You want them to make their ideas clear so that you can understand the point of the presentation. You should be able to restate the speaker's thesis sentence in your own words. You should also be able to recall the main ideas that developed the thesis, and you will often be able to remember some of the more significant supporting materials that the speaker used. Now the people who listen to your speeches should be able to do the same. They will evaluate your presentation according to how easy it was for them to accomplish their listening goals. If you put yourself in their place as you create your speech, you will be able to double-check yourself in advance. Any adjustments that you make from the listeners' perspective will help to give your speech greater clarity.

Goals as a Critic

To be a good **speech critic**, you need to keep in mind the evaluation criteria presented in Chapter 12—the standards of presentation, ethics, and audience adaptation. Although each of these measures a different aspect of the speech, all three must be considered in order to carry out a complete evaluation of the quality of the speech. Most untrained audience members tend to focus on only the presentation skills of the speaker—voice, eye contact, appearance, and smoothness of delivery. More insightful critics will balance their observations of these skills with attention to organization, support, honesty, completeness, and value to the listeners. That is why your instructor may emphasize certain areas that at first may not seem that important to you or your classmates. Your instructor has been trained to keep all of these factors in mind and to balance them while forming a critique of the speaker and of the speech. The critical feedback that you get from an instructor may be in oral or written form or a combination of the two. Very often, an instructor will focus the oral critique on the positive aspects of the speech and save any commentary on weaknesses or areas needing improvement for a written critique. The major factors that a speech critic will keep in mind are the topic, audience adaptation, form or pattern, organization, time allocation, clarity, transitions, use of supporting materials, use of language, and delivery. Notice that for a speech critic, delivery is only one of several areas to be evaluated.

There are ways to combine all aspects of a speech into a coherent evaluation. For reasons of efficiency, the evaluation criteria are often clustered on an evaluation form. Evaluation forms cover major principles of public speaking and allow critics to be specific in their criticism. A professional critique will cover these same areas, although it will probably be in narrative form and many extend to a dozen or more pages. The professional speech communication journals often publish exceptionally well-done pieces of criticism as a way of offering insights into the communication processes of notable speakers. In any case, the two forms shown here differ in areas of emphasis, the second one allowing for more free commentary from the critic. You may use these guides when you are criticizing other speakers or as a tool for self-evaluation. You could also create your own, or perhaps your class has one that everyone can use.

Student Name _____

Topic _____ Date _____

SPEECH EVALUATION
Dr. Zeuschner

Scale: (0-5 points possible per item)

0	=	*Missing or done incorrectly*
1-2	=	*Meets minimum requirements for university-level work*
3-4	=	*Fulfills requirements above university minimum level*
5	=	*Substantially beyond expectation for university minimum*

Outline: Overall impression, coherence, form, clarity, neatness   _____

Topic: Appropriately adapted to audience, substantial   _____

Introduction: Clear, compelling, commanding attention, interesting, relevant, sufficient length   _____

Thesis Sentence: To the point, simple, single sentence   _____

Transitions: Clear relationship of ideas, smooth flow   _____

Body: Logical order, organization, cover the necessary points   _____

Support: Quality of supports, evidence, substance   _____
Variety, impact of supports (incl. visual aid, if used)   _____

Reasoning: Connections and conclusions clearly warranted   _____

Ending: Clear, simple review of major ideas, thesis, introduction   _____

Bibliography: Sources listed clearly at end of outline   _____
Substantial consultation evident   _____
Sources utilized in flow of speech   _____

Communicative Skills: Vocal quality, nonverbal   _____
Direct presentation, non-dependence on notes   _____

TOTAL   _____

(possible 75)

Evaluation: 30-40   points = Average
45-50   points = Excellent
55+   points = Outstanding

SPEECH CRITICISM FORM

Critic: _____ Speaker: _____

Speech subject: _____

Date of Rehearsal: _____ Place of Rehearsal: _____

Time Spent: _____

Significance of topic and value of ideas:

Adequacy and appropriateness of supporting materials:

Clarity of organization:

Adaptation of content to audience:

Choice and fluency of language:

Use of voice and body in delivery:

Either one of these evaluation forms will help to guide feedback and critique.

The main value of being a good critic is your ability to improve your own speeches as well as others' by identifying their specific strengths and weaknesses. Critiques help you specifically to become a better speaker by pinpointing areas where you are already competent or where you demonstrate skillful application of good speaking techniques. They also help by pointing out areas where your speaking skills could be improved. By observing the strengths of others, you learn what techniques are effective and worthy of emulation. By noting the weaknesses of other speakers, you identify speaking behaviors to avoid. In other words, if you can be a good critic of others' speeches, you should be able to took at your own messages more carefully and use your critical insight to improve them.

▶ **IMPROVING COMPETENCY**

The Value of Honest Feedback

One of the best ways to improve your competency as a speaker is to use the power of intrapersonal communication. As you recall, the messages you send yourself about yourself are quite capable of motivating and influencing you. How can you give yourself honest feedback about your speaking abilities? Technology can aid you through the use of a video camera. Try checking one out from your school if you do not have one readily available. Did you find a speech buddy yet? If not, then this is an excellent opportunity to look for one. Have your buddy videotape you, and do the same for your buddy. Then, after you have heard your buddy's comments and suggestions, play back the tape of your speech and look at it in light of the critique. Then try being a critic for yourself, and find out whether it helps to pay attention to the internal monitoring that is your own personal feedback. We are usually our own most severe critics, so be gentle with yourself, but be honest.

Goals as a Consumer of Information

Because you consume information daily and in large doses, it pays to be selective about the messages to which you give your time and attention and those that you can reliably dismiss as being of poor quality. One of your lifelong functions will be that of a **consumer of information** in our information society.

You will continue to receive messages constantly; to some degree, you have already developed a system for evaluating them. Many people do not evaluate the messages that come their way very carefully but simply accept or reject them on the basis of some automatic response pattern that they have developed. Young children, for example, seem to accept messages uncritically. When they become teenagers, they typically begin to reject many messages, especially those from parents or other authority figures. Again, this type of rejection may be automatic, based solely on a rejection of authority rather than on an evaluation of the message.

As you go through a typical day, you are bombarded by informative messages from newspapers, magazines, television, friends, neighbors, instructors, and others. As you evaluate messages in the public domain, remember to look at three areas: their application to you, the trustworthiness of the source, and their demonstration of good communication principles.

A message has application to you if it provides value that you can use. For example, as you listen to the news, look for connections that you can make to your own circumstances. A broadcast on earthquake preparedness in the area that you live in may connect to your need to prepare your living quarters. At the other extreme, the broadcast may be lengthy, sensational, and attention-getting, yet not have any real value for you. Have you ever seen the way some television stations cover a gruesome train wreck? They interview survivors who are frightened and in shock. If there are fatalities, they ask family members, "How do you feel?" and in general exploit the sensational aspects of the story. This kind of information probably has little value for most listeners except to appeal to their emotions with pictures of other peoples' tragedies. A critical evaluator would ask, "How does this apply to me?" Your answer to this question will give you insight into what the source is trying to accomplish and how well it is reaching its goals. If your listening goals are not being met, you should question the value of continuing to listen.

A source that is trustworthy merits your attention more than one that is not. Trustworthiness includes having a record and reputation for furnishing truthful information, carrying out reliable reporting, conducting conscientious research, and having supplied previous information that was substantial and related to the interests of the intended audience. If the person or source has a long-standing and well-earned reputation for being accurate, you can use that credibility as an evaluative criterion. The *New York Times*, for example, has a long-standing record for being truthful and accurate in the stories it publishes. Network news broadcasts on radio and television also make substantial efforts to be accurate in their reporting. You probably have friends whom you can trust to give you accurate information because they have always done so in the past. You probably can think of leaders in your community—in clubs, religious organizations, and business, or political affairs—who have established reputations for accuracy, so you also view them as trustworthy sources of information.

However, if you do not have the source's record, how can you evaluate the trustworthiness of the source? That question can be answered by the third measure of public communication criticism: use of good communication principles.

Good communication principles include all the factors you have been studying in this section, especially the use of the supporting materials. Does the speaker use outside research and cite it during the presentation? Or, does the speaker depend solely on personal anecdotes or experiences, unnamed experts, or undocumented studies? Does the speaker supply names, dates, titles of publications, and qualifications of authorities cited? Is there any support at all? You may hear someone say, "A recent survey shows conclusively that…" While that statement may very well turn out to be a trustworthy support, you have no way to judge its credibility without a specific citation. On the other hand, if the speaker says, "A Gallup poll published last week in *Time* magazine shows conclusively that…," you have a basis for evaluating that support. If the speaker says, "A poll of several neighbors published in a mimeographed flyer proved conclusively that…," you would have another basis for evaluating the information. Check the citations offered.

In addition to verifying the supporting materials, use one of the speech evaluation forms and check for good use of other principles. Is the message well organized? Is the thesis clearly stated? How does the message apply to you? You probably will not be carrying a copy of these forms around with you for the rest of your life, so you will need to make a permanent copy in your mind of the major principles involved. You will remember this system if you apply it regularly by being a critic of others' speeches and of your own presentations. Just as you are a careful consumer of automobiles, electronic equipment, clothing, appliances, and food products, you can become a careful consumer of information. You want value for your money when it comes to purchasing products, so demand value for your time when listening to information presented in the public forum.

In summary, you can apply your evaluation skills as a listener in the classroom or career setting, as a critic looking for specific strengths or weaknesses, and as an everyday consumer. Each of these roles can, in turn, help you to create better messages. Listening to presentations with an open, critical mind will help you become an objective critic of your own work. While perfection is not a reasonable goal, improvement certainly is. Give yourself praise when you do a good job, and always seek to improve a worthy effort so that it meets the requirements of clarity, substance, and impact.

IMPROVING INFORMATIVE SPEAKING COMPETENCY

The four elements of communication competency—repertoire, selection, implementation, and evaluation—have been implicit in the discussion throughout this chapter. Knowing the several approaches that are available to you when you prepare an informative presentation expands your repertoire. You have also learned the guidelines for choosing one or another as well as some techniques to keep in mind when applying any of those choices. Finally, you are now familiar with some detailed methods for evaluating communication choices made by yourself and others.

Among the most important ways for you to improve your communication is to learn to make your meaning clear. Be concerned with your choice of words. Review the material on verbal communication if you like, and apply the suggestions given when preparing informative speeches. Keep your vocabulary at a level that is appropriate for the listeners. Think about what they are likely to know already, and what they probably do not yet know about your topic. Being concrete and specific will help you to achieve clarity. Watch your use of pronouns (e.g., she, he, it, and they) and use specific identifiers when possible (e.g., Adele Komsky, Robert Gomez, Sandy Point State Park on Highway 41, and Mayor Settle). Enliven your specific references with vivid descriptions. Color, size, shape, comparison, and contrast will help your audience to create memorable mental images from your words. "Then I returned home" can be transformed into "After the fire died down, I raced home to tell everyone else about it, but arrived out of breath and too exhausted to speak for several minutes." The latter statement is, to say the least, more interesting, vivid, and memorable for your listeners.

Try to balance your use of exciting language with an effort to be concise. Being concise means to express your thoughts with efficiency, avoiding extra words that do not add information to your ideas. Keep your presentation simple. Your listeners cannot reread your previous sentences as they can in a written essay. If your sentences tend to be complex, compound, and lengthy, apply the principle of conciseness in the selection and implementation of your language choices. Check your language use for economy and brevity.

Clear **transitions** also help an audience to follow your ideas. Connector sentences such as "First we will examine the causes of the war" prepare your listeners to hear that particular part of your presentation. After each major section, you should link your ideas together with a transition sentence such as "Now that we have looked at the causes of the war, let us examine its effect on the people in the region." This sentence lets your listeners know that you are finished with one major section and are moving to the next one. Of course, you could also say, "Next, the war's effects," but this sentence only announces the change; it does not link the two ideas, nor does it help the audience to move smoothly from one idea to the next. Again, the audience cannot reread what you have just said. Oral communication style differs from written style in that it requires clear, frequent transitions.

One method to help the audience listen is related to the transition and is called a **preview.** On the sample outlines you may have noticed the following entry: "III. (Body [preview])." As you begin the main part of your speech, it is useful to let the audience know how you will divide the topics stated in your thesis sentence. By giving listeners a preview, you enable them to identify your information by category. Your listeners will prepare themselves mentally to receive three or four units of information from you. Your organizational pattern will also be made clear in advance, and you will have provided a helpful overall orientation to your presentation. "To explain the effects of the Vietnam war, I will first discuss the causes of the war, then describe some of the effects it has had on the people of the area, and finally talk about several of the major impacts it has had in the United States." This short preview helps your audience to clearly see the pattern of your speech and will help them to pay attention to what you are about to say.

Similar to a preview is an **internal summary.** When you take a moment in the middle of your speech to summarize the major ideas up to that point, you are doing an internal summary. If your speech is longer than eight or ten minutes or contains a very complex sequence of ideas, an occasional internal summary can help your listeners to understand and remember your speech. If you are giving a short, impromptu speech, an internal summary benefits you as well as the audience because it gives you a moment to think about where your speech will go next.

Transitions, previews, reviews, and summaries are all methods of improving your informative speaking abilities. If you make frequent use of them, your speech will flow smoothly, and its meaning will be clear. These techniques help you to remember each section of your speech as you pause mentally and use a transition or a summary to prepare for the next section of your presentation. Get into the habit of employing these tools; they can help you to develop into an effective, informative speaker. If you are not always sure when to use them, it is better to work them into your speech than to risk leaving them out and losing your audience as you move from one idea to the next. Competent speakers always have these tools in their repertoire of skills. They practice which ones to use and when, and they also regularly evaluate the effectiveness of these methods in their speeches.

SUMMARY

Informative speaking consists of speeches that define, demonstrate, or explain. These three styles can be mixed successfully in a single presentation, yet whether you are the listener or the speaker, the goal remains the same: to leave the listeners with a greater understanding of the topic than they had before the presentation. A successful informative presentation has that goal as its main focus.

Informative speaking is a common experience in both classroom and career settings. In this chapter, you learned about being both a competent giver and receiver of messages. Help your listeners by using transitions, being concise and clear in your word choices, and including previews and internal summaries. You can also increase your communication competency by using good critical thinking skills to create and evaluate informative speeches. This chapter was designed to start you on that path.

Key Terms

definition, **251**
demonstration, **253**
exposition, **255**
topic selection, **255**
speech critic, **259**

consumer of information, **261**
transitions, **264**
preview, **264**
internal summary, **264**

EXERCISES

1. Imagine that you have been asked to present a speech of definition to your class. What topic would you choose that would be informative to other students in the class? What resources would you gather to support it? How would you organize it? Go through the same questions for a speech to demonstrate and a speech of exposition.

2. Although many televised speeches are designed to be persuasive, some may be informative. Do news broadcasters follow the patterns of organization presented in this chapter? Watch the network news for three consecutive nights, and keep track of which patterns occur most frequently. What about the nature specials or biographies that you see on television? What patterns do they use? Compare your examples with those of other students in class.

3. As you prepare your own informative speech, try at least two different organizing patterns for the same topic. Select the one that "feels" better, and try to explain why it seems to work and the other does not.

4. Seek out a public speaker on your campus, and attend a presentation by that person. Keep track of the outline, the pattern of organization, the supporting materials, and the style of presentation. How would you rate this person? What did the speaker do that you would like to emulate in your own presentations? Did the speaker do anything that you think should be avoided?

References

Hoar, Nancy. "Genderlect, Powerlect and Politeness" in *Women and Communicative Power*. Annandale, VA: Speech Communication Association, 1988.

Lakoff, Robin. "Stylistic Strategies within a Grammar of Style," in *Language, Sex and Gender*. J. Orasanu, M. Slater, and L. L. Adler, eds. New York: Annals of the New York Academy of Sciences, 1979.

Lakoff, R. T. *Talking Power*. New York: Basic Books, 1990.

Tannen, Deborah. *Talking 9 to 5*. New York: Morrow, 1994.

Persuading Others

After reading this chapter you should be able to:

- Identify the main components of value systems and explain how attitudes change
- Describe a variety of persuasive speeches and the ways they are developed, supported, and presented
- Present your ideas to influence others
- Believe that you have something substantial to say and feel confident to say it
- Develop and present a persuasive speech to your classmates
- Evaluate and critique the persuasive messages of others

When you think of the great speakers of the past, you are probably thinking of the great **persuasive speakers**. The speakers who are remembered are those who influenced the events around them. Ancient Greek orations, many of which are still available for us to read today, were often persuasive discourses about the great issues of the day. Collections of these orations feature both pro and con speeches about a single subject.

From the ancient Greek orations to the Iroquois addresses in the long house; the speeches of the abolitionists and suffragettes; and the President's most recent State of the Union speech, public speeches have dealt persuasively with the great issues of their time. Many of these orators often spoke at great length—from thirty minutes to several hours. These speakers followed the guidelines for effective speaking for their time and place, and many of those guidelines are still appropriate today. Your persuasive speeches will join a several-thousand-year-old tradition of carefully prepared communication about significant, contemporary issues. Those many years have produced proven ideas and insights regarding the way people react to messages that are intended to influence them and how a speaker like you can use those insights to produce messages that successfully persuade an audience to think, feel, or act in a particular way. In addition to the wisdom passed down by a long, rhetorical tradition, modern psychology and other social sciences have provided useful knowledge about how to influence the minds and emotions of other people.

We begin with a definition of persuasion, followed by an examination of three categories of persuasive messages; a discussion of how we form and modify our attitudes; and a description of four types of persuasive speech. The chapter also presents information on supporting materials, organization, and persuasive language and presentation styles. Finally, we look at ways to evaluate and improve persuasive speaking.

A DEFINITION OF PERSUASION

A message that influences the opinions, attitudes, or actions of the receiver is a persuasive message. The definition of a persuasive speech includes the process used to create the message. Whenever you try to convince someone to eat at your favorite restaurant, vote for your preferred candidate, attend a particular religious service, or buy a CD by your favorite group, you are using persuasion. Although the goal of each of these messages is to influence an audience, there are three categories of persuasion that are traditionally identified by the type of information that is the subject of the message.

FACTS, VALUES, AND POLICIES

Typically, you can create a persuasive speech about one of three types of concerns. These concerns, or questions, are related to facts, values, and policies.

DIVERSITY IN COMMUNICATION
The Evolution of Acceptance

It might seem strange to you, but the ability of ordinary citizens to speak in public on important issues is a relatively new concept. Even in the early history of our country, only white males could participate in important meetings, either as advocates or decision-makers. Even in the late 1800s, women seldom attended meetings, much less spoke at them. At some of the early women's suffrage conferences, men ran the entire meeting. At issue was whether to allow such people as Susan B. Anthony or Elizabeth Cady Stanton to speak, and sometimes these women had to sit in a separate section of the auditorium, screened off with a curtain. Even more interesting is the case of Sojourner Truth, a former slave who for years faced the double barrier of being African American and female before finally gaining a large and strong audience of listeners—mostly white males.

Diversity has only recently come to advertising. Before 1970, virtually no people of African, Latino, or Asian ancestry appeared in any television commercials. In 1968, S. I. Hayakawa speculated that it would be revolutionary to include all types of people in commercials, since the companies behind those ads depend on high credibility to make their sales. The current increase in the diversity of people in television commercials demonstrates their inclusion in mainstream society as role models.

Facts are usually the concern of historical and legal persuasion. Did Lincoln issue the Emancipation Proclamation for political reasons? Was John Doe murdered? Was Amelia Earhart a spy? Does that newspaper article libel me? These are questions or propositions of fact.

Values are deeply held beliefs that direct our lives. Do we support public education? Is honesty the best policy? Does a promise of lifelong commitment mean the same thing as marriage? Values represent the area in which some of the most intense and personally involving persuasion takes place.

Finally, questions of **policy** are those that ask what should be done. Should we spend our vacation touring the coast on bicycles, visiting Disney World, or helping to rebuild grandmother's house? Should we take a vacation at all? Should we vote for Candidate X? Should we vote? These actions are the subjects of speeches that discuss policies.

Each of these concerns—fact, value, and policy—might be discussed in the same speech. If an education bond issue is to be successful, its proponents need to convince you of the facts, relate the facts to your values to motivate you, and finally, persuade you to act. A political candidate and the makers of a new brand of detergent both follow the same steps in their efforts to persuade you. However, most persuasive speeches are categorized by their ultimate goal, even if they touch on other, ancillary goals or concerns along the way.

To be successful in your attempts at persuasion, you need to address the motivations of your listeners. These motivators are the values and attitudes that are shared by large groups of people. Let us begin with a quick review of those values and attitudes.

In Chapter 7, values and attitudes were presented in relation to self-concept. Recall that values comprise a person's primary orientation toward life—the principles by which a person's actions are guided. Your **value system** provides you with a general orientation to life situations. Values tend to remain stable and are less likely to change than are attitudes or beliefs. If they do change they will probably change very slowly. Therefore values are difficult to change in a persuasive speech, especially if the speech is a short one. Short speeches are typically given in classrooms, in brief presentations by political candidates, or in television commercials. Instead of trying to change values, these persuaders use the existing values of the audience as a basis for creating a persuasive message. In that way the message can concentrate on attitudes—smaller units of belief—that are more easily modified if listeners perceive the core value from which the attitude stems to be the same as the core value that is implicit in the message.

Suppose that two candidates for office assume that their listeners value education, and each tries to persuade the audience that he or she will do a better job of supporting education. The listeners ask themselves which candidate will better implement their value systems, and this may lead them to adjust their attitudes toward the two office seekers. If you believe that one will do a better job of acting on your values than the other, your attitude toward that person will be more positive than your attitude toward the other.

ATTITUDE CHANGE THEORY

How do attitudes form? More importantly, in the context of persuasive speech, how are they changed? These questions are the subject of research by communication scholars who study **attitude change theory.**

Early studies of persuasion and influence included a definition of the concept of attitude. As you know, attitudes are based on values and more specific applications of those values to the events in the world around you. A simple definition provided by researchers in the 1930s is still valid today and is useful in learning more about persuasive speaking. An attitude can be defined as "primarily a way of being 'set' toward or against certain things" (Murphy et al., 1937).

Because attitudes are internal and cannot be seen directly, we rely on reports about attitudes to tell us what they are. These reports may be simple, and consist of responses to questions and other verbal or nonverbal expressions. For example, a person might say, "I don't like Senator Jones's record on educational issues. I think I'll vote for Smith instead." Answers to a questionnaire about likes and dislikes in general and responses to public opinion polls are also expressions of attitudes.

Attitudes may come from many sources, and many people, especially in the field of psychology, have tried to explain both the development of attitudes and attitude change theory.

Early Approaches

The period before World War II saw the development of several approaches to the study of attitudes. The early work on attitudes followed the work of Pavlov and his experiments in operant conditioning in which dogs were trained to salivate when they heard a bell ring. The sound of the bell had previously been associated with food, and so the bell became a conditioned stimulus for the dogs that caused them to salivate.

Psychologists then applied Pavlov's findings to humans and speculated that attitudes might be a result of some repeated association, or conditioning. An early theory was formulated by B. F. Skinner; instead of forcing an association to create a conditioned response, a reward was provided every time a correct response was given. Although the work was initially done with rats—teaching them to press a lever to get a food pellet—these findings in behavior modification were applied to human behavior. For example, if you expressed a particular opinion as a child and your parents said, "My, what a wonderful child!" or made some other positive response, you may have been reinforced in that opinion. A third approach was taken by Hull, who theorized that both habit and drive worked together to create reinforcement. **Habits** are repeated behaviors; **drives** are needs, such as the need for food, shelter, and the avoidance of pain or injury. As we respond to these needs, we develop predispositions for behaving or believing in certain ways (Hilgard and Bower, 1966).

During World War II, a great deal of attention was focused on the extensive use of propaganda through the use of mass media. Films became a weapon of psychological warfare, and all the countries participating in the war made propaganda films for use in their own countries. They also produced other films for export to persuade people in other countries to be on their side.

The use of training films by the U.S. Army allowed for extensive testing of various types of persuasive messages on the attitudes of soldiers, largely because thousands of them were available to be tested in a fairly controlled setting. Much of this work was connected with Yale psychologist Carl Hovland. His studies concluded that most of the early army training films had little effect on soldiers' attitudes. The government then wanted to discover what kind of messages would produce a predictable change of attitude. Hovland found that sometimes an attitude would change after a period of time. This delayed reaction was called the *sleeper effect*. He also noticed differences in attitude change between the presentation of a message that gave only one side of an issue and that of a message that gave mostly one side and a little of the opposing side as well. The researchers discovered that one-sided messages had a positive effect on audiences who already held the particular attitude, but two-sided messages had an effect on people who were initially unfavorable to the message (Hovland et al., 1949).

Credibility

Later, Hovland and others who were influenced by his work continued to study how attitudes are affected by source credibility and by fear appeals. Briefly,

source credibility theory says that receivers of information are likely to be influenced by a source that they find to be credible. These studies show that immediately after a presentation, audiences are more likely to be influenced by highly credible speakers than by speakers who are not so credible. However, because of the sleeper effect, the influence of both high- and low-credibility sources begins to even out as time passes.

What constitutes high credibility? Researchers have identified four elements associated with credibility: expertise, dynamism, trustworthiness, and goodwill. These factors exist in the minds of the audience as beliefs. In other words, it is important to your credibility that the audience believe that you are an expert, that you are trustworthy, that you have goodwill toward them, and that you are energetic. Sad to say, the phenomenon of source credibility explains why people are taken in by con artists every day. Since we seldom have a good, dependable, or absolute way to determine the existence of these qualities in other people, we instead depend on unreliable criteria such as appearance or whatever people tell us about themselves. Genuine tests of credibility require a little more investigation. These tests were covered in Chapter 12 in the discussion of criteria that are used to evaluate public speeches and in the discussion of ethics and communication.

Source credibility is not a modern concept in persuasive speaking. Early Greek and then Roman rhetoricians wrote extensively about how the speakers of their day could persuade others, and prime among their concerns was source credibility—called *ethos*. Ethos is usually translated to mean the speaker's character, and you can see the root of the word ethics in that term. Good ethos is a blend of expertise, trustworthiness, dynamism, and goodwill.

A good reputation is an important asset for anyone to possess. It either opens up or closes off the potential for communication, depending on the quality of the reputation.

Advertisers depend on creating and using a positive reputation. That is why they hire easily recognizable people who already have a positive reputation to appear in their advertisements. They put actors, sports figures, and celebrities in their ads, and pay them enormous sums of money. Their hope is you will be influenced sufficiently by these people's reputations to transfer their credibility to the products being sold. At the least, they expect the ads to catch your attention.

TECHNOLOGY AND COMMUNICATION
Digitizing Images

Recently, as sophistication and technological capacity have increased, some advertisers have inserted hidden messages in their ads, messages for the purpose of reinforcing the persuasive impact of the ad. The development of digitized sound and images now let us remove, insert, or otherwise alter features of the message. On a home computer, you can change someone's eye color pixel by pixel and give your Uncle Fred's digitized likeness glowing magenta pupils, one orange tooth, or extra ears. "Seeing is believing" is probably on its way out as a truism because of our digitized technology.

Automobile ads constantly tell you how high the product was rated in consumer satisfaction polls or how low it was rated in surveys of automobile repair costs. Lawsuits are filed over defamation of character because a person's reputation, character, or ethos can be demonstrated to have monetary value.

Later, we will discuss how you can develop credibility with your listeners. If you want to affect your audience's attitudes, keep in mind that source credibility is a major factor in bringing about that change. Another factor that has been extensively studied is the use of fear as a persuader.

Fear Appeals

You probably remember seeing films in driver education classes showing the results of terrible accidents. Perhaps your dentist's office has photographs of rotten teeth, bleeding gums, or deformed jaws on the walls of the waiting room. These are obvious **fear appeals**. Do they work?

In a classic study conducted by Janis and Feshbach, fear appeals were used to create better dental hygiene. Building on the work of Hovland, these researchers knew that an attitude could be modified more easily if the subjects of the study were psychologically aroused during the presentation of the persuasive message (Hovland et al., 1953). The subjects, students at a large high school, attended a mild, medium, or strong fear-related lecture on tooth decay. In general, the most improvement in dental hygiene occurred in subjects who had been exposed to the mild fear appeal. The least effective approach turned out to be the strong fear appeal.

Additional research showed that two-sided messages had a stronger positive effect on receivers' resistance to later persuasive efforts by others (Lumsdaine and Janis, 1953). Therefore if you want your audience to resist rebuttals to your presentation by other speakers, you should probably present some of the other side's arguments during your presentation. Another line of research showed that the strength of the fear appeal must be realistically related to the change that is desired. For example, a very simple action, such as brushing your teeth, may be seen as being too simple a way to prevent horrible disfigurement. One strength of these studies was that the measured attitude change was not just a change of answers on a questionnaire, but an actual change in behavior. Another strong point was that attitude changes seemed to be long lasting.

In an effort to account for the variations in the results of studies of fear appeals, researchers later identified three factors that work together to make fear appeals change attitudes (Rogers, 1975). These factors are (1) the degree of harmfulness of an event, (2) the likelihood of the event happening to the listener, and (3) how well the action being recommended is likely to work. For example, if a problem does not seem to be very significant or harmful, it is unlikely to cause fear. On the other hand, if the degree of harm seems overly exaggerated, the audience will dismiss the problem. Or an audience may agree that the problem being discussed is serious but feel that it does not apply to them. It is therefore unlikely that they will feel involved enough to modify an existing attitude or behavior. Finally, an audience may find that the problem presented is indeed terrible and believe that there is a chance it will happen to them, yet they do not adopt the solution or action because they think it won't work.

It appears that all three elements must be relevant to the audience for an appeal to work. The national effort to stop the spread of AIDS is an excellent example of how these elements are used. Almost everyone is convinced that AIDS leads to death, in fact, that it is a direct cause, so there is no need to concentrate on the first element of fear appeals—harm. Instead, it is toward the second element that much of the persuasive effort against AIDS is directed—that it can happen to anyone. At first this statement was not believed by most people. AIDS was associated with members of the gay community, perhaps with Haitians, with a few recipients of blood transfusions, or with drug addicts who share needles. The death of movie star Rock Hudson and the persuasive speaking of Elizabeth Taylor helped to increase discussion about and attention to the disease. However, not until basketball great Earvin "Magic" Johnson became infected with the HIV virus were many Americans able accept the second factor of this appeal to fear—the disease was spreading beyond the groups originally associated with it. The third factor—the effectiveness of the solution to the problem—is still at the center of much debate about safe sex, abstinence, or totally monogamous relationships. How have people's attitudes and behavior been affected by persuasive and informative speeches about AIDS? Public opinion and private practices are monitored constantly by health officials and some positive changes in both opinions and actions are being reported. The worry is that those changes may only be temporary.

If you take a course in persuasion, political communication, or mass media you are likely to study in detail the work of the investigators named here and many others. Modern psychological investigation has provided extensive information about attitudes and how they are changed. For now, these few principles of attitude change theory will help you understand the messages that you receive daily from advertisers, as well as the messages that you create when you try to persuade others.

TYPES OF PERSUASIVE SPEECHES

There are several ways to approach the various persuasive speaking situations that you may encounter. Four general categories of speech seem to cover most of them. They are (1) speeches to convince, (2) speeches to actuate, (3) speeches to reinforce or inspire, and (4) debates and public argumentation.

Speeches to Convince

When the primary audience reaction that the speaker is trying to obtain concerns the listeners' opinions, then it is likely that the speech that is being given is a speech to convince. No direct action is required of the listeners; their attitude will be the focus of attention. For example, if a speaker tells you that Franklin Roosevelt was wrong to try to increase the size of the Supreme Court, that Sara

Teasdale is a better poet than Emily Dickinson, that abortion is wrong, or that more money should be spent on the space program, you are dealing with a speaker who is trying to convince you of something. Once again, very little, if any, action is required. Later on, you may form your opinion of Roosevelt as a president, buy Teasdale's collected works, put a bumper sticker on your car opposing abortion, or vote for a candidate on the basis of that person's position on supporting funding for NASA. However, the immediate goal of the presentation is not to create a sleeper effect in terms of action, but to modify your attitude.

Speakers can certainly discuss controversial issues, and while historical issues may not have any action implications, other issues may. An audience member may be convinced that abortion is wrong and then feel justified in asking the speaker, "So, what do you want me to do about it?" You may be convinced that NASA needs more money, and it seems logical to ask the speaker-advocate, "How can I help get NASA more funding?" Those questions about action are what change speeches to convince into the next type of speech: speeches to actuate.

Speeches to Actuate

Getting people to do what you want them to do is sometimes difficult. You first need to convince them that the action you propose is the right one for them. The next step, taking action, is the goal of the speech to actuate. Nearly all advertising is geared toward action. It does the SuperClean Dishwasher Company little good if you are convinced that the product is good but you do not actually buy it. Advertising can be direct or very subtle, but the intention is clear: to motivate the receivers of the information to engage in some sort of action. On the job, you may hear a speech about improving employee safety behavior or increasing productivity. Clearly, these are persuasive speeches that are designed to actuate. On campus and in your community, you regularly receive persuasive messages asking you to vote for a certain issue or candidate. The keyword in a speech to actuate is usually *should*. You should work harder, you should vote for Joanne, and you should buy a SuperClean Dishwasher.

Speeches to Reinforce or Inspire

These speeches are commonly given to audiences that are already leaning in a favorable direction. A sermon is a good example of such a speech. People seldom come to a religious service seeking to be converted. They usually attend because they already share the religious beliefs of the speaker, and the sermon simply reinforces those beliefs and builds enthusiasm in the congregation. Many public speakers try to make their listeners feel more enthusiastic for one reason or another. One such example is that of a team coach's talk before a game. The coach does not need to make the team want to win, but the coach must energize the players so that they will try harder to win. Speakers at most public ceremonies, such as dedications, awards ceremonies, or graduations, use the inspirational model. The speaker's goal in each of these situations is to remind the audience of the values or commitments its members already hold or once held and then motivates them to become rededicated or reinforced in those values. These speeches are usually filled with inspirational stories and examples; they often appeal more to the emotions of the listeners than to their logic.

Audiences, of course, bring their expectations with them to the occasion, and good inspirational speakers, being sensitive to these anticipations, tailor their speeches accordingly. A graduation is not the time for a speaker to announce support for a presidential candidate or to push the sale of a favorite sports car. One of the most famous speeches of our era, Martin Luther King, Jr.'s "I Have a Dream," is a stunning speech of inspiration. The thousands of people who marched with Dr. King to the Lincoln Memorial in 1963 already supported the cause of civil rights. They were tired and sometimes impatient, so he reinforced their original commitment with the power of his voice and his words.

Debates and Public Argumentation

A special type of persuasive speaking occurs when two people speak—one for and one against the same issue. These forums, usually called **debates**, feature the opportunity to hear opposing views from supporters of both sides. A public forum can be held on a question of fact, value, or policy. Although it is possible to have more than two sides, interactions featuring multiple positions are usually less satisfying to an audience because of the necessity of keeping fine distinctions between the advocates in mind. For example, every four years, during presidential elections, you may see a televised "debate" with five, six, or seven candidates, each of whom is vying for the party's nomination. Although these forums may be

Martin Luther King, Jr.'s inspiring speech "I Have a Dream" reinforced the values of the listeners.

useful for gaining superficial impressions of the candidates, they are less debates than showcases. In fact, the National Communication Association now refers to these events, even when just two people are speaking, as *joint appearances by the candidates*, not as debates.

Public argumentation can be an important part of community involvement and civic awareness. Presentations can include meetings of the city council or board of supervisors, commission and government hearings, and programs sponsored by local interest groups. Republican and Democratic Party organizations are found in most communities, and other groups, such as environmental action associations, religious organizations, other political parties, civil rights leagues, and many others hold public meetings to address issues and questions of importance to them. These meetings, in addition to being a rich source of information about particular topics, continue the long U.S. tradition of freedom of expression.

One thing that all of the presenters in these speaking situations have in common is a desire to motivate the audience. To get people to agree with them, they need to organize and support their ideas in a way that goes beyond what is required of the informative speaker. Speakers in public argumentation can adapt both the supporting material and the organizational patterns used in the persuasive setting.

Developing Motivating Supporting Materials

From before the time of Aristotle, speakers have been concerned with finding the most effective ways to reach others with their messages. Aristotle called these methods proofs and divided them into three main categories: personal proof, which he called ethos; emotional proof, known as pathos; and logical proof, or logos. These categories still represent useful ways of analyzing speeches of persuasion.

Ethos

Ethos, or personal proof, was included in the earlier discussion of source credibility. To create an impact on your listeners, you must tap the four resources within you: expertise, trustworthiness, dynamism, and goodwill.

You can show yourself to be an *expert* by actually being one. That means that you pick topics about which you already know a good deal or about which you can do extensive research. Furthermore, you should have a personal connection to the topic that shows the audience that you have both knowledge of and genuine concern for the topic. During the speech, reveal that you have done extensive research and can quote objective sources and established experts. You want your listeners to credit you with having the competence to be an expert on the topic. Politicians who visit a disaster site or travel to other countries to get firsthand experience are seeking ethos, or personal proof.

Second, your audience is more likely to be persuaded by your speech if they think you are *trustworthy*. Once again, the best way to appear trustworthy is to *be* trustworthy. The reputation for honesty and truthfulness that you may have

The Story of Communication
Quintillian's Notion of the Credible Speaker

THE ROMAN RHETORICIAN Marcus Fabius Quintillian lived from about A.D. 35 to A.D. 95 and is most famous for his twelve-volume book *Institutio Oratorio*, in which he set forth his ideas about the expression and presentation of messages and critiqued many of the great writers of classical times. His ideal speaker was someone who was a "good person, speaking well." With this simple phrase, Quintillian summarized the philosophy of many books, including this one. You need to *be* credible, not just *act* as if you are, and then follow up with a strong presentation. This advice is moving into its third millennium, and is worth teaching to each new generation.

earned in the past will greatly enhance your credibility with your current audience. As was discussed earlier, professional persuaders in advertising and politics constantly try to present to their audiences either the appearance or the substance of honesty. Your classmates will have an impression of you from previous communication interactions, in a formal setting, the person introducing you may mention your trustworthiness in the past.

Dynamism, the third element of ethos, is the one that is most directly under your immediate control. Audiences generally respond favorably to speakers who are lively, energetic, and upbeat if, of course, these behaviors are appropriate to the topic and situation. Voice, posture, gesture, and movement all can contribute to an impression of dynamism. You may need to adjust your delivery style to the size of the room, the audience, and the space available. The delivery skills discussed in Chapter 12 did not come from some abstract idea about an ideal speaker. They are grounded in research that confirms that a skillful delivery style makes audiences more attentive and receptive to the content of your speech. In persuasive speaking, a delivery that communicates sincerity and dedication to the topic will be received by the audience as part of the persuasive message. More information about persuasive delivery styles follows in this chapter.

Goodwill, the fourth element of ethos, requires that you tailor your message to the needs and for the benefit of your listeners. If you have their best interests at heart, they are likely to be responsive to your speech. You can also demonstrate goodwill as you give your presentation. Are you pleasant? Do you observe social courtesy and everyday norms of behavior? Do you communicate positive regard for your audience? All of these factors will help to create a climate of goodwill during your persuasive message. The advertising that you see on television may feature warm family scenes at a fast-food restaurant, a young person coming home to Mom, or a major oil company showing how it cares for the animals and plants in the environment. All are attempts to secure the viewers' goodwill.

In addition to developing your credibility through these methods, you can add persuasive force to your messages by using the other two types of proof that Aristotle identified: emotion and logic.

Pathos

Emotion, or **pathos**, helps your listeners to become involved or aroused. Attitude change theory states that getting the listener to identify with or have feeling for the topic creates a persuasive communication climate. Arousing and using your listeners' feelings can be a highly effective way to get them to pay attention to what you are saying and may also motivate many of them to do what you ask. Consider magazine ads that ask you to send money to help poor children. They may show a picture of a sad-eyed child dressed in ragged clothes, and you may feel a response of sympathy. On television, you may see footage of people in desperate condition in programs that are designed to raise money for worldwide hunger relief. These are examples of emotional proof. However, do not think that sadness and pity are the only emotions that you can use persuasively. Any human emotion can help you get your audience involved in your thesis. Persuaders often used humor, fear, and pride. How do persuaders get you to buy their brand of toothpaste or mouthwash? Fear is usually the motivator. What awful fate awaits you if you have bad breath or dull teeth? Sometimes a funny story or example will make the audience feel good about the topic. Humor, then, can be a persuasive tool, and so can poking fun at something. Political cartoons are an example of using humor to persuade.

Research shows that emotional proof, or pathos, can be very strong in helping to persuade others. Research also indicates that emotion is best used when it is combined with solid reasoning so that your listeners both feel and understand your message. One of the best ways to get emotional support into your persuasive messages is to use compelling stories or examples. Remember, they must be short enough to simply illustrate one or two ideas in your speech. You could include a moving or humorous personal experience, a touching example, a humorous anecdote, or a compelling description of an event that relates to your thesis. Some communicators use emotional proof to the exclusion of any other. This technique is effective only in the short run and with an audience that does not respond thoughtfully to messages. The best use of emotion in persuasive speaking is in conjunction with other forms of proof that also help to make the topic memorable and motivating. Most listeners, especially as their level of education and sophistication increases, demand the inclusion of factual information and a logical interpretation of that information before they make any important commitments.

Logos

Emotional supports are powerful, but they must be used with care and only to heighten interest or command attention. They must not replace other forms of proof. **Logos** was Aristotle's term for logic, or reason. While logic certainly includes making connections from a set of facts and drawing logical conclusions from those facts, as used here the term also includes the entire range of logical supporting materials and the reasoning process that brings them together.

CRITICAL THINKING IN COMMUNICATION

Logical Constructs in the Persuasive Speech

In the chapter on critical thinking, you learned about deduction and induction as logical forms of reasoning. The tests of both truth and validity were used to examine sequences and conclusions. The same processes now apply to material in this chapter as you examine both the facts used in persuasion and the processes used to link those facts together to reach a conclusion. Suggestions drawn from Chapter 4 can now help you to apply those logical elements to your persuasive speaking and listening.

Recall that *inductive reasoning* asks you to find supporting materials that are typical. When you create persuasive messages, select supporting materials that meet this logical test. Have you chosen examples that are representative of other examples that are readily available? Or did you select examples that show only one side of the issue? If so, you not only violated the rules of induction, you also ignored the psychological research that found that it is more effective to introduce arguments for both sides of an issue rather than one side alone. Good induction also takes into consideration the effects of time and requires that you select supporting materials that are recent. Finally, your supports must be sufficient if they are going to help you prove your point.

Applying deductive principles to the selection and use of persuasive supporting materials can be accomplished in several ways. You can adopt a *deductive organization* for the body of your speech by first presenting and then supporting a general principle in the same way that you would lead off with a major premise in a deductive syllogism. Next, the middle part of the speech, the body of the speech, would develop related concepts in the same way that you would phrase minor premises. Finally, a conclusion would constitute the final section of the body of the speech in the same way that a syllogism ends with a conclusion.

You may wish to make causal claims during your speech. Causal claims link events by stating that one event (cause) made another event happen (result). The major shortcomings of causal reasoning involve the fallacies of *hasty generalization*, whereby a conclusion is drawn too quickly from insufficient support and of *post hoc*, whereby a statement is in error because it assumes that if one event follows another in time, the first event must be the cause of the second. As an educated persuader, use the principles of critical thinking to help you avoid these reasoning pitfalls. These elements of formal reasoning are a good place to start, but you might also make use of informal types of critical thinking to augment your use of logos.

Informal Reasoning

The best way to recall the earlier discussion of informal reasoning is to think about the Toulmin Model presented in Chapter 4. Toulmin examined the reasoning process as people use it to help them reach conclusions. He noted that we take some information (grounds) and connect it to a conclusion (claim) by means of some principle (the warrant). For example, several of your friends like Nana's Ice Cream (grounds), so you conclude that it is probably a good place to go after a movie (claim) because your friends' judgments on such matters are usually right (warrant). In your persuasive speech, you will probably offer grounds to support your claims. In so doing, make certain that you examine the warrants that are operating. For example, if nobody knows your friends or, worse, your friends are known but not trusted, then your grounds will not be connected to your claim in the minds of your listeners. Persuasion occurs as a *transaction* between senders and receivers. Failure on the part of many would-be persuaders to consider the warrants of the audience has meant failure to persuade altogether.

Consider your own firmly held core values, such as your religious, moral, ethical, or political values. Others who hold different but also firmly held values are unlikely to be persuaded by your warrants. As illustrated by attitude change theory, you must appeal to the audience members on the basis of their values, because it is within a people's value system that warrants often develop.

Why do different people reach different claims or conclusions when presented with the same data? Members of a jury often differ, even after hearing the same information. The famous O. J. Simpson trial demonstrated that listeners from various backgrounds interpreted the same information very differently (Lacayo, 1995). Why? The answer is that they apply different warrants, or principles, to their reasoning processes. Make certain that when you develop persuasive messages, you examine the warrants that are operating in your own reasoning processes and assumptions. For your persuasive message to be effective, you also need to select supporting materials from the items your research has produced. You should have a variety of resources at your disposal, including statistics, short stories, quotations, examples, visual aids, and illustrations. Use the ideas contained in ethos, pathos, and logos to help you select the best and most appropriate materials. Choose those that will likely motivate your listeners. A review of the principles of audience analysis in Chapter 11 can also help you to make connections between your supporting materials and your listeners. A good rule of thumb is to create variety in your supporting materials, both in their probable effect on your listeners and in their type. For example, avoid using too many statistics, quotations, or personal anecdotes. At the same time, make certain that you appeal at one time or another during your speech to your listeners' sense of logic, their emotions, and their impression of your credibility. How much logic? How much emotion? How much credibility? It all depends, as in any speech, on you, your topic, the audience, the occasion, the time limits, and the circumstances. You can be sure, however, that the best speakers include each of these areas in their speeches.

> ## ▶ IMPROVING COMPETENCY
> ## Identifying with the Audience
>
> Modern rhetorical theorist Kenneth Burke claims that you can persuade people only if you can get them to identify with you or your message. He called the process of identification *consubstantiality*, which means a sharing of attitudes, beliefs, and values between speaker and audience, sender and receiver. When you examine persuasive messages, apply this idea of identification to see how speakers, advertisers, and even you try to make use of values that are common to both senders and receivers of messages.

DEVELOPING PERSUASIVE ORGANIZATION

Although you could certainly use any of the organizational patterns discussed earlier to prepare a persuasive speech, those patterns lack the advantage of being specifically designed to persuade. There are several ways to outline a strong motivational speech that builds a case for your thesis and takes your listeners from one idea to the next. First, we'll look at some logical patterns that are based on what you already know about critical thinking. Then we'll examine a special method of preparing persuasive speeches, called the *motivated sequence*, that has been used and tested for over seventy years.

Logical Patterns

Perhaps the most common way to organize a persuasive message is to use the *problem-solution* pattern. This **logical pattern** outlines one or more problems and then urges the listeners to adopt a particular solution. The body of the speech has only two major divisions: A. Problem(s), followed by B. Solutions. This pattern is easy for a speaker to use and for an audience to follow. The only real difficulties with this pattern are that the problem may not be significant, or the solution offered may be impractical, too expensive, or ineffective at solving the problem. Make certain that you use the principles of cause-and-effect reasoning when preparing a problem-solution speech. In addition, test for fallacies, especially the post hoc fallacy.

If you use a problem-solution format, your outline will look like this:

    I. Introduction (*a compelling story related to problem X*)
   II. Thesis sentence (*you should solve problem X*)
  III. Body (*preview*)
      A. Identify the problem
        1. Supporting material that defines it
        2. Supporting material that shows its significance
        3. Supporting material that shows its extent
        4. Supporting material that applies to listeners
      B. Solution to the problem
        1. Proposed action step
        2. Justification for the proposed action
        3. Probable consequences or benefits of the proposed action
  IV. Conclusion (*brief review of A, B, thesis sentence, and introduction*)
   V. Sources/bibliography

This type of presentation is commonly used in groups, committees, civic organizations, councils, clubs, and even among roommates. You sense a problem and propose a solution. Every problem from cleaning the city streets to cleaning the bathroom that you share with roommates can be organized into the clear and direct problem-solution format.

A format that is related to problem-solution is the *cause-effect* format. If you wanted to convince someone that there is a logical relationship between a suntan and skin cancer, you would use a cause-effect organizational format. This format resembles the problem-solution format in many ways. The first step in both is the same. However, when you consider an historical question—identifying the causes of World War I, for example—it becomes clear that no solution is needed in your format. Instead, you would try to establish causal links between events. Your logical reasoning would have to be clear, compelling, and free of fallacies for your audience to accept your thesis. Your organizational pattern would look like the problem-solution one, but it would not have a solution or an action step.

Motivated Sequence

Perhaps the most widely studied organization pattern is the *motivated sequence* developed by Alan H. Monroe over seventy years ago (Monroe, 1935). The reason that it has gained such popularity is because it works! Its parts are similar to outline sections you have already studied, but their arrangement is designed to lead listeners to the desired conclusion. The five steps of the motivated sequence are: (1) attention, (2) need, (3) satisfaction, (4) visualization, and (5) action.

The *attention* step is similar to the introduction of any speech outline. Here is where you capture the interest of your listeners and turn it into concern for your topic. To establish a *need*, you identify a problem that should be solved. The need can involve factual information—for example, understanding an event or solving a mystery; or a value—for example, reevaluating a position on evolution or safe sex; or a policy—for example, electing a person to office, buying a particular car, or supporting national health insurance.

Once you have the attention of the audience and have presented the need involved in your thesis, you move directly to showing your audience the solution—that is, the *satisfaction* step. This step may be fairly short and is often a restatement of your thesis. This is when you ask your listeners to change their minds or take some action. The next step is *visualization,* and here is where you can be somewhat imaginative. Try to get your audience to *see* the consequences of your solution, to *imagine* the benefits they will get if they adopt your thesis. You can also mention the negative effects of *not* choosing your thesis—the bad things that will happen if your audience does not adopt your idea. Some speakers try to introduce both positive and negative visualization in this step, thereby creating a comparison-contrast form of supporting material.

Finally, you request of your listeners a specific *action.* It is usually a directly focused form of your satisfaction step and may be designed to be inspirational or motivational. "So when you go to the polls tomorrow, remember to place an X next to Jane Doe's name!"

If you were preparing a standard outline for a speech and wanted to put your ideas into a motivated sequence pattern, your outline would look like this one:

    I. Attention Step (*introductory story, example*)
   II. Thesis sentence

III. Body (*preview*)
   A. Need Step (*problem, difficulty*)
      1. Supporting material #1
      2. Supporting material #2
      3. Supporting material #3
      4. Additional supporting materials
   B. Satisfaction Step
      1. Support for your solution
      2. Details of your plan or idea
   C. Visualization Step
      1. Support for the positive effects of your idea
      2. Support for the negative consequences of rejecting the idea
   D. Action Step
      1. Description of steps to take
      2. Support for or details of steps to take
IV. Conclusion (*brief review of A, B, C, D, thesis sentence and attention step*).
V. Sources/bibliography

You can create an influential presentation by using a persuasive format to organize your speech; combining that outline with strong and appropriate supporting materials; and motivating your listeners through your credibility, the strength and logic of your reasoning, and your appeal to their emotions (Gronbeck et al., 1995) .

DEVELOPING PERSUASIVE LANGUAGE

Getting people to do what you advocate is a difficult process, but you can improve your chances of success if you put some time and effort into making language choices that increase your impact. Most effective speakers select their words very carefully.

As in your informative speeches, you want your **persuasive language** to be clear and memorable. One way to create a response in your listeners is to excite their imaginations. When you use the motivated sequence in your organization's plan, you will engage their imaginations directly during the visualization step, but you can also tap into their imaginative processes throughout a speech by using imagery.

Imagery

There are several ways in which language can help you create images or scenes in the minds of your audience. Chapter 6 presents ways in which language affects our thoughts and imagination. One powerful way is by analogy, which is a form of comparison. Analogies are usually divided into two types: figurative and literal. A figurative analogy is the more imaginative because it takes things that are not alike in the real sense and uses comparison to make one of them more colorful and memorable. A literal analogy takes two real things and compares them. For example, an easy chair is like a recliner in many real ways and your college is very much like my college in many real ways.

Examples of figurative analogies are much easier to think of just because they are so colorful and memorable. When people speak of our country as a ship of state and compare the President to a captain, they are using figurative analogy to express an idea about how our country is governed or should be governed. Of course, the President is also very different from a captain in many ways, but nevertheless the point is made. A company may be compared to a bicycle, with each element of the corporation connected somehow to some part of the bicycle, or a family may be compared to a tree, or a community to a beehive, or the object of your affection to "a summer's day."

You probably recall that the type of comparison that uses the word *like* or *as* is a simile, and that other comparisons are called metaphors. Long, extended, story-length comparisons are labeled allegories, and many of our religious teachings come to us in the form of parables, another form of metaphor. Each time you use these types of supporting materials, you are helping your message become clear and memorable to your audiences. In the field of communication, research attention has focused on the use of stories to understand how people receive, organize, remember, and respond to communication (Fisher, 1984, 1985).

As a persuader, take advantage of the knowledge and tools described here to help you make your ideas memorable and effective. Research conducted at Michigan State University demonstrated that speeches that used analogies had a greater persuasive effect on their listeners than those that did not use analogies (McCroskey and Combs, 1969).

Colorful and judicious use of adjectives and adverbs can also enhance your speech and the willingness of your audience to get involved in your ideas. Creative use of description to form images can make your ideas live on in your listeners' minds. You might simply describe someone as being tall, or you could elaborate, saying that he "was a giant of a man, towering over the heads of everyone else in the room." The first description does not create a scene in your listeners' minds, whereas the second one creates a vivid image immediately.

Adjectives and adverbs are the descriptors in our language. They can, of course, also describe the image that your audience is forming about you and your ideas. Your audience is judgmental and can label you as *outgoing and upbeat* or a *talkative, overbearing loudmouth*. The subject of both descriptions could be the same person, but the imagery creates a very different picture. Did the soccer player walk away from the field "slowly," or did she "drag herself along, one aching step at a time, until she finally sank into a heap at the sidelines"? Use the power of language to make your message memorable with images that will remain in your listeners' minds long after you have stopped speaking.

Impact

Another way to create and use persuasive language is to give impact to your message through emphasis, humor, and personal references.

Emphasis means that you alert your audience to important ideas as they emerge by using transitions. A transition might be worded as follows: "This next idea will save you hundreds of dollars on your car repair bills." Notice how the transition calls attention to an important point. The statement, "This problem is not limited to our cities, but can be found right here on campus," emphasizes the direct application of your ideas to your immediate audience. Of course, you must limit your use of emphasis, or everything will seem to be really important. When that happens, your speech never varies from a high pitch, creating a situation that becomes very stressful for the audience.

Humor is another way to give your ideas impact. You may recall that pathos included the use of humor as a persuasive technique. The test of humor, as of all supporting materials, is that it must be appropriate to the situation. A persuasive speech is often about controversial ideas, and while humor can help the audience relax to receive your message, you must be careful not to offend your listeners and turn them against your thesis. Good humor based on wit, surprise, intelligence, and goodwill can enhance your credibility. On the other hand, if your humor is based on sarcasm; vulgar or off-color material; or mean-spirited satire, you can damage or destroy the impact of your message. Sarcasm is usually perceived as pettiness, and vulgarity may offend your listeners. Satire is very hard to do well and may confuse your audience about your real message. Good persuasion does not demean, offend, or confuse your listeners.

Finally, *personal references* command attention and make a connection between you and your material that the audience can appreciate. Your firsthand experience with a topic can be worked into your presentation so that it enhances the listeners' perception of your expertise. The story of your sunburn can be a dramatic support for your speech on sunscreens. Your experience of driving a friend to the hospital after he had drunk too much will give impact to your speech on alcohol abuse. These supports can be powerful, so it is wise not to overdo them. The speech should not turn into a monologue about the great tragedies in your life, or you risk losing your listeners. The topic must remain relevant to your receivers throughout your presentation; and if your personal references are directed to a significant idea in your speech, they can reinforce that relevance.

DEVELOPING PERSUASIVE PRESENTATIONS

Your delivery should match your thesis. You should speak about significant, relevant, important issues—and your presentation should reflect these purposes. Do not hesitate to communicate to your listeners that you find the material you are speaking about to be very important. In comparison to your delivery when you give an informative speech, your delivery of a persuasive speech will probably be more serious, formal, and dynamic; it will also include a greater voice variety and will make use of more pauses. You need not become theatrical or employ dramatic gestures, but your delivery should truly reflect the importance of your ideas in a way that is appropriate to the audience and the situation. Watch yourself practice on videotape to get a feeling for the persuasive impact your presentation is making. Is there anything more that you can do to increase your effectiveness? Do you need to tone down your presentation because it is too jarring? Is your speaking rate too fast for your audience to follow as you tell an important and touching story? Are you making use of pauses so that your listeners feel a sense of drama before you present a key idea? Do you sound cheery and upbeat during your speech on child abuse? Do not forget the test of appropriateness. Your presentation should fit the room, the topic, and the audience.

In addition to vocal considerations in speeches of persuasion, keep in mind nonverbal elements. Gestures and facial expressions must be consistent with the ideas expressed. If your movements are too grandiose or if your facial expressions are inappropriate, your listeners will be distracted from your thesis.

Your persuasive message will be successful if it is about a substantial and worthwhile topic presented in an organized manner with supporting materials that vary in type and function. It will gain polish as you add persuasive language and a persuasive delivery.

ADAPTING PERSUASIVE SPEECHES TO YOUR AUDIENCE

Now that you have a variety of tools from which to select as you prepare your persuasive speech, you need to think about the different conditions you may face as you analyze your listeners. Four distinct types of audiences may be present: supportive, interested, apathetic, and hostile.

If you know that your listeners are already likely to be **supportive** of you, then the goal of your speech can be to inspire or reinforce. You might give your listeners some of the most recent information so that they feel confident that their knowledge is current, and you might use pathos to energize the audience. Perhaps you'll finish your presentation with a reminder of some direct action steps that you want the audience to take.

Suppose your research into your audience reveals that they are **interested** in, but undecided, on the issue. You can then compose your presentation with strong evidence, paying careful attention to expert testimony and statistical supporting materials, if appropriate. These people are likely to have some opposing arguments, so take advantage of the attitude change theory that advises you to mention and address some of the opposing arguments.

A third condition you may face is **apathetic** listeners; they are not yet interested or they do not care about your issue. Sometimes apathy can be traced to lack of knowledge, so you should spend a significant portion of your time developing the problem and its relevance to the listeners. Section A in the outline body should have sufficient materials to underscore the problem. In your outline, include supporting materials that show the extent of the problem and how that problem directly affects your listeners. If your audience is apathetic because the issue really does not apply to them, seek another topic; you would be violating one of the principles of ethical speaking if you tried to persuade audience members to act on an issue of no importance to them.

Finally, you may face a **hostile** audience that is already opposed to your position. Rather than give up, you may be able to reach these listeners if you first spend time developing common ground with them. Using Burke's terminology, seek their identification with you and your perspective. Demonstrate the qualities of goodwill and trustworthiness. Once you have created common ground, use your expertise to connect their interests, concerns, and values with your position.

If you take time to do a considered audience analysis, you stand a better chance of reaching your desired goal of persuasion. Of course, you may face an audience that includes a mixture of all these types; in this case, you may need to combine approaches. Since the hostile group may quit listening first, you might want to begin with common-ground materials and end with your reinforcement and inspirational elements. Attention to these considerations will help you to be evaluated positively by your various listeners.

EVALUATING PERSUASIVE SPEECHES

As with informative speeches, you can evaluate persuasive speeches from the three perspectives of listener, critic, and consumer. Compared to an informative speech, there is more to listen to and listen for in a speech of persuasion. Consequently, there are more elements to evaluate in persuasive speaking.

Listening Goals

When listening to any speech, the listener evaluates the organization, relevance of the topic, main ideas, and supporting materials. When the speech is persuasive, the listener must also be very demanding in evaluating the logic that is used to connect all of these components into a motivating message.

As a listener, first try to decide whether the speech is aimed at convincing, inspiring, or moving you to action. Listen carefully for the thesis; it might not be stated overtly but may merely be implied, as in the case of advertising and political presentations. Listeners should always ask what the value of the proposed action is for them. You can be certain that presenters sense some value in the proposed action for *themselves*, but what motivates them to want *you* to join in? It may be their care and concern for your welfare, that their favorite cause needs more supporters, or that they stand to gain personally or financially from your support. A critical listener uses active listening skills to sort out ideas, discover the thesis, evaluate information, check the quality of supporting materials, and follow the development of the main ideas to determine whether sections build on each other in a logical manner.

Since persuasive speeches usually involve values and attitudes and are often controversial subjects, it may be difficult for you to concentrate on your active listening skills. Suppose the speaker is talking about abortion, gun control, the death penalty, college tuition, nuclear power, or any one of a dozen other topics about which people have strong opinions. If the speaker takes a position that is different from yours, you will have to try hard to keep listening with an open mind. It will be difficult to withhold a quick judgment and avoid mentally preparing a rebuttal while the speaker is still talking. It would seem that when you need the skills of active listening the most, you are least able to use them. Therefore an important listening goal in persuasion presentations is to be very attentive to your own reactions.

Suppose that the speaker has selected a controversial topic and the view that is expressed in the speech is exactly like your own. Again, active listening will be difficult because you may spend your listening time mentally cheering the speaker along and forgetting to activate your listening skills.

You may not be able to be a successful listener every time you listen to a persuasive message, but the effort to do so can still help you to evaluate persuasive messages—as both a critic and a consumer. You will be better prepared for both of those roles if your listening practice has been complete and careful.

Critical Goals

From the previous section, it is clear that you as a listener need a complete set of criteria to function as a competent critic of any message. The evaluation criteria presented in Chapter 12 can serve this purpose. Evaluate the speaker's methods, supporting materials, connection with the audience, and presentation. Examine the logical, emotional, and personal forms of proof that are used in the message, and be especially concerned with the speaker's adaptation (or lack thereof) to a particular audience. Has the speaker taken care to apply the ideas, costs, and benefits of the message to this particular group of listeners? Are the supporting materials directly related to the interests of the group?

Listen to the way the speaker uses language, transitions, interest, and delivery skills. Can you comprehend the vocabulary? Is it offensive? Does it move you? Does the speech follow a sensible and appropriate pattern that you can identify? The critique forms used in class can help you begin to organize your criticism. Later, you will want to come back to the list of items you use to criticize other presentations and apply them to your own messages.

Criticism involves more than just picking out the flaws and successes of others. The goals of a critic are to explain why and how presenters do certain things but not others in their speeches, evaluate the success or failure of the presenters' choices, and suggest alternatives.

In most messages, there are areas of excellence and areas that are in need of improvement. As a critic, you should try to carry out objective evaluations, using the criteria for judging good speeches in a way that is independent of your personal opinions or biases. For example, you may be opposed to handgun controls but still able to judge a speech that advocates such controls as being well organized and convincingly presented. You can also agree with a thesis but dislike the speech. It is challenging to give positive criticism to a speech when you oppose its thesis. It is also a challenge to admit that a speech supporting your favorite cause was not very well done. However, as a critic, you must be able to do exactly that if your objective application of the criteria warrants such a judgment. However, this does not mean that critics can never express their opinions. Opinions are the topic of the next section on being an effective consumer of persuasive messages.

Consumer Goals

The best consumers hold informed opinions that they develop by listening carefully, completely, and critically to the great volume of information with which they are bombarded every day. If you have learned how to be an active listener and an objective critic, you are in an excellent position to draw reasonable conclusions and, consequently, take wise and sensible actions. You will be able to base your decisions on complete information and good judgment. Some people form opinions on the basis of surface impressions or a quick impression. As a trained communicator, you can avoid making superficial responses to advertisements and instead seek out complete and reliable points of view. Persuasive speakers will ask you for your time, your money, or your personal support. To be an effective consumer, you should think very carefully before parting with any of those things. Before you consider such a major commitment, evaluate very carefully any persuasive messages, especially those from advertising and politics, for the value they can give you. Professional persuaders have the job of getting you to part with something. Take on the job of professional consumer, and insist that speakers, including yourself, maintain high standards of clarity, support, ethics, and honesty in the presentations they design to influence you and others.

IMPROVING PERSUASIVE COMMUNICATION COMPETENCY

There are few controls over the kinds of persuasive messages to which you are exposed every day, so you must become competent at measuring the quality of these messages. Being personally competent at persuasion will be valuable to you for the rest of your life as you listen to, react to, and send out persuasive communication.

The first step toward persuasive communication competency is to be aware of the principles and techniques of persuasion. By studying how people can and do change attitudes, you can enlarge your own repertoire of communication options. Attitude change theory, combined with the wisdom inherited from classical rhetoric as well as modern presentation techniques, have given you sophisticated, technical skills as well as an appreciation and knowledge of human behavior. This combination of knowledge, choices, and skills enhances your basic competency.

When developing a speech, use the guidelines to select an appropriate topic from among your options. Construct a message based on your analysis of the topic, yourself, the audience, and the occasion. Work on your speech until you have constructed a solid piece of communication. The selections you make from among your choices of supporting materials are important because they underscore your personal credibility. Logical reasoning and provisions for audience involvement add even more credibility to your presentation. Keep in mind that you have a variety of pattern choices to use for the organization of your speech, so select one that you think is appropriate for both you and your subject.

Once you have made all of the selections mentioned above, it is time to implement these choices in your actual presentation. Practice giving your speech by using appropriate delivery skills, increasing the impact of your vocabulary, viewing yourself on videotape, and having someone listen to and react to your practice sessions. Be sure to follow the guidelines for time allotment as well.

If you work conscientiously on these guidelines and recommendations, you will not only implement and increase your knowledge about persuasion, but you will also be ready to judge the outcome of your efforts through self-evaluation.

You are your own best critic. Using the criteria for judging persuasive messages, review your presentation to see how well it measures up to those standards. Did you focus on your own concerns or those of your listeners? Did you select a topic that was significant to them, as well as to you? Were your supporting materials substantial, relevant, recent, well researched, and credited to their sources? Were you able to introduce variety into both the forms of support and their functions to establish credibility, logic, and emotional proof? You should have presented a message that is rich in content, clear in meaning, and challenging to the intellect of your audience. Did you do that?

Another way to be evaluated is through the responses of your listeners. Did the audience react favorably? Did you get some direct feedback, either from your listeners or from your instructor? Take into account the evaluation of others, and add it to your own evaluative perceptions to obtain a full, balanced evaluation.

SUMMARY

Your attitudes and values give direction to the way you live your life. The development or changing of listeners' attitudes and the ability to influence their actions are at the heart of persuasion. The theories about how these changes come about help us gain a full understanding of ourselves as communicators—both senders and receivers of messages. The various types of persuasive messages—speeches to convince, speeches to reinforce, or speeches to move to action—all have a similar goal: to influence the audience. You can choose claims or questions of fact, value, or policy when selecting your topic. As you plan a persuasive message, pay careful attention to the types of supporting materials that you select. Apply the principles of critical thinking in choosing evidence to substantiate your main ideas. Does your evidence enhance your personal credibility, demonstrate logical connections, and provide an emotional link between your audience and your topic? When you are ready to organize your outline, consider using different patterns, such as the problem-solution and the motivated sequence patterns. Try organizing your information in a variety of ways until you find one that seems to work best for you, your audience, the setting, and the time allotted for your speech. Use the ideas discussed in this chapter for creating an impact through skilled delivery and an enhanced use of language. You can create and maintain listener attention and interest if you apply those suggestions. Follow the now familiar steps of selecting a topic, creating a thesis sentence, organizing the body, selecting effective supporting materials, and creating an interesting introduction and conclusion. These steps parallel the process for preparing an informative speech, but their content and their logical interconnection are specifically directed to the goal of motivating your listeners.

You have also learned how to evaluate a persuasive speech from the perspective of a listener, a critic, and a consumer. Finally, you have seen how you can apply those evaluation techniques to improve your own competency as a persuasive communicator.

Key Terms

persuasive speech, **268**
facts, **269**
values, **269**
policy, **269**
value systems, **270**
attitude change theory, **270**
habits, **271**
drives, **271**
source credibility, **272**
fear appeals, **273**
debates, **276**
public argumentation, **277**

ethos, **277**
pathos, **279**
logos, **279**
emphasis, **286**
humor, **286**
supportive, **287**
interested, **287**
apathetic, **287**
hostile, **288**
logical patterns, **282**
persuasive language, **284**

EXERCISES

1. Watch television for one uninterrupted hour to collect data on the types of persuasive appeals that are used in advertising. Collect examples of the following appeals: fear, humor, and pity. Can you identify other appeals? Then make a note of the different values on which television commercials are based. Prepare a three-to-five-page report about your hour-long observation and share it with the class.

2. If persuasive speech presentations are given in your class, take critical notes on one of them. Then present a brief critique to the class based on your evaluation of the speaker's choice of topic as well as the organization, supports, and delivery.

3. Bring several magazine ads to class, and describe how ethos, pathos, and logos operate in magazine advertising. Do some ads have only one kind of appeal, whereas others use a different appeal? What do you think accounts for these differences?

4. The next time you observe a persuasive speaker in person, notice the adaptations that the speaker employs or misses. For example, does the speaker refer to the specific situation (time, audience, and location)? Is the vocabulary the speaker uses appropriate to the audience? What other specific adaptations do you notice?

5. Present a six-to-eight-minute long persuasive speech to your class following the guidelines presented in this chapter.

References

Cantor, Joanne and Becky Omdahl. "Children's Acceptance of Safety Guidelines After Exposure to Televised Dramas Depicting Accidents." *Western Journal of Communication* 63, 1 (Winter 1999).

Fisher, Walter. "Narration as a Human Communication Paradigm: The Case of Public Moral Argument." *Communication Monographs* 51 (1984).

Fisher, Walter. "The Narrative Paradigm: An Elaboration." *Communication Monographs* 52 (1985): 347.

Gerrend, Mary A., David P. MacKinnon, and Liva Nohre. "High School Students' Knowledge and Beliefs about Television Advisory Warnings." *Journal of Applied Communication Research* 28, 4 (November 2000).

Gronbeck, B., Y. German, D. Ehninger, and A. Monroe. *Principles and Types of Speech Communication,* 12th ed. New York: HarperCollins, 1995.

Hilgard, E. P. and G. H. Bower. *Theories of Learning.* Englewood Cliffs: Prentice-Hall, 1966.

Hovland, C. I., I. L. Janis, and H. H. Kelley. *Communication and Persuasion.* New Haven: Yale University Press, 1953.

Hovland, C. I., A. R. Lumsdaine, and E. D. Sheffield. *Experiments on Mass Communication.* Princeton: Princeton University Press, 1949.

Lacayo, Richard. "An Ugly End to It All." *Time* (9 October 1995): 30–37.

Lumsdaine, A., and I. L. Janis. "Resistance to 'Counter Propaganda' Produced by One-Sided and Two-Sided 'Propaganda' Presentations." *Public Opinion Quarterly* 17 (1953).

McCroskey, J. C. and W. H. Combs. "The Effects of the Use of Analogy on Attitude Change and Source Credibility." *Journal of Communication* 19 (1969): 333.

Monroe, Alan H. *Principles and Types of Speech.* Chicago: Scott, Foresman, 1935.

Murphy, G., L. B. Murphy, and T. M. Newcomb. *Experimental Social Psychology.* New York: Harper & Row, 1937.

Park, Hee Sun. "Self-Controls as Motivating Factors in Opinion Shifts Resulting from Exposure to Majority Opinions." *Communication Reports* 14, 2 (Summer 2001).

Rogers, R. W. "A Protection Motivation Theory of Fear Appeals and Attitude Change." *Journal of Psychology* 91 (1975).

CHAPTER 15

Speaking on Special Occasions

After reading this chapter, you should be able to:

- Describe the occasions and events that might provide you with speaking opportunities

- Understand the methods that you can use to help you speak in a variety of situations

- Feel capable of and willing to present speeches of introduction, commemoration, and thanks, as well as short-notice presentations and oral readings

- Organize and present a short-notice speech

- Prepare and present an oral reading

In addition to the informative and persuasive presentations that you often make in class and on the job, there are special-occasion speeches that require their own preparation guidelines. You might introduce someone to an audience when that person, not you, will be the featured speaker or guest. You could be asked to speak at a commemorative event (such as a graduation), a recognition ceremony, or other similar occasion. Possibly, you will be the person being honored; then you'll need to respond and thank those who are honoring you. In a career setting, you may be asked to present an idea on the spot, or you may need to deliver an impromptu speech about your project, company, or special interest. Sometimes you will read someone else's words in the form of a short story, poem, or religious text. Each of these situations requires good speaking skills, of course, but what follows are some special suggestions to help you get the most out of the experience. Let's start with the speech of introduction.

SPEAKING TO INTRODUCE ANOTHER PERSON

A **speech to introduce** has several requirements. As a member of an organization, you may be asked to introduce a visitor or a guest at a program or event. You may recall your own important occasions, such as your graduation, where someone introduced the main speaker. Keep that experience in mind as you learn about the goals of speeches of introduction.

Goals of the Introduction Speech

Speakers who introduce others usually tell a little about the person and express appreciation for the person's being the main speaker. They may also present the title or theme of the speech. Good speeches of introduction are usually short, and the more the audience already knows about the speaker, the shorter the speech of introduction should be. For example, if you are introducing the head of your company at the annual employee luncheon, all you need to do is make a few goodwill remarks—perhaps some humorous ones, depending on the attitude of the guest of honor. In fact, the official protocol for introducing the President of the United States is, in its entirety, "Ladies and Gentlemen, the President of the United States." That's all, just a single line.

On countless occasions when clubs and other organizations bring in a guest speaker for a program, they will need someone to introduce that person at the appropriate time. It may be the same person who will act as moderator for the event, or it may be a selected person whose sole job will be to introduce the speaker. If that person is you, there are several things you can do to introduce the speaker effectively.

Methods of Organization and Presentation

First, a speech of introduction must focus on the guest speaker, not on you or anything else. Keep the listeners' attention on the person who will be speaking right after you. Place him or her in a favorable and interesting light. If possible, do some research on the person ahead of time. For example, if you have enough time in advance of the speaking date, you can write to the speaker and ask for a biographical sketch. If the person is already well known nationally, you can find detailed information about the person by checking current biographies in the reference room of a library. If possible, arrange interviews with people who know your guest—such as colleagues, co-workers, or family members—or you might arrange to interview the person directly. Interviews take time to set up, and it is difficult to think of good questions in advance. If you are given your assignment shortly before the event, an interview may not be possible.

If information about the person is not available in printed sources and you have not been given much notice in advance, you are limited in the amount of information that you can obtain. Suppose that the guest arrives just a few minutes before the speech is to take place. You will not help yourself or your guest by trying to rush through a hurried, last-minute question-and-answer session. Perhaps you can get a few moments alone with the guest, away from others who will also be trying to get the speaker's attention. Or you can talk with the person who invited the speaker originally and find out a little about the speaker. Then you might review the information briefly with your guest, and ask, "Is this all right? Is there anything I should add or take out?" In that way, you save your guest the task of making up an entire introduction for you. Other alternatives are to conduct a telephone interview beforehand or arrange some time to talk by offering to drive the guest to the event. In any case, it is your responsibility to do some research in advance of the event, and you may be forced into a very cramped time frame.

If you have a few days' notice, do not waste it by waiting until the last minute to prepare your introduction. Speech preparation, any speech preparation, will be enhanced by as much advance work as you can manage to do. Use your time, whatever it is, to your best advantage.

Second, it is very important that you keep your speech concise. Your research may reveal dozens of interesting facts, little-known personality characteristics, or charming stories about the person's early years, school activities, hobbies, adventures, and interests, but do not try to include them all in your speech. Select one or two that are very important or reveal some central aspect of the guest's life or personality. Your goal is to present the person to your audience in a positive and informative way, not to give the main speech. Just include some basic data for the benefit of the audience, and round out that information with one or two anecdotes.

Third, keep your speech short. This advice is easy to follow if the speech is concise. A speech of introduction is rarely more than two or three minutes long, and the better known the person is, the shorter the speech should be. Follow the rules of good speech organization just as you would for any other speech by constructing a clear outline. The introduction will probably begin with a salutation to the audience: "Good morning, everybody. I am happy to welcome all the members of the GoodDay Products engineering division to our annual breakfast." Then move directly to your thesis sentence, which tells your audience the topic of the main speech: "Today I am pleased to introduce our keynote speaker, Chris Masterson, who will be speaking to us about 'Chips and Dips: Variations in the Computer Industry.'"

Next, organize the body of the speech in a pattern—probably the chronological pattern—and include in the body two or three main headings. The chronological pattern is typical for speeches of introduction and usually includes a brief biography and some notable achievements. The body ends with a brief description of the person's most recent activities, and the conclusion states the reason that the person was invited to speak at the particular event. Of course, you could try other patterns. A topical pattern might include personal information, education, and achievements, but these items still have a chronological aspect. If you provide a few specific supporting materials, such as dates, titles of books or articles the person has written, names of schools attended, and one or two very short anecdotes about significant events in the speaker's life, you will have a complete speech. Then you will be ready to conclude with a transition sentence that helps turn the podium over to the speaker: "Ladies and gentlemen, please join me in welcoming today's guest, Chris Masterson." Because your speech will be very short, it is not necessary to review as you would in longer speeches.

Make certain that you say the person's name clearly a few times, and if you have a title for the talk, include that as well. However, do not preview the guest's speech or give away any special information that the speaker plans to announce. The audience should remember the speaker, not the person who introduces the speaker. By remembering to focus on the speaker, doing some background research, preparing a concise outline, keeping the speech short, and creating a positive setting with a clearly expressed transition to the guest, you can present a strong speech of introduction.

SPEAKING TO COMMEMORATE A PERSON OR EVENT

Sometimes, rather than introducing someone else who will speak, your purpose is to express appreciation for, or present an award to, someone. There are many similarities between a speech of introduction and a speech of recognition.

Goals of a Commemorative Speech

Like a speech of introduction, a **commemorative speech** must focus on the person or event being recognized, not on the presenter of the speech. The same processes of research can be followed, and solid, specific information—dates, stories, and accomplishments—should provide the substance of the speech.

The reason for these events is usually to honor or recognize the outstanding achievements of others and perhaps to present them with prizes or awards. Preparation for these speeches begins like the preparation for speeches of introduction.

Methods of Organization and Presentation

Gather information and prepare your speech by focusing on why the person is being honored. Commemorative speeches are much longer than speeches of

TECHNOLOGY AND COMMUNICATION

One Billion Watching!

Thanks to advances in satellite broadcasting, award shows on television, such as the annual Academy Awards each March, are regularly broadcast to huge audiences. It is estimated that the 2002 telecast was transmitted to over one billion viewers worldwide. Our technology truly makes us a global village where news and information can be instantly communicated to the entire planet. Imagine preparing a speech to talk to a billion people! And you thought your classroom audiences were a challenge?

introduction so you can include more supporting materials. Also, you will probably want to include some information about the award itself. State when and why it was started; identify notable previous recipients; and provide any other information that creates a context for the current ceremony and explains its significance to the audience. This part of your presentation will probably be main heading A on your outline. Heading B would begin with the background of the person currently receiving the award, and section C would briefly describe the current activities and future plans of the recipient. For example, the presentation of the annual motion picture Academy Awards on television usually begins with a short speech explaining the background of the award and how the voting is done. You can provide a similar function if you develop section A of your outline as background information. If you have been asked to present an award that is named in honor of someone or is supported by a specific organization, it is appropriate to take a moment and talk about the connection between the award and that person or organization. Again, your focus must be on the award and the recipient, not on yourself, your reactions, or your ideas. Use an outline, select a pattern of organization, and practice your speech aloud several times to establish and maintain a dignified tone for the occasion.

Sometimes, as at the Academy Awards, the name of the recipient is kept secret until the very moment that the award is presented. For most occasions, however, your audience will already know the person and no purpose is served by keeping the recipient of the award a secret. If you try to keep the recipient's identity a secret, as you begin to list details of the recipient's background, life, and achievements, the audience members will be busily telling each other that they have guessed who it is—an audience reaction that takes away from your presentation. Unless there is a serious and compelling reason to build suspense or a purpose for using surprise, you should give the award winner's name in the thesis sentence and perhaps several times afterward during the speech.

Another form of commemoration is the speech of praise, which is usually given when someone reaches a milestone, such as retirement, leaving an organization after many years of service, or completing a term of office. Another form of this speech is given to honor someone who has died.

If the person is leaving an employment situation, you may wish to set a mood focusing on fond remembrances of the past and good wishes for the future. Often, a successful speech of this type mixes humorous stories or examples with a few solemn items. If the person will be missed a great deal, you can say so and acknowledge this feeling but not emphasize it. Your listeners will be sad enough without your dwelling on the sense of loss they will feel when the honoree departs. Keep your remarks positive, or even festive, as a way to balance some of the sadness. Good speeches at retirements will certainly thank the employee for the past, but some humor and positive references to the future will keep the mood upbeat.

If you are speaking to honor someone who has died, use some of the same guidelines that are used in speeches of retirement. A *eulogy*, the praising of someone who has died, usually demands a solemn tone throughout, although a touch of humor can add a positive note if it is appropriate to the person being honored. Suppose the person being honored by your eulogy was lively, outgoing, and always ready with a joke or a funny story. Using a little bit of that tone in the eulogy would seem appropriate. But always make certain that your comments are appropriate to the person. If the deceased was grumpy and not well liked by others, do not fabricate stories about a lovable person or invent personality traits that did not exist. Search for positive things to say and focus on them, but do not create information just for the sake of your speech. Be positive, but be appropriate. On this occasion, you need to analyze your listeners very carefully, and consideration of their feelings must be uppermost in your mind as you prepare and present your speech.

Speeches commemorating the dead or someone who is leaving a company or retiring can be sad, but they can also serve to inspire and honor. Because they mark important turning points in our lives, they deserve care and attention in their preparation and presentation. These are not speeches to trust to last-minute inspiration.

The Story of Communication
The Eulogy as Literature

SOME OF THE GREATEST speeches in human history have been presented as eulogies. In classical Greece, the funeral oration by Pericles honoring Athenian solders provided a model for study; students still study Pericles in public address classes today. You may have already memorized the best-known speech in U.S. history, a speech given by Abraham Lincoln at a cemetery to commemorate the soldiers who were buried in Gettysburg, Pennsylvania.

The combination of the solemn occasion, the greatness of the person being memorialized, the talent and skill of the speaker, and the moment in history at which the occasion takes place can come together in a eulogy to produce a lasting work of oratorical literature. An eloquent statement that examines the struggle of a professed atheist who hopes eventually that he is wrong, is Robert G. Ingersoll's "At His Brother's Grave." Adlai E. Stevenson's eulogy for Eleanor Roosevelt commemorated her life of service and inspired others to follow her example.

SPEAKING TO ACCEPT OR THANK

Sometimes the person being honored at a special event will be *you*. This exciting, uplifting, and sometimes surprising moment will be another opportunity for you to present a short speech.

Goals of the Acceptance Speech

Thanking people is the other side of giving awards or honors. Should you be the one selected to receive an award or prize, you need to thank the presenters appropriately. You may know about the award in advance of the presentation event, so you can prepare a short **acceptance speech** of a minute or two that is well structured and practiced. The exception to this time limit will be when, in conjunction with receiving the award, you are also the featured speaker for the occasion. At graduation ceremonies, colleges sometimes confer an award—often an honorary doctoral degree—on the person who will then give the commencement address. The Nobel Prize ceremonies, especially for literature and peace, often feature the recipient's acceptance speech as a main component of the presentation. In this case, the person getting the prize or award has several months in which to prepare a long speech. At other ceremonies, such as the Academy Awards, the potential winners are narrowed down to a list of five, and each one is instructed to prepare a one-minute speech and be ready to give it at a moment's notice. My

You may be asked to introduce someone, present an award, or give a thank-you speech to a group.

favorite acceptance speech on this occasion was given by Liza Minelli when she was selected best actress in 1972. She walked happily onto the stage, smiling broadly and warmly and said, "Thank you for giving me this award!" Then she strode offstage. Other award winners usually thank people who contributed to their winning the prize or who have been a significant presence in their lives. If the prize is named in honor of someone, mentioning that person adds a nice touch. In expressing thanks for a scholarship, for example, you might want to say, "I am especially appreciative of the Evelyn Johnson family for donating this award, which will help me cover the costs of my tuition next year." Specific comments like these are appropriate if they are kept short and if they relate to the purpose of the award.

Any of these speeches—of introduction, commemoration, and acceptance—are special forms of speaking, but they have in common the following elements: analyzing the purpose and the audience, adhering to time limits, and observing speaker guidelines. These speeches are typically short and often require some special thought about what material to include in the body and what style of delivery is most appropriate to the particular occasion.

SPEAKING ON SHORT NOTICE: IMPROMPTU SPEECHES

In your classroom and later in your community and career settings, there will be times when you will be called on to "say a few words," yet you will not be given a significant amount of time in which to prepare a speech. You may be asked to speak immediately, in which case your specific preparation time is only a few seconds, or you might be given a few hours' notice, as when a company supervisor tells you in the morning that you will be asked to give a report later that day. Or you could be at a civic meeting and decide to speak on the issue being discussed, so you take a few minutes to jot down some notes. This type of **short-notice speech** is called impromptu speaking.

Goals of Impromptu Speaking

The main feature that distinguishes an impromptu speech event from others is that you have limited time to prepare. You can make impromptu speeches that are informative, persuasive, and even entertaining. You can speak to introduce, to thank, to inspire, or to motivate. Even though an impromptu speech is given on short notice, it is still a speech and, if done correctly, has all the elements of a speech.

Even without the luxury of time, you still possess many resources that you can use to prepare and present an impromptu speech. The most important resource you have is yourself. You have enormous amounts of information stored in your memory, and the successful impromptu speaker is one who can tap into that reserve of material and pull out specific stories, facts, numbers, dates, examples, and even visual aids. Effective impromptu speakers are successful because they are able to quickly recall information appropriate to the occasion from a past vacation, newspaper article they once read, favorite story of their grandparents, or a scene from a movie. They can remember songs they heard on the radio, magazine articles, popular television shows, and college classes that captured their interest. From these experiences, they can extract statistics, quotations, or examples. Effective impromptu speakers often give many impromptu speeches, because the practice they get diving into their memory banks helps them to become better and better at finding and using the materials that are stored there. Regular use of these personal resources makes them more easily accessible.

Additional sources of information for impromptu speeches can be the audience and the occasion. What do you know about your listeners that you can use in your presentation? Do they share a theme, common element, motto, or activity that you can include in your remarks? Perhaps you can recall something about their purpose, history, or previous achievements. Previous speakers may have mentioned ideas that you can incorporate into your speech and on which you can elaborate in order to adapt them to your thesis. You can also take a quick look at any program notes, information handouts, or bulletins that have been prepared for the occasion. If you are speaking at a special event, include remarks about the event. If your talk happens to be on a date near a holiday, tie the holiday into your speech. You may be in a special building, city, or college campus that you want to note in your speech. An impromptu speaker must be particularly alert to all aspects of the situation and surroundings to be effective. One of the most-often-used skills in speaking is impromptu speaking, a speaking skill that you can apply in nearly every aspect of your life for many years to come.

The short-notice speech is based on the same principles of good public speaking as any other speech, so let us review those principles and apply them to an impromptu setting.

Methods of Organization and Presentation

The ideas about organization and presentation that you learned in Chapters 11 and 12 can be adapted to the impromptu speech quite easily. Focus on a simple thesis sentence, select an organizational format, include specific supporting materials, add a quick introduction and a conclusion, and observe the time limits— either formal or informal—that may be in effect. One of the best methods for achieving success with a short-notice speech is to outline your remarks—a small piece of scratch paper or even the back of a program is quite suitable. You already know that the spoken part of an outline has four parts: the introduction, thesis sentence, body, and conclusion. If you have time to create a bibliography, you are not doing an impromptu speech. Create an outline with space in the body for two to four main ideas and some space under each of those for a few specific supports.

When creating the body of the speech, remember to choose a chronological, topical, logical, or motivational pattern. Variations on the chronological pattern

▶ IMPROVING COMPETENCY
Outlining the Essay as a Speech

Try this technique the next time you take an essay examination. Before you begin to write, jot down Roman numerals I, II, III, and IV in the left-hand margin of your paper or booklet in small print, leaving a large space between III and IV. Leave I blank for the moment, and note the main point of your answer in a few key words next to II. Next, try to create two, three, or four major ways to explain your thesis, and put these into some order (topical or chronological, for example) under III (as A, B, C, etc.). In other words, make a thumbnail outline of your answer.

It is worth investing a few moments in preparing your answer in this way, because writing down all the key words and ideas right at the beginning will help you to recall details and relationships later. Sometimes fatigue sets in, and an important idea you thought of at the beginning of your writing, that you intended to include in the middle of your writing, simply gets left out because you forgot it. Or you may take off on a tangent, and your answer begins to stray from its main idea. Without an outline, you may be connecting ideas, but they may lead down a path away from your main point.

Once you make your outline, reread the question. Does your thesis sentence provide a direct response to the question? If so, then begin writing, perhaps using a specific item for your introduction or saving a few lines so that you can come back and insert the introduction later. If your outline is not as directly responsive to the question as you like, concentrate on the outline for a few more minutes. Try rephrasing the thesis sentence, developing a new organization pattern, or adding a few more facts or other supporting materials. For long answers, a clear, focused, organized essay can be a lifesaver from both the writer's and the reader's point of view. Don't forget your quick preview at III and a comprehensive review for your conclusion. Your answers will be easier to write and easier to read.

are popular because they are easy for both the speaker and the listeners to remember. As long as the pattern that you select is appropriate to the thesis, the occasion, and the audience, use it. For example, if you were in an American literature class and were suddenly asked to report on your view of the character Jim in *Huckleberry Finn*, you could easily visualize the chronological pattern and divide your answer into "First impressions of Jim," "The river journey," and "Final evaluations." Your presentation would be clear and easy to follow, and you could support each idea with brief examples from the novel. Or you might quickly decide that a good way to analyze Jim's character would be in terms of relationships (using a topical pattern), in which case you would discuss Jim's interactions with other young people, and so on. This topical analysis would probably be more interesting but tougher to do on short notice. However, many students approach the writing of essay exams as if they were speeches, and the relational pattern might occur to you if you were sitting and thinking about your answer during an extended examination period.

If you were at a planning commission meeting in your town and the topic was the approval of a new access road near your house, you might select a persuasive pattern for your impromptu speech. You could cite the inadequacy of the current roads (problem) and the better traffic flow that would result from the proposal (solution). If you were opposed to the road, you could still use a persuasive pattern, but you would present ideas in opposition to its construction. For example, you might use the motivated sequence pattern and begin with a statement about increased traffic being a safety hazard (problem), followed by some specific examples as support. You might then suggest an alternative route for the road (solution). Get your listeners to imagine improved traffic flow and safety as a result of your new idea (visualization), and conclude by urging the rejection of the original idea and the adoption of your idea (action).

In the above examples, several patterns could be used. You could use a chronological pattern for the new road speech or the problem-solution format for discussing the character of Jim. However, there seems to be a rightness to some patterns that warrants their use in certain situations. Practice using the various formats to keep them fresh in your mind and available for your use at a moment's notice.

Once you have decided on a thesis, selected an appropriate organizational pattern, and researched some supporting materials, you need a good idea for an attention-getting introduction. Notice that deciding on an introduction is one of the last things that you do in preparing for an impromptu speech, just as it is in your other speaking situations.

Often one of the last items in the preparation of other kinds of speeches, introductions should be interesting and appropriate and should lead up to the thesis sentence. You can use stories or quotations that you like. Folktales or proverbs can also be included. Fairy tales usually have a moral; if the moral is the same as the point of your thesis, use it. Perhaps your point of view on the new access road is that the benefits of having it are not real, but illusory. A quick reference to the story about the *Emperor's New Clothes* will focus everyone's attention on your point. Parables from the *Bible*, stories of Native Americans, examples from the *Koran*, and stories about your family are all possibilities for introductory material. Make the length of your introductory story appropriate to your overall time frame, and do not get so involved with the details of the story that you do not have time for the rest of your speech. Ten percent of your total time is a good guideline for the length of introductions. Introductory material should be relevant, clear, appropriate, and short.

When it is time to end your impromptu speech, recall the general principles for ending any speech. Do not generate any new ideas; review quickly the main headings but not the supporting details; repeat your thesis; and conclude by referring back to the introduction. Many times, an impromptu speaker will finish the body of the speech and stop there. Remember that the audience still needs a quick review or restatement of the thesis to have a lasting impression of your ideas. Any speech that is longer than three minutes would probably benefit from a review. If the speech is shorter than that, just state a short, simple conclusion to tie your ideas together.

DIVERSITY IN COMMUNICATION
Folktales

Some of the richest sources of material you have for gathering support for your impromptu speeches are folktales from around the world. These tales are handed down because they contain a clear message based on some moral principle and are told in an appealing, engaging, and memorable form. But do folktales really fit the bill for good supporting materials? Yes, these tales survive in our heritage because they are clearly told, are easy to remember, and often contain a universal moral or truth that transcends time and place. While you may be very familiar with some folktales, especially those told at home and in school, do not overlook the vast literature of other cultures. School textbooks have been including non-European literature to a larger and larger extent. Students in elementary school this year will have much greater exposure to literature from around the world than you did, but you can make up for this loss by visiting a library and checking out the collected folktales of a variety of cultures. Even better, can you visit someone from a different culture who tells stories? Perhaps you have a friend or relative who is closely linked to a culture that is different from yours and who could share tales with you personally. Many libraries have reading hours that often feature a particular culture, and they would welcome your attendance. By increasing your knowledge of the stories of many cultures, you not only add to your available storehouse of information to be used in impromptu speeches, you also expose yourself to the wisdom of the world's peoples.

Remember, all speeches have a time limit, either formally imposed, arising from the audience's tolerance, or related to the situation. Since you cannot practice your impromptu speech ahead of time to get an idea of how long it will take, you will have to time your speech in another way to avoid violating the time limit. In some public hearings, speakers are limited to three or perhaps five minutes. Ask someone to give you time signals. Trying to time yourself is difficult because you are already trying to remember to do a dozen other things. People sometimes take off a watch, look at it very carefully, set it down next to their note card outline, and never look at the watch again. Your best strategy is to keep your ideas flowing and try to finish in a little under the time allotted. If you have made your point, clearly supported it, and quickly reviewed it, stop talking. Even if there is a moment or two remaining, resist the temptation to add some new point or a new story. They will be out of sequence and be seen by your listeners as padding. They can also create confusion where once there was clarity. When you are finished with your outline, stop talking.

Even if no absolute time limits are given to you, you need to think about the psychological limits of the situation. At a large public meeting, there may be dozens of people waiting for you to finish so that they can have an opportunity to speak. Be sensitive to these limitations so that your listeners keep listening to you and do not turn their attention away from your content to the amount of time that you are taking up. If you are in a classroom situation with only ten minutes remaining in the period, be careful of using all the remaining time so that no one else gets a chance or so that the instructor needs to keep the class late to make important announcements. By going beyond the time limit, you create an impact on the event that follows. For example, the next class may be waiting to get into the room, or the students in your class may be trying to leave and get to their next classes on time. If your audience is waiting to go to lunch or catch a bus, even one second over the time allotted will be wasted, and you stand a good chance of turning potential supporters into hostile reactors.

These suggestions for short-notice presentations can be put into practice in a few seconds, if necessary. However, you also need to have your delivery skills on tap to be effective in the impromptu situation. Effective delivery of impromptu speeches begins by practicing the suggestions for overcoming nervousness. Deep breathing and muscle-relaxing techniques will help to keep your mind clear so that access to your storehouse of information will be easier. If you had a chance to sketch a rough outline, go over it, making your handwriting neat, clear, and large, while you practice deep breathing. When you give the speech, use your outline if possible. If a speaker stand or lectern is available, place your outline on it so that it is not noticeable. A well-modulated voice, good eye contact, and natural and appropriate gestures work in an impromptu speech as in any other speech. If you do not start in a place where everyone can easily see you, you may need to move around to make eye contact with everyone. Adjust the volume of your voice to the size of the room. Watch the previous speakers—if there have been any—to see how they adapted, and use any information you gain from observing their presentations to the advantage of your own.

In summary, the short-notice speech should look as much as possible like any other speech that you give. The best way to achieve this goal is to give impromptu speeches as often as possible. Take opportunities to comment in class, at work, and in public. Each time you do, you are providing yourself with valuable experience for the next time you speak at a moment's notice.

READING LITERATURE ALOUD

The final area of public speaking on special occasions may involve you in reading literature aloud to an audience. Sometimes this reading is part of a ceremony, such as at many religious functions.

Goals of Performing Literature

In her influential text, Charlotte Lee defined **oral interpretation** as "the art of communicating to an audience a work of literary art in its intellectual, emotional and aesthetic entirety" (Lee and Gura, 2000). Thus the goal of an effective performance of literature is to help the listeners understand, feel, and appreciate the work being read. As in most other types of communication, the focus is not on the person doing the reading or speaking, but on the content of the message. You may find opportunities to read aloud at ceremonies, at reading hours in a library, at organizational programs, to your friends, or to your children. Research in the area of child development demonstrates that reading aloud to very young children has a clear, positive effect on their acquisition of language skills.

Whatever your audience, you might look through the writings of various authors for an appropriate selection to read. Use your personal experiences and feelings as guides in selecting material to share with an audience. The audience will respond, sometimes by visible and audible feedback, letting you know how your reading is being received.

Oral interpretation brings together the author, reader, and audience through the means of literature (Swanson and Zeuschner, 1983). First, the author writes the material and experiences the emotional impact of creativity. Second, the reader searches among the writings of various authors for the proper selections to read, using personal experiences and feelings as guides in selecting pieces to share with an audience. Finally, there is the audience, which by visible and audible responses lets the reader know how a reading is being received. This may sound like a simple thing to do, but to be an effective interpreter of literature you must find good materials to read, be able to analyze the literature to discover the author's intent, and draw on personal experience to put feeling and meaning into your presentation. Practice reading literature aloud to polish both your interpretive and delivery skills. Study the literature you select to read, and during your reading, look at the reactions of listeners to help you improve the audience's understanding and appreciation of the reading. Students who are interested in oral interpretation should read the opinions and ideas of writers in this field as one means of enriching their understanding of what constitutes effective oral reading. You probably can take a course in oral interpretation at your school.

Creative reading is **audience-centered**, in that the "stage" is the audience's imagination. Your responsibility is to use verbal and nonverbal symbols that enable the audience to create appropriate mental images. Through their participation, both the reader and the audience members use their imaginations to draw from their life experiences.

Methods of Presentation

Presenting literature involves trying to keep communication channels with your listeners open; reacting in your mind to the literary situation as an observer of it. Try to keep communication channels with your listeners open when you present literature. Think of yourself as an observer of literature and then communicate your reactions, thoughts, and feelings to your audience using your repertoire of visual, vocal, and nonverbal communication methods (Swanson and Zeuschner, 1983).

There is a difference between acting and oral interpretation. Interpretation is a communicative *presentation*; acting is communication through *representation*. You should deliver your material in a manner that is appropriate to a reading situation. It is difficult to pinpoint the difference between interpretation and acting, but you should avoid attempting to suggest props, perform actions, and portray characters. You should also avoid the use of gestures that go beyond what is considered appropriate for good public speaking.

The following chart should help you sort out the difference between being an interpreter and being an actor (Zeuschner, 1978).

Criteria	Acting (Stage-Centered)	Interpretation (Audience-Centered)
1. Who are you?	A character	Yourself
2. Who is telling the story?	Actors	You
3. Where is the scene?	Stage	Imagination
4. What is your relationship to the situation?	Participant	Observer
5. What kind of expression is used?	Representation	Suggestion
6. What is your relationship to the literature?	The actor tries to portray the writer's concepts by actually representing them.	The reader and the listener share as observers of the writer's concepts.

In the performance of literature, the reader's primary intention is to enable the listeners to imagine the situation from the writer's perspective. When an interpreter's actions and gestures distract the attention of the listeners from the material being read, they forfeit the main purpose of the reading. There should always be economy and focus in the art of oral interpretation.

Presentation Methods

To achieve the response that you desire you must demonstrate the delivery skills of an effective oral reader, including the ability to articulate and enunciate properly. Also, use variety in the pitch and tone of your voice, your patterns of intonation, and your rate of speech. Maintain eye contact with audience members, as you would do in any speaking situation.

You might want to begin with an introduction that leads into the material you will read. An introduction is strongly recommended in a public performance because it helps to identify the material being read and creates a context for your listeners. Sometimes, as in a religious ceremony, the material may be selected for you, and someone else may write the introduction.

Remember, the reader's job is to present an intelligent interpretation of a significant piece of literature. The choice of that literature, like the choice of a speech topic, should be based on an audience analysis.

Evaluation of Performances

Program and Selection of Literature   When you think about selecting and organizing your material, ask the following questions: Is the material of an appropriate quality and type? Is the material appropriate to your ability? Do you have variety in your material, and do your selections complement one another or provide an agreeable contrast? When writing your introductory and transitional comments, think about the following questions: Does the introduction state the purpose of the reading and the material to be read? Does it evoke interest? Do the transitional comments demonstrate your comprehension of the material and lead the audience from one selection to another? Are your introductory and transitional comments presented in an extemporaneous, communicative manner?

Communication Skills   To communicate the author's meaning, you must project both the author's ideas and attitude. Does your interpretation show that you understand the references and the allusions in the material? Are you able to establish a mood that is suitable to the material? Are you using appropriate phrasing, emphasis, subordination, inflection, and articulation?

Finally, make use of vocal and physical imagery to communicate emotion. Take advantage of appropriate sound patterns—alliteration, assonance, and onomatopoeia. Do you employ the rhythmic elements of verse form, prose cadence, tempo, or rhyme? Do the elements of pitch, volume, quality, time, stance, posture, gestures, and facial expressions contribute to your communication?

Readers' Theatre

A special type of oral interpretation takes place in a group ensemble format that is usually called a **readers' theatre.** Its purpose is to give a group the opportunity to present a literary script using their voices and bodies to suggest the intellectual, emotional, and sensory experiences in their presentation of a piece of literature. People who participate in a readers' theatre try to develop the ability to communicate complex ideas and feelings through individual and group manipulation of vocal and physical variables to involve the audience in the literature. A readers' theatre group is usually composed of three or more readers (Lewis, 1991). In a readers' theatre presentation, there are a variety of ways to use eye contact and focus, including direct eye contact with the audience, on-stage focus, and off-stage focus above the heads of the audience. The focus that is used in a readers' theatre presentation is determined by the particular treatment of the literature.

Types and Styles   There are several varieties of readers' theatre programs, including school productions, religious events, and community readings. Presentations might consist of a thematic collage of various literary selections from one or more authors or an excerpt from, or adaptation of, a single piece of prose, poetry, or drama. Props, costuming, lighting, and music may sometimes be used to enhance the program. However, these extra literary devices should not dominate the presentation. Groups may also use physical and vocal variables such as movement, choral and antiphonal reading, and staging.

The interpreters should convey the meaning of the material as well as its feeling and thought. Monologues, dialogues, choral readings, and other forms are used to embellish the intellectual and emotional meaning of the script. Usually members should share equally in the presentation. No one person should dominate or monopolize the program. The readers are expected to give greater insight into the literature than the audience might gain from a silent reading of the script.

Evaluation of Group Performances

Of course, any group wants to know how well its presentation is received. Readers' theatre groups can evaluate their reading in several ways.

Program and Literature Selection   The quality of the material can be judged by examining its literary merit. Is the material fresh and interesting? Does it leave the audience with a sense of having participated in a total experience? You can check for balance in the program by making sure that cast members have an equal share in the presentation. Are the roles of cast members of equal importance?

Presentation Skills   Your vocal action, delivery, and style can be evaluated by asking these questions: Did the material allow for suitable vocal variety? Were flow, pacing, and tempo effective? Was any characterization particularly distinct and believable? How well did group members interrelate? Was there consistency of focus onstage, offstage, and with the audience?

You can evaluate the organizational pattern of the script by examining the unity of purpose in the program. Was the organizational pattern evident in a collection of work united by a single theme, a collage of one author's work, or a compilation of prose, poetry, and drama by several authors?

Finally, you can gauge the overall effect of the program by asking yourself the following questions: Was the program in good taste? Did the program retain the interest of the audience throughout the entire presentation? Did the audience experience a sense of emotional and intellectual fulfillment from the program?

A readers' theatre program of monologues, dialogues, choral readings, or other oral presentation forms embellishes the intellectual and emotional meaning of the script. To learn more about oral interpretation, read a full text that contains additional ideas and details or take a course on the subject.

Finding Materials to Read

Whether you are reading alone or with a group, you will need to select materials if they are not provided for you. How can you find good literature for a reading? In general, you should begin by selecting materials that you understand and enjoy. To a degree, good literature is literature that you like and appreciate. It is wise to begin your search with literature you have previously read and categories of literature with which you feel comfortable. For readings of expository prose, the *Readers' Guide to Periodical Literature* is an excellent source of citations of magazine articles on all kinds of subjects, and it is indexed by topic. The periodicals that are listed include *Saturday Review, Atlantic, Harper's Magazine,* and *The New Yorker* as well as a wide variety of other periodicals. Textbooks and anthologies, particularly those used in literature courses, provide excellent sources of expository prose readings.

Narrative prose differs from expository prose in that it tells a story, making use of characterization, dialogue, and plot. Narrative prose has more emotional content than does expository prose. It is found in journals, diaries, letters, and, of course, novels and short stories. For summaries of plots of novels, consult *Masterpieces of World Literature in Digest Form,* and you should have no difficulty at all finding anthologies of short stories. Book reviews in newspapers and magazines will give you clues to interesting new novels and stories. Bestseller lists in bookstores and magazines also offer good ideas to interested readers.

CRITICAL THINKING IN COMMUNICATION
Criteria for Selecting Literature

Among other factors, there are three important criteria that you can use to help you evaluate the quality of the literature to be selected for reading.

1. The *universality* of literature means that the idea expressed is potentially interesting to all people because it reflects common experiences. The emotional response that is evoked is one that most readers and listeners have felt at one time or another. Universality does not mean that the material will immediately appeal to all people regardless of their intellectual or cultural backgrounds, but it does mean that the potential is there for any person to relate the piece of writing to a personal or common experience.

2. *Individuality* implies that the writer has a fresh approach to a universal subject. While seeming to be the opposite of universality, individuality means that the idea expressed is handled with a personal touch and does not sound like dozens of other writings on the same theme or subject. The key to individuality in writing may be found in language choice, images, and methods of organization. To determine whether a writer has individuality, you first need to become acquainted with a wide variety of literature.

3. *Suggestion* exists when the author has chosen references and words that allow readers to add to or enrich the subject matter using their own backgrounds as sources of ideas. Suggestion means that the writer has not told everything but has given a sufficiently clear direction for the imagination of readers so that they may draw on their own experiences to add meaning and emotional impact to their reading (Cunningham, 1941).

Poetry is usually represented in major literary anthologies. *The Poetry Index* provides one of the best references for poetry selections. Most libraries devote entire sections to works written by poets. Books on literary criticism are also useful to students who are researching poetry, as well as other forms of literature. For drama, the *Play Index* is recommended. In addition, collections of the best plays by year are quite popular and can be found in most libraries. Many publishers print paperback copies of one-act plays, and special publishing services offer monthly publications listing new play titles.

A reader recognizes that there are numerous ways to treat any subject, but some ways are more effective than others. You may be fond of certain poems, plays, or stories because of your early associations with them. Provided that your early associations are similar to those of the audience, relying on these materials can serve as a useful starting place for creating a program. However, it is a good idea to broaden your horizons and not limit yourself to what you already like. It is important to establish criteria for evaluating the literature you select for a reading. Such criteria ought to help you discover new literature and integrate those discoveries into your personal repertoire.

The factors of universality, individuality, and suggestion are closely related and serve to balance each other in effective writing. The universal idea is drawn from an experience that all people are able to share; the individual method of expressing the idea is different from those used by other authors; and the suggestion of associated ideas and responses points the way for the imagination to follow and allows for continuing enrichment on many levels of meaning (Yorden, 2002). Sometimes these factors are not all present in a selection with equal force, nor is it necessary that they be. But if one of them is missing entirely, it is likely that the literature under consideration is low on quality.

Preparing Materials for Reading

After you select a piece of literature for a program, the task of preparing the script and excerpting sections to be read is next. The following guidelines can help you to begin this task (Lee and Galati, 1987).

Arouse interest in the reading. Anything you might say that will leave the audience thinking, "This should be interesting," is appropriate. The art in this is telling enough but leaving enough out that the listener will want to hear the reading.

Establish the correct mood and the proper setting for the particular piece of literature that you have selected. Your introduction should be brief. When you read several different pieces in the same program, introductory remarks may be spaced over the entire reading by making brief statements just before each selection.

Type or neatly write out *all introductory remarks*, the transitions, and the piece(s) making up the program. Place them in a folder or notebook. Folders and notebooks should be neat and not distracting—that is, not covered with a colorful picture or stickers and not torn or worn out. Type, write, or print materials in bold, easy-to-read letters, using double- or even triple-spaced lines for easy access to the material at a glance while reading. Leave space for marginal comments or markings that will be helpful in projecting emphasis while reading. Never become completely dependent on the folder or notebook. The audience should not even be aware of it.

Cutting and Excerpting Materials for Reading

Sometimes the material you select will be too long, or you might want to use only parts of it. Proper cutting and excerpting is both permissible and essential. The following suggestions regarding excerpting may be helpful to you as you prepare your reading (Lee and Gura, 2000).

Know the time limit, and read your selection(s) several times so you can judge the approximate amount of material you can excerpt and still have the selection(s) fall comfortably within the time limits. Next, read the selection(s) for personal impact. Be able to distinguish the essential descriptions, narration, and allusions from the nonessential ones. Discussing your decisions about what is or is not essential with someone else can be helpful. Remember that part of your impact is likely to come from the slowly developed moods that an author builds through carefully selected descriptions and allusions; do not end your excerpt prematurely. Make up sentence bridges between parts. Wherever possible, use the author's own language for your sentence bridges to conform to the author's style. Delete the words *he said* and *she said* throughout the selection(s). Perhaps you can add names to distinguish the characters, but do so only occasionally, not before every line of dialogue. Subplots can be cut, as can minor characters. Cut sections or stanzas from poetry, taking care to preserve the rhythm and cadence of the original piece, as well as its essential theme.

To be an effective reader, you must review your feelings, attitudes, and moods regarding particular pieces of literature. When practicing, let yourself go a little in terms of expressing emotions. Allow your feelings an opportunity to guide your vocal expressions and physical movements. Practice reading aloud and practice often. Whenever possible, record yourself reading part or your entire program. Become a good storyteller by developing a once-upon-a-time quality for every reading. Every time you read aloud, project a first-time atmosphere. Your listeners should be captured by the opening moments of every reading. Listen to others, and learn to recognize how other readers capture your attention. Effective reading bypasses self-consciousness. Study methods and techniques of voice control. Such study should include attention to breath control (exercises in inhalation and exhalation) as well as volume and projection (the loudness and direction of the voice). Your voice must be appropriate for the surroundings and the literature. You must also learn to use your voice to punctuate the literature to read the selections at an appropriate rate of speed (Lee, 1971). All of these suggestions, when put into practice, can help to make you a competent reader of literature with a large repertoire of selections and reading techniques. You will be able to select materials wisely and use effective reading techniques and skills in any situation. You should be able to put these skills into effect if you practice sufficiently. Finally, you will be able to ask and answer evaluative questions to judge your own reading and that of others.

SUMMARY

Speaking on special occasions can help to increase your overall communication competency. By making appropriate presentation choices, you will be able to introduce, thank, commemorate and read literature with thoughtfulness and feeling. Take advantage of opportunities for practice, and your skills will improve. Every special-occasion speech creates a chance to develop and reinforce other elements of good speaking. If you perform well, you make a positive impression on your listeners. Applying evaluation criteria to these speeches lets you round out your communication competency. By learning the various competencies presented in this chapter, you will progress down the road to becoming a polished speaker for any occasion.

Key Terms

speech to introduce, **296**
commemorative speech, **298**
acceptance speech, **301**
short-notice speech, **302**

oral interpretation, **307**
audience-centered, **308**
readers' theatre, **310**

EXERCISES

1. Watch a speech of introduction either in person or on television, and evaluate it according to the suggestions presented in this chapter. Did the speaker put thought and care into the presentation? If so, how?

2. Interview a member of your class, and pretend that you are going to present that person at an important meeting fifteen years from now where that person is the featured speaker. Prepare a two- to three-minute speech of introduction for your classmate, and ask that person to do the same for you. Present your speeches to the class. For this assignment only, you may invent reasonable information to cover the fifteen-year time period (L. R. Zeuschner, 1995).

3. Attend a meeting of your student government, a hearing on campus, a city or county public forum, or a meeting of a political or special-interest group. Listen carefully, select an issue about which you have a clear opinion, and present an impromptu speech. Were you able to follow the suggestions for preparation and presentation offered in this chapter?

4. One of the most satisfying ways you will ever spend an hour on a Saturday morning is to volunteer to read stories to children at your local library. Find out when the library has a story hour and sign up to be a reader for one time. Then follow the guidelines to select, prepare, and present a story or two. You will probably want to volunteer again once you have done so the first time.

References

Cunningham, C. C., *Literature as a Fine Art: Analysis and Interpretation.* New York: Ronald Press, 1941.

Lee, Charlotte I. *Oral Interpretation,* 4th ed. Boston: Houghton-Mifflin, 1971.

———— and F. Galati. *Oral Interpretation,* 5th ed. Boston: Houghton Mifflin, 1987.

———— and T. Gura. *Oral Interpretation,* 9th ed. Boston: Houghton Mifflin, 2000.

Lewis, Todd. *Communicating Literature.* Dubuque: Kendall-Hunt, 1991.

Shugart, Helene A. "Parody as Subversive Performance: Denaturalizing Gender and Reconstructing Desire in *Ellen.*" *Text and Performance Quarterly* 21, 2 (April 2001).

Swanson, Don R. and R. B. Zeuschner. *Participating Collegiate Forensics.* Scottsdale: Gorsuch Scarisbrick, 1983.

"The Last Interp List: 965 Ways to Get to Nationals." *California Speech Bulletin* XXXIV (October 1996).

Yorden, J. E. Roles in Interpretation, 3rd ed. Dubuque: Brown and Benchmark, 2002.

Zeuschner, Linda Rockwell. "Introducing the Speaker Fifteen Years from Now." *GIFTS—Great Ideas For Teaching Speech,* 3rd ed. R. B. Zeuschner, ed. New York: HarperCollins, 1995.

Zeuschner, R. B., ed. *The Handbook of the Pacific Southwest Collegiate Forensics Association.* Los Angeles: PSCFA, 1978.

INDEX

Optional CD-ROM chapter page entries appear in **boldface.**

Abdicratic leadership, 191
Academic Teachers of Public Speaking, 17
Accents, effect during speeches, 237
Acceptance speeches, 301–302
Acting, in contrast to oral interpretation, 309
Active listening, 38–42
   listener responsibilities, 48–49
   removing barriers to, 45–48
   speaker responsibilities, 50
Actuate, speeches to, 275
Adjustment phase, of culture shock, **19-9–19-10**
Adult/child communication, **17-2–17-9**
Advertising
   diversity in,
   persuasive techniques of, 272–273, 279
   vs. public relations, **18-13**
Affection needs, in interpersonal communication, 129
African Americans. *See also* Culture
   and conversation styles, 143
   and free speech, 15
   and storytelling, 7–8
   and variety in American English, 100–101
Afrocentric perspective, 18, 57
Age, **19-16–19-17**
   and communication technology, **19-18, 20-18–20-19**
   as factor in group communication, 189

Age Discrimination Employment Act (1967), 161
Ageism, in language, 102–104
Agenda, of problem-solving groups, 181
Aha! phenomenon, 119
Algonquin nation, and public speaking, 15
All-channel network, of group communication, 185
Allegories, use in speeches, 284–285
Ambiguity
   and using edtalk, **17-9**
   fallacy of, 60
   in nonverbal communication, 81
   tolerance of, **19-10**
American Association of University Women, **17-8**
American Dictionary of the English Language (Webster), 94
American English
   and the International Phonetic Alphabet, 97
   mainstream, 99–100
   variety in, 100–101
American Sign Language (ASL), 78
Americans with Disabilities Act (1990), 161
Analogies, use in speeches, 284–285
Anatomy (Galen), **20-18**
Anecdotes, use in speeches, 215
Anglo-Americans, communication patterns of, 143

Optional CD-ROM chapter page entries appear in **boldface.**

Anthony, Susan B., 15
Anxiety. *See* Communication apprehension
Apathy
    of audience, 287–288
    of community, **17-10**
Appearance, for speeches, 213–214, 239
Appraisal interviews, 154
Appreciation listening, 36, 42–43
Argumentation, public, 277
Aristotelian thinking, 57
Aristotle, 4–5, 9, 212, 277
Articulation, 6, 236–237
Artifacts, 76
Asch, Solomon, 187
Asia
    language development in, 6-8
    pictographic writing in, **20-3**
Assertiveness,
    by women, **19-16**
    in interpersonal communication, 146
Association for Communication
    Administrators, definition of speech
    communication, 17
Assumptions, testing, 58
"At His Brother's Grave" (Ingersoll), 300
Athletes, and visualization, 117
Attitude change theory, 270–274, 279,
    18-10
Attitudes, 115
    and organizational behavior, 16-6
    changing, 270–274
Atwood, Margaret, **17-5**
Audience
    adaptation of persuasive speeches for,
        287–288
    analysis of, 212–213
    and effect of analogies on, 285
    diversity in, 213
    selecting appropriate language for, 263
    show concern for, 235, 244, 269, 276, 278
    visualization by, 283
Augustine, 8
Authoritarian leadership, 191
    and free speech, 14
Autism, 121
Avoidance stage of relationship, 134
Awards, speeches concerning, 298–302

Barnlund, Dean, **19-4**

Barriers
    to effective communication, 28–31, 122,
        19-6–19-10, 19-19
    to effective listening, elimination of,
        45–48
BASICS (Behavioral Assessment Scale
        for Intercultural Competence),
        19-10–19-11
Behavior
    offensive, **19-7–19-8**
    rules for in organizations, **16-8**
Beliefs, 115–116
Bertalanffy, Ludwig von, **16-4**
Bettelheim, Bruno, **17-5**
Bibliography, for speeches, 201, 202–203
Block printing, 6
Bloom, Benjamin, 32
Body image, as factor in intrapersonal
        communication, 112
Body language. *See* Nonverbal communi-
        cation
Body, of speeches, 202
Bonding stage, of relationship develop-
        ment, 132–133
Books. *See also* Literacy
    using for research, 223
Bradbury, Ray, 8
Brainstorming
    as part of creative thinking, 71, 119
    in small-group communication, 180,
        182, 194
Breathing, and preparing for speeches,
        232
Brief History of Time, A (Hawking), **20-18**
British Museum, 3
British Parliament, birth of, 11–12
Broadcast media, as resource for speeches,
        224
Brown, John, 15
Bryan, William Jennings, 15
Bulletin board, electronic, **20-8**
Burke, Edmond, **17-12**
Burke, Kenneth, 281
Bush, George, Sr., **17-10**
Bush, George W., **17-10**

CA. *See* Communication apprehension
Cable TV, **18-8**
Campbell, Joseph, 7

Optional CD-ROM chapter page entries appear in **boldface.**

Canons, of Rome, 5–6

Careers. *See also* Stereotypes; Interviews
    and communication technology, **20-13**
  communication skills, improving,
    16-12–16-13

Carter, Jimmy, 144–145

Caruso, Enrico, 30

Castro, 13

Cause-and-effect pattern
  in systems theory, **16-5**
  of speeches, 210, 283

CDs
  and storage capacity, **20-6**
  and trials, **20-13**
  including with job application, **20-10**
  using for research, 223

Certainty, in defensive communication,
    140–141

Chain pattern, of group communication,
    184, 185

Channel capacity, 119

Channels, 26
  and elimination of listening barriers,
    46–47
  and mass media communication,
    18-2–18-3
  and public relations, **18-12**

Charts, use in speeches, 219–220

Chat rooms, on-line, **20-9**

Chautauquas, 16

Children
  acquisition of language, **17-4**
  and communication with parents,
    17-2–17-6
  and reference behavior, 176
  reading aloud to, 308, **17-5**

China, language development in, 6–7

Chronemics, 76

Chronological pattern, in speeches,
    208–209, 303–304

Churchill, Winston, 12

Cicero, 5, 8, 9

Circle pattern, of group communication, 183

Circumscribing stage of relationships,
    133–134

Citizens, in democracy, **17-12–17-13**

City-states, 3

Civic life, participation in, **17-10**

Civil Rights Act (1964), 161

Civilization, and communication technol-
    ogy, **20-2–20-7**

Claim, in Toulmin Model, 65, 280

Classical approach, to studying organiza-
    tions, **16-2–16-3**

Classrooms, **17-6–17-10**
  and communication technology,
    20-14–20-15
  and e-mail, **20-15**
  and intercultural communication, **19-12**
  listening in, 36, 44
  setting student self-perceptions in, 117
  work groups in, 178

Clear-and-present-danger test, for free
    speech, **18-11**

Climate, for communication, 136–146

Clinton, Bill, **17-10**

Closed system, **16-5**

Closure phase, in group communication,
    188

Cognitive style, 118

Coherence, 69

Colleges, development of in U.S., 16

Commemorative speeches, 298–300

Communication. *See also specific types*
  about health, **19-17–19-19**
  and culture, 79, 81–82, 86, 96,
  and diversity, **19-1–19-22**
  and gender, **19-12–19-15**
  and managing conflict, 141–145
  and relationships, 23, 130–135
  and rumor, 193
  as inevitable and irreversible, 22–23
  between cultures, **19-3–19-6**
  content of, 23, 26, 30
  context of, 23, 26, 45–46
  definition of, 22
  ethical, 244–245
  in the community, **17-10–17-11**
  organizational, **16-2**
  settings for, 24–25
  supportive behaviors for, 136–141

Communication apprehension, 28–31, 122
  coping strategies for, 30–31, 232–236
  physical reactions to, 28–29
  research about, 31
  responses to, 29–30
  sources of, 28, 231–232

Communication climate, 136–146

Optional CD-ROM chapter page entries appear in **boldface.**

Communication competencies, 32, **17-7**
    improving adult-child, **17-9**
Communication environment. *See*
    Communication climate
Communication model, 26–28, 45–48
Communication networks, 183–185
Communication technology, **20-1–20-22**
    definition of, **20-2**
    from papyrus to microchips, 4
    invention of phonograph, 38
Community, communication in,
    17-10–17-11
    and communication technology,
    20-15–20-16
Compact disks. *See* CDs
Completeness
    as condition for premises, 69
    in communication technology, **20-6**
Comprehension listening, 36, 38, 43–44
Computers
    and communication apprehension,
    20-12
    and digitizing images, 272
    and increasing use of, **20-5**
    and language disabilities, **20-18–20-19**
    and mass media communication, 25,
    18-2
    and on-line research services, 223
    and personal messaging, **20-9**
    and physical disabilities, **20-18**
    and visual aids, 254
    history of, 101
    use by troops in field, **20-14**
    use in creating outlines, 207
Computer-speak, 101
Concentration, and listening skills, 39–40
Conclusions
    drawing in Toulmin Model, 65–66
    of deduction, 56, 62
    of induction, 62–65
    of speeches, 202
Confidence, projection of, 245–246
Conflict, 141–143
    in small-group communication,
    186–187
Conflict management, 143–145
Connotation, 93
Consensus phase, in group communica-
    tion, 187–188

Consideration, in interpersonal communi-
    cation, 146
Consistency, as condition for premises, 69
Consumer of information, 261–263, 290,
    18-15
Content, of communication, 23–24
    as message in communication model,
    26, 46
Context
    and elimination of listening barriers,
    45–46
    and interpreting nonverbal communi-
    cation, 86
    in speeches, 252
    of communication, 23, 26
    of listening, 36–37
Contradicting function, of nonverbal com-
    munication, 79
Control
    as conveyed by facial expressions, 84
    in defensive communication, 139–140
    in interpersonal communication, 129
Convince, speeches to, 274–275
Cooperation, between small groups, 193
Corax, 3
Cost-benefits pattern, of speeches, 211
Counseling interview, 154–155
Cowan, Geoff, 103
Creative thinking, 71–72
Creative visualization, and speeches, 233
Credibility
    and media, **18-10**
    and persuasive speeches, 271–273,
    277–278
Crisis phase, of culture shock, **19-9**
Criteria
    for decision-making, 68
    for evaluating speeches, 242–245,
    259–261, 289–290
    for handling conflict, 145
    for selecting literature to read, 312
Critical listening, 36–37, 44–45
Critical thinker, in small groups, 182, 187
Critical thinking, 54–74
    as a consumer, 243, 261–263
    and communication, 138
    and creative thinking, 71–72
    and teacher attention, **17-8**
    definitions of, 54–56

Optional CD-ROM chapter page entries appear in **boldface.**

Cross-cultural communication.
    See Intercultural communication
Crowley, David, **20-2**
Cultural approach, to studying organiza-
    tions, **16-6–16-7**
Culture
    and children, **17-4**
    and conversation styles, 143, 250
    and diversity, **19-1–19-22**
    and facial expressions, **19-11**
    and interpreting nonverbal communi-
        cation, 79, 81–82, 86
    and linguistic patterns, 97
    and media, **18-10**
    and organizational patterns, **16-8**
    and small-group communication, 174
Culture shock, **19-9**
Cultures
    communicating between, **19-3**
    homogenization of, **20-17**
    learning about, **19-6–19-12**
    recognizing differences between, **19-8**
Cuneiform, 2

Darrow, Clarence, 15
Databanks, for research, 223
Debate
    as form of persuasive speaking,
        276–277
    in Renaissance, 9
Debs, Eugene, 15
Deception, in nonverbal communication, 79–80
    indicated by pupil dilation, 163
Decision-making
    cultural premises in, 59
    informed, 64, 68–72
Decision-making groups, 180–182
Declaration of Independence, 16
Decoders, 27
    and elimination of listening barriers, 47
Deductive reasoning, 56–62
    analyzing, 57–58
    and selecting support materials, 280
    vs. inductive, 64–65
Defensive communication, 139–141
Definition, speeches of, 251–253
Definitions, use in speeches, 215
Delegation, in problem-solving groups,
    181–182

Delia, Jesse, 57–58
Delivery
    as used by storyteller, 7
    of speeches, 236–242
    Roman canon, 6
Democratic communication, **17-12–17-13**
    and freedom of speech, 13–15, **18-11,
        18-12, 20-4, 20-15**
    and leadership, 191
Demonstration, speeches of, 253–254
    videotaping, 254
Demosthenes, 27–28
Denotation, 93
De Oratore (Cicero), 9
Descriptions
    in supportive communication, 137
    use in speeches, 215–216
Determination interviews, 154
Devil's advocate, in groups, 182, 187
Dialects. *See* Accents
Dictionary of Sociology, **19-3**
Differentiation stage of relationship, 133
Diffusion, of messages in mass media,
    18-7
Digitizing images, 272
Directive questions, during interviews,
    157
Discrimination, in job interviews, 161
Disputation, 9
Distortion, of messages in organizations,
    16-9–16-10
Diversion, in mass media communication,
    18-10
Diversity. *See also* Culture; Gender
    in communication, 213, **19-1–19-22**
Donaldson, Sam, **18-3**
Douglass, Frederick, 15
Downward distortion, **16-9**
Dress
    and cultural differences, **19-8**
    for speeches, 213–214, 239
Dumbing down, 49
Dylan, Bob, 96
Dynamism, of speaker, 278
Dyslexia, **20-18–20-19**

Economy, global, **19-5–19-6**
Ectomorph, 112
Edison, Thomas, 38

Optional CD-ROM chapter page entries appear in **boldface.**

Education, early methods of, 2–8
  non-Western approaches, 6–8
  Western approaches, 2–6
Edward I, King of England, 11
Effective listening, 37–38
Egypt
  and literacy, **20-4**
  language development in, 3
  pictographic writing in, **20-3**
Einstein, Albert, 72
Electronic bulletin board, **20-8**
Ellison, Ralph, 40
Ellwood, Charles A., **19-3**
Elocution, 6, 16
Eloquence in an Electronic Age (Jamieson),
  20-12
Emoticons, **20-11**
Emotion. *See* Pathos
Emotional proof (Aristotle), 277, 279
Empathy
  and intercultural communication, **19-10**
  in listening, 36, 43
  in supportive communication, 137–138
Emphasis, in persuasive speeches, 286
Endomorph, 112
English
  American, variety in, 93, 100–101
  and the International Phonetic
    Alphabet, 97
  evolution of, 253
  mainstream American, 99–100
Entertainment, from mass media, **18-4,**
  18-7–18-8
Entertainment interviews, 155
Enthymeme, 9, 58, 66
Environmental factors affecting communi-
  cation, 26, 214
  gaining familiarity with, 234
Ephesus, library at, 4, **20-6**
Equal Employment Act (1963), 161
Equal Employment Opportunity Act
  (1972), 161
Equality, in supportive communication, 137
Equivocation, fallacy of, 60
Ethics
  and communication technology,
    20-5–20-7
  in communication, 244–245
Ethnocentrism, **19-6–19-7**

Ethos, 272, 277–278
Eulogy, 300
Euphemisms, 104
Eurocentric perspective, 6, 18
Evaluation
  after listening, 32, 41–42
  and communication technology, **20-20**
  as conveyed by facial expressions, 84
  in defensive communication, 139
  of group performances, 311
  of ideas in small groups, 195
  of information, 68–70
  of oral interpretation, 310
  of sources, 70
  of speeches, 242–245, 259–263,
    288–290
  of supporting materials, 70–71
Evaluation forms, for speeches, 260
Evaluation interviews. *See* Appraisal
  interviews
Evidence, for premises, 58
Examples, use in speeches, 216, 252
Expectations, 116–117
Experiences, as factor in intrapersonal
  communication, 111
Experimenter effect, **16-4**
Experimenting stage, of relationship
  development, 131
Expertise. *See* Credibility
Exposition, speeches of, 255
Expression, care and precision of, **20-6**
Extemporaneous speeches, 229–230
External consistency, 69
Extrasensory perception (ESP), 87
Eye contact, during speeches, 241. *See also*
  Nonverbal communication

Facial expressions, 84. *See also* Nonverbal
  communication
  during speeches, 241
  in cultures, **19-11**
Facial Meaning Sensitivity Test, 84
Facilitators
  and mass media, **18-5**
  in organizations, **16-10–16-11**
Facts, as basis of persuasive speeches, 269
Facts on File, 223
Fahrenheit 451 (Ray Bradbury)
Fairy tales, **17-5**

Optional CD-ROM chapter page entries appear in **boldface.**

Fallacy(ies)
  of ambiguity, 60
  of approval, 30
  of catastrophic failure, 29
  of equivocation, 60
  of hasty generalization, 280, **19-12**
  of obscuration, 60
  of overgeneralization, 30
  of perfection, 29–30
  of vagueness, 60
  post hoc, 210, 258, 280
False claims, in media, **18-11**
Familiarity, and reducing speech anxiety, 234
Family
  and communication technology,
    20-14–20-16
  and self-concept, 177
  communication in, **17-2–17-6**
  definition of, 176
  roles in, **17-5–17-6**
Fear appeals, 273–274, 279
Feedback, 27–28
  and elimination of listening barriers,
    46, 47
  and facilitators, **16-10**
  and public relations, **18-12**
  and self-concept, 116, **16-13**
  in circle networks, 183
  in work groups, 179
  on speech presentation, 259
Feelings. *See also* Emotion; Pathos
  in creative and critical thinking, 71
  in speech communication, 32
Feminist perspective, 18
Figurative language, in persuasive
    speeches, 284–285
Fillers, in gender-related communication,
    19-14
Films, 271, **19-18**. *See also* Mass media
    communication
Filters, psychological
  for mass media messages, **18-6**
  of communication, 120–121
  of intercultural communication,
    19-6–19-10
First Amendment, to U.S. Constitution,
    14, **20-5**
Flight/fight response, 28, 234
Folktales, use in speeches, 305, 306

Ford, Gerald, **18-10**
Formal rules, of organizations, **16-8**
Forum (Roman), 5
Free speech
  and Greece, 4
  and national emergencies, **18-12**
  and revolution, 13
  clear-and-present-danger test for, **18-11**
  in the United States, 14–15, **18-11**
Frost, Joyce, 141
Frost, Robert, 99
Funnel format, for interviews, 166, 167

Galen, **20-18**
Gallup Poll, 64
Galvanic skin response (GSR), 80
Garvey, Marcus, 15
Gatekeepers, 193, **16-10–16-11**
  and mass media, **18-5, 18-6, 18-9**
Gender. *See also* Sexism; Culture;
    Stereotypes
  and communication, **19-12–19-16**
  and communication technology,
    20-17–20-18
  and nonverbal messages, **19-15**
Generalization, in reasoning, 65, 280
General semantics, 93
Generation gap, **19-17**
Gestures, 84, 240. *See also* Nonverbal
    communication
Getting to Yes (Fisher and Ury), 144
Gettysburg Address (Lincoln), 42
Gibb climate factors, 136
Gibb, Jack, 136
Global economy, **19-5–19-6**
Global village, **19-4**
Goldman, Emma, 15
Government. *See* Politics
Graphs, use in speeches, 219–220
Greece
  language development in, 3–5, **20-3**
  orators of, 3–5, 268
Grounds, in Toulmin Model, 65, 280
Group norms, 175
Groups, small, 175–182
Groupthink, 188
Gutenberg Bible, **20-5**
Gutenberg, Johannes, 10
Guthrie, Woody, 85

Optional CD-ROM chapter page entries appear in **boldface.**

Halo effect, 40
Harvard, John, 16
Harvard Negotiation Project, 144, 147
Hasty generalization, fallacy of, 280, **19-12**
Hate speech, 103
Hawking, Stephen, **20-18**
Hawthorne Effect, **16-4**
Hayakawa, S.I., 93
Health
    and communication, **19-17–19-19**
    and communication technology,
        20-18–20-19
Health care system, communicating with,
    19-18
Hearing impairments, and communica-
    tion, **19-17, 20-18**
Hearing vs. listening, 37
Hedges, in gender-related communica-
    tion, **19-14**
Henry, Patrick, 13
Henry VIII, King of England, 11
Heyer, Paul, **20-2**
Hieroglyphics, 2, 3
Hispanic Americans, language of, 101.
    See also Culture
Hitler, Adolf, 41
Hoffman, Dustin, 121
Holmes, Oliver Wendell, **18-11**
Holographic projection, 179
Homogenization of culture, **20-17**
Honeymoon phase, of culture shock, **19-9**
Horizontal direction, of message travel,
    16-11
Hostility, in audience, 288
Hovland, Carl, 271
HUB model, **18-5–18-7**
Human relations approach, to studying
    organizations, **16-3–16-4**
Humor, in persuasive speeches, 286
Humphrey, Hubert, **20-16**
Hybrid differences, in gender communica-
    tion, **19-14–19-15**
Hypercorrection, **19-14**
Hypertext, **20-11, 20-14**

"I Have a Dream" (King), 276
Iffel, Gwen, **18-3**
Imagery, use in persuasive speeches,
    284–285

Imagination. *See* Visualization
Implied evidence, 63
Implementation
    and communication technology, **20-20**
    during an interview, 167
    improving adult-child communication,
        17-9
    of effective communication, 33
    of ideas in small groups, 195
    of speeches, 246
Importance of sequence pattern, of
    speeches, 209
Impression management function, of non-
    verbal communication, 80
Impromptu speeches, 230–231, 302–307
Incas, recording system of, 7
Inclusion needs, in interpersonal commu-
    nication, 129
Individuality, of oral interpretation mate-
    rial, 312
Indo-European language, 2
Inductive reasoning, 62–65, 280
    vs. deductive, 64–65
Informal rules, in organizations, **16-8**
Information
    access to through technology,
        20-15–20-16
    currency of, 71
    distortion of, **16-9–16-10**
    evaluation of, 68–70
    from mass media, **18-4**
Information interviews, 153
Informative speeches, 250–266
    evaluating, 259–263
    improving competency in, 263–265
    patterns of, 256–259
    types of, 251–255
    vs. persuasive, 250
Ingersoll, Robert G., 300
Initiating stage, of relationship develop-
    ment, 130
Innes, Harold, **20-3**
Inspire, speeches to, 275–276
Institutio Oratorio (Quintillian), 278
Integrating stage, of relationship develop-
    ment, 132
Intensifiers, in language, **19-14**
Intensifying stage, of relationship devel-
    opment, 131–132

Optional CD-ROM chapter page entries appear in **boldface.**

Intensity, as conveyed by facial expressions, 84
Interaction, 27
Intercultural communication, 25, **19-2–19-6**
 and communication technology, **20-17–20-19**
 building competency in, **19-10–19-12**
Interdependence, of parties in conflict, 142
Interest, as conveyed by facial expressions, 84
Interference, 27–28
 and conflict, 142
 and elimination of listening barriers, 47–48
International Phonetic Alphabet (IPA), 97
International student exchange, **17-9**
Internet
 and global village, **19-4**
 and plagiarism, **20-6**
 and talk shows, **20-10**
 as resource for speeches, 224
 as source of information, **18-15**
 number of users of, **20-4**
Interpersonal communication, 24, 125–150
 and communication technology, **20-8–20-9**
 and relationship development, 130–135
 definition of, 126
 improving, 146–147
Interpersonal system, in families, **17-2**
Interpretation, 118–119
Interruptions, in gender-related communication, **19-15**
Interviews, 151–170
 and communication technology, **20-9–20-10**
 and organizational behavior, 16-12
 conducting, 156–158
 definition of, 152
 formats of, 166
 improving competency in, 166–168
 performing well on, 159–165
 preparing for, 161
 types of, 153–156
Intrapersonal communication, 24, 109–124
 and communication technology, **20-8**
 definition of, 110
 improving, 106–107

Introduce, speeches to, 296–298
Introduction, for speeches, 201–202
Invention (Roman canon), 5
Invisible Man, The (Ralph Ellison), 40
Iroquois nation, and public speaking, 15, 268
Isidore of Seville, 8–9
Isocrates, 4
Italy, schools of, 9

Jamieson, Kathleen H., **20-12**
Japan. *See also* Culture
 and small-group communication in, 174
 language development in, 7
 organizational behavior in, 16-7
Jargon, 101–102
Jefferson, Thomas, 16, **17-12, 20-15**
Jewish civilization, and mass communication, 8
Johari Window, 127–128
John, King of England, 11
Juarez, 13

Keats, John, 16
Keller, Helen, 22, 23
Kinesics, 83–84
Kinesthetic learning, 118
King, Larry, **18-3, 20-10**
King, Martin Luther Jr., 15, 276
KISS principle, 218
Knapp, Mark, 130
Knowledge
 as communication competency, 32
 early preservation of, 8
 from mass media, **18-8–18-9**
 in creative and critical thinking, 71
Koppel, Ted, **18-3**
Korzybski, Alfred, 93

Lady Astor, 12
Laissez-faire leadership, 191
Language. *See also* Verbal communication
 acquiring skills of, 96–98, 146–147
 and speech evaluation, 244
 and stereotypes, 102–104
 as symbol, 92–94
 emergence of, 2
 gender differences in, **19-13–19-15**

Optional CD-ROM chapter page entries appear in **boldface.**

intensifiers in, **19-14**
persuasive, in speeches, 284–286
qualifiers, use of, **19-14**
syntax of, 95–96
tags, use in, **19-14**
use and misuse of, 99–106
use in syllogisms, 56–65
Lao-Tsu, 7
Leadership, in small groups, 190–191
Learning
    and mass media, **18-8–18-9**
    kinesthetic, 118
    verbal, 118
    visual, 118
Learning disabilities, and computers,
    20-18–20-19
Leathers, Dale, 84, 192, **19-11**
Legends of the Fall, **18-15**
Lehrer, Jim, **18-3**
Lenin, Vladimir, 13
Letters. *See also* Messages; Literacy
    and communication technology, **20-8**
    sent after interviews, 164
Libel, **18-11**
Library research, for speeches, 222–224
Lie detectors, 80, 145, **20-13**
Life scripts, 116
Likert, Rensis, **16-6**
Lincoln, Abraham, 41–42
Line pattern, of group communication,
    184, 185
Linguistic oppression, 102–104
Listeners
    analyzing for speeches, 212–214
    note-taking, 50
    responsibilities of, 48–49
Listening, 36–52. *See also specific type*
    active, 38–42
    adequate vs. effective, 36, 37–42
    as source of inspiration, 49
    consumption, 49–50
    contexts for, 36–37
    improving, 45–50
    in interpersonal communication, 146
    misconceptions about, 37–38
    time spent on, 36, 37
Listening dropouts, 49
Literacy
    associated with political power, **20-3–20-4**
    expansion in Renaissance, 9

Literature, reading. *See* Oral interpretation
Logic. *See also* Logos
    appearance of, 57, 243
    faulty, 57, 63
    of longevity, 63
Logical pattern, of persuasive speeches,
    282–283
Logical proof (Aristotle), 277, 279–280
Logos, 277, 279–280
Louganis, Greg, 117
Luther, Martin, 10
Lyrics, of songs, **18-12**

Macy, Anne Sullivan, 23
Magazines, using for research, 223
Magic, and our verbal code, 104
Magna Carta, 11
Makau, Josina, 55
Manipulation, in defensive communica-
    tion, 140
Manuscripts, delivering speeches from,
    229
Maps, use in speeches, 218
Mass homogenization of culture, **20-17**
Mass media communication, **18-2–18-17**
    and communication technology,
        20-16–20-17
    and false claims, **18-11**
    and propaganda, **18-10**
    definition of, 25
    development of, 3, 8–9
    functions of, **18-3–18-6**
    improving competency in, **18-14–18-15**
    vs. other types of communication, **18-2**
McGregor, Douglas, **16-6**
McLuhan, Marshall, **19-4**
Meaning, created by use, 94
Measurement, of group outcomes, 192
Media. *See also* Mass media communica-
    tion
    bias of, **18-10**
    definition of, **18-2**
Medi-speak, 101
Memorized speeches, 228–229
Memory
    as used by storyteller, 7
    devices, 39
    Roman canon, 6
Men, communicating with women,
    19-12–19-16

Optional CD-ROM chapter page entries appear in **boldface.**

Mentoring, of women, **19-15**
Merzenich, Michael, **20-19**
Mesomorph, 112
Messages, 26
    about health, **19-18**
    and communication technology,
        20-8–20-9
    and digitizing images, 272
    and elimination of listening barriers, 46
    and ethics, 245
    and HUB model, **18-5–18-7**
    and public relations, **18-12**
    censoring of in organizations, **16-9**
    distortion of, 193
    effective, 281
    one-sided vs. two-sided, 271, 273
    sent by nonverbal communication, 78–82
Mesopotamia, 2, **20-3**
Metaphors, use in speeches, 284–285
Microchip circuitry, **20-3**
Middle Ages, communication during, 8–9
Minelli, Liza, 302
Minyan, 174
Miracle Worker, 23
*MLA Handbook for Writers of Research
    Papers*, 203
Models, use in speeches, 218–219
Modern Language Association (MIA)
    format, 203
Mongatari, Shotetsu , 7
Monroe, Alan H., 211, 283
Motivation pattern, in speeches, 210–212,
    283–284
Movement, 76, 83–84
    during speeches, 240
Mudd, Charles, 22
Multi-step approach, to mass media, **18-3**
Muscle relaxation, and preparing for
    speeches, 233
Myths, 7

National Communication Association, 17
Native Americans
    and linguistic patterns, 97–98
    and public speaking, 15
    and small-group communication, 174
    and storytelling, 7
    cultural premises in decision-making, 59
    sign language of, 78
    value system, 213

Neanderthals, **20-3**
Negation, defining by, 252
Neologisms, 102
Nervousness. *See* Communication
    apprehension
Netiquette, **20-7**
Networks, communication, 183–185
Neutrality, in defensive communication,
    140
Newspapers
    in mass media communication,
        18-2, 18-7
    using for research, 223
Nez Percé War, 59
Niemoeller, Martin, **17-13**
Noise, 27–28
    and elimination of learning barriers,
        44, 47
Nondirective questions, during inter-
    views, 157
Nonverbal communication, 75–90
    and cultural differences, 79, 81–82, 86,
        19-7, 19-11
    and gender differences, **19-15**
    as part of active listening, 39
    as part of delivery, 6, 26
    deception in, 79–80
    definition of, 76
    during an interview, 161–162
    functions of, 78
    importance in conveying meaning, 77
    in classroom, **17-7**
    types of, 83–87
Nonverbal skills, for speeches, 239–242
Norms
    in different cultures, **19-11**
    in organizations, **16-6, 16-8**
    in small-group communications, 175
Note taking
    during interviews, 163
    to improve listening comprehension, 50
    to prepare for speeches, 222

Oberg, Kalvero, **19-9**
Objects
    in nonverbal communication, 84–85
    use in speeches, 218–219
Obscuration, fallacy of, 60
"Ode to a Grecian Urn" (Keats), 16
One-on-one interview, 166

Optional CD-ROM chapter page entries appear in **boldface.**

One-step approach, to mass media, **18-3**
On-line research services, 223
Open system, in organization, **16-2, 16-5**
Opinion leaders, **18-3, 18-5**
Oral interpretation, 307–314
    audience-centered, 308
    use of voice in, 314
    vs. acting, 309
Oral traditions. *See* Storytelling
Organization, Roman canon of, 5–6
Organizations, 192–193
    and public relations, **18-13**
    as culture, **16-6–16-8**
    behavior in, **16-2–16-10**
    communication in, 25, **16-2**
    groups working in, 192–193
    rules in, **16-8**
Organizational cultures approach, to
        studying organizations, **16-6–16-8**
Organizational patterns, in speeches,
        208–212, 243, 258, 282–284, 303–307
Orientation phase, in group communica-
        tion, 186
Ouchi, William, **16-7**
Outlines, for speeches
    and extemporaneous presentation, 230,
        303
    and persuasive speeches, 282–284
    computer assistance for, 207
    familiarity with, 246
    general, 200–201
    logical structure of, 203–207
    samples of, 201, 204–205, 256–257,
        283–284
    symbols in, 206–207

Panel interviews, 166
Paper, invention of, 4, 6
Papyrus, 4, **20-3**
Parables, use in speeches, 285
Paralanguage, 83
Parents
    and children, **17-3–17-6**
    and teachers, **17-8**
Parliament (British), birth of, 11–12
Participation, in civic life, **17-10–17-13**
Pathos, 277, 279
Paul, Saint, 4, **20-8**
Pavlov, Ivan, 271

People, in communication, 26, 46, 48–50,
        126–150
Perception
    and media manipulation, **18-10**
    and self-concept, 114, 116
Performance reviews. *See* Appraisal inter-
        views
Pericles, funeral oration by, 300
Personal references, use in speeches, 286
Persuasion, in public relations, **18-13**
Persuasion interviews, 155
Persuasive speeches, 267–294
    adapting to audience, 287–288
    and changing attitudes, 270–274
    evaluating, 288–290
    improving competency in, 290–291
    language of, 284–286
    organization of, 282–284
    subject matter for, 268–270
    types of, 274–281
Personal attributes, as factor in intraper-
        sonal communication, 112–113
Personal proof (Aristotle), 277–278
Phonologics, 94, 95
Physiological preparation, for speeches,
        232–234
Pictographic writing system, 2
Pictures, use in speeches, 218
    digitizing, 272
Pitch of voice, in speeches, 237–238
Plagiarism, and the Internet, **20-6**
Plato, 4–5
Play Index, 313
Poetry Index, 313
Police interviews, 163
Policy, as addressed by persuasive
        speeches, 269
Politics
    and communication, 11–15
    and communication technology, **20-16**
Polygraphs. *See* Lie detectors
Post hoc fallacy, 210, 258, 280
Posture, 83, 239–240
Power, in small-group communication, 189
Power of Myth, The (Joseph Campbell), 7
Practice, of speeches, 246
Praise, speech of, 299
Prayer, in schools, **18-12**
Premises, 56

Optional CD-ROM chapter page entries appear in **boldface.**

accuracy of, 57
  testing, 61, 69–70
  truth of, 58–61
  validity of, 61–62
Presentation standards, for speeches,
    243–244
Presentations. *See* Speeches
Press conferences, **17-12**
"Pretty Boy Floyd" (Guthrie), 85
Preview, including in speeches, 264
Primary group, 176
Principles and Types of Speech (Monroe), 211
Print resources, for research, 222–223
Printing. *See also* Literacy
  and American colonies, **20-12**
  impact of first books, 10
  long-term impact, **20-6**
Probability
  as qualifier, 67
  relying on, 62
Problem orientation, in supportive com-
    munication, 137
Problem-solution pattern, of speeches,
    210, 282
Problem solving, as type of intrapersonal
    communication, 119
Problem-solving groups, 180–181
Problem-solving interviews, 154–155
Progressive value system, 212–213
Pronunciation, 237
Proofs, in persuasive speeches, 277–280
Propaganda
  in media, **18-10**
  in war films, 271
Protestant-Puritan-Peasant value system,
    212
Proverbs, use in impromptu speeches, 305
Provisionalism, in supportive communi-
    cation, 138
Proxemics, 76, 85
Pseudo-listening, 37
Pseudo-relationships, fostered by mass
    media, **18-5**
Psycholinguistics, **17-4**
Psychological preparation, for speeches,
    234–236
Ptah-Hotep, 3
Public argumentation, 277
Public communication, 24–25

Public relations, **18-12–18-14**
  careers in, **18-14**
  definition of, **18-12**
  functions of, **18-13–18-14**
  vs. advertising, **18-13**
Public Relations Society of America, **18-14**
Public speaking. *See also* Speeches
  and preaching, 8
  and revolutions, 12–13
  and technology, **20-11–20-12**
  non-Western approaches to, 6–8
  Roman canons concerning, 5–6
  through debate, 9
  Western approaches to, 2–6
Pupil dilation, and deception, 163

Qualifiers, 67
  in gender-related communication,
    19-14
Quick judgment, 40, 44
Quintillian, Marcus Fabius, 5, 8, 278
Quipu, 7
Quotations, use in speeches, 216

Racism
  and organizational patterns, **16-8**
  discussing, **19-7**
  in language, 102–103
Radio, effect of, **20-3**, **20-12**
Rainman, 121
Rate of speech, 238
Readers' Guide to Periodical Literature, 223,
    312
Readers' theatre, 310–311
Reading
  and political power, **20-3–20-5**
  to children, 308, **17-5**
Reagan, Ronald, **17-10**
Reasoning. *See also* Deductive reasoning;
    Inductive reasoning
  approaches to, 56–68
  informal, 280–281
Reasoning and Communication (Makau), 55
Rebuttal, 67
Receivers, of messages, 27
  and elimination of listening barriers, 47
  in small-group communication, 174
  transaction with sender, 281
Recovery phase, of culture shock, **19-9**

Optional CD-ROM chapter page entries appear in **boldface.**

Red Jacket, 15
Reefer Madness, **19-18**
Reference behavior, 176
Regulating function, of nonverbal
    communication, 79
Reinforce, speeches to, 275–276
Reinforcing function, of nonverbal
    communication, 78
Relationship function, of nonverbal
    communication, 80
Relationship potential, 23
Relationships
    and communication, 23–24
    and interpersonal communication,
        130–135
    and nonverbal communication, 80
    behaviors that help sustain, 136–141
    stages of, 130–135
Religion, communication and, 10
Renaissance
    communication during, 9–10
    schools of, 9
Repertoire of skills, 31–32
Reputation. *See* Credibility
Research, for speeches, 221–225
Resumé, 159–160
Retirement, speeches honoring, 300
Review, after listening, 41–42, 44
Revolutions, and communication, 12–13
Rhetor (Latin), 5
Rhetoric, 4–5, 9, 16
Rhetoric (Aristotle), 4, 212
Rhetorical definition, 252
Risky-shift, 177
Ritual, and our verbal code, 105–106
Roles
    as factor in intrapersonal communica-
        tion, 113–114
    within families, **17-5–17-6**
Rome
    language development in, 5–6
    roads of, **20-4**
Roosevelt, Eleanor, 15
    eulogy for, 300
Roosevelt, Franklin, 15
Roosevelt, Theodore, 15
Rose Parade, **16-7**
Rosetta Stone, 3, 98
Rule of grouping, 203

Rules, organizational, **16-8**
Rumors, 193, **16-11**

Safety needs, in group communication, 177
Sales interviews, 155–156
Samples, used for induction, 63–65
Sanger, Margaret, 15
Sapir-Whorf hypothesis, 97, 103, 110
Sarcasm, 83
Satellite TV, **18-8**
Savants, 121
Schizophrenia, 121
School. *See* Classrooms
Schutz, William, 129–130
Scientific approach, to studying organiza-
    tions, **16-2–16-3**
Screening interviews, 154
Screens
    to communication, 120–121
    to intercultural communication,
        19-6–19-10
Scully, Vin, **17-7**
Seami, 7
Selection interviews, 153–154
Self-concept
    acting as filter, 120
    and aging, **19-16–19-17**
    and classroom, **17-8**
    and communication apprehension, 31
    and communication technology, **20-8**
    and family, 177, **17-5–17-6**
    and linguistic oppression, 103
    and perception, 116
    as factor in intrapersonal communica-
        tion, 111–112
    blind spot in, 128
    derived from interpersonal messages,
        126
    using video or audio to correct, 113
Self-disclosure, 127–128
Self-esteem needs, in group communica-
    tion, 177
Self-fulfilling prophecies, 117
Self-image. *See* Self-concept
Semantics, 94–95
Semiotics, 94–96
Senders, of messages, 26, 46
    in small-group communication, 174
    responsibilities of, 50

Optional CD-ROM chapter page entries appear in **boldface.**

transaction with receivers, 281
Senses, and nonverbal communication, 76, 87
Sequential pattern, in speeches, 208–209
Sexism
    and organizational patterns, **16-8**
    in classrooms, **17-8**
    in families, **17-3**
    in language, 102–104
    in small groups, 190
    reinforced by expectations, 116–117, **19-15**
Shakespeare, William, 98
Shaw, George Bernard, **19-11**
Short-notice speeches. *See* Impromptu speeches
Short stories, use in speeches, 215, 244–245, 279, 286
Shyness. *See* Communication apprehension
Sicard, Abbé, 78
Sign language, 78
Sillars, Malcolm, 22
Size sequence pattern, of speeches, 209
Skills, in communication, 32
Skinner, B.F., 271
Sleeper effect, 271
Small-group communication, 24, 171–197
    and communication technology, **20-10–20-11**
    and organizations, 192–193
    best environments for, 185–186
    common goal of, 174
    definition of, 172–175
    improving competency in, 194–196
    personal influences on, 189–190
    phases of, 186–188
    types of, 175–182
Smiley face, **20-11**
Social communication, and technology, **20-13–20-19**
Social groups, 175–178
Social roles, as factor in intrapersonal communication, 113–114
Social systems approach, to studying organizations, **16-4–16-5**
Solidarity needs, in group communication, 177
Sonnet 18 (Shakespeare), 98
Source credibility theory, 272

Sources, crediting, 245. *See also* Support materials
Sources, of messages 26, 46
    evaluating, 70
    for speeches, 202–203
    responsibilities of, 50
Space, in nonverbal communication, 85–87
Speakers
    credibility of, 272
    effective, 3, 12, 15, 27, 41
    in community communication, **17-11**
    responsibilities of, 50
Speaking and writing, 99
Special-occasion speeches, 295–316
Speech apprehension. *See* Communication apprehension
Speech codes, 103
Speeches. *See also specific types*
    environmental factors affecting, 214
    evaluating, 242–245, 259–263
    improving delivery of, 245–246
    preparing, 199–226
    presenting, 227–248
    skills required for, 236–242
    thesis sentence of, 201, 202, 250, 256
    types of, 228–231
    summaries in, 264
Socrates, 4
Socratic method, 3
Sophists, 5
Space sequence pattern, of speeches, 209
Spanglish, 101
Speech communication, definition of, 17
Spontaneity, in supportive communication, 137
Sports, and mass media entertainment, **18-7–18-8**
Stage fright. *See* Communication apprehension
Stages, of relationships, 130–135
Stagnating stage of relationship, 134
Standards of presentation, for speeches, 243–244
Star pattern, of group communication, 184, 185
Statistics, use in speeches, 217
Status, in small-group communication, 189
Stereotypes. *See also* Culture; Gender
    and cultures, **19-8**

Optional CD-ROM chapter page entries appear in **boldface.**

and family messages, **17-6**
and language, 102–104, 253
and media, **18-10**
and older people, **19-17**
as form of unexpressed warrant, 67
in analyzing audiences, 213
in small groups, 190, 195
Stevenson, Adlai E., 300
Stone, Lucy, 15
Stories, short, use in speeches, 215, 244–245, 279, 286
Story of English, The, 100
Storytelling, 2, 7–8, **17-9**, **19-17**
Strategy, in defensive communication, 140
Structural differences, in gender communication, **19-15**
Style, Roman canon, 6
Subordination, in outlines, 203–206
Substance abuse, **19-18**
Substituting function, of nonverbal communication, 78
Suggestion, in oral interpretation material, 312
Summaries, including in speeches, 264
Superiority, in defensive communication, 139
Support
    for logical arguments, 67
    in interpersonal communication, 147
Support materials
    for decision making, 70
    for speeches, 202, 214–221, 243, 257, 262
Supportive communication, 137–138
Syllogism, 9, 56, 57, 60
    testing, 61
Symbols
    language as, 92–94
    in Mesopotamia, **20-3**
    in nonverbal communication, 77
    in outlines, 206–207
    of Neanderthals, **20-3**
Syntactics, 94
Syntax, 95–96
Systems, 1–4, **16-6–16-7**
Systems approach, to studying organizations, **16-4–16-5**

Taboo, and our verbal code, 104–105
Tag questions, use by women, **19-14**

Talents, as factor in intrapersonal communication, 112–113
Talial, Paula, **20-19**
Task orientation, in work groups, 178–179
Taylor, Elizabeth, 274
Taylor, Frederick, **16-2–16-3**
Teachers
    and building student self-concept, **17-8**
    and parents, **17-8**
    in classroom, **17-7**
Techne (Corax), 3
Technology. See Communication technology
Telecommuting, **20-13**
Teledemocracy, **20-16**
Television, 44–45, **20-12**
    and family communication, **20-14**
    and global village, **19-4**
    and mass media communication, **18-2, 18-7, 18-9, 20-16**
    and v-chips, **20-5**
    sexism in plots, **17-3**
Termination stage of relationship, 134–135
Theatre, readers', 310–311
Theory X, **16-6**
Theory Y, **16-6**
Theory Z, **16-7**
Thesis sentence, for speeches, 202
Thinking. See also Critical thinking; Creative thinking
    styles of, 118–119
"This Land Is Your Land" (Guthrie), 85
Thomas, Dylan, 96
Three-step approach, to mass media, **18-3**
Time
    in nonverbal communication, 76, 85–87
    limits in impromptu speeches, 306–307
    sequence pattern in speeches, 208
Time-and-motion studies, **16-3**
Tolerance
    of ambiguity, **19-10**
    of cultural differences, **19-8**
Tone, of voice, 238–239
Topical patterns, of speeches, 209–210
    impromptu, 230–231, 302–307
    of introduction, 296–298
Toulmin Model, 65–68, 280–281
Toulmin, Stephen, 65
Tower of Babel, 2

Optional CD-ROM chapter page entries appear in **boldface.**

Town crier, 9

Training films, 271

Transaction, 27, 281

Transitions, in speeches, 254, 264

Translations, of Rosetta Stone hieroglyphics, 3

Trump, Donald, **18-11**

Trustworthiness. *See* Credibility

Truth
in communication technology, **20-6**
of premises, 58–61, 69

Truth, Sojourner, 15

Two-step approach, to mass media, **18-3**

Understanding, as conveyed by facial
expressions, 84

Unions, in U.S., **18-12**

Universality, of oral interpretation material, 312

Universities, development of in U.S., 16

Upward distortion, **16-9**

Uses of Enchantment, The (Bettelheim), **17-5**

Vagueness, fallacy of, 60

Validity, of logical arguments, 57, 61–62

Values, 114–115
and audience analysis, 212
and culture, **19-3**
and organizational behavior, **16-6**
in communication technology, **20-7**
in persuasive speeches, 269–270, 281,
288–289

V-chips, for televisions, **20-5**

Vellum, 4

Verbal communication, 91–108
during an interview, 161–164

Verbal learning, 118

Verbal skills, for speeches, 236–239

Verbal supporting materials, for speeches,
215–216

Video, and the telephone, **20-10**

Videotapes
in trials, **20-6, 20-13**
of practice speeches, 240
using for research, 223

Virtual reality games, 179

Vision impairments, and communication,
19-17

Visual learning, 118

Visual aids, for speeches, 217–221, 254

Visualization
and oral interpretation, 308, 309
and speeches, 233, 235–236
by audience, 283

Vita, 159–160

Vocal fillers, **19-14**

Vocalics, 76, 83

Volume, of speech delivery, 236

Wait time, in classroom, **17-7–17-8**

Walters, Barbara, **18-3**

Warner, Margaret, **18-3**

Warrant, in Toulmin Model, 65, 280
as premise, 69

Weber, Shirley, 100

Webster, Noah, 94

Webster's Dictionary, 94

Williams, Montel, 157

Wilmot, William, 141

Wilson, Woodrow, **18-13**

Winfrey, Oprah, 157, **20-10**

Wizard of Oz, The (Baum), 71

Women, communicating with men,
19-12–19-16

Words. *See also* Language
acceptance of new, 95, 102
sound of, 95

Work, and technology, **20-13**

Work groups, 178–179

Writing
development of, 2, 4
speaking and, 99

X pattern, of group communication, 183

Xsosa people, 97

Y pattern, of group communication, 184,
185

Zenger, John Peter, **18-11**

Zimmerman, Robert, 96

Zoku Gunsho Ruiju (Mongatari), 7

THE CASTLE OF PERSEVERANCE

MIDDLE ENGLISH TEXTS SERIES

The Middle English Texts Series is designed for classroom use. Its goal is to make available to teachers, scholars, and students texts that occupy an important place in the literary and cultural canon but have not been readily available in student editions. The series does not include those authors, such as Chaucer, Langland, or Malory, whose English works are normally in print in good student editions. The focus is, instead, upon Middle English literature adjacent to those authors that teachers need in compiling the syllabuses they wish to teach. The editions maintain the linguistic integrity of the original work but within the parameters of modern reading conventions. The texts are printed in the modern alphabet and follow the practices of modern capitalization, word formation, and punctuation. Manuscript abbreviations are silently expanded, and *u/v* and *j/i* spellings are regularized according to modern orthography. Yogh (ȝ) is transcribed as *g*, *gh*, *y*, or *s*, according to the sound in Modern English spelling to which it corresponds; thorn (þ) and eth (ð) are transcribed as *th*. Distinction between the second person pronoun and the definite article is made by spelling the one *thee* and the other *the*, and final *-e* that receives full syllabic value is accented (e.g., *charité*). Hard words, difficult phrases, and unusual idioms are glossed either in the right margin or at the foot of the page. Explanatory and textual notes appear at the end of the text, often along with a glossary. The editions include short introductions on the history of the work, its merits and points of topical interest, and brief working bibliographies.

This series is published in association with the University of Rochester.

Medieval Institute Publications is a program of
The Medieval Institute, College of Arts and Sciences

 WESTERN MICHIGAN UNIVERSITY